GW00480614

VOICES FROM THE SPANISH CIVIL WAR

Personal recollections of Scottish Volunteers
in Republican Spain
1936–39

Ian MacDougall

With recent photographs of the veterans
by Sean Hudson

Polygon
EDINBURGH
1986

First published in Great Britain in 1986
by Polygon, 48 Pleasance, Edinburgh EH8 9TJ.

ISBN   0 948275 19 7

Foreword copyright © Victor G. Kiernan 1986.
Text copyright © Ian MacDougall 1986.
Photographs of the veterans © Sean Hudson
The photograph that appears on page 11 is reproduced by kind
permission of the Glasgow Herald and the photograph on the bottom
of page 75 is copyright © Capital Press.

The publishers acknowledge subsidy from the Scottish Arts Council
towards the publication of this volume.

Design by James Hutcheson

Typeset in 10 pt bembo by Pennart Typesetting (Edinburgh) Ltd.,
6 North Charlotte Street, Edinburgh EH2 4HR.

Printed and bound by Billing & Sons Ltd.,
Hylton Road, Worcester.

Table of Contents

FOREWORD

The civil war that broke out in Spain in July 1936 was one of the great events of our century, this epoch of old things obstinately clinging to life and new things struggling to be born, like a drying up of seas and rearing up of mountains in geological history. It was a prodigious revelation of man's unbelievable capacity for both good and evil. It was a conflict in which one side, army rebels and their fascist and other reactionary allies, committed some follies and enormous crimes, and the defenders of the Republic some crimes and enormous follies, chiefly feudings among themselves.

The entire resistance to the military uprising might indeed be called an act of heroic folly, though it could not be foreseen at the outset how determined fascist Italy, Germany and Portugal would be to make Franco win, or how determined the democracies – Britain, France, America – to let the Republic lose. If the working class in Madrid and Barcelona had not thrown itself into the breach, all might have been over as quickly as most of the plotters must have expected. Return of dictatorship would not have been as bloodless as on the last occasion, in 1923, but the wholesale massacres of workers and peasants that the civil war and fascist victory brought with them might have been escaped. As it was, Spain was left to fight the battle against fascist domination of Europe alone. It is impossible for a historian to measure in cold blood whether such a doomed struggle and its fearful sacrifices were worth while.

Vastly the greater part of history never comes to be recorded, but vanishes with those who have made it or endured it. This makes it hard to write of events accurately later on, and easy to distort them, by intention or otherwise. Even when there is written evidence, it becomes difficult in time to interpret. Memories transmitted by word of mouth can be an invaluable aid; but there is a great difference between an oral tradition left to take its own meandering course, and the testimony of the original participants. Walter Scott shows us amusingly the happenings described in the first part of *Guy Mannering* as they have come to be twenty years later, garbled in the minds of local wiseacres. Even in the minds of those who lived through them, facts may be blurred in course of time by later impressions, changed opinions, or simple dimming of memory. Authentic history cannot be picked up from them ready-made; it has to be constructed out of what they can tell us by much careful sifting, combining, cross-checking. The Spanish civil war has been a prime theme for investigation on these lines, and has been fortunate in much skilled handling of the material by devoted but open-eyed friends of the Republic. A monumental outcome not long ago was Ronald Fraser's *Blood of Spain,* built on the recollections of hundreds of men and women who took part in or were caught up in the contest, on one side or the other.

Ian MacDougall's searches have been within more circumscribed bounds, but they are related to one dramatic feature of the conflict, the services of that unique fighting-force the International Brigade. They have a significance for military history at large, not Spain's only; also for understanding of the Britain of those years, and Scotland in particular. A decade or so ago the History department of Edinburgh University made tape-recordings of interviews with some veterans of the Brigade, for use with a documentary film on the civil war. Ian MacDougall, one of its old students, has taken up a similar plan on a far wider scale, seeking out all surviving members of the Brigade to be found in Scotland; there must be few if any who have slipped through his net. He has brought to his task, besides a glowing interest of many years in the civil war, long familiarity with the practice of oral history, as a leading spirit of the Scottish Labour History Society. It is sufficient to refer to his big book *Militant Miners,* largely about the life of the Fife miners' organizer John McArthur, pieced together from his own memories.

It may be worth while to recall that British soldiers had stood on Spanish soil many times before (as, in Roman times, soldiers from Spain stood on British soil). In 1585 Drake's privateers were plundering Vigo; in 1706, during the War of the Spanish Succession, Lord Peterborough's force helped to beat off the French from Barcelona. In 1704 Britain took possession of Gibraltar, and on several later occasions held it against Spanish attacks. In 1808 when Napoleon occupied Spain and Portugal and a British contingent was sent to reinforce the patriots opposing him, the long-drawn Peninsular War began. In the 1830s during the first Carlist War, a British Legion was campaigning in Spain on the side of a Liberal government against monarchist reaction.

This 'Legion' was not much better than a disorderly rabble, and Wellington's men were remembered as much for the dreadful storm and sack of Badajoz in 1812 as for their part in the liberation of Spain. By contrast with such forerunners, the British battalion of the International Brigade deserves to be reckoned, along with Cromwell's Ironsides, among the bravest and most inspired soldiers that Britain has ever put into the field. They helped to save Madrid, and in the earlier phases of the war, while a new Spanish army was being painfully put together, to save the Republic. Scots had a distinguished place, and, as Christopher Harvie writes in his *Scotland and Nationalism,* 'evoked great sympathy' from their countrymen, and from south of the border as well.

'The portrayal of humanity in its most pitiable and degraded form is an essential part of the tradition of Spanish painting', F. Elgar reminds us in an essay on Picasso, who was faithful to it in his paintings at Barcelona at the beginning of this century, studies of 'invalids, beggars, and pitiful, resigned outcasts'. He took refuge from the spectacle of hopeless poverty by emigrating to France. De Falla the composer was another who went to live abroad, after his endeavours to mould a truly Spanish and modern music: his inspiration was drying up, under a painful sense it has been suggested of Spain's disunity. All nations have always had their discords, but those of Spain were exceptionally acute. Apart from the presence of linguistic minorities, Basque and Catalan and Galician, the country had been welded together by its kings and priests far too much in the pursuit of irrational aims: dynastic interests, conquests in or out of Europe, religious orthodoxy watched over by the Inquisition (not finally abolished until 1835), and 'purity of blood', Europe's first official racialism. All this Don Quixote windmill-fighting, with utilitarian concerns allowed only a meagre share, could generate a nationalistic spirit, but not create a true nation.

Spain had lagged behind most of western Europe, and sunk into a long semi-isolation from it. A community so cut off may acquire strong feeling and sensibility, but development of the rational faculties requires neighbours to exchange and debate ideas with. At any rate, most Spanish political and social thinking has been stunted or abstract, and clogged by religious left-overs like the moraines deposited by an ice-age glacier. Conservatives have accused foreigners of inventing a 'black legend' to traduce Spain, and have been eager to blame them for all Spain's maladies. Some in our day have seriously maintained that the Moriscos, or descendants of the old Moorish inhabitants, had to be persecuted in the 16th century because England was bribing them to revolt – just as Spain had to have a brutal dictatorship to ward off the infection of Moscow gold.

On the other wing, although Marx and Engels paid much attention to Spanish history and problems, chiefly about the time of the Liberal revolution of 1854 and that of the tug of war between Marxist and Anarchist ideas in Spain in the early 1870s, they cannot be said to have read all the riddles of the Spanish sphinx; and it has been pointed out that Spaniards have not yet added much to the corpus of Marxist thinking. What the country inherited from its past – above all from possession for centuries of a vast empire, and the special favour of Heaven, or at least of Rome – was the self-complacency and ingrained fear of change of the conservative classes, the poverty and discontent of the rest, and the impregnable pride and courage, together with willingness both to undergo and to inflict suffering, shared by all. Only such a country could have fought such a war of three years.

Nineteenth-century Spanish liberalism, Siamese twin of a sluggish industry (least feeble in the peripheral Basque and Catalan areas) and semi-feudal agriculture, failed to do more than tinker with Spain's economic, political, educational backwardness. Twentieth-century liberals showed not much more energy. One of their best early spokesmen, Joaquín Costa, reveals some of its besetting weaknesses, even though he had many fresh ideas to offer. In his celebrated book on the condition of Spain, *Oligarchy and Caciquismo,* he complained that Spain was falling further behind Europe, even behind Japan; it was a feeling strong among progressives in the Russia of that day too. He called for a new Liberal spirit, but failed to define it by setting social objectives clearly before it. He denounced the sway of the *cacique* or local boss, but not the entrenched social inequalities and injustices that made it possible.

A new chance came when the fall of the dictator General Primo de Rivera was followed in 1931 by that of the discredited monarchy. A republic was set up mainly by middle-class liberals, all the less effective as reformers because the world slump was intensifying all economic problems; but radical changes could now be discussed, and there was a growing Socialist party to advocate them. Agrarian reform was the most urgent need. Restrictions on rack-renting and evictions by landlords were long overdue; the plight of the landless labourers on southern estates was worst of all. In the late nineteenth century the British government had been obliged at last to introduce reforms in the Irish countryside, and then to go further and buy the landlords out. Spain's Agrarian Statute of 1932 was mild enough, but it stirred up bitter controversy, much like Portugal's still more belated reform law of 1975. Left and Right were each both alarmed and encouraged by what was happening abroad: in the Soviet Union collectivization and the first Five Year Plan, in Germany the coming to power of fascism in 1933, in Austria in 1934; in Italy it had been installed by Mussolini in 1922. Left and Right both made much use of slogans of *action,* appealing to a public tired of the verbiage of politicians, though on one side they stood for a march forward, on the other a march backward, under new foreign labels.

Collision may have been inevitable in any case; it came in July 1936 because a group of army conspirators rebelled. Spanish generals, like their South American cousins, had tenacious habits of intervention in politics; an army supposed to be the nation's protector may really be a watchdog trained to bite some of those under its protection. It was easy for the miscellaneous parties of the Right, and their Church, to flock together under a unified military and political command, because none of them had any practical programme, any ideas beyond hatred of socialism and democracy. Franco and his followers called themselves 'Nationalists', while relying heavily on German and Italian troops as well as arms, and 'crusaders', while hiring 80,000 Muslim tribesmen from Morocco, much as George III hired German regiments to subdue his American subjects. In this light the 'nation' was a pagan deity, a Baal or Moloch, before whom its false prophets prostrated themselves in feigned ecstacies.

Vague but emotive watchwords like 'Traditionalism', the old Carlist monarchism under a new name, and *Españolismo*, 'Spanishism', formed a perfect specimen of 'ideology' in Marx's sense, a patchwork blanket or coat of many colours made up of pretences, illusions, fantasies, for a senile class, like Spain's landlords, or society, to wrap round itself. Since the era of bourgeois revolution ended, it has been the more disoriented, insecure sections of the middle classes that have most needed such a costume. Men with much property, or no property, both look at their world more realistically. Among those whose minds were clouded, or as Marx would say 'bewitched', by spells and sorceries from the past, were large numbers of peasants, the small farmers, owners or tenants, of Castile and Navarre. Many of these fought willingly for the insurgents. Nearly half of Spain had voted just before the war against the republican Popular Front. Marx had long before made his classic analysis of the similar mentality of French peasant-proprietors, denizens of the 'deaf village'.

More progressive sections of the middle classes and intellectuals were loyal to healthier ideals; but the liberal's highest ideal, liberty, however admirable is by itself a negative. July 1936 found Republicans hesitant, divided, and in spite of so many obvious warnings unprepared. They were not the men to direct a desperate and prolonged contest; and some of those at the head of the Socialist party proved less good at biting than they had been at barking. Leadership fell more and more to communists, nearly all of them new recruits – there had been very few before the war – converted by the glaring need to organise and discipline the war effort. Victory over fascism, not communism for Spain in any near future, was their target, the only sensible one there could be. Unfortunately they had too much of the bigotry of converts, fanned by Stalinist emanations from the Soviet Union which was Spain's only friend and supplier of arms. Unluckily also, they were between two indispensable allies, liberals who did not want socialism at all and Anarchists who wanted it unadulterated and immediately. No doubt both stood for precious values, democratic rights in one case, spontaneity and enthusiasm in the other, which communists then and at other times have underrated. Whether more harmony could have counterbalanced the enemy superiority in equipment can only be guessed. But it has been the bane of progressive causes that some curse seems to set their adherents against one another. Dead Caesar's spirit, Brutus lamented at Philippi,

'turns our swords
In our own proper entrails.'

Deepening polarization of Europe between communism and fascism extended itself into Spain, sharpening class confrontations and bringing to the front communism and fascism, neither of them native to Spain, in the two belligerent camps. In turn the splitting in two of Spain helped to divide Europe more completely. Left and Right wrestled on no issue more bitterly than over Spain, and the Republic was frantically, hysterically vilified by Frenchmen who before long would be fraternizing with their own Nazi invaders. In this country Tory hated of the Republic deserves to be remembered as an example of something far commoner in history than is often realized, class prejudice overcoming rational self-interest. Churchill in those years was moving from admiration of fascism in its homelands to fear of the threat it posed to the British empire; yet he had nothing to say against its gaining control of Spain, and endangering the empire's Mediterranean lifeline. 'There seemed no longer to be even the slightest possibility that either England or France would take a firm stand', the American Secretary of State Sumner Welles wrote of his visit to Europe late in 1937. He and Roosevelt deplored 'the pusillanimous role that both had so far played in the Spanish Civil War'; the U.S.A., Welles 'sadly admitted' in his memoirs, did no better.

Just as communists came to the front in Spain, communists elsewhere saw more clearly than others how urgently all Europe needed a halt to be called in Spain to the triumphant advance of fascism. There was a high proportion of them in the International Brigade, and its setting up was the finest achievement of the Third International, quite enough to lend lustre to a generally disappointing balance-sheet. In occupied Europe during the Second World War communists were everywhere to the fore in resistance movements, and each country where such a movement sprang up – France and Yugoslavia notably – had sent contingents to the Brigade, whose fight set an example to them all. Britain's resistance to the Nazis was of a different kind, but it too must have caught many sparks from the still bright memory of the Spanish Republic.

Fascism conversely was emboldened by the successful co-operation between the dictators, and between them and their protégé Franco, in Spain; also by the approval of many, and the timid inaction of others, in the democracies. There could be no prospect of its being turned aside by further appeasement from further aggression; and its onrush seemed irresistible until it was stopped at the gates of Moscow, as its vanguard in Spain had been stopped at the gates of Madrid. To Hitler's disgust, Franco was compelled by Spain's exhaustion to take only a limited part in the war; he sent troops to aid the Nazi invasion of Russia, as Hitler and Mussolini had sent troops into Spain. He gave the Axis every 'moral' support. Much about this can be learned from the book by Sir Samuel

Hoare (Lord Templewood) about his wartime mission to Spain. Even that hardened Tory found Franco a detestable tyrant.

The dog returns to its vomit, and the washed sow to the mire, in the twentieth century as well as in Biblical days. Scarcely was the war over before Western governments went back to their former ways. Britain led by intervening on the reactionary side in a civil war in Greece, in very much the same fashion that the dictators had intervened in a civil war in Spain. Franco was propped up by the U.S.A., because of the general preference of American imperialism, now fully fledged, for right-wing military dictators, and because Spanish bases were wanted for war-preparations against the Soviet Union. He was propped up at home by the Church, whose subservience to him was another thing that struck Hoare unpleasantly. Since then the Spanish Church has expressed contrition for its un-Christian vindictiveness against its political opponents. It may be conjectured that the very remarkable, and until not many years ago unforeseeable, improvement in the Catholic Church's social outlook all over the world has owed much to this chastening lesson.

Since Franco's death there have been sweeping changes for the better in Spain, but he left a legacy of multiple difficulties, political and economic, and an army command accustomed to regard political power as its birthright. No class-divided country is ever truly 'united', but in the Spanish case disunity remains unusually sharp, and the danger of reaction very real. Franco is regretted not only by landowners and big business, but by those of the middle classes who prospered under his reign, the same kind of people who welcomed the murder of Allende in Chile. There has been one attempt at an army coup, and more than once there have been rumours of imminent trouble. Abroad too, especially in Washington, there are unquestionably many who would like to see Spain cajoled or coerced back on to the strait and narrow path. Friends of Spain, and of European enlightenment, have a duty to study and remind others of the lessons of what happened in July 1936, and to be ready to join in opposing any attempt to repeat it, under whatever pretext.

As a survivor of the generation of the 1930s for whom the Spanish Republic's struggle was the most heroic thing of our lifetime, and its defeat the most tragic, I rejoice to know that the fiftieth anniversary of that fateful month is not being allowed to pass unnoticed; and, very particularly, that such a tribute as this volume represents is being paid to the International Brigade, in whose ranks some of my earliest friends gave their lives, and to which some of my oldest friends have looked back as the great adventure and virtue of their lives.

V.G. Kiernan,
Emeritus Professor,
University of Edinburgh.

INTRODUCTION

This book presents recollections by twenty Scots who volunteered to go to Spain to assist the Republicans and oppose Fascism in the Civil War of 1936-39. An effort was made to trace every volunteer surviving in Scotland. At least two or three survive who, however, were either not traced in time, or are now too frail, to be invited to contribute their recollections here.

Of the twenty veterans four are now dead. Tom Murray and Garry McCartney died within a few months of recording their recollections. Those of Donald Renton and George Watters, who died in 1977 and 1980 respectively, were recorded a decade or so ago in interviews by Professor Victor Kiernan as part of a project by the History and other Departments of the University of Edinburgh. The project culminated in the production of an impressive documentary film about the Spanish Civil War. Professor Kiernan with characteristic helpfulness let me know during the preparation of this book of the existence of these two recordings and also of one made at that time by John Dunlop. A few extracts from this last recording have, with permission, been added to my own below.

The value and the shortcomings of oral history are well known. About the relatively recent past it can provide testimony and insight that may or would otherwise be lost. Since very few 'ordinary' working men and women keep personal diaries or ever write down their experiences oral history enables especially "the common five-eight, the hewer of wood and the drawer of water", as one of the veterans below described himself, to contribute his or her testimony. Equipped with tape-recorder the student of history has unlimited opportunity to record and contribute to the preservation of personal experiences that are, or may be, small but significant parts of the vast mosaic of the past.

The problems or shortcomings of oral history obviously include the subjective and retrospective nature of recollection, especially when perhaps, as in the case of the Spanish Civil War, the events described took place half a century earlier. How accurate and typical are the personal experiences related in the pages that follow here? There is obviously the perennial possibility, even likelihood, that experience, reading and reflection after the events described will tend subtly, even

1

unconsciously, to affect the accuracy of recall of what actually happened and how things seemed at the time they happened. Of the twenty veterans who recall their experiences here only Hugh Sloan appears to have kept a diary at the time – but that diary, alas, as he tells us, was among the casualties of the Ebro offensive in 1938. Those academic historians who dismiss oral history as subjective and as 'old men drooling in their cups', surely need no reminder that documents, even those written at the time of the events they describe, can and very often do contain sins of omission and commission. In the recollections below there are at any rate plenty of opportunities for the reader to compare and contrast the testimonies offered. One's impression in recording them was that the veterans were speaking with honesty and sincerity of matters that had generally etched a very deep impression on them. Of course that does not mean they may not be mistaken or biased or that they recall everything of importance. Indeed the reader will find that often the veterans frankly admit they cannot be sure if some particular recollection is accurate or their understanding complete and reliable. These veterans are people, not philosophical or historical encyclopedias. What they give us are their personal recollections. These are not, and make no claim to constitute, an objective, scholarly history of the Spanish Civil War. They are personal accounts, half a century after the War, of what it felt like to be there at the time.

So far as is known little or nothing of these accounts has hitherto been published. Short interviews with Donald Renton, Steve Fullarton, Tommy Bloomfield and Tom Murray by my friend and colleague Ian S. Wood were published in May 1977 in the *Scottish Labour History Society Journal*. An extract from part of my interview with Tom Murray was included in the autumn 1984 number of *Cencrastus*. Some of the veterans below evidently gave some information to Bill Alexander in the compilation of his book, published in 1982, *British Volunteers for Liberty: Spain 1936-39*. Phil Gillan was the author of a pamphlet *The Defence of Madrid*, published by the Communist Party in 1937. And John Dunlop, who began to write up his memoirs a few years ago, contributed two or three short instalments from them to a periodical, *The Blue Blanket*. Judith Cook included in her *Apprentices of Freedom* (London, 1979) a few sentences or paragraphs of recollections by Eddie Brown, George Drever, Garry McCartney, and George Murray.

The accounts below inevitably vary in length, detail, vividness and surety of recall. Inevitably also, most of the veterans could recall some parts of their experience in Spain more fully and clearly than other parts. Two accounts – those of John Dunlop and Hugh Sloan – are particularly full and detailed, a tribute to what at times seems the almost photographic quality of their memories.

The order of presentation of the recollections is basically that in which the volunteers themselves went to Spain. An exception is Annie Murray, who went to Spain in September 1936, the same month as Phil Gillan – the two first of the score here to go. But she has been placed further down the sequence so that her medical experiences may be read beside those of two men who went out in January 1937: Tom Clarke, a stretcher bearer with the International Brigade, and Roderick MacFarquhar, who went out with the Scottish Ambulance Unit but soon left it in disagreement with certain policies or tendencies it was following, and, along with some colleagues, transferred to the International Brigade where he continued his work in organising the bringing out of wounded from the front line and helping to do so.

In the interviews there was a basic common framework of questions put to each veteran: reasons for volunteering to go to Spain; political affiliation, if any, at the time; how and by whom the application to go was processed; the journey to Spain; training, equipment and weapons, uniform, food and drink; volunteers and others encountered in Spain; the enemy – Moors, German and Italian as well as Spanish Fascist forces; particular battles or campaigns personally engaged in; wounds and deaths; aerial bombing; relations with the Spanish population; return home and aftermath; service, if any, in the 1939-45 War; retrospective view of the Spanish War and its impact on the veteran personally. Such basic questions were of course supplemented by others relevant to the individual veteran's experience, contacts, subsequent views, etc. Once the recordings were transcribed further questions were put or clarifications sought. The sixteen surviving veterans were sent a copy of the edited transcript of their own recording and asked to check it for accuracy.

In editing the verbatim transcript of these recordings a continuous attempt has been made to preserve and present the actual words used by the veterans. One of the great attractions of oral history, in addition to the personal relationships struck up between interviewers and interviewees, is of course the directness, pungency and sometimes poetic quality of spoken recollection. How to render these qualities faithfully in editing the transcripts is one of the challenges of oral history. The main modifications made below to the transcripts have been in cutting out repetitious matter, and in transpositions in the order of presentation so that a basically chronological narrative resulted. Footnotes to oral recollections of this kind can become prolific. An attempt has been made to limit these to providing where possible a little additional information about persons or matters mentioned in the text.

It has been estimated that about 500 volunteers went from Scotland to Spain to oppose Fascism and assist the Republican Government. How typical of those volunteers are the twenty whose recollections are presented below? Their political affiliations at the time may not have been wholly typical. Fifteen of the twenty were members of the Communist Party when they went to Spain. Several of these, such as Donald Renton, Hugh Sloan, George Watters and John Londragan, had been Party members for several years beforehand. Some others, such as Annie Murray, John Dunlop and David Anderson were relatively recent members. A further two – Tommy Bloomfield and Steve Fullarton – joined the Communist Party during and as a result of their Spanish experiences. One of the twenty – Roderick MacFarquhar – was a member of the Labour Party. Of the two remaining, Frank McCusker was a member of the National Unemployed Workers' Movement but not of any political party – though he indicates he would have remained a member of the Communist Party, to which he had earlier subscribed, had he not been chronically unemployed and unable to afford the subscription; while Bill Cranston was not a member of any political party or other organisation, personally and politically he appears to have been influenced by the example of Donald Renton, his brother-in-law. The Communist Party may be rather more strongly represented among the twenty than among the 500, though it seems certain that a majority, even a sizeable majority, of all volunteers from Scotland were in that Party when they went to Spain. None of the twenty was a member of the Independent Labour Party and since some members of that Party were among the volunteers in Spain, the veterans below are not at least for that reason (setting aside the question of any Liberals, Conservatives, Scottish Nationalists, Anarchists or members of other smaller Parties of the Left such as the British Section of the International Socialist Labour Party mentioned by Donald Renton) a complete cross-section politically. Whatever their actual Party affiliation what they appear to have felt strongly they had in common was what prompted them to go to Spain in the first place: a commitment to turn back the rising tide of Fascism in Spain, Europe, the world. Setting aside the few adventurers who for reasons other than that made their way to Spain, the twenty veterans below (none of whom could, in my opinion, be regarded in the least as an adventurer) may be regarded in that fundamental sense as typical volunteers.

Two of them, Donald Renton and Tom Murray, served as political commissars in the International Brigade, and Tom Murray in particular offers the reader a useful description of the work of a commissar. Five served at one time or another with the anti-tank unit of the XVth International Brigade. Their accounts are not, however, repetitious but on the whole complementary. Of the nineteen men, eleven were wounded, several of them seriously. Five of the nineteen were taken prisoner by Franco's forces. Three of them were captured at the battle of Jarama in early 1937, and after their release from captivity one of them, Tommy Bloomfield, returned to Spain to fight again. The other two of the five, Garry McCartney and George

Drever, were captured in the spring of 1938 and not released and repatriated until virtually the end of the War.

About half of the nineteen men had already had military experience or at least military training before they went to Spain. Three had served in the British Regular army: David Anderson and Tom Clarke had completed seven or eight years' service respectively in the Gordon and the Cameron Highlanders, while Tommy Bloomfield had served for six months in 1931 with the Black Watch, until his mother proved he was under age and her only support. Tom Murray had been conscripted into the army for three weeks at the end of the 1914–18 War, but had served earlier in local defence volunteers. At least five others of the nineteen had been in the Territorial army, and one other (John Dunlop) had been a member of the Officers' Training Corps at school.

The occupations of the twenty volunteers were, at the time of their going to Spain, predominantly manual and reflected the fact that they were almost all members of the working class. Two were miners, two railwaymen (one of them a railway clerk), and there was a printer, an engineer, a blacksmith, a nurse, a housepainter, a chimney sweep, a transport worker, a labourer, a political organiser, a Temperance organiser, an accountant, and a research chemist. Four were unemployed (or at any rate longer term unemployed): a jute worker, two ex-Regular army, and one other.

The places of origin of the twenty were almost certainly not in proportion to those others of the 500 who went to Spain from Scotland. Four belonged to Glasgow, four to Edinburgh (excluding Tom Murray, who though a Town Councillor there, had been born and brought up in Aberdeenshire and Kincardine), two each to Aberdeen, Dundee and Fife, and one each to East Lothian, Perthshire and Inverness. Two others, Annie and George Murray, could be said to belong to both Perthshire and (with their brother Tom) to Aberdeenshire, though at the time of their going to Spain Annie was completing her training as a nurse in Edinburgh, and George was employed as a printer in Glasgow. But Lanarkshire, Ayrshire and Dumbartonshire (Vale of Leven), from which numbers of volunteers went to Spain, are not represented at all among the twenty below, and Glasgow and Dundee seem distinctly under-represented.

The three Murrays were of course brothers and sister, and Donald Renton and Bill Cranston were brothers-in-law. Some others of the twenty knew each other before they went to Spain: Donald Renton and George Watters, for example, and John Dunlop and George Murray, and the latter and Eddie Brown were apparently already close friends. No doubt these relationships and friendships influenced the volunteers to some extent in reaching their decisions to go to Spain but they seem not to have been a cardinal factor.

In the preparation of this book my thanks are due to all those people and institutions that have given practical help and encouragement. No one but myself is to be blamed for any shortcomings in the book. The eighteen veterans whom I interviewed were unfailingly helpful, patient and courteous. Some were interviewed in their own homes and I am indebted also to them for their hospitality: John and Mrs Anne Dunlop, Hugh and Mrs Jeannie Sloan, Mrs Annie Murray Knight and her husband, and Tommy Bloomfield and the late Tom Murray. Particular thanks are due to John Dunlop for a good deal of additional practical help that he gave. John Londragan and Tom Clarke were very helpful, as were Jim Torrance and Ronnie Webster, respectively secretaries of Dundee and Aberdeen Trades Councils, in arranging a room for interviews of veterans in Council premises. I am grateful also for similar help given by Iain Flett, Archivist, and Veronica Hartwich, Assistant Keeper, at the Archives Centre and Museum and Art Gallery respectively in Dundee. To the British Broadcasting Corporation, and especially to John Arnott, Senior Producer, and David Jackson Young, Producer, B.B.C. Radio Scotland Talks Department, I owe special thanks for a great deal of practical help and encouragement in the preparation of the radio programme based on these recollections that was broadcast in February 1986. That the B.B.C. readily agreed that tape-recordings made for the programme could be added to the other tapes I had already made and the whole collection deposited for permanent preservation and public access in the School of Scottish Studies at the University of Edinburgh, places in their debt anyone in future who wishes to listen to these tapes. Verbatim transcripts of all the tapes will also be placed in the School of Scottish Studies. Thanks are therefore also due to Professor John MacQueen, Head of the School, for his willingness to house these materials and make them accessible to anyone interested. To Ian S. Wood, Editor, and the Scottish Labour History Society I am grateful for permission to quote from interviews of Donald Renton and Tommy Bloomfield published in the Society's *Journal* of May 1977. My indebtedness to Emeritus Professor V.G. Kiernan is apparent. To several other members, present or past, of the History and other supporting Departments of Edinburgh University, thanks are due for permission to make use of material recorded for the Department of History in interviews by Professor Kiernan with John Dunlop and the late Donald Renton and George Watters, in connection with the Inter-University History Film Consortium a decade or so ago: Dr Paul Addison, Dr Anthony Aldgate, Dr Owen Dudley Edwards, Rosemary Gentleman, Eric Lucey, and Michael Reilly. The Transport and General Workers' Union, Scottish Region, made a donation towards the cost of publication and the Scottish Arts Council provided an indispensable grant that enabled typing of the material for publication to be completed in time to meet the publisher's deadline. Warm thanks are also due two efficient and patient typists, Mrs Jean Singh and Mrs Margaret Thomson. My friend and former student Arthur Moncrieff of East Linton and my brother George provided lifts in their cars when distances proved too much for my push bike. Polygon Books deserve credit for their rapid decision to publish the material, and my particular thanks are due to Neville Moir and Peter Kravitz and their "ancestral ghost". Above all, the tolerance, encouragement and practical help of my wife Sandra have been indispensable as ever.

Ian MacDougall,
Edinburgh
May 1986

SOME RELEVANT EVENTS

1808–13:	Peninsular War
1812:	Liberal constitution
1820:	Army revolt in favour of 1812 constitution
1823:	Absolute monarchy restored by French army intervention
1833–39:	First Carlist War – British and French volunteers support liberals
1872–75:	Second Carlist War
1873–74:	First Spanish Republic
1875–1923:	Constitutional monarchy
1898:	Spanish-American war
1914–18:	Great War – Spain neutral
1917:	Russian Revolution. Revolutionary general strike in Spain
1917–23:	C.N.T. (Anarcho-Syndicalist) and employers' gunmen wage war on each other in Barcelona
1920:	Spanish Foreign Legion formed
1921:	Tribesmen defeat Spanish army in Morocco
1922:	Mussolini and Fascists take power in Italy
1923–30:	Dictatorship by General Primo de Rivera
1926:	Fascist regime established in Portugal
1928–32:	First Five Year Plan in Soviet Union
1929:	Wall Street Crash – world slump begins
1931:	Abdication of King Alphonso XIII. Republic established. Japanese invasion of Manchuria
1932:	Unsuccessful coup by General Sanjurjo
1933:	Hitler and Nazis in power in Germany. Falange (Spanish Fascist Party) founded
1934:	Left-wing rising against right-wing Republican Government severely repressed. Socialist rising in Austria crushed by Dollfuss
1935:	French-Soviet Pact. Mussolini invades Ethiopia (Abyssinia). Hoare-Laval Pact. Conscription and formation of Air Force announced by Hitler. Anglo-German Naval Agreement

1936:   Feb: Electoral victory by Popular Front
           Mar: Re-militarisation of Rhineland by Hitler
           Jun: Popular Front Government (Blum) in France
           Jul: 17-20:   Military rebellion begins in Spain and
                         Morocco. Hitler and Mussolini aid it
           Aug: France closes border with Spain
           Sep: General Franco appointed head of rebels.
                International Brigades formed to defend Republic.
                First meeting of Non-Intervention Committee in
                London. Moscow Trials begin
           Oct: Russian aid for Republican Spain begins to arrive
           Nov: Franco begins siege of Madrid. Republican
                Government moves from Madrid to Valencia. Nazi
                Germany and Fascist Italy formally recognise
                Franco's regime
1937:   Feb: Battle of Jarama
           Mar: Battle of Guadalajara
           Apr: Non-Intervention patrols established. Guernica
                bombed by Franco's planes
           May: Street fighting in Barcelona – Anarchists and
                P.O.U.M. versus Communists and Government.
                Neville Chamberlain becomes Prime Minister in
                Britain
           Jun: Franco's forces capture Bilbao. Fall of Blum
                Government in France
           Jul: Republican offensive at Brunete. Japan begins war on
                China
           Aug: Republican offensive in Aragon – Belchite captured.
                Franco's forces conquer Basque Provinces
           Nov: Republican Government moves from Valencia to
                Barcelona
           Dec: Republican offensive begins at Teruel
1938:   Jan: Republicans capture Teruel
           Feb: Eden resigns as British Foreign Secretary, replaced
                by Lord Halifax. Franco recaptures Teruel
           Mar: Franco begins offensive in Aragon. *Anschluss*: Hitler
                takes Austria
           Apr: Franco's troops reach Mediterranean – Republican
                Spain cut in two
           May: Republican Government issues thirteen-point
                programme of War Aims
           Jul: Republican offensive on the Ebro begins.
                Non-Intervention Committee plan for withdrawal of
                volunteers from Spain
           Sep: Munich Crisis and Pact
           Oct: Final parade of International Brigades at Barcelona

Nov: End of Battle of the Ebro

1939:   Jan: Fall of Barcelona to Franco

Feb: British and French Governments recognise Franco's regime

Mar: Fighting between Communists and Colonel Casado's supporters in Madrid. Franco occupies Madrid. Hitler occupies Prague. British and French Governments give guarantees to Poland

Apr: Franco formally declares War in Spain ended

Aug: Nazi-Soviet Non-Aggression Pact

Sep 1: Hitler invades Poland: beginning of World War Two

The Lord Provost of Glasgow, John Stewart, bids farewell to the Scottish Ambulance Unit outside Glasgow City Chambers in January 1937 as it sets out on its second mission to Republican Spain. Miss Fernanda Jacobsen is in centre, with, on the extreme left, George Burleigh. (See below recollections of Roderick MacFarquhar.)

Born in 1912 in the Gorbals, Glasgow, and brought up there, Phil Gillan was unemployed for many years in the 1920s and early 1930s. He was a member of the National Unemployed Workers' Movement and played a side drum in the Gorbals Unemployed Flute Band. In the 1939-45 War, although employed in a reserved occupation as driver of a road petrol tanker, Phil Gillan volunteered to join the Royal Air Force as a flight engineer and was accepted – only to be subsequently discharged as "surplus to requirements", following intervention by the Petroleum Board.

PHIL GILLAN

It is on record that I was the first to go from Scotland. I can remember the date I arrived in Spain. It was on my passport. It was September 19th 1936. The War had only been two months old at that time.

In the early 1930s I was a member of the Young Communist League in the Gorbals and very active politically. When the Spanish War broke out it hit the news very, very much. And we did feel that the particular governments of the day were not assisting the Spanish Republican Government as they should have. We felt that, all right, we were very limited in what we could do here but it would be a nice gesture if we could get to Spain some way or another and participate in the War.

I had already been a lance-corporal, for what it was worth, in the Territorials. I joined the Territorials in 1929, not out of patriotism, no way, it was the only way we could get a holiday. And you got money. You got your bounty, boot allowances and your pay when you were away at camp for a fortnight. You got two weeks' holiday and you were well fed. I think that was the main reason why most people joined the Territorial Army, simply to get some money and a holiday and well fed while you were on that holiday.

It used to happen that we went to do our drills at the drill hall with our ordinary civvy clothes with a web belt and bayonet round our jacket and carrying our rifle. You kept the rifle at home. I'd see me maybe going to a branch meeting of the Young Communist League, after a drill, hanging up my web belt and bayonet and putting my rifle in the corner while I attended the meeting of the Y.C.L.

Anyway, being a member of the Young Communist League it was arranged for me through the Communist Party to go to Spain. When I went to Spain my family did not know, nobody knew. There were only two persons knew that I was going to Spain: Peter Kerrigan and a lad called Davie Burke, he was the Scottish Secretary of the Young Communist League.[1] That's the only ones that knew. Well, they were the only ones that I knew who were aware that I was going to Spain. My family were quite surprised, I would imagine, because they would lose all sight of me until they got the first letter to tell them where I was – I was in Spain. So I suppose like all other parents and families they were quite concerned that in fact you were in a War. And from that point of view they would be concerned. But they knew my politics and they knew that I was doing something which I believed in, which I thought was right. I didn't tell my family before I went because, well, I suppose at that time, being the first person to go, you wanted to know any difficulties or anything like that – the authorities might try and stop it – and to try and find out all the pitfalls that might arise or to get the experience of it. After that it wasn't so bad and they could sail over right up until the time of the ban on volunteers. The boys then had to cross over the Pyrenees. I think they first started to cross the Pyrenees round about March or April 1937.

So it was arranged for me to go to Spain and I left early in September 1936. I travelled overnight on the train to London and there I got the fare to take me over to Paris, along with a letter. I arrived in Paris and the headquarters of the French Communist Party in turn gave me another letter which I should take to Spain. I then travelled overnight from Paris by train to Perpiguan and then I came to the frontier.

At the frontier there was a large force of the French gendarmes on the French side, and on the other side about 100 yards away were the Spanish militia, who were the customs officials and what have you. I handed over the letter from Paris to one of the Spanish militia officials and he took it away. He came back about ten minutes after that and took me through the frontier. I was put in a taxi. In the taxi was quite a swarthy looking gentleman with his wife, quite a good looking woman. He turned out be the Mexican consul on his way to Barcelona.

We were taken to a hotel in Port Bou, had a lovely four course meal and some Spanish vino. Then we went back on to the taxi, down to the train, and we travelled on the train down to Barcelona. There I reported to an office in the station and I was taken by a lorry to the Karl Marx Barracks in the city. I was there for about three days. There was no one I could speak to, because no one could speak English. A Spanish officer came to me one day and told me that in another barracks there were about half-a-dozen British lads. Would I like to go there? Of course I went there and there we formed the Tom Mann Centuria. That was before the International Brigades were formed.[2]

In our barracks was the Thaelmann Centuria, who were Germans. Then later on we were transferred down to Albacete, which was the base where the International Brigades were formed and trained. We got the option of joining either a French battalion or a German battalion. We chose to join the Thaelmann battalion, which was German.

We went for training. We were supposed to go for a concentrated six weeks' training at a wee place called Villa de la Franca. We got up the next morning and went out into the fields to start our training. But we got no training whatever because we hadn't time. At that particular time – this would be early November 1936 – Franco had launched everything against Madrid. Round about midday there were two motorcyclists came flashing on to the fields where we were. They had a quick word with our commanders and we were withdrawn from the field and put into lorries. We went to a place called Chinchón. We arrived there about four o'clock in the afternoon. We were woken up about two in the morning. We got into lorries again and we travelled pretty far down south where we were engaged on our first action, at a place called the Hill of the Angels. On top of the hill there was what we called a fort but I think it was a monastery. The Moorish forces were in there and our job was to attack it and put them out. Anyway it didn't work out that way and the losses on our side were fairly heavy, fairly substantial.

We were in what we called the XIIth Brigade. The XIth Brigade were straight into University City in Madrid.[3]

We were withdrawn from the Hill of Angels. We were put on to lorries and went fairly fast up to University City. We passed right through the centre of Madrid. When we got there apparently the XIth Brigade had taken quite a lot of punishment, and they merged the two, the XIth and the XIIth, into the XIth Brigade. And then we were in University City, you know, the different buildings and all that sort of thing. We were there for maybe four or five weeks. It was quite a long continuing battle. It wasn't like many of the other battles, which lasted maybe three or four days and then there was a lull after it. This was continuous, night and day, just going up the lines and back down, up the line and back down.

The object of the battle from Franco's side was to capture Madrid and overthrow the Republican Government. That was the time Franco's colleague, General Mola, said that he was attacking Madrid with five columns, four under his command and the Fifth Column inside.[4]

We weren't so much in the streets where we were. It was a barracks. And on the right hand side of the barracks was a red building. I don't know what sort of building that was. But then the other University buildings were about three or four hundred yards in front of us. There was quite a space there. But it was a case of fighting continuing inside the barracks and what we called the red house. It was a case of we would throw them out, they would throw us out, all this sort of thing. We'd be released for maybe three or four days, we'd go back up. And we'd go into the place that we had vacated or three or four hundred yards further up, where the previous troops had advanced or retreated. And this went on for about six or seven weeks.

The bulk of the troops that we were up against were Moors, because the way the fighting was going, advance and retreating, there was quite a substantial number of corpses all over the place.[5] And one of the sort of awe-inspiring scenes that we saw were three Moors who had been climbing over these railings – there was a small wall and railings – and it must have been in the previous battle. They'd been coming over and had been shot and killed and they had fallen over. But their ankles, their feet, had caught on the top of the spikes. And they were hanging down like big bats. They wore blankets over them, and they had *alpargatas*, sort of white canvas shoes, and a uniform and a fez. Their arms were outstretched and they just looked like bats hanging over.

So the bulk of the troops we were fighting was the African army, the Moors. If we advanced they would disappear rapidly, and if they were advancing we would disappear back the other way as quickly as we could. But we were very, very close. The distance was only 150 yards from their outpost to our outpost. Actually it was Sefton Delmer, who was up from the *Daily Express* visiting us one night and he told us that this was the closest in the whole of the University City.[6] See it stretched a fair distance, because it went from the Casa del Campo and right beyond. But this was a salient right into University City and that's where we were. And they were really expecting to take Madrid at any time. We were getting the newspapers and it did look very, very tough.

One of the strong features of Franco's army, as any other International Brigader will tell you, was the amount of tanks that they had. You could always hear the tanks, you know. We had tanks too but not as many as them. It was regular feature, you could see their tanks. And they'd get quite close, and you'd get the order maybe to retreat. Then on the other hand they might retreat, and the tanks would go back. But in this particular section where we were for about six or seven weeks, we were back at precisely the same spot within 300 or 400 yards, backwards or forwards. It was something like *All Quiet on the Western Front*, you know, where they just kept on going back and forward. And that's what happened for about six or seven weeks.

Our tanks were quite small tanks, quite small tanks. Their tanks were a bit bigger but not the sort of tanks that you saw in the Second World War or the tanks that we've got now. They were little, what you'd call whippet tanks, light tanks. I didnae see any particularly heavy tanks but nevertheless they were equally as frightening, you know.

Casualties were very, very high. How you saw it was on the lorries. Each *zug*, which was more or less a platoon, that's the German for a platoon, would be on that lorry going up and the lorry would be full. But coming back you could see all the lorries and they were really looking quite empty. But some of the older soldiers used to say, "Well, that's the way we're losing, they must be losing the same on the other side." So the losses on both sides were very, very substantial.

Fascist planes coming over was a regular feature at that time. One of the horrifying things that we saw were thirty-three – we counted them – there were thirty-three planes in formation flying over Madrid. And on at least three occasions they would fly over our lines and strafe the lines. But the amazing thing was that the amount of casualties was negligible. And I think the Franco forces must have got to know that because they stopped strafing the lines because it wasn't worth their while. Once the shout went round, "Avión!", you started to hide anything that shone or anything that looked from the air like the front line. And I suppose they would do as much damage to their own troops as they did do with us.

During the fighting we managed to get to know civilian Spaniards because we were actually in Madrid, being in University City. When we came back for rest there was a wee place called Fuencarral, which was a suburb of Madrid, where we'd spend maybe two or three days before going back up the line. But we could go out there and go into a cafe and talk to the people. It was amazing to see how these people, to be so close to the front line, how they lived and how they behaved. And they were really solid on our side and solid against Franco. Their morale was extraordinary under the circumstances. The food was obviously limited. You could see the queues at bread shops and things like that. In comparison we were much better fed because the International Brigades at that time were used probably as shock troops and I think they got the better of the food.

We were far, far better equipped than the Spanish troops. We had sort of corduroy trousers and khaki jackets. We had a blanket and we had a sort of raincoat. Later on we were supplied with steel helmets. We had machine guns but I was not a machine gunner. Our machine gunners were Germans. The only other weapon that I used was a trench mortar, a very, very old-fashioned type of trench mortar which we were using in University City.

It was really hard fighting. It was a crucial battle for control of Madrid. That's what it was because Franco, I think, threw everything into it that he could. Then it settled down. Then he knew that he wasn't going to get Madrid. It wasn't to be. He just never captured Madrid. Madrid never surrendered. Right up until the very, very last Madrid held out.

I remember an incident that happened. When you compare the International Brigades with the modern British army, you know, and the type of officering, officers came from the ranks and they had to prove themselves. And I remember we got a new company commander. He was a young fellow called Oswald. He was quite young, he'd be about twenty-four, something like that. A real harum scarum lad. I remember one time he got a revolver – that was officer status when you got a revolver. He was on the balcony of this house that we were in. He fired about four or five shots into the air. We reprimanded him for you never know where these bullets were going. We weren't too happy with him, not because he was inefficient or anything like that, but too foolhardy, much too foolhardy. Some of the other Germans thought the same. And we used to have these meetings after an action, to discuss the weak points, the strong points and that sort of thing. And we were critical of Oswald and so were the rest. As a result he was replaced as a company commander. Now how could you do that in the British army? Or any other army? You just couldn't do that. Oswald was replaced by another young lad. But Oswald, being what he was, harum scarum, a very brave young man, he was placed in charge of patrols and used to go out at night on patrol. On two occasions, I understand, he brought back some prisoners. But he went out one night and never came back. The patrol never came back. So that was that. That was Oswald.

I remember another young lad with us. He was only eighteen – in fact, later on it turned out that he was only seventeen. With a right polished accent, obviously well schooled, he spoke very good French. He turned out to be Winston Churchill's nephew, Esmond Romilly. But in fairness to young Romilly he never at any time advertised who he was. He kept it very secret. He came back to Britain and wrote a very, very good book, very anti-Fascist. He was quite a character. He married Jessica Mitford and went back to Spain. The British Government sent a cruiser or a destroyer to Spain to try and get him back out. He hit the news. But he went to the United States and then he joined the Royal Canadian Air Force and was killed in 1941 in a raid over Norway.[7]

That was one lad. But there were lots of lads there who were very, very good. Well, they were your comrades. You became very attached to them.

Well, we were in the fighting at Madrid for maybe four or five weeks. Then from there we went down to a place called Boadilla. And things didn't work out right for us at all. There were ten of us in our little British section. I got wounded first. Then about ten minutes after that another seven of the lads got killed. Then the other two who were left they came back home.

I was wounded in the neck. It was rather a peculiar wound because the bullet went in the left side and passed right through the neck, between my windpipe and my spinal column. And when you think of all the nerves and tendons and arteries that pass through the neck, that bullet at the end of the day turned out to be a flesh wound and did no permanent damage at all. The doctors over there said it was quite a miraculous wound. I'm sure it was. It was about seven months after that before I got the full use of my left arm. I suppose it would be shock round about the tendons and that sort of thing. But at the end of the day, you know, it was a flesh wound and it left no long term effects. I was exceptionally lucky. After being in hospital in Madrid I was sent to convalesce at Castilla de la Plana. Then I was repatriated back home. I came back in February or March 1937. I didn't return to the War in Spain after being wounded. I had to attend hospitals here at home for quite a long time for physiotherapy.

After I returned here I spent a fair amount of time as secretary of the Scottish Youth Foodship Committee, gathering in food for Spain. We had a very, very good Youth Foodship Committee and we did very well. One of the things we used to do was go round a lot of churches and speak to the people in the churches for food for Spain, you know. The response was really excellent, really excellent the response we got from many of those churches.

Looking back with fifty years of hindsight on the Spanish Civil War there's no way I could fault myself for going there. I think it was absolutely right and the longer I think about it the more convinced I am that I was right. And I think that events proved conclusively that we were right. Because after the War was finished Franco was *persona non grata* so far as Western Europe was concerned. He was barred from NATO and from the European Economic Community. He just was not accepted. He was a great ally of Hitler during the War. All these things all add up to the fact that we did the right thing.

Those who did the wrong things were the governments of the day. They did not give to the Spanish Republican Government the aid that they were entitled to under International Law. If the British Government let the country down then there were some of us who were prepared to say, "Well, what the Government should have done and won't do we'll have a crack at and we'll try and do something about it."

Although it was a short time it was nevertheless a big piece of our lives. But looking back with hindsight the War, and meeting. International Brigaders from other countries – Poles, Czechs, Germans, French, Spanish – was an experience one could only have once in a lifetime.

Donald Renton, who died in 1977 at the age of 65, was a well known labour leader in Edinburgh all his life. He joined the Labour Party soon after the General Strike, in which he had taken part, in 1926. Three years later he left the Labour Party and became a member of the Communist Party until his resignation from it in protest against the crushing of the Hungarian rising in 1956. He rejoined the Labour Party and became a Town Councillor in Edinburgh from 1962 until his death. In the Second World War he served in the Royal Artillery, taking part in the anti-aircraft defence of London and several other cities throughout the German blitz.

DONALD RENTON

I saw the War in Spain as part and parcel of the general offensive by the Fascist Powers against working class rights and liberties all over the world, including our own country. I had been active in the labour movement in this country since I was a boy of fourteen and was a member at that time of the Communist Party. So after taking part in the National Hunger March in November 1936 – I was an unemployed man at the time – immediately after that I decided that I had to be part and parcel of the struggle not only of the Spanish people but for the British people, who were then being menaced by the threat constituted by Fascist Germany and by the existence of the Axis grouping on a world scale.

Among the men who left Edinburgh in November 1936 there was my very, very good friend George Watters and a number of others: Harry Fry, who was destined to become one of the commanders of the British Battalion of the International Brigade; George Bridges, who was killed at Jarama, who was not a member of the Communist Party but of the British Section of the International Socialist Labour Party; and a lad called Forrester, who also was a member of the B.S.I.S.L.P. It was an all-party grouping, seeing the struggle in Spain as part and parcel of a united effort to help the Spanish people not only to maintain their own liberties but to enable us to maintain ours against the growing Fascist threat.

On our way through from Perpignan to Figueras we had none of the tight security that became part of the experience of comrades who were to arrive in Spain after us. We crossed the frontier in relative comfort, and the guards at the frontier, in broad measure, appeared to indicate to us considerable sympathy for the aims that we were seeking to achieve in terms of support for the Spanish Republic. Of course this was before the creation of Non-Intervention patrols, which were Non-Intervention in name only in the sense that they never precluded assistance arriving for the Fascists in the shape of men or material. On the other hand these patrols did operate quite considerably to detract from the volume of support that the Spanish Republican cause in our view demanded and should have been afforded by the so-called democratic countries of the West.[8]

The first place we arrived at in Spain was Figueras and here I had an experience I can always recall with a thrill of pride. While we had often talked about the role to be played by women in the general struggle, there for the first time we saw the militia women, comrades who like ourselves were either going to have or already had had first line experience in battle against the Fascist enemy. These were wonderful comrades, people who had – so far as I was concerned at least – a very, very powerful inspirational effect on arriving inside Spain itself. It brought home to me that here was a general struggle that, despite the backwardness of Spain by and large, here for the first time were women beginning to play the kind of role without which the general emancipation of ordinary working people on a world scale from any form of exploitation is impossible.

When we arrived in Barcelona we were welcomed by mass enthusiastic demonstrations of the population. And although I have heard it said that demonstrations can be swept up, there is one thing that can never be instilled into the minds of ordinary people and that is to stimulate an enthusiasm that they don't possess. And there in Barcelona I felt for the first time that the ideas that we had talked about, of unity against the common enemy, were being reflected in the welcome afforded us.

We were only in Barcelona for a very, very short time. We proceeded down through Valencia, which we passed through at night time, so I can't tell you anything about Valencia itself other than the blacked out stations which, in retrospect, were reminiscent of experiences we had during the Second World War. We went through Valencia and up to Albacete and here we were kitted up. We were all provided with very, very good khaki and boots. But at that juncture no actual weapons were issued to us in the mass. In other words, what little training we got at Albacete was training based on weapons that were completely obsolete and liable to explode in your face if they were actually used. Most of them were donkey's years old and of no use whatsoever in actual battle conditions.

Albacete had of course been a place where Franco had succeeded temporarily in establishing power. In fact, it was his own home town. But his power was overthrown by the uprising of the people of the area. Nevertheless it was this background that required one to be very, very careful in one's movements in Albacete. Wherever you went you had to move in groups in order to avoid isolation and the possibility of attacks by the Fifth Column. You had to be vigilant and on your guard all the time that you were in Albacete.

We moved up to Madrigueras and here I was to make the acquaintance of Tom Wintringham for the first time. Now this man, while a supremely modest person, was an absolute genius not only in his ability to inspire, but in his capacity to create weapons. He established for us that even in the worst of conditions it became possible for ordinary men and women who were fighting for proper causes to find the means through which, in one way or another, they could fight back against the enemy. I remember that among the other training weapons that we had in Madrigueras there were a couple of old Lewis guns, battered almost out of recognition. But Tom managed to bring them back into service. One of the first things that Tom taught us, using these old Lewis guns, was how to fire at aircraft.[9]

Other weapons that we had in Madrigueras then were the old French Chauchat, a shockingly poor automatic weapon, and again the terribly poor rifles, if one could describe them as such, with which we continued to be issued right up until the first Company of what was to become the British Battalion came up from the front at Córdoba.

Now that was an occasion I'll never forget. These comrades had already been through the mill on the Córdoba front, at Boadilla and elsewhere in the southern regions, and they carried scars of battle. Many of them had already been wounded. Some of the best known characters in the British labour movement had already been killed in the fighting in these areas: John Cornford, for example, and Ralph Fox, who didn't live to bring out all of the tremendous promise that he possessed as a writer and as a leader of men.[10]

When this Company came back they had among them a comrade who was to play an outstanding part in the subsequent history of the Battalion, at least until I was taken prisoner and beyond that stage too until his final repatriation: Jock Cunningham. It's strange that I should first meet Cunningham in Spain because I knew of him through my eldest brother, who had served with the Argyll and Sutherland Highlanders in the West Indies. Cunningham had served with the Argylls there, too, and when a revolt developed in the British garrison at Kingston, Jamaica, over a number of issues affecting the troops, Jock Cunningham was made the fall guy.[11] Jock went to prison in Britain for quite a time. After his release he was active in the London area in the Unemployed organisation, then he went to Spain. In Spain very rapidly he established his claim to be dubbed the British Chapiev – one of the great partisan leaders immediately after the Russian Revolution.[12]

This point links up with the point about weapons because it was in Madrigueras that for the first time we saw Russian rifles. I'll never forget that day because at that time I literally worshipped the Soviet Union. And when one finally had a rifle on which one could depend for killing Fascists, and not killing yourself, with a hammer and sickle emblazoned on it, then one felt a real thrill of pride. Here was the great Workers' Republic coming to the aid of the Spanish people in their effort to preserve democracy inside their own country. Because please bear in mind this fact: the struggle in Spain was not a struggle to establish Communism. It was a struggle to preserve democracy against the Fascist threat not only to liberties and the rights of working people, to progressive people in Spain, it was part and parcel of the general defence of a movement that was beginning to develop on a world scale.

Anyway that Russian rifle was for me the greatest prize I ever received at any time. I remember all of our comrades very, very rapidly proved what remarkably fine marksmen they were because these rifles – although I wouldn't have compared them with the British Lee Enfield for sturdiness – were wonderfully accurate. Practically anyone could become a sharpshooter with the Russian rifle in a very short space of time.

We were fortunate too in that here we got hold of those heavy Russian Maxim machine guns. In the training period we very quickly discovered they were capable of creating terrible disorder in the ranks of the Fascist enemy.

During the training period of the Battalion at Madrigueras we had some problems arising from drink. A strict order had been issued by the Popular Front organisation in Madrigueras itself that during training no drink would be served to any of the Internationals.[13] Notwithstanding this there were lads turning up very, very much under the influence. We discovered by pure accident that the way round the problem of getting drink even when there was a complete prohibition was to order what they called *cafe frío*, cold coffee, a mixture of rum and coffee. The cafe owner who had been selling this landed in prison in Albacete.

The other point that illustrates the general reaction of the International Brigade and Spanish Republican leaderships to this problem of drink was that Harold Fry as our officer – and Fry was the kind of man who liked a pint himself – made it clear that no one in his Company would under any circumstances be in the line either with drink in his posession or under the influence of it. And Fry made a specific point of inspecting every water bottle, to make certain that water and not alcoholic drink was in it.

I don't want to say much more about what transpired in Madrigueras during the training period except to say that here one of the political errors that, in my view, remains to be sorted out in connection with the Spanish War was in fact created. There had been brought into being an Irish Company. In the light of the struggle of the Irish people for their own national independence this Company should have been, in my view, quite a separate organisation, even although attached to the British Battalion and part of the International Brigade. In practice, however, the Irish national struggle as a related factor to the Spanish fight was not in my opinion concretely enough recognised. So it brought about one or two ugly situations at Madrigueras during the training period. Nevertheless these were overcome and largely through the activity of a chap called Prendergast, who had formerly been a member of what they called the Irish

Republican Congress. Through his efforts and those of Frank Ryan these things were resolved in a manner that enabled the Battalion finally to go into the line at Jarama in early February 1937.[14]

The Jarama Valley is an important approach to the Madrid–Valencia road. The attack being made by the Fascists at that time was aimed at cutting the single life-line to Madrid that was then still open. Notwithstanding the massacre of our own Battalion and many other Battalions of the International Brigade in the course of the battle of Jarama, the line that we held there remained the line until the end of the War, until Casado and company betrayed the Spanish Republic by their capitulation to the Fascist enemy.[15]

I don't want to go into great detail about the actual course of the battle of Jarama. But I do want to correct a mistaken impression which in whatever way it got about bears no actual relation to the truth. On both sides of the lines there were people who were dressed in almost identical garb. True enough we were dressed in khaki but by and large ordinary Republican Army units and also elements of the Spanish Fascist army, such as the *Tercio*, the Spanish Fascist Foreign Legion, were dressed in similar garb. And no error of judgement would have been made in the course of the actual taking of that position from us if it had been a question of the Moors trying to masquerade as Internationalists singing *The Internationale* and aproaching us with raised fists and all that. The contrary is true. Because of the very mixed up pattern of the battle, the nature of the dress and all the rest of it, it became possible for them to pull a fast one. Yet even then, in our section at that juncture, there were different voices raised, you know, to keep firing. Others were for cease fire – "These are our own comrades," And it all arose because of the tremendous confusion of the battle and the circumstance that we, a heavy machine-gun Company, which normally is a Company held in support to give covering fire in advances or retreats, were compelled by the situation that developed in the battle of Jarama to become the forward Company of the entire British Battalion and indeed of all the battalions of the International Brigade that were then involved in the Jarama action.

Before that point, however, our Battalion had suffered too from grossly bad administration. This was because a character who proved completely unreliable was in charge of the ammunition truck for these heavy Maxim guns. The bulk of our boys in the Battalion had already become casualties before the Maxim ammunition arrived in position. But they arrived in time to prevent what could have been a complete debacle, to convert that into its opposite, and to enable the line to be held there until the end of the War.

In the event, because of the circumstances I've already described, we were surrounded. Our Company at the beginning of that encirclement probably had around 120 men. When we finally were in Fascist hands there were only some thirty of us left, the bulk of whom in one way or another had been knocked about rather badly. I'd been wounded in the legs, Harry Fry had a broken arm, shattered with machine gun bullets, Jimmy Rutherford was battered soft, George Watters had gone down.

The Fascists couldn't understand the kind of resistance that was being made to them in the course of their offensive along the Jarama Valley towards Organda Bridge and so on. And I suppose from their point of view to take some prisoners possibly proffered some hope of intelligence secrets and all the rest of it. Well, if that was the hope of the Fascists then I'm very, very proud to say it didn't come anywhere near realisation. Like any other soldiers in similar circumstances our business was to try and mislead the enemy about the actual strength. So when we were being questioned we built up a picture of an enormous mass of men and material there ready to resist the Fascist onslaught. Harry Fry and I, as his commissar, were instrumental in quite considerable measure in building up this picture of a complete wall of opposition, something against which the Fascists would be completely destroyed. I think it's just possible – it's a conjecture – that this may have had an effect in slowing down the impact of the Fascist assault at that juncture.

When we were taken prisoner we were compelled to march through this valley in such a manner that we were under fire from our own line. There was a lot of dead ground in this area and the Fascists who were escorting us, while able to keep a certain amount of cover themselves, compelled us to appear in the sight of our own comrades who were manning the sunken road. A number of our comrades were killed in the course of this march through Death Valley.

An experience of mine then helped illustrate how absurd it is for many people to place their faith in sky pilots, padres, whatever their religious persuasion. As already mentioned some of our comrades were dressed in exactly the same way as the Fascists were. One of our boys had got a very bad one and was very obviously dying. One of their chaplains went forward to this boy to place the cross on his lips. The boy was obviously on his way out. Around him there arose the shout, "Rojo! Rojo!" – Red! And that crucifix came back before it ever touched the lips of the comrade concerned. As an example of Christian charity that has helped to convince me in my own general approach to the whole issue of religion since that day.

At the end of this valley there was a sharp turn and here Ted Dickinson was executed. Now Ted was an Australian by origin. He had been very, very active in the Jewish Ex-Servicemen's Movement for Peace in East London. He was a comrade of outstanding ability in military terms and in being able to lift and rouse people in the most difficult conditions. Well, the Fascists sorted this man out as a very, very obvious leader of men. A Fascist officer pointed at Ted and pointed at a tree. They carried through a form of execution with rifles lined up only a few inches from the head of the person so that the whole effect is to blow the complete top of the head off. Well, Ted before dying gave us all the Republican salute. "Salud, comrades," said Ted, and we responded in like manner. Inspired by his example, frightened though we were, expecting the same thing to happen to us, at least we felt it was absolutely necessary to carry the splendid example, if necessity arose, that Ted had shown in his last few minutes.

We were taken over then by a party of Moors. They were mounted on horseback. Our wrists were all bound, some of us were wounded, it was a very, very difficult situation. But these Moorish horsemen were whipping us on. International Brigaders will recall a particular sign that became famous inside Spain indicating what was going to happen to you, something about which we can laugh rather grimly now but which at that time appeared a very, very likely prospect in the light of all that had taken place until that moment. [16]

We were finally put in *camions* under heavy guard and taken to a little town called Navalcarnero. There we were put in prison. One of the experiences I am able to recall very well is how the Italian Fascist officers used to bring their senoritas into the prison to look at the prisoners, jeer at them, and very often to encourage the Moors to come into the cells to knock you about. It was a good thing that the Moors as a general rule didn't know very much about how to knock people about, other than with rifle and bayonet. Luckily they weren't booted or shoed in a way that enabled them to do very much damage.

We were in prison at Navalcarnero for quite some time and then we were transported to a place called Talavera de la Reina. There a concentration camp had been established on the site of an old pottery factory. There were prisoners there not only from Britain but from other countries on which the International Brigades were based – German and French and other comrades. Notwithstanding all the pressures of the Fascists, the efforts they made to create conflict between one group and another on food and other questions, the general solidarity of the comrades in the prison or concentration camp, as it really was, remained superbly high. Real friendships in fact were built among the different groupings. Spanish Fascism was Fascist without a doubt – but the Spanish Fascists had not yet acquired the kind of skill characteristic of the Nazis in Auschwitz, Belsen, Buchenwald, and all their other concentration camps.

The Fascists ultimately decided that they were fetching us to trial. The charge laid against us comrades in the International Brigade was military rebellion. In other words, the Fascist characters who had risen in military rebellion against the legally elected Spanish Republican Government were the same characters charging us with military rebellion. In the event, a number of our comrades, including Jimmy

Rutherford from Edinburgh, were sentenced to death. Others of us were sentenced to thirty years' imprisonment and George Watters from Prestonpans to solitary confinement for life.

At that trial the entire proceedings were in Spanish. No effort was made to translate any part of the proceedings for any of us. Although a few of our boys, rather more gifted in languages than I am, had begun to pick up a few Spanish phrases, in broad terms it was quite impossible really to know what was being said inside that court.

The spectators' gallery provided further evidence to me that priests and prelates of any description couldn't be relied upon, because the most interested spectators during the trial were clergymen obviously gloating over the fate they felt was going to befall us.

So back we went to the concentration camp, awaiting the sentences to be carried through. Meantime we were put to work digging a great pit in the cemetery at Talavera de la Reina. This great pit was the place at which the executions were carried through. It was no uncommon thing while you were working down there enlarging these pits for Fascist firing squads to be busy with their dirty work of exterminating the people whose crime was to hold trade union cards, to believe in democracy, and things of that nature.

We were in Talavera de la Reina for some time. Perhaps fortunately for us a chap called Pembroke Stephens, who was then one of the international correspondents of the *Daily Telegarph,* in one way or another had got wind of the fact that there were Britishers among the prisoners held in Talavera de la Reina. I'll give Pembroke Stephens his due. Pembroke Stephens went out of his way to try and establish contact with the people who were then being held in prison by the Fascists. Now Pembroke Stephens made no secret of the fact that he himself supported Franco and the general Fascist cause expressed in either Germany or Italy. But sometimes one does encounter a peculiar insularity, and the insularity in Pembroke Stepens' case was that we were British and if he could do anything to help us he was prepared to step out of his way to that extent. It's an ironic comment that Pembroke Stephens was killed some time later by a Japanese bomb when he was covering the war in China. He was killed in Nanking during one of the Japanese bombardments of that town. He himself had been of course one of the supporters of the Berlin-Rome-Tokyo Axis.[17]

Well, after some time in Talavera de la Reina we were moved up to a prison in Salamanca. And here in Salamanca prison there were close on 3,000 prisoners. The overwhelming majority of them were under sentence of death. We hadn't known at this juncture that as soon as we had been captured at Jarama our boys in the International Brigade and the Spanish Republican Government had taken quick action to make known to the world that Britishers were among the people who had been taken by the Fascists. And the Republican Government, through del Vayo at the League of Nations, had put into motion action to secure an exchange of prisoners.[18] Side by side with this the Spanish Republican Government made it plain that for any one of us who was executed similar action would be taken on the Republican side as far as Fascists were concerned, and more particularly German and Italian Fascists.

Anyway we were in Salamanca prison and it was there that we finally learnt that the negotiations for our exchange were nearing completion. One of the things that was done at this stage was to supply us with a "suit" of civilian clothing. Now it's quite impossible to describe this "suit". If you think of a very loosely meshed sack and of a cloth very similar to that then you've got the kind of garb in which they finally decked us out. But they had taken away our uniforms from us. And here it was a wonderful thing to see the reactions of the Spanish people. Spanish jails are rather different from jails in other parts of the world – and I've been in jails in this country, too, in the course of and for my political activities. In Spain very often quite considerable masses of people are able to move about in the patios of the jails. We ourselves were kept incommunicado from the prisoners in general but the Spaniards managed to find ways of communicating with us. The Fascists were in the process of clearing out our uniforms, obviously intending to re-use, them possibly for further actions and the same type of subterfuge that had resulted in our own capture. I recall these Spanish comrades' message very well: "They've taken your uniforms, comrades. We hope they haven't taken your politics." And of course for every one of us that remained a challenge at that particular time, just as it remained a challenge thereafter.

Some of these experiences in prison help to illustrate the actual character of the Fascist enemy no matter where Fascism rears its head. One other aspect was the story of Jimmy Rutherford from Edinburgh. Jimmy was a young lad, little more than eighteen years of age, when he was taken prisoner at Jarama. He wasn't quite eighteen before he went out to Spain. While we were prisoners he was questioned by a character called the Marquis Merry del Val.[19] Anyway, Jimmy was among those of us who were exchanged at that time, but Jimmy and Harry Fry later returned to Spain. In my own case a decision was taken that I should be in charge of the anti-Fascist work in the East End of London and particularly among the unemployed where Mosley was making some inroads at that stage.[20] Anyhow, Jimmy returned to Spain but was once more taken prisoner. He was incarcerated at Miranda del Ebro, one of the most notorious concentration camps in Fascist Spain and one that corresponded rather more closely to the German model than anything we had experienced during our incarceration in Fascist territory. Merry del Val was again the person who interrogated him and as soon as he saw Jimmy he recognised him. The comrades had made up their minds to cover Jimmy up and had dubbed him with a new name. But there was one thing Jimmy couldn't prevent and that was the recognition of his finger prints. We had all been dabbed in the process of being repatriated to our own countries. One other thing I think I should say, and this is that all of my recollections of the very, very fine comrades who died in the course of battle in Spain, or who were executed by the Fascists after capture, as Jimmy Rutherford finally was, add up to my conviction that every one of the sacrifices of those comrades was a worthwhile sacrifice. Such scarifice should inspire in my view every one inside the labour movement to do more to bring about the kind of solidarity movement that will really help the Spanish people. We in Britain still have our responsibility, those of us who were in the Brigade, who were alongside the Spanish people in the course of their struggle to help to life and rouse still greater support for the Spanish people to enable something to be implemented that should have been implemented years ago. That is the declaration that was made at Potsdam by the representatives of the Allied Powers after the victory over Hitler. And this was that Fascism had to be extirpated everywhere. Everywhere includes Spain in my view, and that's still our task.[21]

INTERNATIONAL BRIGADE

Edinburgh and District Ex-Members' Association.

Hon. Treasurer—JOHN P. C. DUNLOP,
9 East Fettes Avenue, Edinburgh, 4.   'Phone 20754.
Office and Central Food Depot:
c/o DOTT, 8 Grosvenor Crescent, Edinburgh, 12,

The I.B.

FOOD CONVOY FOR SPAIN

**Will arrive in Edinburgh on Saturday, 21st January.
The Mound, 4 p.m.; Foot of Leith Walk, 4.30 p.m.**

Donations, in Cash, for I.B. Disabled Ex-Members, Widows and Orphans and Non-Perishable Food for Spain **Urgently** required.

You are invited to make a collection from your Household. Kindly **place Cash** in this Envelope, and **have Parcel of Food Ready** for Collector.   (Chocolate, Sugar, Rice and Tinned Milk, Meat, Beans, Peas, Fish, Butter, etc.).

GREAT "AID SPAIN" RALLY

On SATURDAY, 21st JANUARY, at 7.30 p.m., In the MUSIC HALL, GEORGE STREET.

Members of Convoy and Prominent Local Speakers. Musical Programme.   Come and Bring Your Friends. Pay tribute to heroic Spanish People & International Brigade.

IMPORTANT.—Complete this Space before handing back.

Name,...

Address,...

Cash Enclosed, £   :   :

WARWICK & SONS LTD., EDINBURGH.

Envelope for donation to International Brigade Food Convoy for Spain, organised by Edinburgh and District Ex-Members' Association, and probably dating from 1939.

George Watters, a Prestonpans, East Lothian, miner and general labourer, was born in 1904 and died in 1980. He joined the Communist Party in the early 1920s and remained a member until his death. His brother-in-law William Dickson was killed in the Spanish Civil War, fighting in the International Brigade at Brunete in 1937. George Watters' own fate in the battle of Jarama remained unknown for many months to his family, who were forced to assume he was dead until, happening to visit a cinema, they saw a Movietone Newsreel showing him among prisoners-of-war being repatriated.

GEORGE WATTERS

Strange to say, I was in the Territorial Army in the early 1920s. After the strike in the mines in 1921 I realised clearly with the beating the miners got at that time, the struggle that had developed, the setback generally in the working class movement by the Tories driving against the workers at that time, that we had to do something about the situation. I also had a brother killed in the pits just previous to this. This helped get my mind fixed that there was something far wrong.

And from that time on I began to look round about me as to where I could find the movement that really would express the views I had. My career started in the political movement as far back as 1922. And later I began to take more and more part in politics. Unfortunately, not having much opportunity of schooling or anything else in Prestonpans, away from everything, all that I received regularly was ten dozen copies of the *Weekly Worker* or *Workers' Weekly*. The name changed periodically because of the fines it had to pay, and if the paper was unable to carry on they just brought out another paper.[22]

This was followed of course by the strike in 1926, when I became involved in pickets and had taken part in activities all round the area, coming to Edinburgh to attend meetings, and all the time gaining experience. Ye began tae become more and more involved in the political movement. There were more and more of us coming into Edinburgh, taking part in events, and building up in the fight against Mosley at that particular time. I remember gaun tae a meeting in the Usher Hall, having been supplied wi' a ticket by some of the students at Edinburgh University. I landed down right in the second front seat in the Usher Hall. You'll know what sort of position I was in. My job was to get up and create a disturbance right away by challenging Sir Oswald Mosley, which I did. At that time I had a pretty loud voice. And Sir Oswald Mosley wasn't being heard. I was warned by William Joyce, better known later on as Lord Haw Haw, what would happen to me unless I kept quiet.[23] There was a rush and in the rush I got a bit o' a knockin' about, and taken up to High Street.[24] We were released wi' the Party phoning up and letting them know any bail that was being tabled. It finished up wi' us being fined £5 each. But when I was in the High Street I was accused by one o' the Fascists o' having kicked him in the eye. His eye was split right across. So I jist said at the time,

"I wish tae Christ it had been me. I'd at least felt some satisfaction."

But this all led up of course to the outbreak of the War in Spain. Right from the commencement I had the feeling that something should be done about it. The intervention of the Germans and Italians into Spain naturally worried us, and we were afraid of the situation developing, of what was likely to happen with the Spanish Government, which at that particular time was carrying through some very good measures so far as the ordinary people, and even the middle class, in Spain were concerned. The eight hours' day, compulsory education for all children, a guaranteed wage they couldn't go below a ten peseta minimum, and a number o' other features considered a great advance as far as the Spanish people were concerned. This didn't meet of course with the approval of the upper classes, the Fascist element. So the War developed, wi' Franco having the assistance o' March, a tobacconist millionaire, financing the sending of Moors and that to Spain.[25] Then the intervention of the Germans and Italians made the situation critical.

As far as we were concerned we felt that something had to be done. The British Government was claiming there was no proof the Germans and Italians were intervening, and was supporting the policy of Non-Intervention. Unfortunately at that time the Labour Party were supporting this line, which I considered a very unfortunate thing.[26] The whole of the press, except for the Left papers, were publishing articles saying there was no proof of the Germans and Italians being in Spain. The situation became critical.

So when we heard about the formation of the International Brigades I finally held a meeting at Ayres Wynd, the common place for holding meetings in the centre of Prestonpans, and told the crowd I intended to go to Spain. I told them that more and more should take more interest in what was taking place in Spain as it would affect them directly later on with Hitler and Mussolini becoming involved.

By this time I had a wife and three children, but fortunately the wife was like myself, supporting the fight of the International Brigade.

I then went to Edinburgh where we had the Communist Party centre. I got two other lads along wi' me, Jock Gilmour and Jimmy Kempton, and the three of us went up and volunteered to go away to Spain. J.C. Park, the Party secretary in Edinburgh, was the boy that was taking the recruits and passing them through. He was a wily lad and one that knew his business all right. I mean, fellows going in before us had got away with getting a certain amount of money and never being seen again. Parkie wasn't having anything of that. The first thing that he asked if anybody came in who volunteered for going to Spain: "Why do you want to go to Spain? Any particular reason?" And unless he came forward with a satisfactory reason there was no chance of passing through.

Once you did get through, you came to Edinburgh. We got buses frae Edinburgh to Glasgow and then at Glasgow we got buses again that took us right down to London. And then in London when it came to getting across to France, we met wi' an important comrade that we went up to see. Donald Renton was put in charge of a group. I was put in charge of a group. And we got the money to buy their tickets, return tickets – who they went tae for coming back, I don't know – so there was no chance o' anyone disappearing wi' the money. Things were like that. Naturally ye had the adventurer and the boy that was tryin' tae get somethin'. It was necessary to be very careful in the approach they took to the thing at that time.

But we got the returns, landed in France, went right to Paris and stayed for a night. The following night we went right down on the train to Perpignan, right on the border. At Perpignan there were buses arrived, and they came in and checked ye had a passport to go on to Spain. One fellow in the bus has a passport, he was sitting on the right hand side. Whenever they came in he showed his passport and they were quite satisfied. They were quite obviously all sympathetic and knew what was happening. We went through quite easily.

After we left Figueras we made for Albacete. And in Albacete there was a barracks and in it we were supplied with equipment, every bit as good as what we got in the British army. I mean, it was khaki, just somewhat similar. We had puttees. They weren't too particular what you put on. Ye could have leggings. But on the whole we had a sort of puttee. The uniform was good and we were issued with Russian rifles.

We were pretty fortunate as far as food was concerned. Despite the difficulties we seemed to get just enough to do us. We were't looking for much. We knew that certain things had to be for the Spanish children. And because of that I never heard a complaint yet regarding the food. It wasn't just what we would have expected at home but we understood the difficulties and were quite happy wi' what we got all the time that we were there.

We had a bit of training in Albacete and we also had the experience of being fired on there by spies or supporters of Franco, from windows and that. Fortunately enough we picked up one of the places, reported it to the Spaniards – that is what we were informed to do, not to do anything about it ourselves, but to immediately inform them. Some of the Spaniards went in and they soon dealt with the situation. We didn't have really much time for training. We shifted from Albacete after, say, a week and went up to Madrigueras. At Madrigueras we did a bit of training and it was there we met with Jock Cunningham and Tom Wintringham. Colonel McCartney was at the time the commander but something happened. He was wounded, it was some mistake that they made, and Tom Wintringham took over after McCartney moved up.[27] Under Tom Wintringham we had Jock Cunningham taking charge of the Company. Jock Cunningham was a very good lad that everybody understood. He knew how to deal with men. He knew how to be severe. He knew also to get men along with him.

I mean ye met with some elements that were deliberately causing strife. One in particular. After Cunningham got us all ready and we went on a march this man had struck one of the young lads. And Cunningham when he got us right out, Cunningham says, "Now we'll have a bit o' teachin," he says, "what you can do and what you can't do." He says "We're all here as volunteers and we're all here to do a job," and he says, "we've got to do that job, and nobody's going to interfere with you." And he challenged this Glasgow fellow who had struck the young lad, and gave him the hidin' o' his life. This fellow left, was sent back home as bein' no use to the International Brigade. We had a few experiences of these things.

From Madrigueras we went right up tae the line. We were rushed up because o' the attack that was being made on Madrid. We landed up intae Jarama Valley. When we went in the Fascists were advancing at the time and here ye had instances of where, as a result of no proper trainin' and that, no' the men making mistakes, but one of the commanders o' a company goin' forward. When he was informed by the French and two or three others about the Fascists coming forward, he says: "The English go forward." So we went forward, and unfortunately we lost quite a lot of men in that incident wi' him goin' right forward instead of making a line there where he was and gettin' his men entrenched.

We got into positions and held on to them when the others were compelled to retreat on both our sides. A matter of three days we were in them and we were completely surrounded. We were using the Maxim machine gun in our particular part. In the other parts they were usin' other types o' guns. My mate from Prestonpans he was badly wounded just the day before we were surrounded and I advised him to wait on them comin' up wi' the ambulance men that would take him down on stretchers. But he felt that the stretchers were needed for men that were more severely wounded than he was. He didn't realise how bad he was and unfortunately he died as a result of the wound. He was pumping out blood a' the time.[28]

Followin' that, well, it was jist a case o' fightin' and carryin' on. We got some lad bringing up ammunition for a day and we had plenty of ammo. We carried on wi' this and I think we did a very good job so far as the effects it had on the enemy. Because wi' their advance naturally on all sides of us we were able to get them wi' the machine gun. How we got to know the effects it had had was wi' the Fascists themselves after we were captured referring to us as "Mucho fuerte" – strong. That was what the consequence of our stand had been against them.

Finally, they came in from both sides. Someone had cried out that it was our own fellows that were coming up from the rear. So we didn't pay attention. We were paying attention to the front. A' I know about it was that I got hit on the head wi' it must ha' been the butt end o' a rifle. Donald Renton was wounded and quite a lot o' things had happened. When I came to they were all standin' wi' them wi' their hands up. Well, I'm afraid they got the gun that I was on because I was keeping firing right up till I got hit and that was that.

Before we were captured we had an experience during the night. We had one fellow calling for help and it sounded a good English voice and that. We were warned by Tom Wintringham not to pay attention to anything like that, that the Fascists would try everything to get prisoners. One of our fellows was insisting that we should do something about it. So foolishly or otherwise, I don't know, I volunteered to go out. I said to this other fellow, "You're so big in the mouth you can come out behind me with a grenade, and if there is any chance o' them gettin' us throw the grenade and get out o' it." Well, I went away out but I lost touch with our friend with the grenade. He'd apparently gone right back after he had gone a little bit out. I went out and my experience was that the voice was going further and further away, travelling all the time. Finally, I had to make up my mind. I says, "Well, it's going to be difficult getting back here during the night to our own place." And wi' no touch wi' the fellow that had come out wi' me I finally made an effort to get back. Luckily enough I contacted one of our own fellows right at the extreme outside. He brought me along to get me checked up to see that I was really one of the International Brigade. That was the experience I had of goin' out for some apparently wounded lad.

In that sector where we were fighting at Jarama we saw a lot of Moors. At the same time we saw a lot of others, and amongst them was one Welsh-speaking fellow that was shouting at us about being Communist so-and-sos and that. I'll give the enemy troops this much, they appeared to be fighting all right. But the Moors, while being quite good riflemen, the weather was against them and there was great difficulty in getting them going up into the line at times. There was a cartoon, I remember in the *Daily Worker* at the time, o' the Moors being outside round about a camp fire, and inside were Mussolini, Hitler and Franco. And Hitler's sayin' tae Franco: "Why the hell did ye no' get Eskimos instead o' Moors?" It was the type o' weather they were gettin' at that particular time.

They were using the Moors for taking us back as prisoners, back in trucks and that. We had one amusing incident. We were passing through a big town when we were going back as prisoners, and there was one fellow came out with a big club, a prehistoric club, threatening us with this club, ye ken, shouting at us. Ah says, "He's a cheerful bastard." Donald Renton says to me, "Let it go, let it go." I felt like hitting the man wi' the club at the time. We had many o' these experiences when we were prisoners.

Looking back on the War in later years my only regret is that the Spanish Republican Government wasnae successful. But I always felt that it was necessary to do it at that time. We carried through a job. We had some expressions from some o' thae comrades that maybe we were a bit previous and that. I don't think so. I always thought that we played a little part, and alongside that we had a demonstration o' courage by the Spaniards that I never could experience any other where. And our own lads too – I mean Jimmy Rutherford, Harry Fry, Ted Dickinson, great examples to anybody.[29] Fellows that you could be proud of. And I mean ye had Tom Wintringham, Tom Wintringham comin' up to us and heavy machine fire all round about, Tom walkin' wi' a stick. I felt it was a bit foolish at the time that he should do this kind o' thing. But it was for the morale o' the younger element I think he was concerned.

Our instructions frae the start – and I felt they were the right instructions – were tae take as many precautions for your own life as possible in order to do the utmost damage to the enemy. And that I felt was really good advice. And that's what I tried to carry through all the time I was there.

One day in particular we were paraded in two lines and given a cigarette each – but no matches were given . . . [see page 50].

Edinburgh Spain Emergency Committee

SPAIN is NOT Defeated

BUT

SPAIN'S DANGER IS OURS

ACT FOR SPAIN.   *ACT FOR BRITAIN.*

SAVE PEACE.

DEMAND ARMS and FOOD for SPAIN

Protect British Ships and British Seamen

Parliament meets on TUESDAY
Make Your Voice Heard

Rally to the Mound,
MONDAY FIRST, 30th January
At 10 p.m.

MANY PROMINENT AND REPRESENTATIVE SPEAKERS

Preliminary Notice—

    G. R. STRAUSS, M.P.

    KINGSLEY MARTIN (New Statesman)

    G. J. MITCHELL, Advocate, and others,

speak on

"THE CRISIS"

On *FRIDAY FIRST*, 3rd February, at 7.30 *p.m.*

In the MUSIC HALL, George Street.

Reserved Seats—3d   **Unreserved—Collection**

BISHOP & SONS, LTD., PRINTERS, EDINB.

Leaflet for an Edinburgh rally shows that support for the Republican cause persisted even after Franco's victory.

Frank McCusker, now in his late seventies, worked in a Dundee jute mill from the age of twelve until he was paid off at the age of eighteen, soon after the 1926 General Strike. Apart from occasional casual work he remained unemployed for many years. As he lived at home with his parents and his father was in employment, Frank's weekly income for four or five years before his marriage in 1931 enabled him to claim a larger unemployment benefit, was 12½ pence a week. He was a Hunger Marcher in the 1930s. After his discharge form the British army in 1940 he spent the rest of the War working on the construction of aerodromes.

FRANK McCUSKER

Just readin' about what was happenin' in Spain and what the people were fightin' for or fightin' against, fighting against Fascism, which I loathe, I decided to try and get to Spain at all costs.

I went up to see Mr Hodgson, he was organising the men for Spain here in Dundee. He was the secretary of the Communist Party. I wasn't a member of the Communist Party at that time. I had left the Communist Party – not because of any political thing but just because the money – payin' fees – was bad at that time. I was a member of the N.U.W.M., the National Unemployed Workers' Movement, at the time.

I was in the Territorial Army before I went to Spain. I had some military experience, handlin' a rifle and things like that, in the Territorial Army. That was aboot 1935 or 1936. I was still in it when I went to Spain. I could ha' been charged for enterin' Spain and joinin' a foreign army while I was a member o' the British army. But they never bothered. I joined the Territorial Army about two year before I went to Spain, never knowin' of couse that I was gonnae finish up in Spain! It was jist for the money I joined the Territorials. Ye got a fortnight's holiday and ye got paid for it, and that's what I joined it for.

I cannae mind actually the date I went to Spain. I was in Spain for about two year. I never got a medical in Dundee but when I went to Glasgow I got a medical examination there and told: "Now, if you want to back out you can back out if you want and nobody'll say anything about it." But I was determined to go.

I went down to London then a couple of days after that, and I had another medical. And the very same thing happened: "You can leave if you want to, nobody'll say anything, nobody'll say anything about you at all." But it was decided.

I went over to Paris and got the last medical there, because we were gonnae walk over the Pyrenees mountains. One of the chaps that was wi' me was medically unfit for that and was sent back tae Dundee again. But they told you then: "You're committed now to Spain once you go on from Paris tae down the Border, you're committed. You can't turn back or anything like that."

But I did turn back because the police caught me in a place called

41

Perpignan on the borders o' France. They picked me up and I was charged wi' vagrancy. They knew what they were doin', of course. They took me to court and they says to me: "Go back to England again." Ah says, "Ah can't go back to England again, I've no money." "Oh, we'll provide for that."

So they put me on the train, then they put me on the boat and put me back into London again. That was on the Wednesday. On the Friday I was on the boat back tae France again and I got right through then.

I was in Paris for four of five days and then we right down to the borders o' Spain and we were picked up there by a Spanish or French guide – I can't remember what he was – and he took us over the Pyrenees mountains. He knew the paths. We were there on the Pyrenees for a day and a half, marchin' or walkin' till we got over the borders. At one place we had to wait for about two hoors because there was a guard on the road, a Frenchman. We had to wait tae he came on guard before we could cross over the border. He came past us and he never saw us but he knew we were there. And he had to be whistlin', whistlin' *The Marseillaise*. And when he kent, and when he got out o' sight – we didnae want tae commit this chap any – we over the fence, across the road, over another fence, and we were in Spain. There was no question that that French guard was sympathetic. That chap must have been a member o' the Communist Party o' France, or he was a sympathiser anyway, because he turned his back on us.

When we were crossin' the Pyrenees there were about twelve of us. We left four on the Pyrenees that couldn't do it, four Americans that we'd already picked up in Paris when we went down. But it was their own fault. They must ha' been journalists or students o' some kind. They were carrying typewriters and things like that, which was stupid. They might have known that goin' over the Pyrenees mountains ye needed all your faculties and no' carryin' typewriters and things like that. When we got half roads over the Pyrenees they just couldnae go any further. I never saw them chaps again so I don't know whether they ever got to Spain, or whether they went back or what.

It really was the worst experience ever I had in my life. And if it wasnae for what I was doin' I'd ha' went back. Only I knew what I was doin' and it kept is going. But the other Dundee chap that came down wi' me he couldn't pass the medical and he was left in Paris. But he wouldnae go home, he wouldn't leave Paris. He stayed there for about two month till eventually he saw that it was hopeless, that he couldnae go over. He came back. But he was that keen to get to Spain.

After we got into Spain we went to a place called Figueras and the chap that was in charge there was Tito, leader o' the Yugoslavs later on. [30] It was a big garrison place, a castle, a big fort. We stayed there jist for a night and we went right on to Barcelona and right down –

this was on the train – to a place called Albacete.

We got kitted out wi' our uniforms and what-not in Albacete and then we were sent to Madrigueras. We did wir trainin' in Madrigueras for about six weeks.

We had a Russian machine gun, an automatic rifle it was. It fired, I think it was forty rounds and we got leave to fire about five o' them. That was our trainin' as far as firin' a gun was concerned.

We had a rifle, of course. The one I had, you had to put the butt on the ground and put your foot on the bolt tae get it out – ye couldnae pull it out wi' your hands. So that was the kind o' rifle I got at the start. But when we finished up we had Lee Enfield rifles, got frae somewhere in Britain, I suppose.

We were very, very short o' ammunition o' all kinds, and the same wi' guns. When I went, the first Company I went intil there were about twelve guns atween the lot of us – and there were twenty men in the Company. The shortage was because there was a blockade on in Spain frae the British Government and the French Government and they allowed nothing to go in. Actually, when we were goin' there we were goin' to fight for the legitimate Government o' Spain, the elected Government of the people, which was entitled to get munitions and help from France and Britain. But they refused to give it 'cause they said they didnae want tae get involved. Hitler and Mussolini were involved and they were poppin' it intae the other side but the ban was on our side. Of course the British Government was bannin' anything goin' to the Fascists an' a', which didnae mean a thing when they were gettin' Mussolini and Hitler to give them stuff and men.

After Madrigueras I went tae Jarama. I was up there for about eight weeks at Jarama, in the battle of Jarama. Well, it wisnae a battle at a', it wis a bloody slaughter as far as we were concerned. They had everything and we had nothing. And that's where we lost the majority o' oor men, at Jarama. We lost about ten men from Dundee alone. That's no' coontin' a' the men frae Glasgow and all the rest o' the places. The International Brigade got a real beatin' up there.

About two or three times the Fascists tried to get over but we were entrenched by that time and they never managed it. I remember the Moors comin' over one time and they had their cloaks, big black cloaks, thrown o'er their shoulder, telescopic sights on their rifles. But we had barbed wire and we just mowed them down because we were in a position to do that to them. They seemed to be fanatics. Ye could hear them singin' and screamin'. But they must ha' pulled them back again. But ye knew by the way they were dressed that they were Moors. They had a bad reputation because they were bloody brutal, I suppose. They took one o' our boys a prisoner, a boy called Tom Picton, an' he jist put his hand to take a cigarette oot and they shot him dead. This was one o' their officers. But they jist wanted excuses, I suppose, for shootin' him. I was at the Jarama for about eight weeks,

as I said. Then we were taken out o' there, and we got taken to just
outside o' Madrid for a relief. But before we went out the Germans –
anti-fascist Germans – that were on our flank, they said, "If the British
are gaun out we're gaun out an' a' for a rest." Some of them had been
in there for nearly three month. So we had to go back again and stay
for aboot another fortnight.

Professor Haldane and Harry Pollitt came up to see us.[31] I
remember when Haldane came up jist wi' that the Fascists made a
charge for us and he ran down the communication trench. And the
boys were saying, "Look at him away!" But he came back again. He
came back wi' a rifle. I dinnae think he'd ever had a rifle in his hands
before, because he had the butt the opposite way. But he was comin'
up the trench, but we kept him back anyway.

Professor Haldane had come up to check the air at Jarama, to see
whether it was possible for the Fascists to pit over gas to us. But the
word that we got, he said it wasnae likely: if they were puttin' over
gas they wad ha' got it theirself because of where we were situated.
We had a gas mask, of course, but there were never any gas. They
never put any gas over.

So we were taken out anyway o' Jarama and went into Madrid for
about three or four days. Than that was the time o' the battle o'
Brunete. We went up there at Brunete and that's where I got
wounded, well, jist outside o' Brunete, in a little village cried
Villanueva de la Cañada. And I never saw any more fightin' efter that.
I got wounded in the arm by an explosive bullet. It went in there and it
came right oot up there. And gangrene had set in til it. I was taken to
hospital in Madrid. It was an American that operated on me. They cut
all this rotten stuff away from my arm. I was in Spain for about a year
after that because they couldnae get my arm tae heal and they didnae
want to send me back to Britain in that condition. I was goin' from
'ospital to 'ospital and they were tryin' tae get my arm back to normal
before they sent is back to Britain, ye see.

Some other things I remember about the War. I saw Italians at
Brunete, just before I was wounded. I think there were aboot nine or
ten Italians and Germans mixed in this village that we were takin', and
I saw them gettin' taken away as prisoners. In fact, I saw plenty o'
Italian prisoners. They were givin' theirsel' up as quick as they were
gettin' over there, 'cause they didnae want tae fight. The only yins
that was fightin' actually was the Nazi Germans. Possibly the Nazi
Germans I saw at Brunete were air force men. But we couldnae shoot
them down at a' because they came over us and ye could see them
wavin' out their planes. They were that confident, and we had
nothing to shoot against them. We had no anti-aircraft guns with us at
the front. We had anti-aircraft guns in the like of Barcelona and places
like that, guardin' the towns, but as far as the front was concerned the
Germans jist played wi' us, as far as their planes were concerned. Ye

could see them wavin' their arms out the planes. Then they just ssshhhcccccrrrhhh, and you had to run for your life then.

There were some real characters in the International Brigade. Tom Picton, he was a Welshman, he was the chap I told you aboot that got shot by the Moors. But he was a real character. He was chucked out the British navy at one time. And have you ever seen Desperate Dan? He had a face like that, his chin, and he was a real tough guy, a boxer. But we christened him Tom Vino. Instead o' puttin' water in his bottle he put vino in.

And we had another chap, he was an American, a Jew, Benny Rubens. And he wanted away frae the Americans a' thegither. He wanted tae be a Scotsman. And we christened him MacRubens. And he was wi' us right up, in the Jarama, and he was with us at Brunete. I dinnae ken what happened til him after that because I lost touch wi' a lot o' them after I got wounded. He was a character, this MacRubens. He always wanted to see Scotland.

The Spanish civilians were marvellous, real marvellous. They were really good, especially the ones in the country, you know, the peasants in the country. Aye, one time, after I got wounded, I met this Spanish couple, oldish couple, and they took me up to their farmhouse and they had a couple o' kids there as well, and they gave me, you know, *comida,* plenty of *comida.*[32]

I was in Spain for about two years before I came back to Britain. I got a big operation down in London, in Middlesex Hospital. And they grafted a nerve into my arm but it never took on.

After the Spanish War I was victimised in the sense that, when the Second World War broke out, I went into the British army and went tae France at the start. I went to see the Medical about getting a glove for ma hand because it was cold. That was in the first six months o' the War, 1939. The Medical says, "What are you wantin' a glove for?" Ah says, "Because I've got this bullet wound in ma arm." "Where did you get the bullet wound?" Ah says, "A got that in Spain." I was back in Britain in two days – throwed out o' France, because I was in tae the Spanish War, discharged from the British army.

Looking back now on the Spanish War I say it was well worth while because even though Franco won, he never won – in the sense that they've got a socialist government now in Spain. So I think the International Brigade did one little thing anyway in helping to get a real democratic government elected in Spain later on.

Oh, the War was the biggest event in my life, all right, there's no question about that. And I'm gled I was there. I'm gled I came back of course, but I'm gled I was there.

Born in 1914 Tommy Bloomfield worked for many years as a miner in Fife and was in hospital having a lung removed when an explosion and fire caused the closing down of the pit in which he had been working, the Michael Colliery at East Wemyss, some twenty years ago. He served in the Royal Navy in the 1939-45 War. Tommy Bloomfield was one of those volunteers who went twice to Spain to fight in the International Brigade – the second time as a repatriated prisoner of war.

TOMMY BLOOMFIELD

The reason I went to Spain was in the Hungry Thirties I was navvying at a bob an hour and if you straightened your back you were off the job. Finally, I got a job wi' a contractor. The gaffer was a pig. He shouted frae one end o' King Street in Kirkcaldy to the other: "Hurry up, come up here!" When I got up I says, "You didn't want me to run?" He says, "Hurry up, hurry up!" I says, "Look, gie's the books. I'd rather go tae Spain and shoot bastards like you."

So I went to a meeting where Willie Gallacher was speakin' in Thornton and I volunteered there and then.[33] I was informed I would go to Spain one Friday in December 1936. I was not a member of any political party. But I had had a little previous military experience because I had joined the Black Watch in 1931 at the age of sixteen when I was unemployed and there was no work available to alleviate the circumstances at home. I was in the Black Watch roughly about six months. Then my mother claimed me out as I was under age and was her only support.

So I went to Spain in December 1936. And wee Jock MacGregor, the greatest wee lad in Kirkcaldy, his wife complained and John MacGregor was out. He would have made a good political commissar. We got the bus at the foot of Glassworks Street in Kirkcaldy to Glasgow. There we were taken under the wing of various people and put on buses and sent to King Street, the headquarters of the Communist Party, in London. It was the Communists who were doing the brunt of the work.

We got the week-end ticket to Paris. Roughly 200 British crossed the Channel that December to go to Spain. I was the only one from Fife that I know of. But Harry Fry, Jimmy Rutherford, Donald Renton, they were all there. They were from Edinburgh and Leith.

We went to a place in Paris cried the Place de Combat. From there we were put into small boarding houses or hotels, and as we grew in numbers we went to the station in parties and got on the train to Perpignan. There we were put in hotels and collected, and we went through the frontier in a motor coach. That was the first time, when the frontiers were open. But the second time I went, a year later, in December 1937, you had to climb the Pyrenees from dusk to dawn, with the French police hunting you, taking pot shots at you. And you went over with guides. But the first time – no problem in going.

You hit Figueras, a frontier town. You only touched it and then you were loaded on to trains to Barcelona, where you were put into the Karl Marx Barracks. From there you travelled to Albacete, headquarters of the International Brigades. Your depot was Madrigueras.

The training in the International Brigade was very elementary. Ye had no butts or anything like that. Everything had to be carefully done, because ye had men that had never handled a rifle, never seen anything. Now we got rifle training, open order, advance by sections, fired a few rounds. We had no machine guns. We got our officers, our sergeants, and we were a unit prior to going up the line. You all looked after each other. They were a type of men it was a privilege to have been in the body of them – the greatest ever. What's yours was mine and what's mine was yours. They were welded in one thing from all walks of life, all political parties – a love of democracy.

We had twelve hours training on the Russian water-cooled Maxim machine gun in Chinchón on the 11th of February, prior to going up the line the next morning into the Jarama. On the 12th we moved up into the Jarama. Now the four International Brigades consisted of somewhere around 15,000 men. They went up against roughly 30,000 crack German troops, Italian troops and Moors – the foolhardiness of the attack astonished them and stopped them. And that front never altered from that day until the last phase of the War.

Now when we were captured No. 1 Company and No. 2 Company had been beat back from Suicide Hill, which was a hill slightly to our left of the machine gun Company. We gave them covering fire for their retreat and then we held the line. We held it over the 12th and on the 13th No. 4 Company broke under heavy anti-aircraft fire, overhead shrapnel, and didn't send word to No. 2 Machine Gun Company. And the Fascists got right round us. What had happened was there were a few persons who rose out the dead ground in front of our guns, giving the clenched fist salute, saying, "Kamerad, Kamerad", and some trying to sing *The Internationale*. Well, some guns kept firing, others ceased firing and it was just pure hell, Out of the original 120 finally twenty-nine of us were herded together.

Harry Fry, the Company commander, was wounded in the arm with a dum-dum bullet. Ted Dickinson, an Australian, a lawyer to trade, who was the second-in-command, gave Harry medical aid and destroyed his papers so that there would be no repercussions on Harry. But being taken with his own papers still on him Ted was singled out by the Fascists and told he would have to fight for Fascism or die. That man chose death. He marched up to a tree like a soldier on parade, did a military about-turn, and said: "Salute, comrades!" the second he died. I felt like fainting. But when I saw that man die he put the backbone right back in my body, and I said to myself: "Tam, if you get out of this ye're coming back to have another go." Which I eventually did. Donald Renton, Harry Fry, Ted Dickinson, and a Canadian who came from Windsor, Ontario – 'Yank' Levy – were the backbone of our Company. We would have followed them from here to hell. Incidentally, in the Far East during the Second World War while I was in the Navy I picked up a *Life* magazine and 'Yank' Levy was mentioned in it – he was instructing the American army on guerrilla warfare. You name them, we had them: all walks of life, the greatest men ever.

We had been prisoners less than 24 hours when we were interrogated by a person who had an Oxford accent and whose first words were: "By Jove, jolly fine mess you've got yourselves into, what, what!"

We were marched off to a place cried Navalcarnero, about twenty miles to the south west of Madrid, by Moorish cavalry who were using their sabres across our heads and shoulders to chase us on. I pitied Fry because he had an arm wound and Donald Renton because he had a bullet wound in the leg. Some of us were maybe in pairs or threes, and it was just little pieces of wire tying your thumbs together and they were extremely tight. When we got to Navalcarnero we were placed into cells, three cells with twenty-seven in them, nine to a cell. On the way Phil Elias had put his hand in his pocket for a cigarette and he was shot out of hand.

At Navalcarnero we were put to work for a brief period at the railway terminal, which was a distribution centre on the Lisbon-Madrid line. You should have seen the stuff made in Britain which was coming up into Spain and Portugal – everything from tins of Skipper sardines to Lewis guns. The trouble was that we couldn't sabotage the guns, we were so closely guarded. The army or the Civil Guards never left us.[34] After Jarama it was a tour of the prison camps for us. We dug burial pits for each new batch of anti-Fascists captured locally and brought to the prisons where we were held.

When we were at Talavera we were subject to mental torture. The guards would tell us, "Esta tarde todos muerto" – "This afternoon you all die." When the death wagon had gone with its average of thirty men who were shot for the simple reason they had voted for a Republican front Government, the guards would then inform us, "Esta noche todos muerto" – "Tonight you all die." On the death wagon leaving at night we were then told, "Mañana por a la mañana" – "Tomorrow morning you all die." Just imagine – the Fascists executed ninety men per day at Talavera over a period of months. On one occasion a German volunteer of the International Brigade who had been wounded between the eyes, whose sight came and went and who had become a mute, was questioned in front of us by a German Fascist officer and his Spanish girlfriend. As the German prisoner could not speak he showed his contempt for them by urinating on their feet. The German Fascist officer then ordered that he be taken out and shot. The German Brigader knew that he would be shot anyway.

One day in particular we were paraded in two lines and given a cigarette each – but no matches were given, a sample of the treatment the Fascists were giving us. There were cameras there that day taking pictures of us but they were not close enough to show the body lice crawling on the outside of our clothes. Eventually, in the late summer of 1937, we were repatriated to Britain in an exchange of prisoners. It was a relief, I can tell you, especially since before we were released we were given a court-martial. Our defending officer was a lieutenant in the *Tercio,* the Spanish Fascist Foreign Legion. Not one word was said in our defence and we ourselves were not allowed to speak. The sentences handed out were that two were condemned to death, four to solitary confinement for life, and all the rest of us got thirty years' imprisonment. When we were released from the San Sebastian prison we had our first wash in three and a half months. We were given three safety razor blades between twenty-seven of us. We tossed a coin to determine our turn. I was unlucky, I was ninth.

When I came back from Spain that first time I joined the Communist Party. My reason was I saw the Republican Government, how the civilians were, how they were treated, how everything worked out, the democracy of it. And I saw the Fascist side of it as a prisoner, where men who had voted for a Republican Government were shot because of that, for the least thing. And their troops were led from behind with the dog-whip and the revolver in the other hand – not like the International Brigade or the Spanish Republican army, with their officers at the front leading their men. It was a difference, a vast difference. And it was just like an empty stomach makes an empty head think. And when you looked at these things, with my upbringing, always hungry, and seeing Republican Spain, then experiencing Franco Spain, I could differentiate. Therefore I joined the Communist Party. I spoke at a few meetings then I went back to Spain because I was bitter at the treatment I had had from the Franco regime. I went back out the second time along with six others from the twenty-nine who were taken prisoner out of the 120 men of the machine gun Company at the Jarama. The rest had been killed, with the exception of three that went back for ammunition.

During the second time I was in Spain the Foreign Office used to sent my mother bills, wanting the money that it had cost to take me back into Scotland from Spain. And they wanted to know the whereabouts of her son. They knew damned well where I was.

If I had been married I would never have gone, because I would have had obligations to a wife. I didn't believe that married men should have gone.

Altogether I was in Spain roughly two years. I always wrote home to my mother. And I got my Woodbine and my razor blades through the letters – thirty Woodbine in a long envelope. And they queried it at Kirkcaldy post office. They didn't like the Woodbine and the razor blades going in a letter to me in Spain.[35]

Now as for food and drink in Spain, well, at first you all had queasy stomachs because of oil in the food. They fried rice. You had fried fish in the oil. Everything was in oil. And gradually you got inured to the oil and you began to like it. And the *arroz y carne*, that was rice fried with meat, was very good. Rice with fish was very good. You name them we had them. Eventually of course we had our own cooks. We got rissoles of corned beef. We sometimes had chips, fish and chips, and various things. The Battalion cookhouse was a great place. They did a good job and they were well worth their place.

At times we had enough to eat. But when you were on the run you were lucky if you had a hard bit of bread in your knapsack to keep you going. Ah've sat and ate raw onions like an apple, the tears runnin' doon ma cheeks, that hungry. In the morning, the mules came up with your food and ammunition. And you got a hardtack for the middle of the day, maybe a tin of sardines or a tin of bully beef between so many of ye, and at night you got a hot meal as well, providing there was no attack on. It was haphazard. That's a soldier's life. You've got to bear up with these things.

As far as getting fruit went, well, you were lying in amongst the grapes and the orange groves. There was no problem there. The only problem was ye had slack bowels. Dysentery and diarrhoea were quite common.

Personally, I didn't drink myself. I never tasted alcohol in Spain. But no one was allowed to take spirits of any sort up to the front line or in the reserve line. Although it was done I've known them tae fill up the Russian water-cooled Maxim with cognac, empty it out and – they couldn't use their drinking water because it was precious – they urinated in it. And, by the holy, you want to have smelt that gun when it was firin'. I drank water or lemonade. The water was drinkable because it was boiled when it came up with the wagon. And you always had your cup of coffee. You only got the lemonade when you were out the line. Very often I was thirsty when I was in the line. But drink doesnae quench your thirst so I was better off than them that took it, I think.

Now as regards officers and N.C.O.s they were men who had the position because they proved their worth. In the line you were under their command. But out of the line there was no, "Yes, sir, no, sir, three bags full, sir." They were just ordinary soldiers like yourself. They ate the same as you. They went through the same as you. Your officers were at your head, not behind you. They were real men, there because of the capabilities. There was no election of officers and N.C.O.s – the men proved themselves in battle. If they were fit to lead men they were given the job. If they weren't fit they were taken from the job and a better man put in. It was a sort of communal decision. There were get-togethers and a battle was discussed and then if a man was found wanting, no disrespect to him, a better man was put in his position and he understood that. We were there for a purpose: fighting for the Spanish Republican Government and democracy. We werenae there as individuals. We were there as a body, the finest body ever.

In the International Brigades we had contact with other nationalities because they were on your right or left flank. We had contact with Germans, Italians, Czechs – forty-seven different languages were spoken. It was a big thing to get around and make yourself understood. Sometimes Esperanto was the language used. Young Duffy that belonged London Road way in Glasgow who had a big birth mark on one side of his face, and who lasted five minutes in his first action – he got us out of difficulties when we were passing through southern France because he spoke Esperanto.[36]

When Spanish civilians asked us what nationality we were we said, "Inglés" – English. They stared at us with open mouths, because Chamberlain was the man who was beating Republican Spain. But we got over it. We said, "No es Inglés – Escocés" – "We're Scotch." That went down quite well. The Spanish civilians were very friendly and everywhere you went if there was a meal on their table they would invite you to partake of that meal. It was marvellous. There was a family I went about in Madrigueras. There were two daughters. You know, if I wanted to court them I had to court them in front of their father and mother. I sat and ate with them. I gave them cigarettes. They gave me whatever they could spare. I had a little social life, it broke the monotony after the training. And that man and his wife wrote to my mother in Kirkcaldy, and Grahl, that had the 'New Age' bookshop at the top of the arcade, where the Palais de Danse was, he translated the letter and rewrote my mother's letter in Spanish and sent it back to Spain.[37] So we had great relations.

But most of the time your were not relaxing with civilians. Either you were in the line or in reserve or moving from front to front, because the British Battalion was the spearhead of the attack and the rearguard of the retreat. We were the shock battalion of the shock brigades. We were top dogs in Spain as regards shock troops.

Of the British volunteers I knew in Spain I would say three-quarters were Communists, and the rest Labour Party, and Tory party, if you like. They loved democracy. There were quite a few Tories there. Winston Churchill had a nephew fought there. And there was Professor David Guest. I dunno what he was a professor of, but he was a slight lad, and he was just a common rifleman. He was killed on the Aragon as a common rifleman – a professor. What a waste – but just a man who had a love of democracy. A direct descendant of Clive of India, Lewis Clive, was killed on the Ebro. Clem Beckett, your great speedway rider, was killed at Jarama. So was Art Doran, flight lieutenant in the British Air Force. Tudor-Hart, our doctor on the Jarama, was a Harley Street bone specialist. He perfected a technique whereby they could put a multiple injury to a bone with a bullet or shrapnel in a plaster cast and save the person's arm or leg, whereas in the 1914–18 War he would have lost it. So that did the troops in the 1939–45 War a world of good. We had the greatest lads ever. Malcolm Dunbar, Chief of Operations, Ebro Offensive, son of titled people from Dunbar across the water from here in Fife.[38] Jock Cunningham, who had tramped England in search of work, joined the Brigade and became a commander of the British Battalion. Tito fought in Spain. You name them, we had them.

I think the best thing I did for Spain the second time I went out was to take a young lad, Tommy McGuire, who lived in Greenock. Tommy was commended for bravery in the field and promoted sergeant. He died a sergeant paratrooper in the Second World War. He was a great lad and one of the toughest soldiers I ever saw. So was Geordie Robertson of Kirkcaldy, who lived rough and they thought was a drunkard and a lazy sort, but he was a braw soldier in Spain.

Did I see German tanks in action in Spain? We were chased roon' the olive groves wi' the German whippet tanks! Small tanks. And the liquid fire. That was where they first used this whippet tank in warfare and the liquid fire. And the first time they used Stuka dive-bombers was at Belchite, where everything, you thought, was hitting you on the back of the neck.[39] When one building was hit you moved into it in the hope that it wouldnae be hit again. And how we came out o' Belchite I'll never know. Belchite is completely devastated, it's left as a monument to the Civil War. I saw it in 1982 when I was in Spain touring the fronts. Franco accused the Spanish Repubican Government of devastating Belchite. It wasn't. It was the Stukas. Oh, it was terrible. They came in droves. Ye had no answer to them. And the anti-aircraft guns, overhead shrapnel, landshells – everything. You couldn't stand it, you had to retreat. I wasn't impressed by the fighting qualities of Mussolini's Italian troops in Spain, no. The toughest of the lot were the Germans, and the Moors next. But the Italians! I saw the Garibaldis o' the International Brigade. They were different: they had men that were fighting for a belief. It was bred in them. They werenae there because they were sent there. They were volunteers. And there's quite a difference between a volunteer and a man ramrodded into a thing.[40]

Now a few years ago I met a German sailor in the Buccaneer pub here in Templehall, Kirkcaldy. His wife used to work in a local bookshop. When he saw the little badge I had he said, "Oh, International Brigade?" I said, "Yes." He says, "How you stopped us at Jarama I will never know." He had been there – on the Fascist side. Look, if I had known, or the International Brigades had known, the material and the troops that was advancing against them I quite believe they wouldn't have stopped running till they got to the Pyrenees. The Fascists' artillery was wheel to wheel. Moorish cavalry – oh, they had everything. We had a draft company behind us of 200 strong, waiting on us dying so they could get our rifles to fight with. It is as simple as that.

After I went back to Spain the second time the battle I really remember most was the Ebro offensive and Hill 481. It was attacked twelve times in the matter of thirty-six hours and when you got to the top, almost to the top, it was just a ring o' fire. And if you took any more than three steps down that hill you were a dead man. There was one Spaniard, a company commander, who only understood a few words of English. He had a Colt revolver in either hand, and all he could say was, "Come on, boys, come on, boys," and ye had to follow him. It was murderous. On the night we were relieved as we came out the line the Fascists attacked and we were handing over our rifles to the battalion that was relieving us. So you'll have an idea of the chaos that was there.

Dum–dum bullets? It seemed like the Fascists used all dum–dum bullets, and when ye copped one o' these you had a big hole where it came out. Under the Geneva Convention they were illegal.[41] And if I had had my way of it, the way our men were wounded, I would have put a criss-cross in every nickel bullet that I fired and made it spray out on them, just the same as they did to us.

We had our first aid men, our stretcher-bearers and they did a grand job. But it took guts to walk into a front line where you made an attack and were beat back and you went crawling out at night, in the grey dark to pick up the wounded. It took guts. Very few of us had guts like that.

Now at the latter end of the Ebro offensive the word came the International Brigades were being disbanded. We were withdrawn from the line. But the first day we were withdrawn the Battalion commander and the Battalion commissar had a meeting with the men and asked them to go back into the line voluntarily for a couple of days to give the Republican forces a chance to get some troops up to consolidate their line. We did do and what a hammering we took. We lost a great deal of men in these two days, men who would have come home. But it shows the heart was behind the Spanish Republican people.

From the Ebro we went into camp and then we were taken to Barcelona. We marched down the Ramblas into a big arena, where the heads of state, the government, spoke to us and thanked us for the job we had done for the Spanish people. The final one was Dolores Ibarruri, La Pasionara. Her final speech was: "Goodbye, my sons. Come back to us. You have made history. You are a legend." Then we were sent home.[42]

We went through the frontier by bus and then train through France, then across the Channel. We were taken to homes in London. We were kept there for a few days and we marched through the Fascist stronghold in the East End of London – and not one peep out of the Fascist element to us. They knew full well that sticks and stones held no fear for us. They knew if they started any business they would get the fight of their life. Therefore they allowed us to do our marching in peace and quiet.

I came home to Kirkcaldy and there was a Welcome Home held in the Adam Smith Halls. There was a blind organist. He played Chopin that night. And there was a meeting where various persons spoke and welcomed me home and thanked me for the work I had done in Spain.

I was the only person welcomed back at that time in Kirkcaldy. The others were back earlier, wounded, and various other things, ill-health. I was lucky. I had good health bar up to the last time when I ta'en the jaundice, yellow jaundice. I wasn't wounded in Spain. I was unfortunate: it's a lucky man that gets a wound and gets a wee bit rest!

Roughly I think there was round about forty men from Fife that went to Spain. I believe thirteen were killed. I knew of nine who went from Kirkcaldy but I think there were one or two more than that. Two were killed and one came home to die with typhus fever: young Andrew Hillock. Fraser Crombie was killed at Brunete and Dick Henderson went missing on the Aragon retreat, alongside a friend of mine Johnny Lobban from the Vale of Leven.[43]

When the 1939-45 War broke out I volunteered the first week o' the War. And they wouldn't take me beause I fought in Spain, because I'd corrupt the troops. Willie Gallacher fought it out in the House of Commons as regards International Brigaders. He said they could be an asset to the British army as they understood modernised warfare. Then they agreed to take us. I registered for the Royal navy. I got in Black Watch papers. I went in front of a Board. I was liable to a £100 fine or hanged, drawn and quartered. Anyway, I told them: "The Navy, or nothing else. If I don't get the Navy score out my preference and put down, 'Conscientious Objector. Grounds – can't get the unit I prefer.' "

Looking back now on the Spanish War it was important to me, because I was one of the downtrodden masses. And if Spain had pulled through I wasn't going to be in a capitalistic country, I was going to be in a socialistic country. I would have made my home in Spain.

We proved that we were one hundred per cent correct because it was not a Revolution, it wasn't a Civil War. It was a War of Intervention by Hitler, Mussolini and Moors. It was what you would term the Grand Rehearsal. They trained their troops in Spain in realistic manoeuvre for the 1939-45 War. And if Chamberlain hadn't done what he did, closed the frontier, and had given instead the Republican Government its rights by International Law, the 1939-45 War might not have taken place.

Tom Clarke, now aged 78, was brought up in Dundee. He served as a Regular soldier in the Cameron Highlanders from 1925 to 1933. After completing his service he was unable to find employment, joined the Communist Party in Dundee, and took part in the National Hunger March to London in 1934. After his return from Spain Tom Clarke eventually found employment in the jute mills.

TOM CLARKE

The reasons I got involved in the Spanish War started off maybe about the time of Mussolini's invasion of Ethiopia in 1935. At that time I was still on the army Reserve. I had been in the Regular Army for about eight years and I had about four years of Reserve service still to do. And I was expecting to be recalled up. But I remember one of the local lads saying, "You won't be called up. We'll do nothing to help Ethiopia. We'll probably back up Mussolini in the long run." That eventually turned out to be more or less the truth.

It was from then on the way things were going. We'd already seen what had happened in Nazi Germany. I was on the Hunger March in 1934 when Dimitrov slayed the Nazi court and he had to be released.[44] But these were the sort of things that kept building up. And reading about the state of world affairs – my old man used to get the *Daily Worker* every day and of course I read it as well – no doubt at that time made me think a lot about how people were being threatened, how the world was becoming threatened.[45] And when the War did break out in Spain we were getting reports back about the atrocities and suchlike being committed by the Fascists, and how the Spaniards were untrained, had no weapons, nothing at all. And it was about that time that that French deputy André Marty put forward the idea of the International Brigade.[46]

It would be about the end of 1936, December 1936, when a friend of mine, Bob Cooney, was down from Aberdeen staying with us, and we were talking about this, saying, "Well, I'm thinking about having a go, you know, going over there."[47] As I say I already had eight years' experience at least in how to handle weapons and suchlike. So I went down in January and saw Jimmy Hodgson, who was the secretary of the Communist Party at that time in Dundee. I said, "What about putting my name down for this International Brigade?" he was fairly cagey at the time. This was when Eden had got through the Non-Intervention Plan.[48] But eventually later on in January Jimmy Hodgson told me I could go.

So there were three of us left Dundee that day – Bill McGuire, a young lad who was in the Young Communist League, and another lad whose name I can't remember, and me.[49] We went through to Glasgow, met George Middleton who was in the Communist Party at that time, and we got something to eat and then our train fare down to London.[50] There was no medical examination, they accepted that we were fit. In London we met someone – I can't recall now who it was – but there were two or three there. They asked if anybody could speak French. Well, I had a smattering, having had it at school, so I said, "But it's only . . . ." "Oh, well, that'll do." So I was given a packet of cigarettes and told to hand this over when I got to Paris. I also got a number of letters and suchlike to hand over to Peter Kerrigan when I got to Spain. So I was put in charge of this group.

There'd be about twenty or thirty of us. We had week-end tickets to Paris. When we were on board the Channel ship an announcement came over: "All those without passports to proceed to the purser's office." So Bill McGuire and I went along. It was a French ship we were on and this officer asked us what we were doing. We told him we were students and had just finished our exams. If he'd known anything he'd have understood it was a phoney. We said, "We're just going over there to have a week-end." "Oh, well, have a good time." And we got a white card from him.

When we arrived in Calais I said to Bill McGuire, "Come on we'll get off quick and get our money changed and then on to the train." But when we got on to the train there were no other International Brigaders on it, we couldn't see the others anywhere. Anyway we got to Paris eventually and got a taxi, which we'd been told to do, to the *Maison de Syndicat,* the trade union centre. When we got there an old woman came out and she told me it was across the road we'd to go. Here it was a big cafe and there were ever so many people in it. This was where they were gathering all the Internationals. I said, "Well, I'll have to go and see about these other fellows that we lost at Calais." I was going along the street when I saw them and half of them were canned by this time. When they saw me they accused me of deserting them! They had got on a different train. One or two of the fellows had diced caps on, you know, glengarrys, and they were dancing round one or two French couples who were kissing in the street. So I had to get them along the road in case there was trouble with the police.

The next day a little German lad appeared who was in charge, an interpreter, and said to me: "Have you got anything for me?" "Oh, aye," I says, "a packet of cigarettes." But I'd smoked one and that was the one that was most important – there had been a message on it! I normally smoked a pipe but this time I'd just smoked a cigarette, not thinking. I explained to the little German and he said it was all right. I think it was only a question of being sure who we were, you see. And as I say Eden's Non-Intervention policy by this time was beginning to work but fortunately we didn't have to walk over the Pyrenees or sail round by Port Bou or anything like that.

In Paris we ate up in the Co-operative. Then the little German told us, "Now when you're leaving tonight you'll each have a bottle of wine – no more, only one bottle of wine." So we got down to the station. I noticed a fellow there and he had a hacking jacket and jodhpurs and a soft hat. There was nobody speaking to him. So I went over and asked him: "Are you British?" He says, "Yes." He had a real Oxford accent. I said, "Where are you going?" He said, "I'll be going along with you chaps." I says, "Where?". He says, "International Brigade." I says, "Who are you, what are you?" He said his name was John Cameron. He had been a major in some Indian cavalry regiment. He came from Edinburgh. When the rest of the fellows saw me speaking to him they gathered round. John by this time had got sort of worked up and he says, "If it's my good fortune to lead you lads over the top, by God we'll give them . . ." And one bloke says, "Not by God, by Marx" – and he was really serious about it!

We got on the train and the little German said to me, "Now come on, we'll go along and see if everybody has got their wine" and suchlike. We came to this compartment and there were two or three Czechs in it. Two of them had more than one bottle of wine. This little German tore a strip off them and was going to put them off the train. One of the Czechs, an elderly bloke – well, he looked older than me anyway – was pleading. So the German says to me, "Here, you take them." So I had two bottles of wine. Eventually I finished up with six bottles of wine from different people. I says, "What am I going to do with it?" The little German says, "You keep them."

Eventually we got through to Perpignan. We were there for maybe about a day then we were taken over the border into Spain in little buses. We were told when we got on the bus, "Now you'll be stopped by the French police and they'll ask you questions. Don't answer any questions – just sit dumb." So we were stopped at the border, the French stopped us and asked, but nobody spoke. And we went right on and we landed in Figueras.

It was a huge fortress. I think the Moors had built it. Where we were they had originally been stables, there was room for about 5,000 horses. We just accepted that, whether it was true or not. The next morning when we were leaving they had a little sort of orchestral band march us down to the station. They had fiddles and guitars and trombones – it was a real mixture of instruments. But we marched down and got on the train and it took us to Barcelona. There was a big demonstration through Barcelona and then we got on the train for Valencia.

Unfortunately after that the food situation began to get a wee bit awkward. There was no food came on. But every place we stopped the Spanish people were throwing in oranges and we were about knee deep in oranges in every compartment.

There was a whole host of Yanks, they'd been at Figueras and they were along with us. After we left Valencia the engine broke down but some of the Yanks, I think, got it going again. We arrived at Albacete about two in the morning, anyway it was pitch dark. We hadn't a clue where we were and were falling all over the place. But we got into Albacete then.

Next day we had our food and then we were paraded in the bull ring. And it was there I saw this André Marty. There were lots of Frenchmen there and lots of them were wearing red bandanas round their neck. Marty went up to one of them and he says, "Take it off. You don't wear these things if you're going into action." So we were a little more circumspect. I gave Kerrigan the letters and suchlike.

Then we were sent up to Madrigueras, that's where the British Battalion's headquarters were. I met Donald Renton there. He was sort of Company officer or something like that. They were beginning by this time to give you some sort of training. It was pretty poor training on the whole. They didn't have much. By this time, I think, they'd had a supply of Russian rifles. I didn't like them. They were too long in the butt and they only held five bullets in the magazine. I preferred the Lee Enfield but you'd to make the best of what you could.

They were getting gunners, riflemen, and suchlike, but then they said: "What about stretcher bearers?" Nobody was volunteering for stretcher bearers. One bloke was pointing to me and says, "He'll do, he's a first-aid man." I tried to dodge this but, no, I was eventually put over on to the first-aid, on to the stretchers. They were like beds, and there were only two of you to a stretcher.

We left the following night by train. We had already got our gear, packs and uniform and so on. I didn't know where we were going. And I always remember that night there was a little Cuban singing this song, *Ay, ay, ay*. Unfortunately there was also a broken window in our compartment with a hell of a wind blowing through it. So it took the edge off the song. But we finished up in a little place called Chinchón for the day. This lad I pal-ed up with, Alex Alexander, he came from Liverpool, he says, "We'll have a look out for beer." He could speak a little Spanish so we went away looking for beer but there was none. So we finished up in a little winery or suchlike. The fellows who were working there were eulogising the qualities of the different wines and of course we had to sample them. So we sampled ever so many different qualities that night. We got back safe enough to our billets. But the next morning there was a whole line of drunks. And I remember McCartney, the fellow who wrote *Walls have Mouths*, he was the company commander or something like that, and he says: "Now any other body coming up drunk" – he had all the drunks lined up, and I remember one of them had been a cartoonist for the *Daily Worker* who was later killed, unfortunately – "Now any more of this and there won't be one of you to go to the front." After that they were sending all the drunks up the front!

However, we got clear that night and went on to another place. The following night Alex Alexander and I were detailed to go away on the *camión* up to Chinchón. I don't know why we were detailed to go there, but we got up there and landed in this farmhouse. There was nothing to eat but we eventually got a little place where we slept. And by the time we got up in the morning the rest of the Battalion, the British Battalion, were up. We went out and here this bloke Fred Copeman comes along. We were being charged with desertion.

I think Copeman was a bit of a nut. He was one of the lads who had led the mutiny at Invergordon in the Navy, but in my opinion he was a bit of a nut. He was going about with one of those great big revolvers all the time. However, we were being charged with desertion. I asked how the hell you can desert when you're going up the front! But this thing was smoothed out and eventually we set off on the way.[51]

There was some humour. I remember a little London Jewish lad, Davidovitch. "Oh, aye," he says "this is just like manouevres." There was a shell exploded not very far from where we were and that sort of stopped the kidding! But eventually we got up. We were on our way up the Jarama.[52]

To me there was no organised approach, no organised advance or anything like that once we got up there as far as what a company was doing. I remember No. 1 Company went out on to a hill that was terrain something like where in Dundee we've got the Sidlaw Hills. And they'd got away out in the front and you had a deep valley in between where they were and the rest of the Battalion. And unfortunately you had fellows who, more out of bravado than anything else, when they were firing, instead of lying down and taking cover, they were standing up. It was just a slaughter.

The call went out for stretcher bearers and I was one of the unfortunates on the stretchers. So we went up and the first fellow we took out was a lad called Campeau. I think he was a secretary of the Y.C.L. in London at one time. Great big fellow he was, I think he must have weighed about sixteen stone. There were only two of us on this stretcher and the bullets were coming just like bees buzzing around all the place. We got him across but he died ultimately in hospital.[53] And we were steady at that time cutting across, bringing people back and forward. It was really just a slaughter.

That night we got a sort of break when darkness fell. And I remember this lad, Ollie Diamond. Someone said he was an Egyptian, but he was maybe a Frenchman, I don't know. He was in charge of the section I got in touch with. Then I had to take a fellow up the the first-aid station. By this time it was getting dark. I didn't know any Spanish, I hadn't a clue what Spanish was like. I spoke a wee bit of French, but other than that . . . So I took this fellow up to this first-aid station and left him there. Coming back I saw a bloke lying there and went over to ask him where it was. But here the bloke was dead. There were a few bodies lying around. But it was all in the dark, you didn't know where you were. Eventually I found my way back by more good luck than anything else.

Next morning again we were on the move. We started work again, but I can't remember now whether No. 1 Company had been recalled, because they got a hell of a cutting up. They had been recalled from this hill anyway, to be organised better. We were still getting one or two wounded and had to take them back up. One time we were going up there was a Fifer on this stretcher with me. I can't remember his name but he was a pretty hard nut. Coming back he says, "Och, we'll have a seat down here and a smoke." So we were sitting by the roadway and having a smoke and here Copeman comes along again and starts on us. He was going to shoot us! So this bloke, this Fifer, says, "Just you try it, lad." Copeman says, "What do you think you're doing?" The Fifer says, "We're carrying bodies up here. We're coming back and forrit. Are we no' entitled tae a blaw?" Copeman calmed down a bit and went away.

After that things sort of quietened down for a day or two. I remember we got a load of fruit, oranges and lemons, and it was left to us again the stretcher bearers to take them up and dish them round. There was this sunken road and I said, "How the hell are we going to get across here?" There was a machine gun just trained on this. So we got a bit o' rope and we got a basket and we tied the rope round our waist and through our legs and crept along this way. But by the time we got across to these fellows on the other side it was nearly all lemons that were left – the oranges had been all taken by the lads we came to first. There was quite a shindy. They wanted us to go back and get oranges for them but we told them it wasn't on. They had to take what there was.

I remember there was a bit of a retreat. There was a rumour went round, I can't remember what it was, and they started retreating. We'd gone back a bit, and some of them were actually running. And here we came across three women sitting behind a machine gun just past where we were, Spanish women. I saw them looking at us. You know, I don't know whether it shamed us or what. But these women they sat there. There was some other body – it may have been Jock Cunningham – managed to reorganise a lot and get the thing controlled again. It was just one of these panicky things. We sort of stabilised the line.

There was one time, things were fairly quiet, and some blokes were sitting down playing cards and suchlike and there was a Spaniard came over. He was loaded up with grenades and what-not, all sorts of things. He said something and we just told him where to go. A wee while later Jock Cunningham came up – he was the captain. He says, "Did any of you lads see a Spaniard coming across here?" "Aye." He says, "What did you say to him?" "Aw, fuck off." He says, "He was a deserter. He's a Fascist. He deserted to come over. He could have blown us up if he'd been trying." It was things like that happened because of these problems of language. We had a system of interpreters but ye couldnae have interpreters to everybody. And little things like that happened. Fortunately, nobody suffered through our ignorance.

Another time I went out, the planes came over this time – fighter planes. And this lad and I we dived below this *camión*. When we got out after they'd passed – they had been machine gunning us – we looked to see if there was anything to eat or drink in the *camión*. But here it was loaded with ammunition. We had been lying under an ammunition truck!

I think it was a day or so later. We were retired and taken back a good bit and we were getting the first half decent feed we'd had. It was a big dixie of rice, I remember that. The next thing I got a blow on the head and I finished up in the rice, with blood coming out my head into the rice. So they thought I was a gonner. I'd got a bullet in the head. But that didn't put them off the rice.

I was taken away the first-aid section and kept there until they had got an ambulance and it was loaded up. We got on board. There would be about ten of us and there must have been some horrible cases. It was the little Cuban fellow I mentioned earlier who was driving the ambulance. He was a wonderful driver. But the planes came over. Well, on the ambulances they had red crosses all round them, on the roof and everything. But this didn't stop the Germans from coming. He drove off the road and you know it must have been hellish for some. It was bad enough for me but some of them were awful wounds, you know. And they were being tossed around all over the place.

We eventually got into this town where they had a clearance hospital. And I met a Dundee lad there, a little lad Danny Gibbon. He'd been shot through the jaw. It came out through the jaw – and through his eye.

Then I was carried on further to Valencia. They started sharing out the wounded and I finished up in a little place called Castellón. I was put in a hospital there and they asked where I had been wounded. I says, "In the head." And of course they looked and says, "Ach, there's just a lump there." So I was in hospital for two or three days and the lump was still there. One of the doctors spoke French and one of the nurses too, and that was the only communication. I told them: "Look, I've been wounded. I think I've got a bullet in the head." The doctor says, "Aw, well, we'll send you up for an X-ray." So they got the X-ray and it was there. This doctor came in and looked at the X-ray and started, "Right." So here he started cutting in to my head, but there was nae anaesthetic. I don't know if it was pliers he was using but he couldn't get hold of the bullet and you could hear the ding.

There was an old bloke in there, a fellow Donnelly, he came from Birkenhead, a bit of a character. He had shrapnel wounds in the back and was pretty bad. He says to the doctor, "Stop, you bastard. You're killing him." He called him Doctor Crippen after that. But the doctor just turned round and laughed. He didn't know what Donnelly was saying of course.

They left me alone for a couple of days then a little dapper chap came in. He was a dentist. He said, "Have you got a bullet in your head?" "Aye." He says, "Aw, well, I'll see to that." So they brought me in. It was like one of these Hollywood things, they had everybody in, even the cleaners were in to see what was happening. He pulled the bullet out right enough. He had the pliers. He asked me if I wanted the bullet. I said, "No, you can keep it." But it was unusual and I thought myself if you got a bullet in the head you were a gonner.

In the next bed to mine there was an Irishman. He was a young lad, a student in Dublin University. He was an I.R.A. man, and when they asked him where he came from he told them, "Ireland." But they didn't know where that was. I think this killed him more than anything, though he had a nasty wound – the mere fact they didn't know where Ireland was. They didnae even know where Scotland was. They knew of England but that was about all.

After they took the bullet out I was allowed to wander round, there were no restrictions. One night I was in seeing a film, *Oil for the Lamps of China*.[54] There was a revolution going on and it seemed to me very real. When I came out that night, going back to hospital, along the street I was called on. There had been a lot of children playing and the town had actually been shelled by an Italian gunboat. And I had to help where these kids had been. You know they were just a mess. It wasnae a military town, nothing at a'. And they couldn't do anything. The gunboat just stayed out of the harbour, about a mile off, and just pumped the shells in. The kids were massacred. I was in hospital for altogether about three month between that and going down to convalesce at Benicasim. I was there too when the P.O.U.M. caused a lot of trouble in Barcelona. I think they termed it the equivalent to the Independent Labour Party or something at that time. But it was a well-to-do Party. They had plenty of money.[55]

Benicasim was a convalescent centre, a beautiful place that I heard had been a millionaires' resort. So there was one of the large villas to each nationality. Unfortunately, I was made political commissar when I was down there and I had to put my foot down two or three times! We had a doctor in charge of us, a Mexican who had been at the Olympics in Berlin.[56] He was in the table tennis team. He'd married a German girl and she came with him to Spain. I don't know whether they ever got back to Mexico or what happened to them. But he was a very nice fellow, very competent.

I was at Benicasim altogether for maybe about three months and then I was sent up to Albacete, the centre for the International Brigade. The board there marked me unfit. So I was asked, "Do you want to go home or what do you want to do?" So I got a job in the cadre service. It was a documentation place, where you were keeping fiches, keeping track of everybody who was there. There were a couple of Yanks with me in the same office and a Belgian and a Czechoslovak. One fellow there was a brilliant linguist and when I came in they introduced me to him. He said, "I too am a Scotsman." "Oh," I said, "where do you come from?" "Edinboorge." He was a brilliant linguist this fellow, he was a ship's engineer originally, I heard. After dinner we used to go to this place for a coffee. They worked you all day, day and night practically. He'd be sitting there talking to you then someone would throw a question at him in Russian or Polish or something and he would just turn round and answer them in their own language.

I was there for a while then they sent me up to a place called the Bank of Spain. I was put in charge of the British documentation there. There was a German who was in charge of the whole place, the whole Bank of Spain. There was a Canadian and one or two other English speakers as well as myself, and this German always sat and talked with us. One time he came in and he looked rather long in the face. I asked him what was wrong, "Oh," he said, "they want me to go away to Benissa." "Benissa? You're lucky." You know, we were in Albacete at this time in the middle of the summer and it was just like an oven. Benissa was on the sea front. But he didn't want to go. So we got talking about it and we decided, "Och, we'll send in a letter to headquarters saying 'Why do you want to send so-and-so to Benissa?'" (I can't remember his name now). We all signed the letter and sent it. But here the German disappeared. A day or two after he went away the knock came to the door. A couple of Spanish civil police came in. They spoke English. "You Tom Clarke? Did you sign this letter?" I says, "Yes, why? The bloke said he wasnae wantin' to go. Now he's shifted." Here it turned out this German bloke was a Nazi spy. He had come from South America. Someone had written to somebody in South America and said, "So-and-so's down here and he's doing a great job." And they wrote back saying, "He's a bloody Nazi." So he was removed. I don't know what happened to him. I never heard of him again. But it just showed you how efficient the Nazi machine was, their secret service. I don't know what he'd been able to spy out and give away and suchlike but he had carried on like this. If we hadn't written we'd probably never have found out about him.

After that I was sent up to Tarazona, to what they called an engineers' company. These were fellows who had been wounded and suchlike. I was put in there as political commissar. Again ye'd tae tak a'body's girns and suchlike. I was up there for quite a while and then I was eventually sent to Barcelona. While I was in Barcelona you'd get these Italian planes coming over, and a little Italian beside me he used to call them the 'Chamberlins'. Sometimes there was no opposition to these planes. We had an airfield outside Barcelona but sometimes there was no gasoline for our aeroplanes to take off.

And I remember, too, one of the Russian ships – a beautiful ship, I saw it in Dundee in 1934, one of their most modern ships – the *Komsomol* was sunk bringing stuff in to Barcelona. Of course, this was the racket with the Non-Intervention, which was purely anti-working class. Eden wasn't interested in peace. But they were interested in keeping the workers down and he proved it later on. All sorts of people used to think Eden was a gentleman. Well, he wore an Anthony Eden hat. But other than that and maybe his manners, I mean, there was nothing gentlemanly about him. His politics were like the rest of them, filthy.

I never came across any atrocities when I was in Spain. There was only one time, I think it was in Barcelona, I saw a girl. She was a bonny lassie. But there was something peculiar about her. She had no hair. Her head had been shaved but she had escaped from the Nazis and she was still great looking. She would have been quite a swell under present day circumstances. She looked wonderful. It was just something you just couldn't make out. But that was the only thing ever I saw. I remember seeing that on the films just after the 1939-45 War – the French did that with women who were collaborators with the Nazis and suchlike. But this girl certainly looked swell.

Well, from Barcelona eventually I was sent home. This was about July 1938. I had gone out there at the beginning of January '37.

Looking back on the Spanish War now I think that if we had been able to win there the possibility is you would never have had a Second World War. I remember seeing on a Pathé newsreel before I went out there, a ship leaving New York with arms for the Spanish Republican Government. And it had hardly left the harbour when the American coast guards came round and turned it back again. This was during the time of Roosevelt's presidency. So he had a lot to answer for as well as Britain and France.[57] It was a Tory who was sent out to the Canary Islands in a plane to bring Franco back into Morocco and then start off the War there[58] against – well, it depends what you term democracy, capitalist democracy, socialist democracy, or what do you mean by democracy? This great 'Christian gentleman' as he was called ultimately had two prisons specially for priests in Spain who were opposed to his ruling. You can never forget – you maybe forgive, but you don't forget – the reasons for these sorts of things. Churchill also backed up Franco. He never thought about the Empire and Gibraltar at that time, he backed up Franco. He thought it was a Communist Government.[59] In fact as far a I remember there were only two Communists in it, Jesus Hernández and Dolores Ibarruri. It wasn't a

Communist Government by any means. But this was what its enemies put about.[60]

What I did personally was very little. But what I tried to do was really worthwhile. Ye can hold back but if you carry on and do something to prevent Fascism gaining ground, well, you're at least trying to do something. 123 Dundonians were there in the Spanish War and there were seventeen Dundonians killed, which was a very high percentage. Lots of them were wounded. Once you were wounded, sometimes you were scattered, sometimes they thought you were dead, and sometimes people came up and said, "I thought you were dead!"

I think the War was fought in the wrong way. Well, they had this 1914 approach to war – sort of trench warfare and suchlike. I thought about this over the years. When I used to read about the Russian guerrilla movement during the last War. They were able to harass the Nazis and suchlike. If we had tried something like that in Spain, or thought about something along these lines it might have had a different effect. Because obviously the Moors and the Italians – the Italians weren't, you would say, very keen on the War either – weren't capable of this sort of thing. If we had thought maybe about this at that time it might have been more beneficial.

After I came back home I never felt victimised because I had been in the Spanish War. But I did come across one or two workers who, because of their religious convictions at that time, were still anti-Spanish working class., They were trying to make out, you know, you were raping nuns and killing priests in Spain. After I came back I was asked if I had seen any desecration of churches. I had seen one or two churches where there had been some damage, but never desecration where it was destroyed, because this was against the policy of the Republican Government. There was a great deal of anti-Church feeling in Spain.[61]

Annie Murray was born in Aberdeenshire in 1906 but spent her girlhood in Perthshire. Her two brothers, Tom and George, fought with the International Brigade in the Spanish War. During and after the Second World War she worked in children's nurseries in London, then found employment in the Post Office at Mount Pleasant until her retirement in 1964. She married and became Mrs Annie Knight in 1948. She now lives with her husband in Fife.

ANNIE MURRAY

I was very interested in the Spanish situation even before the Civil War, and I volunteered in 1936 through the British Medical Aid Association to go out to Spain to help the Spanish people. I went to Spain because I beleived in the cause of the Spanish Republican Government. I didn't believe in Fascism and I had heard many stories of what happened to people who were under Fascist rule.

The British Medical Aid Committee was composed mostly of London doctors or British doctors, and Labour MPs, left wing MPs mostly, people like that. It had been set up specially for Spanish war aid.[62]

When I started nursing I was twenty-four. I had trained as a nurse in Edinburgh Royal Infirmary and became a fully registered trained nurse. I had finished my training just at the beginning of the Spanish War then I went out to Spain.

I was politically active even in the Royal Infirmary, you know. I had started being active just before I had begun my training. I had led nurses to protest against conditions in the Infirmary and we used to have huge meetings in my room. We got certain things done but very little from the colonel who was in charge of the whole hospital. I wasn't in a union at that time. After the Spanish War broke out, just before I finished my training, I joined the Communist Party.

So it was in September 1936 I went to Spain. I went through France to Spain with a visa. There was really nothing memorable about the journey. It was easy enough for us nurses at that time to get to Spain. We weren't stopped at the frontier, nothing like that.

I arrived at a small Spanish hospital at Huete, more or less on the Barcelona front. Huete was a little village north-east of Barcelona. Two nurses had gone in the first lot of nurses from London and they were in the hospital at the time. And then a few more of us went there. We had I think about twelve nurses altogether in the hospital at Huete, and also there were Spanish nurses, and, you know, untrained people helping, Spanish people. We had many little Spanish nurses. Spain had no real trained nurses. They used the nuns. So these little girls only had about three months' training. But they were very keen and very good for the time they had trained.

We were at Huete for quite a number of months, till I thought I

would like to join a completely Spanish contingent and joined a
surgeon, called Dr Quemada, at a big hospital in Barcelona. I've
forgotten the name of the hospital but it was right in the centre of
Barcelona. I worked with Dr Quemada for the rest of the time I was in
Spain as his theatre nurse.

And then from the hospital in Barcelona we used to go out in the
hospital trains all round the area, behind offensives, and when there
was more work to do outside of the hospital than inside. In the
hospital train it was pretty gruelling, you know. On one occasion we
went under a bridge to operate when bombs were falling.

Hours of duty at the hospital depended on the work, because we
had many casualties at one time and not so many at other times. We
just worked when we had to even if you had to get out of bed in the
middle of the night, you know.

We had a lot of casualties even in the little hospital at Huete, very
serious ones, terribly serious ones. Young, young men calling for
their mothers. It was very sad, terrifically sad. Many of the wounds
were very serious – open holes, stomachs opened up, legs off, arms
off, oh, terrible, terrible. I never saw anybody shell-shocked. It was a
different kind of war from the First World War. We didn't have any
cases of shell-shock in the hospital. We had lots of cases of frozen feet,
and that was a terrible thing because when their feet were coming
round to get their blood flowing again it was a terrible painful thing.
We had an awful job with that, and of course we hadn't really got the
equipment to treat that sort of thing very easily. So there was a terrible
lot of suffering from frozen feet. It was terribly cold in the winter,
very cold up in the hills in the winter where we were, extremely cold.
You talk about Scotland! It was colder than that, I think.

Most of the casualties in our hospital of course were our own. At
least eighty per cent I should think were Spaniards, the remaining
were Internationals from all the countries. I met masses of
Internationals. Lots of Americans, Germans, Italians, Russians and,
oh, every country you could think about that sent volunteers –
French, Yugoslavs. I think every country almost you could mention
there were volunteers from to the anti-Fascist side.

We never had women patients in the hospital but there were women
fighting. I think it didn't last, having women in the fighting lines and
they gave it up soon after the War started.[63]

We got a wounded Fascist in. He was a Fascist officer, a high sort of
ranking Spanish officer. And of course we had to treat everybody,
you know. But the young Spaniards, the casualties, were shouting at
us, "Leave him to die, leave him to die." But of couse we were just
there to treat all the people. We weren't sorry, though, when that man
died brcause he looked a nasty little man.

I don't remember having any Nazi German or Fascist Italian
casualties but we had Moors in the hospital. They were given money

by the Fascists that wasn't of any value. They thought they had
money but it was completely worthless. Mostly these Moors couldn't
read or write and they were just forced to fight, you know. They were
mostly men of between thirty and forty I should think.

Ours were all military patients. We didn't have any civilian patients.
It hadn't been an all-military hospital before the War, it was just a
general hospital.

Most of the nurses who came out that I met were politically
conscious and knew why they were coming out. But there were a few
who just went out to be nurses for a humanitarian reason and had no
idea which side they were on even when they went out there, until
they went out. But most of them came back and have been very active
anti-Fascist workers since. None of the British nurses stayed on in
Spain after the War but some of the other Internationals could have
done, I don't know. None of the nurses I knew got married in Spain
during the War. One went back and married the Spanish surgeon we
used to have in the hospital in Huete up in the north-east.

The Spanish doctors were very good, comparable to ours, very
good men indeed. Some of our own doctors went out to Spain. Dr
Tudor Hart was one. I think he came from London, I'm not awfully
sure. I didn't know many London doctors then at all, because we
weren't working with London people. We were working with
Spanish doctors all the time. The general standard of equipment was
quite good. We weren't seriously short, because of getting stuff from
London. The hospital at Huete was very well equipped, for the same
reason. And even when I was in Barcelona the surgeon used to say
what he would like, and I used to send to London to get it. And then
of course we had taken mosquito nets out with us. We had to give
those to the patients because there was a terrible lot of mosquitoes out
there. It was a terrible problem. It was so sunny that the doctors were
rather keen to try to get the sun to heal a lot of the wounds, and it was
marvellous how it does it, too. So of course we had to put on
mosquito nets over the patients if they were being treated like that. It
was terribly sad to see them.

I didn't speak Spanish before I went out there. But we had a young
man from London who taught us quite a lot of Spanish when we were
free. I got to know Spanish families, though I couldn't say their
names. I was very friendly with all the villagers. I used to go to their
houses. Their houses were under the ground and they were just
hovels, completely dark inside. These were their normal homes, it
was all they had. They had bottles with oil in them and a wick
hanging out the side. And that was their light. I used to go into their
houses with them and they were very friendly. They used to shout
through the village, "Anna, Anna," you know. They really got to like
me. I was more interested, I think, than most of the nurses in the
villagers. And I think I understood what they were going through,

more than some of the others did anyway. The villagers had a donkey and they used to make me ride the donkey. It was terrific, you know.

We mixed with the population in Barcelona and of course the people we met and most of the people in Barcelona in fact seemed to be against the Fascists. I knew there was fighting in Barcelona itself in the summer of 1937 between the P.O.U.M., the Anarchists and the Communists. But we were so busy in the hospital we didn't see much of the outside life really. Oh, I knew the Anarchists! They would shoot anybody if they thought they were well off. Yes, they would just take them round the corner. You could hear the shots sometimes. They weren't very scientific in their approach, you know. We had them working in the hospitals and everything. They were a part of the International Brigade actually. But as I say they weren't very scientific in their approach to the whole cause. Nice enough blokes but they would shoot somebody if they thought they were well off – even just by the way they were dressed, you know.[64]

I remember the food was very poor, very poor indeed. Sometimes we were really hungry. The Spaniards did their best and cooked what they could. It was mostly beans and oil. Coffee of course was just nothing, it was just like sand and water almost, it was so poor. I remember being in a train once and I was so hungry I was picking up beans from the floor to eat. From London they used to send us some chocolate and cigarettes about once a month, a little packet of chocolate or a packet of cigarettes. Of course we used to give them away to the patients. I didn't smoke.

I kept up contacts with my family at home. Well, I had five sisters and two brothers. They kept writing. I always managed to get mail. We got it through the Medical Committee in London. We never actually got personal food parcels from home. I was sent a parcel once but I never knew what was in it because it got bombed on a lorry. Once I came home on leave, I think it was a fortnight at home in Scotland. And once I had some leave in Spain and went to a seaside place where the hotel belonged to anti-Fascists, Spanish people, and they took nurses for a week, I think it was, to give them a convalescence.

Of course my brothers were out in Spain. They came after me a bit. George was wounded, he had a bullet right through his chest and it just avoided his lungs. And of course my brother Tom was also out there. I didn't see much of them of course because I was in the hospitals. Occasionally they managed to come to see me. They were in the International Brigade, of course. Tom was a commissar. George was in the Anti-Tank Battalion. George was in Spain for two years and Tom, I think for about six months. He volunteered to come to Spain but the people in the Communist Party – he was in the Communist Party in Scotland – they didn't want him to come because it was thought that he was too valuable in Scotland. But he said, "Oh,

I must go out there. I just feel as if I've got to help the Spanish people." My brother George, who was wounded, went back to the front we thought far too quickly. However, he survived.

In fact, in the hospital at Barcelona we had not only wounded men but some of them came to us for convalesence as well and sometimes we told them that we thought they should stay a bit longer because they weren't quite fit. But they said, "No." Most of them said, "We must get back to the front."

Most of the casualties came into the hospital pretty quickly from the front. Motor ambulances were used. Of course, they had many ambulances from Britain, you know, a terrific number in fact. And you heard them when we were going through points, you know, the guard used to say, "Ambulancias ingleses," and they got through of course. There were ambulances donated by the people of different countries. Ours were British, of course, with British drivers as well.

There weren't many air raids on Barcelona while I was there at all. But on the other hand maybe there was more bombing than I know because, being in the hospital and being so busy, unless they were fairly close to the hospital I didn't have much experience of them. The hospital I was in in Barcelona was never bombed while I was there anyway. One time, I remember, we took a patient outside to operate on a table because we had so many patients in the hospital we couldn't operate inside. And we had him on the table and we had just amputated his leg, because he had a very infected leg, when a bomb was dropped nearby. So we had to take him off the table in the middle of the operation. Later on I was in London during the Blitz. It was much worse in London than it had been in Barcelona, because I was right in the middle of it there.

I was in Spain for altogether two-and-a-half years. As we were coming out of Spain – the Fascists were getting to Barcelona as we were getting out – I was with the Spanish surgeon and some of the others as we came through Barcelona. We found a whole lot of children, oh, dozens of them, with their hands off, completely off. The Italians had dropped anti-personnel bombs marked 'Chocolate', 'Chocolatti'. The children were picking up these things – they hadn't had chocolate for years – and they just blew their hands off. This Spanish surgeon that I worked with, he was in tears. We all were. This sort of thing was so horrible. It left a big impression on me.

From Barcelona we went to France. I went with the patients into a hospital in France. They were prepared to take the casualties that we had with us. There were nuns running this hospital and they were very kind to us nurses, really nice to us. But the French doctors didn't seem to bother about the patients. They were left there lying on the floor. It was terrible. We were trying to tell them that they'd have to do something about these poor things, they were bleeding and dying. But they didn't seem to be interested. And we thought they were

Fascist types of doctors there.

I wasn't there very long, about a few days, I think, then I flew to Toulouse and came home to London. There was no big crowd at the station in London, nothing like that. I don't think they knew when I was coming and when I came back I was on my own.

I went to Dulwich Hospital and worked there for a time. Then I was in the Civil Defence for a bit at the beginning of the 1939–45 War. And then I became a matron of a children's nursery in Stepney and I was there for quite a few years.

The Spanish War had a terrific impact on me personally, a terrific impact. It was the most important thing in my life. It was a terrific experience I would never like to have missed. I have certainly no regrets at having gone there at all. I know what a struggle the Spanish people had and how cheerful and good they were to us. The spirit of the people was terrific. I've never known anything like it. I would never expect to see anything like it again. It was a terrible, terrible thing when the whole struggle collapsed, you know. The Fascists got the upper hand. In the Republic it wasn't a Communist or a Labour Government even, it was a Liberal type of Government.

It was all terribly sad really, the whole thing was very sad, the whole political situation, because the Spanish people were so buoyed up to thinking they were going to win until the Germans and Italians came to bomb. And of course that settled it. And that was the saddest thing of the whole lot. They were so wanting to win. And there was such a spitit amongst the Spanish people, terrific, you can't believe it hardly. And then the sadness of seeing all the terribly wounded youngsters, eighteen, nineteen, and twenty.

After the War I didn't keep in touch with the people that I knew in Spain. I was very sorry afterward that I hadn't because I had had letters but I wasn't sure who they were. They couldn't write English for one thing and I didn't really have their addresses. I haven't resumed any acquaintance with the Spanish people since and I haven't been back to Spain either. I wouldn't have been frightened to go back or anything like that. I suppose it's because I've been so busy working most of the time, you see. I worked till I was retiring age.

Annie Murray (centre) and other nurses drying and folding bandages to be used again.

Unveiling of the memorial in East Princes Street Gardens, Edinburgh, 1982, to the Spanish Civil War and local volunteers in the International Brigade killed in it. Annie Murray is speaking at microphone. Her brother Tom (in beret) is immediately to her right, and her brother George is at left rear of photo (with bowed head). Phil Gillan (bareheaded) is to left of Tom Murray. Garry McCartney is behind Tom Murray, to right. Bill Cranston is immediately to left of Phil Gillan.

Roderick MacFarquhar was born and brought up in Inverness. As a railway clerk he took part in the 1926 General Strike. During the 1939-45 War he was commissioned into the Reconnaissance Corps at Sandhurst and subsequently was appointed to serve with the G.H.Q. Liaison Regiment (Phantom). He served in Europe as a Staff Captain. After the War he became secretary of the Highland Fund Ltd. He now lives in Glasgow.

RODERICK MacFARQUHAR

I was a student of politics and watched the rise of Mussolini and then the development and activities of Hitler with very great alarm – the possible menace that this represented to my own country. I was a member of the Labour Party and I was involved also at that time with my trade union, the Railway Clerks' Association, in which some of our members were also very interested in these dangerous events. And so I had observed the sudden outbreak of War in Spain, the immediate arrival of Italian troops from North Africa and Caproni troop-carrying planes. And of course the subsequent and very obvious involvement of the German Nazis, with their contribution in disciplined troops and in arms and ammunition. So that I was looking at this with very considerable unease and realised that unless people could stop this further encroachment on liberty in Europe then we would all be involved, Britain included, in war with Hitler and Mussolini.

I felt that by December 1936 the situation was critical in Spain – Madrid was almost surrounded. To my astonishment, the *Glasgow Herald* – I think it was on December 11th (I still have the editorial somewhere) – exulted in the anticipated fall of Madrid.[65] I found this so obnoxious that in a democratic country our press should give dictatorial support to the Nazis and Mussolini's Fascists. The opportunity to do something came up at that time. The Scottish Ambulance Unit was asking for volunteers to go to Spain to assist the Spanish Republic. Having volunteered and been accepted I went in January 1937 to Spain.

The purpose of my going was what Sir Daniel M. Stevenson, a former Lord Provost of Glasgow, who financed or helped to finance the Ambulance Unit and certainly gave a good deal of support otherwise to it, called the support of the Republican Government.[66] I recall distinctly his comment when the newspapers gave a very black picture of what was happening in Spain. "Well," he said, "if Madrid does fall you still have all the rest of Spain to fall back on."

The primary purpose of the Scottish Ambulance Unit, as far as Sir D.M. Stevenson was concerned, was to supply an ambulance service on the front to the wounded of the Republican Army. It also had, through the generosity of the Scottish people several truckloads of

77

food which it was taking out to supply to the people of Spain. It was of course a quite well known fact that the food supplies were down to their lowest level by that time and particularly children and babies were suffering as a consequence. And these were the primary aims, that had been given to the Unit.

The Unit had actually been in Spain prior to that. I believe it went out in September 1936 and it returned to replenish supplies and obtain fresh recruits.

The leader of this Unit was a Miss Jacobsen.[67] I think there were about nine or ten of us went out with it in January 1937. We were all volunteers of course, and people like myself had a certain amount of experience of first-aid. I had also been in the Territorials for a period as well. So some of us had some kind of background of this nature. I don't think the others were members of political parties or otherwise politically active. For example, I don't think George Burleigh was. He was a miner from Kirkintilloch but he was with the Ambulance Unit as a driver. I met him when I joined the Unit on the day we were virtually leaving Glasgow, or the day before. George had been walking round looking at the various people and he came up to me and said would I act as his mate on this trip? You know, I liked George very much, he was a nice strong man, of I would say quite liberal views really, honest to the core. And I was delighted to be with him.

We travelled overland through France to Spain and down to Barcelona and on to Valencia, which we reached one evening in January. The British Embassy had been moved from Madrid, in expectation of its fall, to Valencia. The ambassador was, I think, Mr Ogilvie Forbes.[68] We were taken to a building in Valencia where we were invited to have a fairly rough scrimpy meal. At the same time there arrived the British military attaché. He greeted Miss Jacobsen, in my hearing, with the remark, "Oh, I am so glad you've arrived." He said, "Since the Belgian attaché was bumped off on the Madrid front in December we've had no information at all about the movement of the Republican forces."[69] I thought this remark was a most strange introduction as far as I was concerned to the struggle that I had realised was confronting us. And I expressed some doubts about it to my colleague George Burleigh. "Well, I know," he said, "about that, too. And we're taking steps to make sure that we do not give away any information to the enemy."

Thereafter we left Valencia very early in the morning for Madrid. The road into Madrid was being shelled fairly often and we had to arrive at a certain point in order to get through after dusk. We eventually were lodged in Madrid in buildings close to what had been the British Embassy. And from there we were sent out to the front, the University City front to start with, and also to the front on the river Manzanares, where I had my first experience of real fire and the tasks that we were there to deal with – rescue of the wounded and bringing them to hospital.

We also went to Chinchón and just at the point when the battle of Jarama was being fought, and we had certain tasks to carry out there, with similar rescue of wounded and bringing them to hospital.

We also had the rather – I thought so anyway – unnecessary task of issuing food from our trucks to the people of various suburbs of Madrid, which I personally did not like because I thought it was not properly organised and should have been left to the Spanish authorities to do and not us. We were there till March when again there was an attack, this time by the Italian Fascist army on Guadalajara, with the intention of sealing of Madrid from the rest of Republican Spain.

But before I deal with that let me go back to our arrival in Madrid in January, in darkness, in silence, but with the searchlights moving on the dark sky above. The city had of course been bombed and shelled most intensively during the time since the Fascists had failed in their attacks and efforts to take Madrid in December. This destruction of a modern city under such a siege and in constant attack by shellfire and by bombers was a unique experience and, in the weeks after our arrival, a first experience as far as I was concerned. During the day the city, a beautiful city, looked in the clear sunlight of early spring most charming and pleasing. But regularly during these mornings the Franco forces would start shelling and inevitably casualties appeared: the women out shopping, children with them, and girls at offices. And it was not an infrequent experience, in fact my own personal experience, to see a child badly injured by shells, and picking him up and taking him straight to the hospital in the centre of the city.

These experiences were of course quite normal and in an amazing way the Madrileños were very courageous and firm and to a certain extent philosophical about it. The hotels were virtually closed. They were used now as hosptials. There were bars open and there were shops open, at which the girls would scramble for any costumes and hats that came their way. As Dr Len Crome of our Ambulance Unit remarked once, "Girls are girls the world over whether they are in a war situation or not."[70]

The Unit was based on Madrid, then, but went out to the fronts as I have said, the University City front to start with and later to the Jarama front. The University City, as it was called, was on the outskirts, to the west of Madrid. It had been devastated by the conflict during December when the Fascists made an immense effort to take it and were resisted by the International Brigade and by our Spanish comrades too, who were by this time well enough trained to carry out the defence of Madrid. The women and girls also helped with the sandbagging and the preparation of defences of that nature. These occasions in University City were to my eye of course, having never seen a bombarded city before, quite unique. Buildings, obviously beautiful buildings, had been torn apart by shellfire and bombs and bombing. And there were a number of trenches built to shelter the defensive forces and keep the Fascists out. The casualties of course in these conditions, where there was a very large concentration of stone and concrete, were quite heavy because the splinters from these emplacements were quite severe.

The Unit was moved out on to the University City and brought in casualties and then it moved up to the Jarama front, to the south east of the city. The countryside was beautiful. Spring was just beginning. The Government had made valiant efforts to see that the agricultural production was not interfered with by the War, and you could see the braided corn or wheat coming up. And the countryside in general was very industrious indeed in its efforts to support the Government in its campaign to make sure there was enough food, in spite of the blockade that was taking place. Our quarters on the Jarama front were at Chinchón, where we brought our wounded in from the front to be dealt with by the nurses and doctors in these units. The conditions were quite primitive. Schools were taken over for this purpose, and the doctors and nurses made a very great effort to make sure that their patients were looked after and carefully treated.

Again of course there was also the threat of bombings. The Russians, who had supplied fighter planes particularly to safeguard Madrid, were training the Spanish Air Force to use these planes – called Chatos – to combat the enemy squadrons that were coming over to bomb the city.

We had periods in Madrid when conditions were quiet and we had an opportunity to visit various parts of the city or go to a bar or a cafe. I remember being at one of these one day and being accosted by a man who obviously had lived in Spain for a very long time. He was English. He had looked at my uniform and decided that I must be in support of the Franco forces rather than the forces which I was trying to assist. And quite openly he said, "Of course, you're helpless" and so forth. I was so astonished and so enfuriated by this, I said: "What do you think I came here for? To assist Franco and his forces?" I said, "I came here specifically, and so did this Ambulance Unit come here specifically to help Republican Spain." But this was another kind of indication that, to me anyway, all was not quite well and that somehow the role of the Unit was being misinterpreted.

Later the Unit assembled. Miss Jacobsen said we were going to take a convoy down to Valencia. After a certain amount of investigation I found that the Unit was in fact going to collect all manner of people who were sheltering in the various embassies, sympathisers with General Franco, and take them down to Valencia. I personally refused to go because I thought that this was not the kind of role that the Scottish Ambulance Unit should have been carrying on. With reflection I think that I was probably wrong in this because the

Spanish Republican Government were quite aware of what was going on. They were finding it burdensome to have these people sheltering in those embassies and were quite happy to see them all being delivered to Valencia and put on board British warships. The links between this Unit of ours and the British Government were quite informative and strong, and it caused me and certain members of the Unit a certain uneasiness.

Anyway that operation was carried out and the Unit returned to Madrid. Six ambulances were involved in this evacuation of people from the embassies. I don't know quite how many people there were who were evacuated. But there were also trucks which we had which could be used for that purpose too and I think some of these went as well. But in general there was a certain amount of uneasiness, at least on the part of Dr Crome, another colleague Maurice Linden and myself and George Burleigh. And it was a reflection of George Burleigh's previous admonitions to me.

However, a very serious situation was developing in a threat to Guadalajara by the Italian army which was by this time at least two divisions strong. Their attack was to be against Guadalajara and ultimately to cut off Madrid from the rest of Spain, which would have been a singular triumph for the Fascists if they had succeeded. Guadalajara was to the north-east of Madrid and the attack was to come down through Guadalajara to cut the main road into Madrid, the main Valencia-Madrid road, and seal off that area of the country. In fact, Mussolini in advance of his expected triumph had announced to the world that he was about to cut off Madrid from the rest of Spain. Unfortunately for him the reverse took place, it was a complete disaster as far as he was concerned. His two divisions were cut to pieces. Ironically enough, the International Brigade which helped to stem this attack was led by International Brigaders from Italy, the Garibaldi Battalion. And it was a devastating rout for Mussolini's Italians, from which they had very great difficulty in recovering both in the world sense and in the local sense.

But while this drama was beginning to develop Miss Jacobsen had asked me, because I had been made the senior man in the Ambulance Unit under Dr Crome, what she should do in these circumstances if Madrid was cut off. I said, "Well," repeating Sir D.M. Stevenson's words, "we should deliver the food that we have left to the Spanish authorities and move out along with the Republican Army, if this is necessary." I also quoted Sir D.M., when he sent us off, as saying that even if Madrid were cut off there was the whole of the rest of Spain to work in.

Miss Jacobsen, however, had different views and objected to mine. She said that we were there to help both sides, which of course I immediately claimed was not a proper account of the view of the Scottish people who were contributing towards the support of a

Republican Government and a Republican victory. I said, "Should we in the course of battle pick up enemy troops then obviously we would succour them. But we are not here to help the Fascist forces."

But this conflict within the Unit went on and caused very great disturbance, at least among the three or four of us who took a different view of things. And we said so. There were certain features of the activity by Miss Jacobsen in particular – who was meeting a Captian Lance, a military attaché, I think, who was in the British Embassy, and meeting him after any visits made to and at the fronts – which I personally did not like at all.[71]

There was quite a dramatic scene in the flat in Madrid where we were lodged when we indicated that we were no longer prepared to operate with the Scottish Ambulance Unit and that we intended to join the International Brigade. Miss Jacobsen was furious and uttered various threats to both our reputation and our future, which we rather discounted as they were the words of a distracted and frustrated woman. She then said that we couldn't go, we couldn't do anything of that kind, we would have to go back to Britain. We in answer said, well, we were going whether she liked it or not. In desperation she then asked us if we would meet the British consul in Madrid, a man by the name of Planellyas. She obviously wanted him to instruct us to obey her orders.

So we agreed that we would meet Planellyas and he turned up at the flat fairly late in the evening. Miss Jacobsen said to him: "Order these men back to Britain." He replied, "Miss Jacobsen, that's not in my power to do." And of course she was quite furious about this. We said, "Right, we're going now." We took our kitbags and started walking out. And Planellyas – I never forget this courageous man, who had no reason to expect his fate to be any better than that of other people who had been shot by Franco when he won, stopped us at the door and said: "Gentlemen, allow me to thank you, shake your hand, thank you and wish you God speed." These remarks of course added further to the great fury of Miss Jacobsen.

We left there and arranged to go and meet the great Canadian doctor Bethune, who was taking us next day out to the International Brigade in a location near Madrid. This was, I think, sometime in March 1937 that we parted company from the Scottish Ambulance Unit. We left behind our uniforms, very comfortable as they were. We should have kept them of course because they were of no use to anybody but us. The Ambulance Unit uniform consisted of khaki breeches and khaki jacket, flat caps, and long boots. There was an insignia on one pocket, 'Scottish Ambulance Unit', with I think the British flag on it, too. I suppose it was rather like the British army cavalry uniform of the period.

There were just the four of us – Dr Crome, Maurice Linden, George Burleigh and myself – who resisted the efforts to get us involved in those kinds of undercover activities. I would say that the other members of the Ambulance Unit – I may be wrong in this and I don't want to malign anybody about it – were not, as it were, so politically informed of the struggle that was going on. There were one or two others but they weren't sufficiently influenced to come with us. In fact, we didn't even ask them, we just said we were going. If anybody wanted to come they could do so. The result was very negative, of course. George Burleigh actually went home, because, as he had said to me on the road up to Madrid in January when I had expressed some concern about the remark by the British military attaché on our arrival at Valencia, I had certainly to avoid getting killed with this lot. I had remarked, "Well, George, it's not the very best of times to tell me this!"

However, the three of us when we left the Ambulance Unit joined the International Brigade and were unified into it.

We simply joined the Brigade and we carried on the kind of routine with ambulances and stretchers and dealing with wounded as and when we had to, or when there was a battle. I was mainly on the front line organising the bringing out of wounded and helping to do so. That was really the main kind of role. If it had been the British Army I would have been in the Medical Corps, as it were, rather than in the infantry.

We transformed ourselves very quickly into International Brigaders with a collection of clothes we got from our comrades in the Brigade. I met a man there who became a very close friend of mine, George Green. He turned out his kitbag and dressed me in a pair of, as I would call them now, jeans of some kind, and a jersey which I needed because the weather was still cold, and a shirt of some nature.

George, I found, was a marvellous man, a musician. He played the cello and had been in various orchestras in London. I knew him until the last days in Spain and in fact when we went for the last battle in Spain, when he was killed. George was a most gallant and selfless member of the International Brigade.[72]

The Scottish Ambulance Unit didn't stay long after we left it. It broke up and as far as I recollect it went back to Scotland. I don't know what happened to the ambulances or anything else, but there was no further recollection of seeing them after the Sierra Nevada battles, which took place, I think, in early May. I think what happened was that the Spanish Republican Government got increasingly alarmed at the amount of opportunities there were for this Unit to observe the movements of the Republican forces. You must realise that at that time in particular the appearance of the International Brigade and of course various Spanish divisions – some of which became famous, like the Campesinos and the Listers – on a front almost inevitably meant that there was some kind of attack about to take place.[73] And therefore information about their appearance on a front was almost automatic recognition that there was some attack being prepared. So that the Spanish Republican Government and army could not afford these kinds of potential leakages in a war of this character. I do know that the Scottish Ambulance Unit were barred from going to the front ultimately and I presume that after that they just returned home.[74]

I don't know what happened to Miss Jacobsen at all. I don't want to talk about that particular aspect of it. She went back to Scotland of course. But, in my view anyway, she was not carrying out the duties and instructions that Sir D.M. Stevenson had laid upon the expedition. At least that is my interpretation of it.

I had only met Sir D.M. briefly, when we were leaving for Spain but I got the strong impression that he was a man of liberal tendencies. He certainly had business interests in Spain too. But he had made it quite clear to us before we went that his interests were subordinate to his desire for a democratic Republican Spain. And he in fact helped to organise and finance the whole expedition. He made it quite clear when we were leaving that he wanted to see a Republican victory. But there was the dichotomy between what we were instructed we were there to do and what in a sense I suspect we were being involved in – which was quite a different picture.

Sir D.M. Stevenson was not of course the sole financier of the Scottish Ambulance Unit. There was a tremendous amount of money being poured into the expedition by the people of Scotland. It was a quite extraordinary and exhilarating manifestation of the spirit of the Scottish people that in spite of their – I would almost say – abject poverty at that time, with enormous unemployment and industrial depression, they were still eager to give towards the support of Republican Spain what little they could from the little that they got. It had engendered an enormous patriotic spirit amongst people and a sense of kinship between the Spanish peasantry and workers and the Scottish people. And the result was that large sums of money were given, in small amounts often enough. But the accumulation was enough to send this expedition out. I have no doubt that Sir D.M. Stevenson also helped finance it, as did the various trade unions, and the Co-operative Movement assisted. But the remarkable thing was the affection and sympathy with which the Scottish people viewed the struggle.

After I left the Ambulance Unit the first battle I was involved in was up in the Sierra de Guadaramas. A battle went on there in May/June 1937 up in the mountains. The casualties came down by ambulance to the hospitals to be dealt with. They had the same kinds of wounds and injuries that you get in a mountain area where there is so much rock about and rock splinters too to increase the dangers. They were really trying to break through to Segovia but it failed.

Mainly these offensives failed not because the Republican forces were not brave and determined but because they just didn't have enough fighting equipment to do it with. We were blockaded and we were getting very few things like tanks or guns in, or for that matter ammunition. They did build ammunition factories somewhere. But there was never enough to sustain a prolonged attack and the consequence was that it always failed at a certain point. It was very disappointing of course, but we couldn't do very much about it.

In mountain fighting there were quite a lot of head wounds. The surgeons I must say were quite extraordinary in many respects in the way that they were able to deal with these. And then of course you had the like of gangrene and you had various sepsis and that type of thing taking place. The experience that the surgeons had and their methods of dealing with these things was very much a pioneering development in these areas. They saved very many lives as a result of it.

They had this blood transfusion unit which Dr Norman Bethune pioneered on the front. He was a Canadian.[75] And then they had also Dr Tudor Hart, an English surgeon, who pioneered the use of mawks of some kind for eating up the poison that was in the wounds and cleaning up these things. And they got the wounded away from the front as fast as they could, which was very important towards survival. And there was a very valiant corps of nurses that had come over from England and Scotland, and Wales too, who helped in these cases. They were great people. Nurses I remember included Patience Darton, Ann Murray, and Winifred Bates.[76]

There was a shortage of doctors all round, particularly of course in battle conditions, where I have seen at the Escorial,[77] for instance, the wounded had been pouring in and there were a limited number of doctors and they had to take the more seriously wounded and attend to them first. And of course there was a serious shortage of nurses as well. But that is not to say that the Spanish Republic had no men of very considerable skills, surgeons and doctors, in the army too. There were some very splendid professional men who were ardent supporters of the Republic. And by aiding and abetting the Republicans they were also of course endangering their own lives eventually.

There was a shortage of medical supplies, too, because there was an illicit blockade of the Spanish coast by German and Italian submarines. And the French refused to allow cross-border traffic to go through, even of medical things. The main supplier of these things was the Soviet Union. The so-called Non-Intervention Agreement organised by Chamberlain and Eden throttled the Republic.

My own main role was orgnising the getting of the wounded out of the front. There were quite a lot of incidents where people went in and, you know, risked their own lives to bring the wounded. I remember one very gallant Basque doctor. It is interesting that when you are involved in these situations, example is of very great importance. There was heavy shelling going on at the time and this Basque doctor had gone out to pick up the wounded that were falling about. The courage and the determination of that doctor were quite remarkable. It was a great example. There were many of these kinds of incidents during the Spanish. War.

I came on one or two cases where wounds had been caused by dum-dum bullets being fired by Franco's troops. They cut the bullet before they put it in and the effect of that, once it struck, was to spread the wound. I vividly remember one young man who had got a dum-dum bullet in his thigh which made a terrible mess of the thigh. Probably he'd lose his leg if he didn't lose his life. I can't say there was a general campaign of using dum-dum bullets. I don't think it was common but there was some of it went on. I can only speak as I saw it and I only saw about one or two of these. It was of course contrary to the Geneva Convention. But, oh, how many things were contrary to the Geneva Convention? There were a lot of other things that went on that were contrary to the Convention. They shot prisoners.

I think of course that the Republican Government made a mistake in not offering the Moors in Morocco independence. The Government should have said, "All right, we'll give you independence when we win this War." I think they should have done that.[78] And of course we had similar kinds of problems in Catalonia and in the Basque country, which if they had been handled wisely might have assisted us very much in our struggles. But of course it is all very well to speak with hindsight. I may indeed find that there were voices in the Government who were urging this too in order to assist them in their struggles.

It was a disgraceful period in European history, I personally think, where all the democracies were conspiring to destroy the Republican Government, which had been elected democratically irrespective of what the propagandists tried to say. It was very well supported by the people. I recollect in the period in the trenches in Madrid, when once I had joined the International Brigade and went down to the Manzanares, where there was a local struggle going on, I remember the Campesinos were in the trenches at the time and they were mostly young peasant boys. El Campesino was a member of the Communist Party. It was one of the crack divisions of the Republican Army. And these boys were in their trenches there and they were being taught to read and write in the middle of this kind of attack. It was quite an instructive lesson because these boys were fighting for what they were deprived of and should have had an opportunity to learn – and they knew it. And this is why the Republic was so strongly supported by the peasantry and the people.

It was a very exciting period, well, in my life too of course, and in the lives of many, many people who came out to Spain to assist the defence of the Republic. Our political education was practically a day-to-day experience because we certainly knew what was going on in Europe and the world generally. We could assess what dangers the Republic was suffering from. We knew the lies that were being propagated by the other side – for instance, about the destruction by bombing by the German Air Force of Guernica,[79] and about the so-called mutilations and tortures which sections of the British press had been very strongly propagating in order to weaken the Republican cause. We knew all these things. We were quite well aware also that Hitler and Mussolini were intent on conquering the whole of Europe. All these things we were aware of. And it reinforced both our determination and our political understanding of the situation. In fact, there were very few people in the International Brigade who didn't have a very clear and practical knowledge of the dangers that were in front of us if the Republicans didn't win.

When I came back home to Britain it was quite astonishing to find that I was regarded with almost some degree of horror by some of the more sedate members of my union, the Railway Clerks' Association. In fact I met with this kind of attitude many, many years later even, when the lessons of the Spanish War were clear for everybody to see. They all seemed to assume quite wrongly that everybody that went to Spain was a member of the Communist Party. I am not decrying the membership of the Communist Party, because they were at that time a devoted and idealistic and disciplined group of people. I had a great admiration for the people I met in Spain who were members of the Communist Party. But I personally felt very astonished. I was there on the simple task of saving, or hoping to save, the Spanish Republic – a democratic elected Government. And I would have thought that the people of my country would have been unanimous in their support for it, particularly the trade union movement. Certainly, the leading members of the trade union movement were. But there were a number of members who were, I suppose you would say, between right wing and left wing – classify me as left wing – who found themselves objects of suspicion.

And of course as far as the British Government was concerned we were regarded with very grave suspicion indeed. That's another story of course. But when I went into the British Army in 1941 it was very, very strongly biased against people like myself who had been in the Spanish War.

David Anderson was born in 1912 in Aberdeen and was brought up there. He joined the Gordon Highlanders at the age of sixteen. When the Second World war broke out he served at first with the Gordons then transferred in 1941 to the R.A.F. Regiment, where he became a Flight/Sergeant Instructor. After the war he became a bricklayer in Aberdeen.

DAVID ANDERSON

Well, by 1936 I had become a member of the Communist Party and I was an anti-Fascist. I wanted to go to Spain and fight against the Fascists. Everything was organised by the Communist Party. I made it quite clear that I wanted to go to Spain and they helped me.

There were five of us altogether that left Aberdeen for Spain on the 12th of February 1937. One lad, John Flett from Pack Street in Aberdeen, was older than we were. He would be about forty-five. Three of us were members of the Communist Party: Alex Gibb, Archie Dewar[80] and myself, but the other two weren't members of any particular party as far as I know.

Before I went to Spain I had had seven years' experience as a regular in the Gordon Highlanders. I had joined the army in November 1928 and I finished in November 1935. Out of that time I spent three-and-a-half years in India and a year-and-a-half in Palestine. For most of my time in India I was stationed on the North West frontier. I was in Lundi Kotal, seven miles from Afghanistan, on the Khyber Pass, a year-and-a-half, I think, and then I came down to Peshawar for about another two years.

I became interested in politics before I came out of the army because of things that had happened, things that I had seen, things that influenced me in quite a number of ways. When I came back home I was twenty-three years old and I thought that a person who was unemployed was simply unemployed because he didn't want to work. But I changed my opinion because I tried hard for ten months to get a job and didn't succeed. Eventually, through the Gordon Highlanders' Association, I got a job as a waiter at £2 a week, for a fortnight at a camp for the 5th/7th Battalion of the Gordon Highlanders. That was the only job I got after ten months in civilian life.

I knew that there was something wrong with the system. My brother had been in the army. He'd done seven years before me, he was seven years older than I was. He'd come home and faced unemployment. He'd got jobs here and there.

So when I came out of the army he and I went around to different meetings that were in vogue at the market stance in Aberdeen. We listened to the speakers but I wasn't convinced of anything until I went to a meeting at the Belmont cinema. Peter Kerrigan, secretary of the Scottish branch of the Communist Party, was a speaker and what he had to say was to me just plain common sense. And it was then I started to take an interest in Communism.

At that time I wasn't married. I wanted to go to Spain. I wanted to fight against the Fascists. So as I say five of us left Aberdeen together and went to Glasgow and from there to London. From London we took a week-end ticket over to Paris, got in contact with the International Brigade headquarters in Paris. From there we went on by train to Perpignan where there was a great open area with about five or six field kitchens set up. There was every nationality practically you could think of – Finns, Danes, Europeans of every description, and all segregated into their different nationalities. From Perpignan we went by bus right through the Spanish frontier to Figueras, no obstructions or anything like that. All the people we met on the way they knew where we were going. We were met all the way with clenched fists. I can remember in particular the fellows working on the telegraph lines. They were up above and they were hanging on and waving down with the clenched fist salute.

At Figueras there was a great square where we did our drill and things of that sort. Underground was our sleeping accommodation. Beds had been set up, just beds and straw mattresses. We slept there. There were even one or two women there, you know, who had come across to be of help to the Spanish Government, to act as nurses. The only one I remember was a German woman. She was a very, very nice person. Her husband was in the International Brigade, too, and she came along with him and volunteered to serve in the nurses' organisation.

Quite a number of Englishmen joined us at Figueras. I think there were about seventeen or eighteen of us. There was a commandant and he had an interpreter, a young fellow who spoke several languages and he came up to us and said, "We want you to organise and to elect a military commander and a political commander." I was elected military commander and Archie Dewar, who also came from Aberdeen, was elected political commissar. I was the only one there with any previous military experience and that was the reason I was elected, nothing else! I was able to take over command and give them drill instructions, things of that sort. That came easy enough. I was just simply known as the military commander and that was all. Nobody had ranks at that particular time.

Then there were quite a number of Americans who came over and they joined the English-speaking group, which eventually amounted to about twenty-four. See, we were all separated into different groups, Finns, Danes, Italians, Germans, and so on. They were all under their own commanders.

We were at Figueras for about fourteen days, I think. And every day practically after the drill and things of that sort we marched down to the village, singing our songs. Then we were entertained and we went to Albacete. At Albacete we were rigged out with uniform. We were only at Albacete more or less one night and then from there we went to Madrigueras. At Madrigueras we were in our different groups. There were the French, the English-speaking. There were very few Americans at that time and they were all incorporated into the British squad.

We were a few weeks at Madrigueras. We did a certain amount of training, one thing and another. After that there was an officer took over, commandante we called him. And he sent me to officers' school just before the rest of them went down to the front line. Well, I went to Albacete. Albacete was supposed to be an officers' training school but whilst I'd been in the army I'd spent six years of the seven in the machine Gun Company, and I knew the machine gun from A to Z. And when I got to Albacete the main training was on the machine gun. It was a Maxim but very, very similar to the Vickers. The only difference was that the recalling portions were in the opposite direction. I didn't care for this very much, it got a wee bit monotonous. I wanted to get up to the front line. So I left the school and went back to Madrigueras, hoping to be sent up to the front line.

Now when I got back to Madrigueras quite a number of Americans and Canadians had arrived and a new battalian was being formed. When someone was instructing on the machine gun I asked if I could give a hand and when I gave a hand there were exclamations like, "Oh, you should be an officer." Anyway that night one of the Canadians, he was the commander of the Third Company of what was the beginning of the Mackenzie-Papineau Battalion, asked me if I would be prepared to be a platoon commander in his company.[81] And I said I would. Then I became a commander in one of his platoons. Later on that company were formed into the Mackenzie-Papineau Battalion. This comrade became the commander of the Battalion and I became his second-in-command.

A few weeks after that we went up to the first offensive that the Government had launched, at Brunete. At Brunete, it was a triangle of villages. There was Brunete, Villanueva del Pardillo and Villanueva de la Cañada. These were the three villages that commanded the road to Madrid. The object of the Republican Government was to try and push back Franco's troops from Madrid, so that no longer could he bombard it with his artillery. We attacked Villanueva de la Cañada. That was our objective. And the other Battalions in the International Brigade were fighting at Brunete and Pardillo.

But it was a long time before Villanueva de la Cañada fell. Actually I was wounded at that particular time and I was taken back to hospital in Madrid. The Villa Rosa, I remember, was the name of a hotel that had been turned into a military hospital, and I was sent back there for a few days. We were very, very well looked after. It was very, very modern. Everything was very, very good indeed.

Well, I had got wounded in the face. I thought my face had been distorted out of all proportion altogether. But I had a look in the mirror after I took off my bandage. I saw that there was nothing more than a bullet graze. It was an explosive bullet that had been used. And I realised that there was nothing really wrong with me. As soon as I saw that I began to feel, "What will my comrades think?" So I left the hospital without being discharged, I left the hospital and made to a place where I knew there would be transport up to the front.

Now when I went up to the front at Brunete it was a place called Mosquito Hill. And I was met by a lad that I had left in charge. And out of the Company of 106 only twenty-four were left. All the rest had been killed or injured. The boy I had left in charge was quite happy to hand over the command of what remained to me. I was on the right flank of the Battalion, facing this Mosquito Hill which the Fascists occupied, and on the right side of me was a river bed, about thirty yards wide, that had been dried up. I got twelve fox-holes dug, like, two in each fox-hole. But I had two men to patrol the river bed right up to the bottom of Mosquito Hill, in order that we shouldn't be taken unawares from this flank. They would go up for an hour, patrol this river bed, come back, waken the next two in the next fox-hole. They would go up, they would come back, and then the next two would go on, and so on right through the night. This was our only means of defending our positions at that particular time, because we were in a very, very precarious position.

Mosquito Hill was a position that we couldn't capture with the means that we had. It was absolutely impossible. I mean, they had domination. and as a matter of fact as we lay in that position down below Mosquito Hill, we could see right behind, the lights of the supplies going up to the Fascists' positions. It wasn't long before we realised that the position we occupied was absolutely impossible. And then of course we had to withdraw. It was the end of the offensive as far as the Republican Government was concerned.

It was a big disappointment but at the same time we realised that we weren't being forced back by Spaniards. We were being forced back by the help that Hitler and Mussolini were giving to Franco at this particular time. Because Non-Intervention was a ridiculous thing that was invented. A Government which has been elected by the people has the right to purchase weapons for its defence against any uprising. But this was denied the Spanish Government, a Popular Front Government, a Government that had been elected by the people – it was refused the right to purchase weapons from abroad. But in support of Franco, Hitler and Mussolini intervened. On the other hand, France closed the frontiers. No longer were any people who wanted to help the Spanish Government able to get through the Spanish frontier. The volunteers for the International brigade had to go over the Pyrenees. To me it wasn't a civil war. It wasn't a war of the Spanish people fighting against each other, it was a war of the

Spanish people fighting for independence against Fascism, against the guns, the planes, the weapons of Hitler, the artillery and guns of Italy, and the Moorish mercenaries. That was my opinion.

The Republican army were short of every weapon, practically every weapon. As a matter of fact, when we went into action at Brunete we had one automatic rifle, similar to a Bren gun. And we had six Maxim machine guns for a Battalion. Now that in itself was ridiculous. That was all that we had. The remainder were simply rifles, you know, the ordinary rifle.

Mortars, tanks, artillery and everything – they were all on the Fascist side. They had everything. We used to lie on the ground when Fascist planes came across. They used to come across in droves and circle round our positions. They used to sort of figure-of-eight and they came diving down and bombed and strafed us while we were lying in our positions. All we could do was lie on our backs and try and retard them with rifle shots and things of that sort. The whole thing was ridiculous. But it was the only thing in our power to do. That remained the position all the time. Every position we took up we were bombarded by planes.

But funnily enough, casualties with the strafing and bombing were not great. It was more or less the terror of the plane, coming down bombing and strafing . . . . But after the attack had gone we found that the casualties were very, very few. The main casualties came in actual combat with the Fascists, approaching their positions. Because they had machine guns, oh, twenty times the machine gun power that we had. And that was when the casualties were inflicted, not by bombing or from the air.

We didn't have bayonet charges or anything like that. Well, not what you see in the films, like, charging each other with bayonets fixed and things of that sort, no. But we've had trenches about 100 yards from the Fascists' positions. Mostly the ones that I came in combat with were the Moors. There was a terrific amount of Moorish infantry and cavalry, as well as Italian infantry and cavalry. These were the ones that we were fighting against.

Now the Moors were very, very stubborn fighters. And I remember, I think it was at Gandesa – a lot of hilly country there, and a great many caves in the vicinity. And when we were making the advance, the Moors went into these caves and took their machine guns back in with them. They just kept on firing and we were throwing grenades.

I remember one lad, he came from Lancashire. He was very, very slightly made. He weighed, I would reckon, about 7 stones 7 lbs, eight stones at the very most. But I had seen this little lad pulling a Maxim machine gun for miles, you know. And he had run past the cave where the Moors were and threw in a grenade. There was a machine gun burst of fire and his arm went swinging round his side, and he said, "Gee whiz, I thought my arm was off." Well, he didn't realise like that his arm was only hanging by a tendon. Then I remember when I was back in hospital and here was the same lad that had shown a terrific amount of courage, and he was lying in bed. "What am I going to do now when I go back into civilian life?" he said. His arm had been amputated, or what had been left of it was amputated. His whole future seemed gone, he had just given up hope. He died the following day.

We saw quite a number of Moors. I remember one came running towards us, you know. He was giving up, his hands in the air, and he had a beard and he looked about fifty – well, at that time of course I was a young lad, and forty or fifty seemed old to me. One particular time we'd occupied a position where we had overcome Moors and they were lying there dead, on their backs, lying in the sun, a blazing sun. I thought it was snakes that were crawling from their stomachs. It was actually their insides, you know, their entrails, that had burst out with the heat of the sun.

The Moors were the most ferocious enemy in the world. But I don't think they were feared, and they weren't treated with contempt. They were just treated as an enemy and that was all there was to it.

The Italians on the other hand were different entirely. Mussolini's troops were Regulars and they put up no fight at all, not because they were bad soldiers but simply because they didn't have the urge to fight against something that they didn't want to fight.

There was no German infantry. What we were fighting against was Moorish infantry and cavalry, Italian infantry, cavalry and artillery, and German tanks and aviation. Those were the main people that we were fighting. That's the reason why I say it wasn't a civil war. It was a war of the Spanish people against Fascism. In the International Brigade, taking everyone into consideration, there were only a few thousand. But in the Fascist camp there were tens of thousands of Italians, Moors and Germans. That's what we were fighting against. We had no arms whatsoever to combat them.

We had to fight against Non-Intervention, which prevented the Spanish Government from even getting food into the Republican parts of Spain. I've eaten snails, I've eaten snakes, not because I wanted to but because we were hungry and we had to. I remember this commander, Ed Cecil Smith, who was later editor of the *Daily Clarion*.[82] I was his second-in-command of the Mackenzie-Papineau Battalion. It was a day of rain, the rain came down in torrents that day. And he said, "Are you hungry?" I said, "I'm starving." He says, "What about some snails?" So I went and collected some. There were groves there, you know, and the snails were quite numerous and quite big, with tortoise shells. So we lit a fire and got an old tin and put the snails in. We ate them without salt or anything like that. You see, these were the sort of things you were driven to,

because of the conditions that existed, because of this so-called
Non-Intervention, which acted on behalf of the Fascist Powers and
acted against the Republic. It's difficult for me to speak because I feel,
you know, that we were completely let down. We were completely
let down as far as aid and support which should have been given to the
Spanish Government failed to materialise and everything acted to the
benefit of the Fascists.

Well, after Mosquito Hill we were withdrawn after quite a while.
We were taken into rest not very far from Madrid. We camped there
for quite a few days. After that we were reorganised. The battalions
had been decimated. There were two battalions of Americans, for
instance, the Abraham Lincoln and the George Washington. They
were united into one. The Mackenzie-Papineau Battalion survived but
only to a certain extent, its numbers greatly reduced. The British
Battalion was in the same position. The casualty rate was very heavy.

I was never in the Abraham Lincoln Battalion – they were the first
of the American Battalions that had been formed – but I was in the
George Washington Battalion. I thought the Americans were extremely good organisers. In some ways I thought they were childish,
you know, because they were hero worshippers. I've already
mentioned what they said when I was able to show them how the
Maxim machine gun worked. But for organisation, they were very,
very good. For instance, when we went to Madrigueras we had lofts,
you know, for sleeping accommodation, and we had a blanket which
we used as mattress and bedding combined, see. The British just
accepted this blanket and slept on the floor. But the Americans – no.
Later on when I was with the Americans at Tarazona de la Mancha
they went out and they organised wood and built two-tier bunks.
They got linen and made palliasses and filled them with straw. They
had a wall board, you know, put up and everybody could give their
opinion of different things. They found it was a wee bit more
inexpensive to open up a shop of their own, see, to drink in, with their
own wine. The Americans were good organisers, exceptionally good
organisers. But at the same time they were childish in their outlooks.
If you were good at anything, to them you were exceptional. The
British, down to earth, just accepted things and that was that; but the
Americans were different entirely, they organised things for their own
comfort.

That was the difference I found between the Americans and the
British. I think too that the British were better fighters. They could
accept hardships and the hardships were really bad. The Americans
couldn't, didn't, accept hardships to the same extent. That's what I
found. I'm not going to try and denigrate them but this is what I felt.
They weren't the fighters that, I think, the British were, but maybe
that's a prejudice on my part. I think the British were exceptional, you
know, as far as fighting was concerned.

Among the Americans you had some terrific characters. I remember one, an opera singer. He was really good. He used to go in front of the battalion and sing, "We are the fighting anti-Fascists", and his voice just echoed back, you know. "We are soldiers of the International Brigade." That's where we all joined in – "We are the fighting anti-Fascists." And his voice was as loud as all of us put together.

We had quite a number of Americans that had been well known and had vocations that were well beyond what the normal British had. We'd a few among the British, like David Guest and people like that, from Oxford, Cambridge. But in the main these Americans were people that were actually established in their positions in America and yet they forsook this and came to Spain to fight for the Republic. And they were great people.

There was a proportion of Red Indians among the Americans, not very many but a proportion, but very few blacks. The one that I appreciated most, though he didn't come in combat, was Paul Robeson. Paul Robeson came out along with his wife, and they had set up a stage and his wife accompanied him on ·the piano.[83] I remember to a certain extent his words. He says, "I have been gifted by God with a voice and this voice I am going to use on behalf of my people. A great many people will tell you that niggers stink. But wouldn't white people be the same if they had to exist in the same conditions that the negro people in America have to?" This was only part of what he said, of course, I mean, there was a lot more than that. Then he went on to ask for songs, and of course we're all shouting, everybody's shouting, you know, "Sing Ol' Man River!" And he sang for quite a long time. He was one of the greatest people I have met.

I can remember I met Ernest Hemingway. Well, he was easily met if you ever happened to be in Madrid, he'd be there in one of the cafes and would listen to anybody that had to say anything. I didn't care much for the story of For Whom the Bell Tolls at all. It wasn't like the real thing. Then there was Major Attlee, you know, Clement Attlee, the leader of the Labour Party, he came out to Spain, and so did Pandit Nehru, and quite a number of others.[84]

But what I can remember is this that when things got very, very hard, there was always a member of the Communist Party came to the fore and tried to explain things. They were always the ones that gave the lead and took the risks and things of that sort.

Now again the same thing applied as far as the papers were concerned. I met many reporters – I cannae remember their names now. They wouldn't come up to the front, they would meet you in Madrid or Barcelona or Valencia. But the only reporters I actually saw, you know, in the front line and shooting at times along with us were the Daily Worker reporters. That is true. They were the ones, members of the Communist Party, that had the guts to come right into the front to get their report. The others sat back in Madrid, Valencia.

As for the ordinary Spanish people I found they were very, very sympathetic towards us. They were comradely. For instance, there was a family I got to know. He was a tailor. He was lame. Luz was one of his nieces. Luz means light and I became very friendly with her and used to call her *Luz de mi corazón*, you know, light of my heart. And they used to take us out to the field where the crop was beans, big haricot beans. They would go out with leather bags of wine. That was a picnic to them. It was to gather the beans but at the same time to have a picnic. To me the Spanish people were exemplary. They were friendliness personified. I love the Spanish people. I think that they were great.

There were quite a number of songs sung by the International Brigaders. *The Internationale* was sung all the time. Any time you went on the march you didn't go without singing. As I said, the American Battalion used to sing:

> *We are the fighting anti-Fascists,*
> *We're soldiers of the International Brigade.*
> *We are the fighting anti-Fascists,*
> *We'll stay here till the Fascist doom is laid.*

The last stages of the war, as far as I was concerned, came when we launched the Ebro offensive in the summer of 1938. We had been forced back over the River Ebro earlier that year. After a few weeks or so all our training was on crossing rivers. And eventually the attack came – I think it was against Gandesa. But anyway we crossed the River Ebro. We crossed in little rowboats, little rafts, and things of that sort. We crossed the River Ebro and we all gathered on the other side. And then we launched our attack. We overcame, without a great deal of resistance, the first perimeters of the defence of the Fascists. And we advanced seventeen miles without a halt. I cannae remember how long it took or anything like that. I remember we got as far as Gandesa, maybe about a mile or so from Gandesa.

But the approaches to Gandesa were governed by high hills. Between the positions that the Fascists occupied and ours there was also a great big valley. We were firing with the machine guns that we did have. We were 600 yards on the sights. You have to understand that the valley was all in terraces. well, that was well down below the height of the hills. But eventually we were ordered to attack the Fascists' positions. Well, we went down and the machine guns of the Fascists they just rained bullets. I was caught on the arm. I got a wound on the arm. My arm just went stiff and the rifle just dropped out of my hands. My hands were just rigid. I couldn't half-clench, like, and I couldn't open them up.

This was all my participation as far as that battle was concerned. So

I got up. I knew it was stupid to continue any longer, my aim was to get back now. I had a few hundred yards to get up and over the hills from our own machine guns. The first-aid was in another valley down below the hills. I went down there and got the arm dressed. I was sent to hospital, see, with the rest of the wounded, and I finished up in Barcelona.

I wasn't in hospital for long, the wound was only more or less superficial. But I was given a permit to stay outside. Being an officer I was given a pass to stay in a hotel. At this time I was engaged to a girl at Tarazona de la Mancha, a Spanish girl. She was in the other part of Republican Spain, of course: when Franco had cut through to the sea, earlier in 1938, he had separated all that part from where I was in Barcelona. There was no longer any chance of me getting through to see her. So I was in a cafe one night in Barcelona and I met these two fellows. I think they were Lithuanians. They said if I wanted to get away I could.

I knew the War was over. I mean, it was obvious to me that the war was finished. There was no longer any hope. So I went on this ship, the *Stanhope* it was. It was trading between Barcelona and Marseilles. The crew hid me. They had to hide me from the captain. So anyway we got to Marseilles. And the crew took up a collection. They gave me so many francs. So I lived for three days in Marseilles. I had no passport. Then eventually my money became finished. So I went to the British Consulate. My father was an old age pensioner at the time, you know, he must have been nearing seventy. So they said, "Well, have you got any money?" I said, "No money." "Well, could your father . . .?" "My father's a pensioner. He gets ten shillings a week. How the hell can he afford to get me?" So they wouldn't have anything to do with me.

I eventually decided to hitch-hike to Paris. But never a lift did I get. I got as far as Avignon. Two gendarmes there asked me if I had a passport or money. When I said I didn't have either they put me in a cell for the night. In fact I was there for quite a few days and I was charged with vagrancy. I was brought up before the court and the judge gave me a minimum of one month in prison. This prison was bug-infested. You had to put your clothes outside every night, you know. You weren't allowed anything apart from your shirt. You were locked in at four o'clock. There were two other fellows in the cells, an Italian and an English lad. When I came out of this bug-infested prison I went back to Marseilles again, along with the English lad. I went up to the consul's office again and said, "Look, we've just spent a month in prison." I just lost my temper and eventually they gave me enough money and a pass to get to London. But they wouldn't give the same to the English lad, he didn't get anything at all. So I had to smuggle him on the train and when the inspector came around for the tickets the English lad hid underneath the seats. But I had to leave him at Paris. Later on he wrote me a letter – I've still got the letter yet. He had met some good Samaritan that took him in to Paris and then paid his fare aboard a ship.

So I got back home to London and I went to the Communist Party headquarters. They sent me out and got me a suit. I had at that time only a shirt that had once upon a time been white, an old pair of khaki denim trousers, and a pair of rope-soled slippers. I felt an oddity coming across on the boat. But the Communist Party headquarters gave me the money to get this suit and paid my fare back home to Aberdeen. And that was it.

I spoke in the Music Hall in Aberdeen maybe a week or two after, to an audience there. I got back home about November '38, just before the end of the war. The International Brigade came back just a few weeks after me.

Now looking back after fifty years I think it was a War that was necessary. I think that the Spanish people were let down by Britain, France and others, that could have had the say at that particular time.

I think it was a War that was only a preparation for Hitler to instigate the Second World War. He knew what he could get away with. It gave him greater confidence in his demands as far as the Allies were concerned. It led to his demands being accepted at Munich. And it led to him being able to take over the rest of Czechoslovakia.[85] And all this built up to such an extent that he thought he could get away with murder. And that's it – Hitler was allowed to get away with murder.

George Murray was born in Aberdeenshire on Hogmanay 1909 but as a young boy moved with his family to live in Perthshire. He became a printer and was a member of the Scottish Typographical Association, now merged into the Society of Graphical and Allied Trades (SOGAT). He joined the Independent Labour Party then, before he went to Spain, the Communist Party. During the Second World War he worked in the Clyde shipyards but returned afterward to the printing industry until his retirement.

GEORGE MURRAY

Well, I was active in left-wing politics and of course when the Spanish War started all my mates were of like opinion more or less. A lot of them were going to Spain, you know, and I decided to go too. It was one of the things you wanted to do at that particular time. I had left wing ideals and was a member of the Communist Party. I was also a trade unionist. I was working in a printer's in Glasgow, and you can't be a printer without being a trade unionist. But I wasn't particularly active in the trade union.

I'd be about 25 or so then. Actually it was Jack Morrison that more or less recruited us. He was very active in the Spanish Aid Committee. He was the chap that usually conducted parties down to London and got them tickets. I actually had a passport but some of them had just week-end tickets. I went out about May 1937, I think. I think that was about the time. I don't recall all the dates but it was about May.

I joined in London. I don't know whether you'd call it 'joined' but, I mean, once you got in with Jack Morrison to go with a band of people, that was you joined, more or less. We went across in the usual boat. I had a passport because I had been abroad before. We went to Paris, where there was a big organisation with various places, hotels and others, you could go to. Professor Haldane's wife Charlotte was the organiser of this.[86] I left the money I had with her but I never saw it again! No doubt it was put into the funds. There at any rate in Paris we were gathered into various groups and we went to Lyons. I remember it was a Russian that had this cafe. He was very generous with the liquor. But after that we split into smaller groups and leap-frogged down to the Pyrenees. Then of course we climbed the Pyrenees and got over during the night. It wasn't terrifically difficult so long as you weren't caught. The French police actually weren't bothering much, I don't think. They were supposed to stop you but their heart wasn't in it, as you would say. Well, I don't know if the police were sympathetic but the French Government was more or less sympathetic, or slightly sympathetic. It was the time of Leon Blum.[87]

So we got into Spain then we went to a fortress place, Figueras, and eventually down to Madrigueras, where we did our training. I had no military experience before I went to Spain. At Madrigueras we had a month of training – which was more or less useless. And of course that shows you the kind of army we had, you know. It was all amateurs. Well, there were some people had military experience, a few. But the training was useless because it takes longer than that – four weeks or three weeks – to make a soldier, you know. I mean, we were formed up in military units and so forth but it takes a bit more than that to make an army.

Well, after this training we were made up into an anti-tank battery, where we had three Russian anti-tank guns. That was apart from the British Battalion altogether.

We went up to Jarama and I was promptly shot through the ribs. I was out quite a while for that. That would be about June 1937. When we were up at Jarama the big battle was finished. We were only exercising our guns, without much effect.

So I was wounded right through the chest. I thought I had had it, you know, naturally enough. I was taken down to a kind of hospital, well, two rooms it was. I don't know what it would be, a hall or something. About a week later I wakened up. I think the Spanish doctors at that time weren't up to standard. Anyway, the first thing they gave me was a big glass of vino Malaga. It's a sweet wine, you know. And I felt as if I was up in the air!

There were two incidents I remember about that hospital. There was one fellow lying across from me with his head more or less half off, you know. The blokes used to go along and lift up the cloth that he was in, you know, and have a look at him. The Spaniards were very insensitive, as far as that was concerned. And the second thing was that I was amazed to see this Swiss coming through from one room to the other, walking on his hands. He had a wound in his leg. Later on when I went to a university hospital there was a swimming pool at it, and there was the Swiss swimming away. I thought he had made a remarkable recovery. But I saw the plaster of paris on his leg still on.

After that I was taken down to Murcia, where they had been building a few hotels, a very tourist sort of place. This new hotel, which had never been used, was used as a hospital. And there was another next door. Anyway we used to walk about this town with just pyjamas on. Those were the only clothes we had at that particular time. On one occasion we had to mount a sort of guard of honour. This officer had been killed and we were standing with our rifles, in our pyjamas, outside as the guard of honour.

So I walked about there for a few weeks until a Swiss doctor examined me and she said, "You have water." She couldn't speak English very well. And, oh, an awful operation of taking some sort of substance out of my back. Anyway I gradually recovered. Most of the other boys went to the coast for convalescence. But my sister was a nurse up in Huete, in Catalonia. So I asked if I could go there instead of the coast. So I went up there and convalesced for a while and then went back to the Brigade. That was just before the battle of Teruel, at the turn of the year 1937-38. Brunete took place while I was in hospital.

My sister Ann, the nurse, was in Spain before me. She just went. She had more or less the same sentiments as the rest of us. She was a trained nurse. When I got to the hospital at Huete, there was a Polish bloke wounded very badly, and I remember my sister had given him five blood transfusions of her own blood. She had to be connected up to him in these days. You got the blood run from you to them

I was in the battle of Teruel. Our side captured Teruel but they lost it again later on. Actually, we had a great celebration after this successful battle of Teruel. We were all being taken up to Barcelona. So the train trundled up to Valencia, and we thought it had been shunting or something, for it was going back the way again, you see. But the reason was the Fascists had broken through. We went back to Teruel again.

I was the Battalion agent for the S.I.M. (Military Investigation Service), guarding against insertion of enemy agents, etc.[88] I was all through the campaign of the North, and eventually we were pushed back of course. Actually they cut Republican Spain in two at that time, in the spring of 1938, when they broke through to the Mediterranean about half way between Valencia and Barcelona.

After that I was of course in all the Ebro battles in the summer of 1938. They weren't any more severe than the previous battles but, aye, they were pretty severe. I think the Fascists were better organised by that time, you know.

When the War begain in 1936 some units of the army stayed loyal and fought for the Republic, but most of them were over on the other side. The Franco armies of course were pretty well professional soldiers, you know, which didn't give us much of a chance. We ran up against Italians and Moors in the fighting. We captured a lot of Moors. They didn't know whether to do this or that! Oh, they were just conscripts, I mean. But the Italians were pretty easy to capture, you know. Well, you know what happened to the Italians later on in the Second World War. I mean, they didn't fancy fighting at all, because they are a peaceful kind of people, Italians. But the Moors were mainly properly trained soldiers with maybe seven years' experience or more, I don't know. But the Italians weren't of any consequence. I didn't see or come into contact with any Germans on the Fascist side, except for the air force, of course. Aye, German aeroplanes. I don't think there were German tanks, there were more Italian tanks. Of course they weren't very formidable tanks. They were small tanks, you know. We used to keep them at bay with rifle fire. Of course, maybe it was Italians that were in them, I don't know.

But we were withdrawn towards the end of the battle of the Ebro. I took part in the last march of the International Brigade through

Barcelona. It was a very emotional sort of thing. I mean, young girls were coming over and kissing you, all this kind of thing. Which is surprising, you know, after all that time. But that was the end, as far as we were concerned. We came home. We got a train through to France and that was it.

Well, you know, looking back on the War after half a century, I would say the International Brigade was something unique. There was every nationality you could possibly think of, practically even Chinese. To build an army at all with that was really something of a great achievement. The spirit was very good. If it hadn't been so good, an amateur army would never have survived for the time it did. I suppose the War was a sort of forerunner to the Second World War. Many people, you know, saw what was coming so we tried to stop that.

I never had any regrets about what I did. My only regret was having a bullet through my chest. But, no, no, I have no regrets. I'm quite proud of it. I was badly wounded in Spain but I'm still living after all these years so my health can't be too bad.

After my return from Spain I wasn't victimised at work by employers. Well, the employers didn't know so they never victimised me. When I came back I didn't get my job back with the firm I had been with, actually J. and J. Clark it was called. One of the bosses – I think he was a supporter of Hitler – used to go and buy all his machinery in Germany. And they put round books with Hitler's picture in them. But you wouldn't say I was victimised because I had left the place, you know. But I got a good job quite easily in other places.

In any further communication
on this subject, please quote
No. K 14742/2563/241(1938)
and address—
not to any person by name
but to—
"The Under-Secretary of State,"
Foreign Office,
London, S.W.1.

FOREIGN OFFICE.

S.W.1.

11th September, 1940.

Sir,

        I am directed by His Majesty's Principal Secretary of State for Foreign Affairs to inform you that the sum of £3. 19. 3d. has been expended from public funds in connexion with your repatriation to the United Kingdom on evacuation from Spain.

        2. I am to request you to be good enough to refund this amount to this department either by crossed money or crossed postal order made payable to the Finance Officer of the Foreign Office.

        3. If your present financial position does not enable you to repay the amount due either in one sum or by weekly or monthly instalments, I am to request you to notify this department and, at the same time, to submit proposals for repayment at some future date when you may be in a position to do so, without undue hardship to yourself and your dependents, if any.

        4. You will be informed in due course of any further expenditure which may have been incurred on your behalf.

              I am,
                Sir,
          Your obedient Servant,

E. Brown, Esq.,
    11, Commercial Street,
      Coupar Angus,
        Perthshire,
          Scotland.

Letter from the Foreign Office to Eddie Brown asking him to refund the money for his fare home from the War.

Eddie Brown was born in 1906 in Coupar Angus, Perthshire, and brought up there. His father had a small fishmonger's business. In the Second World War Eddie Brown worked first in the Clyde shipyards then joined the Highland Light Infantry in 1942 and served in the Middle East. He landed with his regiment in Normandy on D-Day. After the War he returned to his trade as a housepainter until his retirement.

EDDIE BROWN

I was a housepainter but in the 1920s and '30s conditions were bad as far as employment was concerned. You had to get out, there was no work in the place you belonged. So you drove yourself further afield – Dundee, Perth, Glasgow, Edinburgh, then down to London, picking up work wherever you could. For four or five years, I would say, after my time was out I had this. I mean ye just chased around getting jobs and naturally you became interested in politics. I joined the Independent Labour Party in Glasgow around 1930 or 1932. I was in Glasgow for roughly three or four years and then found that work there was hopeless so I went back to Perth. In Perth I was accepted as a tradesman and found work in a good shop. I could have carried on there but for what was taking place in Spain. I mean ye felt that ye wished to do something and ye decided to go and have a go at it.

I had carried on as a member of I.L.P. roughly up until around 1934 and then when I went to Perth I joined up in the Communist Party. And it was through them that I made my way to Spain. That was in May 1937.

I came of a very large family. There were sixteen of us in the family. My father had a business on his own. But there was such a difference in ages in the family there were never any more than roughly around eight people stayed in the house at one time. I was the only one in the family that had a Labour connection or was interested in the trade unions or anything of that description. I had one brother who came to Glasgow to work, one of my elder brothers. He was the only one that really supported me in everything I had done. The rest were kind of dubious. But nobody tried to stop me going to Spain. I just decided and went.

Before I went to Spain I had some earlier experience of opposing Fascism in Perth. Mosley came to Perth and the people were very high. I was a member of the Scottish Painters' Society, but also a member of the Communist Party at that time.[89] And when you went and put your ideas in front of the Painters' Committee you got little support from them, as far as your politics were concerned. But when Mosley arrived ye found these same individuals on the Committee that were opposing you were giving you a hand to push him into the Tay and push him out of Perth completely. I mean he only really twice tried to make hay in Perth and he was completely baulked. What happened was, well, in Perth there's the North Inch and the South Inch. Well, the North Inch is where Mosley came down and he had his car planked there and they were shouting the odds from that. But those of us who opposed Fascism we gave his car a push and it landed just simply in the Tay, you know. That finished the speechifying at that time. It just broke up. There was no fighting really of any description, just the force of weight and and his car went down into the Tay. That was roughly 1935–36, just before the Spanish Civil War began. It showed you just exactly how the people were thinking. I mean, whilst they didnae agree wi' your politics they were definitely anti–Fascist. And that was the whole thing, they were right opposed to Fascism.

So I decided to volunteer to go to Spain. I came through to Glasgow and said I wanted to volunteer. The only people that were organising it of course was the Communist Party. They asked me why and so forth. And I told them the reason. It was through them that I was sent from Glasgow to London, stayed a day or two in London, and got a week–end's trip over to Paris. There was a group o' people with us, in fact I was along wi' an Aberdeen fellow, John Londragan. What happened there, we couldnae go and buy the tickets so there was an individual that went and had the tickets and he passed them to you. He had the Communist Party's paper, *L'Humanité*, in his pocket.[90] And when he passed you gave him the go-by. Well, John was the leader. I said to John, "There's the man I think we're looking for." And I put my finger on it. He came in and gave us these tickets to Lyons. And we stayed there with a White Russian who had a hotel, a sort of workingman's hotel. And from there there was tickets bought from Lyons up to Montpellier. And we arrived there and we were given a meal in a restaurant and then at night taken away in taxis to the foot of the Pyrenees. It was quite dark. And then we just crossed the bridge over the river and then we just carried on.

We walked over the Pyrenees, up and up, until it was daylight and by then we were on the Spanish frontier. We walked down from there and arrived at Figueras. I had no encounters, no problems whatsoever with the frontier. We walked over these bridges which were being guarded. And of course the guards split and that was your time. You had rope-soled shoes to keep you from making a noise and you just skipped across them.

I was very fit in these days. I found crossing the Pyrenees quite easy. But there was quite a number that found it very difficult. There were some of them we had to give a hand tae in certain parts to get them up and over. It was a stiff climb for anybody that wasnae really fit. I had done a wee bit of climbing in my time, being country bred. I had climbed a few hills in my time. The time limit to get over was really short. The only time you could relax was when you were on the

Pyrenees on the Spanish side. You could sit down then and have a rest. You were sure there was nobody coming to pick you up then. I would say it took roughly eight hours until we reached our destination.

At Figueras there were French, there were Americans, there were Germans, there were everything. So they decided that we'd do a bit of training. And the French had their *garde-à-vous,* they used to call it.[91] And the Americans had theirs, and the British had theirs. And they were drilled up in sort of fashion, getting them into becoming soldiers. Of course half of us had had some drilling at school. But at Figueras they had nothing to teach us with weapons. Again that was one of the problems, getting the weapons, because they had very few to teach people with. And very few bullets. Luckily, being country bred, I was a fair shot with a rifle before I even went to Spain.

We were in Figueras maybe a week or a fortnight, not more than that. I just cannae recall. We went through Barcelona very quietly because of the fact there were disturbances there. Well, they reckoned that it was the P.O.U.M. They were much like the Independent Labour Party, and quite a number of I.L.P. members were in Barcelona at that time. And what had taken place I really don't know. We just knew that there was a sort of eruption. But when we went through Barcelona the blinds and everything were pulled down so that we just passed on without having anything at all to do with the disturbance that was going on there. I mean seemingly it was quite laughable when you heard exactly what did take place there. I mean in Catalonia they didnae believe in just sending their soldiers up to the front and remaining there. Seemingly they could come back and stay in their house at night and go up and fight the War the following morning. This sort of thing was going on.

We werenae told anything by those in charge of us what was going on in Barcelona. It was only afterwards that ye actually began to see the facts and know the facts. After we had arrived in Albacete and places of that description you knew then there had been something going on. And it came to you in the news always how it leaks out. We didn't know just why at that particular time our carriages were thingied off, didna know that. But we did learn later on that that was the reason.

So we left Barcelona and went on to Albacete, and from Albacete to Madrigueras. We did a bit of training there but again there was nothing to train with as far as rifles and things like that were concerned. And no bullets, so what they used to do was they cut a hole in the centre of a card and they looked through it, them that were training you. They were looking through to see that you were pulling the trigger and the thing wasn't moving. You were dead on the bull. That was the only way they could teach you to use a rifle, and actually you never used the rifle until you really were in action. They didn't have ammunition to train you with at all. The British Government had started this Non-Intervention and they were denying the Spanish Republic and whys and wherefores. I believe that Blum would have still given the stuff to Spain had this Non-Intervention not taken place. But they couldnae get anything through at all.

The kind of rifles we used in training were a bit antique. I mean they were never anything up to the standard that we had in this country at all. But you could fire straight wi' them, put it that way. You could kill. But there was nothing like we had – well, I was in the British army afterwards – we had nothing like, no way, rifles or anything at all, what we had in the British army. No ammunition or anything – everything like that had to be carefully watched. I mean, even your bullets you tried tae kill wi' one, it was a case o' preserving them even in battle, because you could be left wi' nothing. Ye didnae go around firin' like mad, as you could do in the British army, fire these new type o' weapons and keep goin' on firin' them as long as you saw somebody. In Spain ye just had to preserve it for the individual you could see and do something about. Ye couldnae waste ammunition. We had none to waste.

The recollections I have o' Madrigueras were ones of a Londoner – he was in the anti-tanks, too, I just forget his name now – he was a great lad on the stage, and he had big Jock Dunlop from Edinburgh dressed up as a woman and a wee Manchester lad dressed up as a man. And they had the tins over John Dunlop's tits – falsies, aye. We had thoroughly enjoyable nights through things of this description. I mean you enjoyed them just as much as you had enjoyed the theatre in full going fun. It was very good for morale. I mean our morale was never broken. I mean ye did get down when some of the lads that ye knew were getting killed. Sometimes these had a great effect on you. But it was essential just to push on, make the best of it.

We went from Madrigueras to Albacete. And then the unit was formed. There were three anti-tank guns. And we left Albacete and went up to the Jarama. That must have been in June 1937. And this was really to try out the new type of anti-tank gun that we were using, to give the lads the feeling of it before we went on the first offensive. When we were on the Jarama we were still on the defensive, defending the ground there, keeping the Fascists out. There was no offensive at that particular point. We were only getting training on the guns. The big battle of the Jarama had already been fought. It was Spanish comrades that were holding the Jarama.

There were signs still about of the big battle. Any village that we were in – I forget the name of all the villages, cannae recall them – but when we passed through them, yes, they had been badly shelled. There were still some people hovering around but ye could see what had taken place. Civilians had suffered quite a lot, and a lot of houses were uninhabited, and one or two folk would come out the holes, you know. That's what I do remember. The people were carrying on just the same. The War was quite near them. The Fascists were shelling every night at a certain time. Over came the shelling all the time. They had the stuff to do that but I don't think we replied so much. What we did try to do with the guns that we had was to train them on to their trenches but it was given up after a trial or two. They thought they could maybe burst up their trench wi' it but it was too low to do that. The trajectory of our guns wasn't high enough to do that. It was possibly creating havoc behind but that we couldnae see. What we wanted to do was create havoc on their front line.

Our anti-tank guns were Russian and they were good. But ye had to watch your ammunition. It was very, very scarce and one time, in Brunete, when a shell had hit our dump we were all trying to pull back and get the stuff that hadnae been blown up. This sort of thing took place fairly regularly. Funnily enough, when a shell did explode in the dump the anti-tank shells were easier to get out than the bullets because the bullets were flying everywhere. And that was the ammunition for the rifles. They were harder to get at, because you could go and pull out a shell. They exploded and exploded up the way. And ye would get out some of them, but see the bullets, they were flying everywhere, up, down, ye ken what I mean. Ye couldnae get near them. Ye just wondered when it happened where the hell we were gonnae get more ammunition from! The ammunition was so scarce that we had to try and take out what we could.

In our anti-tank unit everyone I think was British, except one Italian who spoke English. He was on No 3 gun, I think. There were around seven of us to each gun, because there were so many carrying the shells, and then there were always three on the gun. The man in charge of our gun was a Londoner, ginger-heided. Oh, I see him. He got killed. I can see him but I cannae remember his name.

The commander of the anti-tank unit was Malcolm Dunbar and Hugh Slater was the commissar.[92] Malcolm Dunbar, I didn't know him intimately but I thought he was a great guy. I mean, he was a great guy to be beside when things were going bad because he just seemed to keep a cool head. On this particular occasion I went over the hill instead of going round it and when I arrived with the ammunition Dunbar asked me was I fired on? 'Yes, I was fired on,' I said, 'but there were tracks there that I fell down on.' He says, 'you took a bloody chance, you fool.' I said, 'Well, it was a long, long way roond, roond that hill to come wi' this stuff.' But I think on the whole he was rather pleased that I had come because of the fact that it gave him a better idea of how things were shaping up front, you know. The Fascists had gone back a wee bit further than he expected them to be. In the Second World War Malcolm Dunbar was a private. I don't understand it, I mean they made me a sergeant in the British army, Bill Alexander became a captain, and Jock Dunlop he was a sergeant.

But they tell me all Malcolm Dunbar ever was was a private, showing that they deliberately smacked him. He was a good individual to be under when things were going bad. I never saw him lose the place. He never said much at any time. In fact, Hugh Slater, the political commissar, had more to say than ever he had. Hugh always had a load to say. Dunbar was a very brave man, a very brave man. Even a wound didnae keep Malky in hospital. He got wounded in the neck and was back the following day wi' a bandage round his neck, in amongst things. That's the type of individual he was. I couldn't tell you if he was a member of a political party. Possibly he was but I don't know, I never heard him divulge his politics. He was very quiet, plus the fact that he knew the game as far as up front was concerned. He seemed to be at home there.

In the anti-tank battery there must have been about ten Scotsmen at least, about half the men. One of them was killed at Brunete. There was one from Dundee and one from Fife, three I think from Edinburgh, one from Aberdeen, and then there was George Murray and mysel' from Perth. I think that more or less was it.

From the Jarama we went up to Brunete. That was the first big Republican ofensive, in July 1937. I got wounded there. Well, what I remember about Brunete was the lack of arms that the Republicans had. It was so obvious. And when we did fire our anti-tank guns to stir them up a bit, over came the planes, just one after the other. They were picking you off at their leisure. We had no anti-aircraft guns. We had nothing like that. They could come over and bomb us just whenever they liked and spy out the land and then the next thing, if they saw men, over came their shells, shelling that particular point.

The planes flew quite low, almost tree height some of them. They were Italian and German planes, all Italian and German. Ye could see the German crosses on them. Ye knew the Italian planes too, they were a lighter type o' plane, the Italians. I didn't know them but I mean ye just listened and everybody seemed to know. When the planes came down far enough they had to be fired on, when they were out reconnoitering your position. I mean they were fired on by rifles. I never recall o' seeing any being brought down by rifle fire. The Republicans had no aeroplanes up at the front. The only place ever I saw aeroplanes was in Madrid. That was when I was wounded and going through there. I was in a Madrid hospital for a while. And when they were bombing Madrid the Spaniards used to call the Republican planes Moscas, 'the wee ones' – meaning flies – when they were up fighting the German and Italian planes. They were Chatos.

At Brunete the busiest individual ever I met was the doctor. Ah wis blown up. I knew I had left my water bottle in the truck that we came up wi' and I went back to get this water bottle, because the water in Brunete was undrinkable. And I'm standing on the top of this truck but I never got the bottle yet. Over came a shell and blew the thing up. And it blew my clothes off and I didn't know all what had happened but my leg was bleeding and all this sort of thing. But a Yank told me the road to the dressing rooms, so I carried on down there. It was still shelling away and there they were in the dressing room, a Canadian doctor and a Welshman, Alan Williams.[93] They were as busy as hell. Alan Williams he came and picked oot shrapnel thingies and put on patches to stem the blood and so forth. And he says, 'If you can make it back to your unit all the better.' Something had happened the ambulance that was coming up to take the other casualties away, some of them very badly injured. So he asked me if I could make it back. I said, 'Oh, I'll make it back.' So I did but my ankle started swelling up after I got back. And Malky Dunbar, he's looking. He says, 'Where the hell did ye get that?' I told him, I said, 'Ye're minus a truck. I was down looking for my water bottle and got blawn up.' So at night my leg started swellin' and swellin', and when the grub truck came up around six o'clock at night, Alan Gilchrist was on it and he said: 'Get him away doon to hospital.' And that was it. It was even worse than I thought, I mean, because it kept me oot o' the front for quite a while that did.

I was on the sick list for about three month, aye, maybe more, maybe four. But I landed in – oh, I forget the name of the place now. But I know it went on until around Christmas, because they emptied all the hospitals when the battle of Teruel started. A' the lads that were in the hospital along wi' me were a' goin'. Ah wis down for goin' too but we were oot and we were kickin' a ball aboot and the ball came to me and I headed it and the next thing there was a crack. That was the ankle that I was wounded in, that was it away again, broken. So that kept me frae goin' up there. I was left while they went away up to Teruel. That was at the turn of the year '37 and '38. By the time I was cleared up the Fascists had sort of stemmed the Republican offensive at Teruel. They werenae able to keep Teruel. They just had to leave that. Then the next thing was the Fascists had cut the Ebro and we had to get back over, over to the Catalonian side. And I think we were amongst the last trains o' wounded people to get over before the bridges were a' blown there, you know. But by that time I had healed up again. And we got into Barcelona.

Then the next thing we were taken out and shoved up the Ebro. We re-crossed the Ebro. This was the Republican offensive in the summer of 1938. We went over there again and that was it.

The anti-tank unit had lost their guns just shortly after the retreat from Belchite and these places.

When we went up the Ebro we crossed the river by paddling boats. I mean, it was the only way we could get across. And we went across and chased the Fascists back to Gandesa. Well, before we came to Gandesa. I was along wi' Jock Dunlop from Edinburgh and we were going up the *barrancos* – hills they've cultivated for the crops of grapes

– and when we got up a certain length I got hit. I said to Jock, "Get down. We're being fired on." And I rolled down. And Jock he rolled down. And then he says, "Where are you hit?" "In my ankle." And he off wi' my shoe. He says, "Ye're no' hit at a'." And then he says, "Just a minute," and here he looked up and here there's blood comin' oot at the back o' ma knee. A bullet had gone through there. And he says, "God, you're shoutin' it's your ankle." And that's where the pain was, in my ankle, no' in my leg at a'.

Night had come on us by this time. I says to Jock, "Look, if you take me up that hill I'll lie up there. Somebody'll find me. Down here it might be the Fascists that'll find me. I don't want that!" So this Irishman and Jock gave me a lift up and left me there. By this time, well, I was quite happy lying there. I knew that some of the lads would find me when they were carrying the wounded down, you know. And in the morning when the light came I heard the voices and gave them a shout and they went and got the stretcher and took me back in.

Then I was taken down to a small house. And the Fascists were shelling that good style. An ambulance came along the following day and took is out there and over the Ebro. We found they had built a bridge there, a wooden bridge, and the ambulances could get over. It was the first time I'd seen anti-aircraft guns. And what a job they were doing, firing away. One would be firing, keeping the planes away. As soon as they ran out o' ammunition the other one would start. This was the only time I had seen anti-aircraft guns all the time I'd been in the War.

That was the end of the War for me because when I was in hospital the big shots from England came round enquiring, wantin' to know your name and address. They were representing the British Government. They were all done up, they could have been majors or colonels. They were all in blue full dress uniform anyway and they had all the paraphernalia round them. They were asking you, did you want to go home? Well, the only thing we could say wis, we wanted to go hme. That was just possibly everybody's thingie but the point is we were prepared to stay there if the Fascists werenae prepared to accept the conditions the Republican Government had put to them, you know. We would have stayed in Spain until the very last. I mean they would have had to chase us over the Pyrenees. Some of them did stay and the Fascists had to chase them over the Pyrenees. There was a huge thingie to get the War finished as far as we could see and that's why these British representatives were there. I mean the War could have gone on for long enough after that, I dare say.

It was in December 1938 I came back. We left Ripoll in Spain and came through by train, right through to the boats at Calais, and then we got on the boat home. We got a great reception both in London and in Glasgow. We had two receptions, as far as the Scotch were concerned. A great reception in England and then a big reception in Glasgow when we came back.

I thought my leg had all cleared up but I came home and I was limpin'. But they gave me shoes and so forth in London. So I put them on and they fitted well and a' the rest o' it. Then we started up to Glasgow, and on the march frae the train intae St Andrews Hall, Eddie – oh, he's dead now – he's saying to me, "There's blood comin' oot your shoe." And I looked down and here it is. So when I went in to the Hall there was a doctor and he came to see it and he says, "You've no feeling there?" He was pushing a pin in on the sole of my feet and I couldnae even feel it. So that meant he gave me a thingie to report. I wasnae stayin' in Glasgow, I was goin' to go on to Perth, to Coupar Angus – the only way I had anywhere to stay. So they took me into the Perth Infirmary and started treatin' the leg. Seemingly what had happened, the bullet had burned all the nerves at the back of my leg, you know. It was a' affectin' the feet. I mean I never felt any pain with it. And even to this day I get these sensations in the feet and in the knee.

I spent a week in the Infirmary and then they gave me exercises to do and suggested I should, if I could do it, get a bicycle and cycle from Coupar Angus where by this time I was staying, into Perth so many days of the week.

So I wasnae able to start working as soon as I came back from Spain. I was a painter by trade and did a bit o' sign-writing but when I came back I couldnae do a job off a plank, I couldnae stand up on a plank. This foot had no feeling in it, and you always had to make sure that if you were on a plank you had a grip. But McLean, the secretary of the painters' trade union,[94] says to me, "There's a job here that'll suit you." I went down to Dumbarton, to Dunbartonshire Council. And they were doin' the roads, it was the first time o' the paintin' o' the roads, you know, the halt signs and a' the rest o't. Goin' along wi' a squad o' men, just doin' that. That was the thing that brought my feet back to life again.

Another effect of the War on me was dysentery. It still has an effect on me yet. Fifty years after the War I'm still suffering physically.

After I came back from Spain I couldnae say that I was victimised or discriminated against. Even in the British army, when I joined it in 1942, they knew that I had been in Spain, and, oh, you found one or two that would ha' done things to you if they could. But on the whole no. I was called up and fought through the War from 1942 onwards.

Looking back on my Spanish War experience I would do the same again, put it that way. I would do the same again.

John Dunlop was born in 1915 in Winnipeg, Canada, but was brought up in Edinburgh, where he was educated at George Watson's College. In the Second World War he served in the Scots Guards. Until his retirement a few years ago he ran a printing business in Edinburgh.

JOHN DUNLOP

When the War in Spain broke out I was a young Chartered
Accountant student in Glasgow. A few months before that I had
begun to take an interest in politics and had in fact gone so far as to
join the Communist Party. It seemed to me at that time that was the
Party to join. And of course reading the *Daily Worker* and the other
press of the day I was very well aware of what was happening in
Spain. It seemed to me that great injustice was being perpetrated on
the people there by the organisations that had revolted against the
legal government of the day.

I was also disgusted at the fact that the other democratic
governments in Europe were not doing anything at all to help the
legal government in Spain against an attack which obviously was
being supported by both the Fascist Government of Italy and the Nazi
Government in Germany. I felt very strongly that if they were
allowed to continue their attack on the people of Spain it wouldn't be
so very long before the rest of Europe was engulfed in war, and the
war would be definitely provoked and begun by the German and
Italian Governments – as indeed proved to be the case.

I was also upset that my relatives and the people I worked among in
the office I was in, which was quite a big Glasgow office, didn't see
the matter in the same light as I did. I was extremely anxious to go and
take part in the War in Spain in the fight against Fascism because I felt
that my own personal example might help to bring more vividly and
closely to my friends, who were not at all politically conscious like
myself, the danger that this war of intervention by the Fascist Powers
of Italy and Germany against the Republican Government had for this
country. The apathy towards the War in Spain seemed to me to be
quite astounding and insupportable. I felt the best way to do
something about it was by going and joining the International
Brigade. There was a natural desire in me to join this new force, partly
from the excitement that it offered. As far as my own personal
background was concerned, it was more or less traditional for the
members of my family to go out into the world when they were quite
young. So it didn't seem to me a difficult thing to go and join the
International Brigade in Spain.

Early in 1937 Peter Kerrigan spoke to a conference of the Scottish

Communist Party and appealed for volunteers to join the British Battalion which had then been formed in Spain. Peter Kerrigan was a leading national official of the Communist Party in Great Britain, and a Glasgow man. He had recently been visiting Spain as a representative of the Party, or possibly the *Daily Worker* – I'm not exactly sure. Later on he was Scottish Organiser of the Communist Party, after I came back from Spain. But at that time he had just returned from Spain and he had been with the British Battalion for some time and he knew very well what was going on there. He described the situation to us.

At the end of this meeting, I said to Bob McElhone, who was my principal confidant in the Party in Glasgow, the first Communist whom I had met in fact, that I had decided I wanted to go to Spain. He told me to leave it to him. Shortly after that I was asked to go and have a meeting with Peter Kerrigan. Peter told me that things were pretty tough, and asked me whether I had any military experience. I said I had been in the Officers' Training Corps at school and knew how to handle a British Army rifle and had some experience in target shooting and manoeuvring in the countryside.

Thereafter I had to go up to Aberdeen on an audit for my firm and I was told to get in touch with Bob Cooney, who was the Communist Party Organiser in Aberdeen at that time. He told me that I had been accepted to go to Spain.

When I got back to my office in Glasgow I got in touch right away with Bob McElhone of the Communist Party and I was told that arrangements had been made for me and another member of the Overnewton Party Branch, George Murray, to go down to London.

At that time, although my family lived in Edinburgh I was staying with an uncle and aunt in Bothwell during the week. I never said anything to any members of my family, but I did mention the fact that I had decided to go to Spain to an older clerk in the firm, who had been a soldier in the First World War and whom I had been milking for his experiences as to what I could expect. And on the very afternoon that I was leaving for London I told him that I was going. He was very upset about it. However, George Murray and I went down to the train at Central Station with some other Party comrades, Bob McElhone and his wife, and there was another man there whom I didn't know, who was a close friend of George, Eddie Brown, from Perth. And then we travelled down on the overnight train to London, unaware that some of my relatives had arrived at the next train to leave for London, hoping to meet me and persuade me not to go. I discovered later that my friend in the office had been so worried that he had told one of the partners who had got in touch with my uncles in Glasgow.

When we got to London it was in fact on the morning of the May Day Rally. We immediately went off to see this. Although not actually taking part in the Rally we were among the crowds who were lining the roads, cheering on the demonstration. We then went to the house of one of George's sisters who lived in London. George went off to the Party offices and came back with our tickets for Paris.

We went by train to Folkestone and crossed on the boat to Boulogne. When we were coming into France there was no problem really, because being British subjects you didn't even have to show a passport. All you had to produce was some kind of identification. I showed my Golf Club membership card, which was adequate, although I did in fact have my passport with me. We got on the train from Boulogne to Paris, where we stayed overnight in a small bed-and-breakfast place which we found ourselves. On the following day George, who had got the address to go to in Paris, went on to this address and Eddie and I sat in a cafe on one of the boulevards. When George came back we all went off to the famous Trade Union Club in Paris at which the International Brigaders were collected and then from there were forwarded on their way.

When we got to this Club we were given a meal and we ate our meals there for the few days we were in Paris. There was an extensive area upstairs with tables and forms at which we sat. We ate just whatever was provided to us. In fact we were given snails in one of the dishes. I must say I enjoyed them very well though it was the first time I had tasted them. The food was extremely good. What the cost of it was I don't know because we weren't asked to pay for it.

In the evenings we were allocated to certain small private hotels in working class districts in Paris. The accommodation was fairly primitive. There were several beds in a room. We only stayed in them one night at a time because it was illegal both in Britain and in France to go to Spain to fight. Therefore every effort was made by the comrades who were organising our onward progress to make it difficult for anyone who might be trying to prevent our going there.

We got, I think, a breakfast of a roll and coffee and then we went off to the Club for the day.

One time we had a meeting at which Charlotte Haldane, Professor J.B.S. Haldane's wife, spoke to us and greatly insulted some of our puritanical members by telling us that we had to watch out for casual women, otherwise there was serious risk of us contracting an unpleasant disease. Some of the comrades took strong exception to this advice, coming from a woman. However advanced their political views were, their moral views were puritan. I confess I was mildly amused by that.

We spent one pleasant day wandering around one of the little parks. Then the time came for us to move and we were taken to a large railway station, where we were told to follow the people that we knew. In charge of each group of us there was a French comrade, and the one in charge of our group was a chap called Henri, who was a

Parisian. We got on the train which took us to Lyons. I shared a
compartment with Bill Alexander, who later became commander of
the British Battalion of the International Brigade, and two Cypriots
from London.[95] We were told not to converse with each other or with
French people. The carriage was packed with French people all the
way to Lyons. Occasionally we saw Henri passing up and down the
corridor, just making sure that everybody was getting on all right.

When we arrived at Lyons we were taken to a restaurant which was
attached to a small hotel, not very far from the station. There seemed
to be a fair number of International Brigaders in the restaurant. After
we had had a meal we were taken out again and told to get into two or
three charabancs which were open. We piled into these. Then an
American comrade came along and told all of us who didn't have
passports to get off the charabanc. Well, as I had a passport I stayed on
the charabanc, and so did Bill Alexander and the two Cypriot
comrades. Everybody else got off, including George Murray.
Although he had a passport his close friend Eddie did not, so George
went along with Eddie. I didn't see George until later on when we
arrived in Spain, at Madrigueras.

Then a group of Americans and Canadians came and filled up the
charabanc and it set off towards the north, out of Lyons, We drove
through wonderful country up to a small town called Oyonnax. It
was not far from the Swiss border. It was a centre of resistance to the
Nazis during the Second World War.

We were put into the best hotel in the town. It was an AA hotel,
owned, I believe, by the mayor of the town, who was also the local
Communist Party Organiser. We sat at a long table in the dining
room there with a group of Canadians and Americans. The rest of the
guests just seemed to be ordinary French people who were staying on
business or holiday.

We spent several days in Oyonnax. We went for walks in the
surrounding district and generally enjoyed ourselves. We went down
to the rugby ground and the Americans had got hold of an American
rugby ball. I learnt to play American Rugby, which I enjoyed very
much.

We had also to attend occasionally political meetings, where we
were told about what was happening in Spain. At one of them we
were very thrilled to meet a Cuban comrade who showed us a pistol,
and how to take it to pieces and put it together again. It was the only
time I ever touched a pistol from then on. but it helped make us feel
we were really going to do some fighting.

Of course being young we were interested in the local talent,
particularly myself and two or three of the American lads. We got
friendly with some of the girls there and we had arranged to meet
them on what was going to be our last evening. However, Bill
Alexander, who was a very regimental type, insisted that I go to a

final political meeting the night that we were leaving. So I didn't get any chance to make closer acquaintance with the girl that I had met the previous day.

The following morning we were away early in the charabanc, back down to Lyons where we were put on the train and taken right down the Rhône valley to Sète, where we were taken off the train, went to a working class district and into a workmen's restaurant and had a good meal. Then a taxi called and took Bill Alexander and me and the two Cypriot lads, Jack George and Basil Pantelides, off to another little town, Agde.

From then on we were told to keep ourselves as inconspicuous as possible because in a town like this we stuck out like sore thumbs. We were taken from the station to a small restaurant and workmen's hostel at the top of a small square. We were given a room upstairs where we had to have our meals and where we had to stay all day. The only time we were allowed out was to go to the public lavatory, which was just down beyond the foot of the square on the edge of a river which ran through this little town. We were allowed to sit at the riverside provided we weren't away too long.

The food here was very good and the company also was very good. We had a highly amusing French character who I think had been a sailor. Anyway he wore a jersey that was like a striped football jersey and trousers with flared bottoms. He was greatly amused at the English comrades. We provided him with a good deal of amusement, just why I don't know. Anyway we got on well with him.

One day we got some new arrivals. Three Italians came in. They had recently crossed the border from Italy. All of them were soldiers in the Italian army and they had come home on leave from Ethiopia, where they had been taking part in Mussolini's conquest. This was their first leave. As soon as they got to their homes they promptly volunteered for the International Brigade and joined us. We thought they were very fine chaps indeed.

We shared, I think, two bedrooms. There were three in a bed. Basil Pantelides, Jack George and I shared one huge bed. The Frenchman, whom we called Bicyclette, occupied one of the other beds with two of his comrades. As we had a fair amount of beans in our diet you can imagine what the night was like. This provoked our friend Bicyclette to great hilarity. The reason he was called Bicyclette was because the first time he let rip with a series of colossal farts, I remarked "Ah, moto-bicyclette". It sounded just like one of those little moto-bicyclettes that one saw going round the French streets. This provoked him to tremendous hilarity.

We were in Agde for several days. Then the word came for us to move and as I was the one member of the four British in the group there (the Cypriots were British subjects then) who could speak a little French I was sent up to the station to buy train tickets to Sète. I came back and gave the tickets to Bill Alexander and the two Cypriot comrades. We then made our own separate ways up to the station and waited for the train.

When we got off the train at Sète we saw Henri, the French guide whom I mentioned earlier. He had tickets for us to get on the next train to Perpignan. As before, we followed people we knew in little groups of two or three. Bill and I kept together and we followed Henri and got on the train. When the train arrived at Perpignan we got off there and Henri told us to follow him. We marched off out of the station in groups of two or three.

Bill and I were rather conspicuous. Bill was dressed in a sports jacket and flannels and I was wearing a light grey double-breasted suit. We were totally unlike all the French people who were moving around at that time.

It must have been round about five o'clock because the station was pretty busy and when we got out of the station we merged with the crowds who were obviously hurrying home from work. We went down the street and Henri went through a little park and out of the park at the other side and down one or two streets. We came to a little restaurant in a side street. It was a narrow room with a row of small tables on both sides, some comrades that we knew by sight were already sitting at tables and the rest of us went in. There didn't appear to be many other people but International Brigaders in the place. We had a marvellous meal. I sat at the same table as Henri and we had a flagon of wine which was sour red stuff but Henri liked it very much. So he ordered another flagon for our table. Everybody else only got one bottle. Anyway I appreciated the stuff as much as Henri did and by the end of the meal I was feeling fit for anything.

After the meal was over we went out and down the street and we came to a place where there were some trucks, or *camions* as the French call them, with a group of Polish-Canadian volunteers that we had met in Oyonnax earlier. We then set off, again in our groups of two or three, back up towards the station, where we crossed through into the goods yard and over the tracks and out of the station at the other side, where we came on a road which was leading out into the country

Dusk was falling and there were a number of the locals going for an evening stroll. We merged with these people but gradually we left them behind as we got out into the country. We went along the road for some time and eventually it got so dark we could just dimly make out one or two people in front of us and one or two others behind. There were thousands of bull frogs singing away in the dark in a marsh at one side of the road.

Suddenly the strollers in front of us disappeared and when we got up to the spot there was a man who directed us into the bushes. We went down off the road in behind the bushes and crouched down in long grass. There were already quite a number of our comrades all crouching down there. We had to keep quiet. We were not supposed to smoke. But those who did want to smoke cupped their hands and bent very low towards the ground, in order to prevent the glow of their cigarettes being seen from the roadside.

Periodically vehicles – cars or buses or trucks – came along the valley which was lined with poplars. The shadows of these poplars were thrown in long lines which moved round past us as the trucks and other vehicles went by. Eventually a vehicle came along and stopped. We were signalled to get out of the bushes and up to the side of the road where we found an old charabanc with its hood up and the driver standing at the side of the road hurrying us into its seats.

Shortly after that a car could be seen coming along. We were told to get down so that we couldn't be seen. We had to crouch down in our seats so that all that a passing driver would see would be an empty charabanc standing at the side of the road with its driver having a run off. When this vehicle passed our driver got in and drove away. But whenever other vehicles were seen we had to bob down below the seats, so they would think ours was an empty charabanc.

We passed through villages which by that time were quiet, with nobody moving around. When we passed through these places we had again to bend down so that it appeared to be an empty bus.

Soon we swung left and the road started to rise. We knew then we were moving towards the border. As we rattled through dark and low-roofed villages bending low in our seats each time, exhilaration frothed in our veins. Eventually we came up a hill and we could see faint lights flickering beyond that. We stopped before we reached the top of the road and got out. There we found a guide waiting for us. He took us down the hill, off the road. We saw a most extraordinary sight. We were on the side of a deep, wide valley and on the other side we could dimly make out the Pyrenees, huge mountains which were being lit by long lancing pencils of light from searchlights which were placed every couple of miles apart for as far as we could see. They were sweeping round continuously. They were the lights of the Non-Intervention Committee. They were searching for people who were trying to cross the border into Spain.

Spain was a member of the League of Nations and the Spanish Republican Government had appealed to the League for assistance in preventing weapons and war materials and troops coming to the aid of the rebellious Franco and his supporters. But instead what happened was the Non-intervention Committee was formed by the League ostensibly in order to prevent foreign troops and supplies going into Spain to either of the two sides involved in the war. The Committee operated of course inequitably because Franco was supported by Italy and by Germany, both Fascist countries, who openly flouted the Non-Intervention rules. Unfortunately for the Republican Government the British and French Governments, who could have done most to help it, refused to do so and used the Non-Intervention Committee as the excuse. This was a very serious mistake on their part because by allowing the Spanish Fascist rebels to be assisted by the Fascist Governments of Italy and Germany, Britain and France were in fact ensuring that they themselves were going to be drawn into the world war that inevitably followed after the fall of Republican Spain.

Well, we made our way down the hillside on a road which was going to cross a main road which we could see quite clearly because of the number of cars that were travelling along it rapidly. This road led, I think, to Port Bou, at the coast at the Spanish-French border. When we got down near to the main road we hid behind some farm buildings at the side of the road, where we were allowed to light up and have a smoke. Then in groups of one or two we crossed the road in between the passage of cars and other vehicles which were going backwards and forwards along the road. When we got across to the other side we found ourselves in a field with rows of high vegetables and we hid in the rows between the stalks there. Then our guide indicated to us that we had to follow him and we moved off in single file up towards the foothills of the Pyrenees.

At one time a halt was called and it was discovered that, owing to the darkness and the silence in which we had been enjoined to move, half of the group had wandered off in a different direction. So one guide went off to look for them and we were taken off further up into the hills.

We moved off from here almost at a running pace higher up into the mountains. Eventually we reached a dip and here we had to halt because the circling rays of the searchlights were getting very near to us. A few feet above us they were striking the hillside. We were in the shadow of a small knoll which effectively concealed us from the lights. But it was a most eerie experience to see this light passing two or three feet above our heads. The lights moved on but then would suddenly swing back erratically. It was never possible to know exactly when we might be caught in them.

Some time passed and then we were taken off over the dangerous part quickly, then again we lay just below a track which was moving right up into the top of the hills. We hid behind some bushes. We could hear our guide talking to some men who had come marching down the road. We assumed that they were frontier guards, some of whom we had been told were friendly towards our venture. Then these men went on down the hill and when they had gone we climbed up on to this track and made our way straight up the hillside. By this time it was beginning to get light and we could see dawn rising over Port Bou on the Mediterranean. It was really quite a marvellous sight. From then on it was just a race to the frontier.

It was quite extraordinary the number of different nationalities that there were among us. I remember there was a Dutchman who could speak a bit of English. There were people who were obviously Poles. There were Germans. There were one or two Britishers like myself and Bill Alexander. And some of our Canadian and American friends we had met earlier.

When at last we got up to the frontier, which appeared to be more or less on the crest of this particular mountain, and got over it we were standing in a group just looking at the view in front of us. It was a green hillside interspersed with rocks, and further down the hillside there was a peculiar, almost ecclesiastical-looking small building. And out of it came a man who waved to us. He was wearing green khaki baggy trousers caught in at the ankles. This was the first we had seen of the Spanish army. It wasn't to be long before we were dressed in a similar outfit ourselves. The man waving was young and looked every inch a Spaniard to us, with his black hair and moustache and handsome face. We swept down towards the place and got into this building, which must have been a chapel at one time. The walls were massive, but inside there was just more or less one room. There was a huge cauldron of coffee steaming on a log fire, and there were loaves of bread for us. We were handed out steaming hot mugs of coffee and hunks of bread which tasted absolutely marvellous after our long hike over the mountains. Once we were all in and had all got our mugs of coffee the singing started up. This was really the most marvellous experience of my life. The Germans sang the German songs of the working class movement in Germany before Hitler. The French were singing, and the Italians were singing. About the only people that weren't singing were the British, who merely joined in with tunes that they knew.

But then, at last, somebody started up singing *The Internationale*, which of course we all knew, and we joined in. I find it extremely difficult to explain the feelings that swept through me when this singing of *The Internationale* started up. Here were we, all young men from really all the nations in Europe, and some from outside Europe as well, joining in this one song in their own language which seemed to express a yearning for the unity of mankind. I find it extremely difficult to explain how exhilarating this was. I don't think I've ever felt the same feeling at any other time in my life.

After we had all been fed we started our trip down the mountainside. For the rest of the day we went down through cork oaks and across streams. We had to wade across the streams. And I remember one little Polish fellow who was about half my size – the water came up to his waist, it came up to just not far over my knees – I'm 6 foot 3¼ inches in my stocking soles. So I was really quite amused at this little chap. And he could see the funny side of it, too.

Finally we got down to a roadway and it was an earthen road. It seemed to be totally covered in a kind of white dust. And there were some trucks with canopies on the backs of them. We came to know them later as *camions*, a Spanish (and a French) word for a lorry. We climbed into these and there were seats on them. And then we set off through the groves of the cork oaks towards our next destination. The weather was very dry at that time and the dust rose up from the wheels of the lorries. And by the time we had gone half-a-dozen miles we were all thickly coated in this white clay dust.

Eventually we came to a town that we went through and then we were driven up a road to a fantastic fortress. This was the famous fortress of Figueras, an amazing place which covered a very considerable area. The walls must have been about a mile long all round. It was situated on an eminence and from the top of the walls the ground sloped down – and I mean the top of the walls, not the bottom of the walls – in a gentle slope all round. Because the place was kept completely free of bushes any infantry or cavalry trying to advance up these slopes had absolutely no cover at all. And the fortress, I believe, was so strong that even Napoleon had been unable to take it.

When we got inside we were greeted by the French commandant, a marvellous character famous in the International Brigades as Garde-à-vous, or, as the English said, Gardez-vous, because this was the one word of command he used that we all came to understand – Stand to Attention.

The place was absolutely swarming with Spanish troops. We discovered that these were Anarchist troops who had been disbanded from the militias and had been reformed by the Government and disarmed. They had no firearms but every one of them was armed with a huge dagger like the Roman short sword. They were friendly to us and we shared quarters with them underneath the earthen walls, and ate alongside them. I got quite friendly with one of them who could speak a little English. His English had been learnt entirely from books so that his pronunciation was the most curious that I have ever heard. But it preserved characteristics of the Spanish language which made it very easy for me later on to recognise any Spaniard speaking English.

I naturally asked this young man about the political situation and he explained that his comrades were mostly Anarchists but he himself was not an Anarchist, he was a Left Republican. And he begged me not to speak too loudly on this matter as his comrades might twig that he was not of their own political beliefs. He felt that they were sufficiently antagonistic to the Left Republicans for his life to be in danger. This seemed to me quite amazing considering that we were all supposed to be united in fighting Franco. This was the first real indication I had of the divisions within the ranks of the Republican forces, and the Republican Government too for that matter.[96]

A day or two after we arrived in Figueras we all had to go to the barber. The barber was quite a joker. He would get you on to the chair, run his clippers right across your head from forehead to the nape of your neck in one direction and then from ear to ear in the other direction. He said "Now that's you finished." He refused to do any more, so you had to get up from the chair and walk around with a cross, a very broad cross, all over your skull. This provoked great amusement among us. And it was only after we'd been in the place a couple of days that he would allow us to come back and get the rest of our hair shaved off. We all had our heads shaved closely for health reasons really, to avoid lice or nits. We saw that practically all the Spanish comrades had their heads closely shaven, and a lot of the Spanish peasants had too. Certainly, we didn't get infected with lice at that time and it was only once we had been in the trenches or on the front for some time that we started to suffer from these little beasts.

Garde-à-vous had a young American adjutant. Apparently he had been kept there because they thought he was really too young to go on to the front. This boy must have been no more than sixteen years old. How he managed to get into Spain at so young an age I don't know. But he was tremendously enthusiastic and said to us: "Now, you know, really we're in the Red Army." And this of course caused a great impression on us: we really felt that we were at one with the workers in Russia and Spain too.

The German comrades that we met there were all young men, most of whom had escaped from Hitler's Germany and come to fight in the International Brigade. They were marvellous chaps and they had marvellous songs. Among them were a few Austrians as well, with one of whom, Heinrich Vogeler, I got very friendly indeed. He came from Vienna and was a keep-fit fanatic. He organised us into running round the walls two or three times every day just to keep us fit. The walls must have been at least a mile round. Heinrich also organised football and basketball. The Germans were extremely good at football, a lot better than even the Scots among us. Later on, in July 1937, Heinrich was killed in the attack round the north of Madrid against Brunete and Villanueva de la Cañada. I was wounded there myself and I met one of the Austrian comrades in one of the transit hospitals. He was looking very down in the dumps indeed. I asked him about Heinrich and he just said one word: "Todt." which expressed to me the tragedy of one young life which seemed to me so full of promise. Heinrich really was a magnetic character, who seemed to be full of life and the joy of it.

During one of the meal times I was sitting beside a man who seemed to me to be a little bit odd. He was a German, but he was totally different from the rest of the men. He seemed to be very much on edge. He didn't seem to be popular with the other Germans and seemed to try to keep away from them. I remember that I was sitting at this table along with my friend Bicyclette, the Frenchman from our sojourn in the little French hotel across the border. We thought that this man was really not one of us. That was the feeling that we had about him, because he did not seem to talk the same kind of language as ourselves. The whole atmosphere about him was different. Well, a day or two later we were taken in trucks and put on the train to go to Barcelona. Our groups were in the last two carriages on the train. There were a number of Spanish soldiers on the train as guards. We hadn't gone more than about twenty or thirty miles down the track through a mountainous area when we saw our strange friend walking down the track. The train had passed him and gone round a bend. Bicyclette pulled the communication cord and the train came to a stop. He and some of the Frenchmen dashed away round, back up the track the way we had come. The next thing we knew here they were back again, hustling along this German. He was brought on the train and he was pushed into a seat opposite me, against the window, and a crowd of us round about so the chap had really no chance to escape at all.

There was a Dutchman on the train whom I had met on the race to the frontier, who could speak a little English and also seemed to be able to speak a bit of French as well. And he seemed a curious character. We discovered in Figueras that he was a chap who couldn't hold his drink at all. He got very drunk and he was really quite obnoxious when he was drunk. He seemed to take exception to the fact that this German had virtually been arrested and he called the Spanish guards. The Spanish guards came along, interested to find out what was going on, and they were told that we had captured this bloke. The Dutchman was getting so obnoxious that I put my foot on his stomach and shoved him back into his seat. He collapsed and never said any more.

When we got into Barcelona the German was taken away and we never heard of or saw him again. But the curious fact about him was he was wearing three suits of clothes. He had three pairs of trousers on and three jackets, and he was walking along this railway track on a very hot day in the middle of May. So either he must have been a bit off his head or else he was not what we in Scotland would call the clean tattie. We assumed, and I think rightly, that the man was a spy who had been sent in from Germany.

We eventually got to Barcelona, were put on another train, and went down through the fields of Catalonia along the coast. Everywhere we went we were hailed by peasants in the fields. We all knew the Communist clenched fist salute but we saw a lot of the peasants in the fields holding their hands clasped above their heads, which we discovered later on was the Anarchist salute. This is the sign that they used on their flags and so on, the two hands clenched together signifying the brotherhood of man.

I don't remember very much of the rest of the journey, except that quite often at wayside halts we were besieged by groups of peasants handing us in baskets of oranges, which were just about the last of the crop, and other things for us to eat. In some places they would bring us marvellous sausages which we could eat raw. Everywhere it was perfectly obvious that we were very popular people indeed.

We eventually got to Albacete, capital of the province of Albacete, and headquarters of the International Brigades. I believe Albacete was the birthplace of General Franco himself. The reason it was chosen as the headquarters of the International Brigade, I think, was that it was an excellent training area, although certainly it was some distance from Madrigueras, which was the place where the English, French and Germans were receiving their infantry training. The countryside round about Albacete was very suitable for training purposes, as we found out ourselves later on, when I was one of the members of the Anti-Tank Battery. We had our artillery park in Albacete and did our training in the countryside round about.

When we got to Albacete we stayed there for a short time in the barracks of the Guardia Nacional, a very large building in the western part of the town, not far from the bullring, as far as I remember. When we got into this place it was packed with International Brigaders from all the countries in the world, it seemed. There were even some Africans there among the French. I think they were Senegalese, and there were some from Portuguese Africa as well. I remember one chap there whom I got to know because I used to come up against him at different places from time to time. He was even taller than myself. He was about 6 feet 5 inches tall. We used to sort of smile and wave to each other, but without being able to converse, because he couldn't speak a word of English and I couldn't speak a word of Portuguese. But his name was Timontero. I used to come up against him later on from time to time.

The barracks were really like a block of flats built in a square. There was a large square in the centre of them. The only entrance to this was through one gateway in the west side of the square. That was the way in to the barracks and it was the only way out, unless you wanted to drop down from the windows. But this wasn't easy because they were barred. In any case there was no reason why you would want to go out that way, unless you were one of the unfortunate members of the Brigade who had been committing some misdemeanour and were shoved into the jail, which was on the top floor. It wasn't very nice being one of the people in that jail because they used to have to clean out the latrines in the place. There was no system of sewers in Albacete. And as there were latrines on each floor, and they were all situated one above the other, everything that came down in the morning piled up in a pit down below. Those poor devils who had been guilty of some misdemeanour were detailed every day to shovel all this stuff up into carts which would take it away. I think there was not much margin in being disobedient, failing to carry out orders.

We were there for a short time and then we were sorted out into our various national groups and all our particulars were taken down and recorded. Then we moved out to the training areas. The training area for the British, the French and the Germans was centred round a village called Madrigueras.

Madrigueras was like many another Spanish village in the district. You approached it over a long wide plain. The first thing you saw was the church tower. Miles and miles after that you began to see the roofs of the village. It's typical of the villages in that part of Spain, certainly at that time. No doubt there are considerable changes taking place now, as I know, because I've been back to Madrigueras since then. A considerable amount of new building has taken place round it. In those days they were low houses, at the most two or three storeys high, clustered round a huge church building.

When we got to Madrigueras we were welcomed by the British group who were already there. The commandant was a young man, Malcolm Dunbar, whom I later came to know well as commander of the Anti-Tank Battery. The political commissar was another young man, Hugh Slater, who was later appointed to the same job in the Anti-Tank Battery.

We were housed in the village hall, which had quite a large gallery round it. Some of us slept on the floor of the hall round the sides, and others slept up in the gallery. There was a stage at the end of this where later on we gave an entertainment in which I took part along with Wilf Winnick, the younger brother of a famous British dance band leader.[97]

Life then settled down to the real business of training us for going up to the front. For the next fortnight or so we marched out into the countryside every day. We learned how to use the Russian rifle, and we learned how to attack and take cover.

The International Brigades had been formed some months before in the early autumn of 1936, when it was clear to quite a number of the young volunteers who had flocked into Spain without any urging from any political party but from their own conviction, that they ought to go and help the Spanish Republican Government against the attack of what they considered to be Fascist generals, who were supported obviously by the Italian Fascists and the German Nazis. I've just been reading some of John Cornford's writings and apparently he had gone to Spain at the start of the war and had been fighting with the militias in the Aragon. He had then gone back to Britain and he had put forward the idea among his friends at Cambridge and elsewhere in England of the necessity for groups of disciplined, trained fighters from outside Spain to help the Spanish militias, who were untrained and totally unversed in the arts of warfare. This apparently seems to have coincided with a feeling in the inner circles of the Communist International or Comintern that this was the way in which Germany and Italy could be stopped in their attack on Spain.[98] They realised the tremendous feeling that there ws among people in all the democratic countries of Europe that the Spanish Government should be assisted. They decided to take advantage of this, and they in fact supplied the organisational facilities for the establishment of a considerable force of international volunteers in Spain.

So the reason why they were Russian rifles was that the Russian Government were the only government outside Spain who were willing to give material assistance to the Spanish Republican Government. They supplied rifles, aircraft, machine guns, artillery and so on. The only Russian weapons that I had direct experience of were the rifles, the anti-tank guns and the Maxim machine guns, because I became both an anti-tank gunner and later on a machine gunner. As far as the aircraft were concerned the snub-nosed Russian planes, Chatos, helped to defend Madrid from the attack of the Fascist aircraft.

The days spent in the fields training at Madrigueras were mostly very enjoyable. In the evening we paraded up and down the one long street in Madrigueras, looking at the girls. But the girls always went in twos and threes and they were mostly completely unapproachable, first of all because most of us didn't speak their language, and secondly because they were well watched by their mothers and relatives. This apparently was the traditional scene in a Spanish village. When dusk fell people went out and walked up and down in the pleasant evening air. The girls and boys went in their separate groups and never the twain shall meet, so to speak. I got very friendly with one or two English chaps, and with George Murray we used to go to a small cafe or tavern in the evenings, which was run by a young woman who it seems was the principal Communist official in the village. She was in fact married to an English International Brigader. She had been a widow and had a lovely little daughter of about seven or eight who was a great favourite of ours. We spent many pleasant evenings in there. Alan Gilchrist was one of the group that I remember very well. Although he had a Scottish name he was an Englishman and a teacher. Alan later on, in the Second World War, was parachuted into Yugoslavia, along with Brigadier Fitzroy Maclean. Alan died a few years ago and in a later visit to Spain by members of the International Brigade his ashes were spread on the ground of an olive grove.

So far as food and drink were concerned when we got to Madrigueras we got wine supplied to us. We got a cup of wine with our meals. We got coffee in the morning, or a kind of coffee. But for midday meal and evening meal at Madrigueras we got wine. But later on in the anti-tank battery, as far as I remember, we didn't have wine – we may have had a wine ration but it doesn't stick in my mind certainly. It was coffee mainly. In the training period of the anti-tank battery, which I shall deal with presently, we were getting plenty of food. There was no lack of food. It wasn't until later on in the war, when we were in the north in Catalonia, and cut off from the south, rations were getting very short indeed. Bascially when we first went there we were fed on things called *garbanzos*. I think the English name is chick-peas. But the British soldier corrupted it into 'carabunchies', you know. We got these stewed 'carabunchies' for every meal. Whenever possible I used to go over to the Spanish group in the Machine Gun Company and feed with them, because they had a lot more and the food that they got was better. It was better cooked than the food that we got from Hookey Walker and his crowd. He cooked, he and some English cooks, for the British, and he had Spanish cooks as well who prepared food for the Spaniards. But our cooks were very insular in their attitude to Spanish food and they wouldn't take a lot of things that the Spaniards would take. Well, for instance, the Spaniards cooked with olive oil; the British wouldn't have the olive oil. And you need olive oil with *garbanzos*. To have them just stewed in water they were pretty grim.

After we had been at Madrigueras for two or three weeks half of the British were moved out to join the British Battalion. A group of us were left and we were told we were going to be trained to use new Russian anti-tank guns, which were the first that had been seen in Spain. This was when the first Anti-Tank Unit was formed for all the International Brigades. We were taken back to Albacete where we were put in quarters along with German comrades whom we had got to know very well in Madrigueras. We were shown the three guns which were to become our weapons from then on. Every day we were taken out into the countryside with the guns and we were instructed how to operate them. Now these really were absolutely marvellous weapons. At that time I believe they were the most advanced artillery pieces in the world. They had a semi-automatic action. As soon as you slammed the projectile home into the barrel the lock rose up and the gun-layer just had to press the trigger, and when using the special anti-tank shell the firing was almost completely automatic. The calibre of gun was 37mm, which was about twice the calibre of anti-tank guns in use in other armies in Europe. The guns were much lighter than the French 45mm and very easily manoeuvrable. They could be manhandled on to a lorry quite easily. They had a marvellous sighting mechanism. The sights were optical sights, which gave one a very good view of what one was firing at and the effect of one's shells. We saw some captured enemy anti-tank guns and they were mere pop-guns compared to the kind of guns that we had. Of course it gave us a great feeling of confidence seeing these and knowing the superiority of our own weapons. The trajectory of the projectiles that were used was very flat indeed, not unlike a rifle bullet. Therefore it was easy to aim them. We had great fun out in the fields learning to fire them. I was appointed observer for the battery.

I think there were about thirty in the battery altogether and ten men in each gun team. There was the gun commander, the gun layer, the gun loader and then there was a group of men who were bringing up supplies of ammunition to the gun. They were also required to manhandle the gun from place to place.

Once we had received our basic training on the guns we were sent on an exercise which occupied at least two days some distance out from Madrigueras. After our first day out in the *campo* or countryside, we came back from our manoeuvres tired and hungry and expecting to find a good meal waiting for us. However, we discovered that while there was a certain amount of food being prepared by the cooks there was no bread at all. We were naturally a bit upset about this because bread was quite a large part of our diet. Malcolm Dunbar and Hugh Slater went off to see the chap who was responsible for supplies for the whole outfit. We discovered that he was a Frenchman and he had acted on the assumption that the French eat a lot of bread, the British do not eat a lot of bread, so therefore the British weren't to get any bread. So a big row developed. However, we British were not entirely unresourceful, and while our commanders were arguing about the supplies we moved in on the French cookhouse. It was all done more or less under cover of darkness and nobody saw who took the loaves and where they went to. But they ended up round the British camp fire. We discovered later on that this was not an uncommon thing to happen in the International Brigades because shortages of all kinds of things were so great that it was common practice for people to be sent out to "organise" the supplies. So this matter of theft received a new name and was sanctioned under the title of "organising". The units that had good "organisers" in charge of their cookhouse fed well or as well as one could be fed under conditions as they were in Spain in those days.

If a unit needed a truck to transport itself and the truck broke down and they couldn't get it mended, well then if the next higher up element or echelon in command could not supply the necessary vehicle or whatever it was incumbent on the commander of that unit to find one some way or other and he usually managed to do so, no doubt at the expense of some other unit. This of course was one of the great difficulties that the Republican forces fought under, because they did not have a well organised commissariat. Their logistical support was dependent very much upon what could be got through the Non-Intervention blockade of Spain.

Our equipment and the uniforms that we wore were very similar to those of the Spanish Army. The Spanish Army wore long trousers which were caught in at the ankles. This may seem a strange kind of uniform to wear but in fact it was very practical because for many months in the year the ground was very dry, there was a lot of dust raised as you marched along and the fact that your trousers were caught in at the ankles kept the dust from moving up inside your trouser legs. The same type of trousers were worn by many of the peasants too. Some of the uniforms were French. Most of our steel helmets were French, obviously old stock from the First World War. Steel helmets were issued to most of us when we got to Madrigueras but not all of us had them, and not all of us were particularly keen on wearing them for that matter. Occasionally one came across chaps wearing a Spanish army type of steel helmet. I had one of these later. It was much more like the German helmet. It fitted more tightly to one's head, it didn't have a brim the way the French *poilu* helmet had or the British Tommy's steel helmet. It came down over the ears and round the back of the neck. I think possibly it did give better protection than the British Tommy's steel helmet. I think the British steel helmet must have been designed to protect soldiers in trench warfare from shrapnel shells bursting in the air. The French *poilu's* helmet gave a similar sort of protection. Both gave greater protection for one's shoulders, whereas I think the Spanish type of helmet gave better protection to the sides of the head and the back of the neck from actual shell bursts on the ground and in open warfare, which was largely what we were involved in.

Some of us had webbing belts but most of them were leather as far as I remember. They were leather ammunition pouches and leather belts and leather straps. We did have canvas knapsacks, as far as I remember, but I don't remember us having kitbags. We didn't have very many personal belongings to carry around with us. Blankets were rolled up and carried over our shoulders and tied with a bit of string or a bit of cord at the ends. Not that one, in summertime anyway, in Spain, required very much cover at night, because the nights were warm and dry.

I was fortunate in that I had good Spanish leather boots, which were issued to me when we arrived there. But many of the Spanish troops didn't wear boots at all. They wore the traditional *alpargatas,* which were grass-soled shoes. They were made of esparto grass which was first of all formed into long plaits and then these plaits were rolled up into the shape of soles of shoes and stitched together with strong twine. Then canvas toe-pieces and heel-pieces were sewed on to them and tapes were sewed on to them, which you tied round your ankles. They were comfortable and very functional. Provided you managed to get them soaked with water at the start of the day they were very good wearing. If they weren't soaked with water from time to time the grass tended to dry out, shrink and become loose and they would wear away very much more quickly than they needed to if they were properly damped.

I had an overcoat some of the time, not all of the time. As far as raincoats were concerned I think we were issued initially with oilskins but I don't remember during my stay in Spain having an oilskin for any great length of time. Once I was wounded I lost all that kind of impedimenta, and when you came back from hospital, back to the troops, you just had to take what was available and if there were no oilskins available you didn't get an oilskin. If there was an overcoat for you, well, you got an overcoat; if there wasn't, well, you were out of luck. If you wanted extra blankets you just had to try and scrounge one from somewhere or other.

The rifles we used were all Russian rifles. Some of them were very old, dating from the First World War. You could tell how old they were because the date was actually stamped into the metal work of the gun. The latest rifles, the 1937 rifles, which some of us had were very good, and the older ones from the First World War time were very good, but the ones produced in between had a very serious fault and that was that the bolt and the breech were made of two different kinds of steel, with different coefficients of expansion. The result was that once you had fired three or four shots the bolt heated up to such an extent that it expanded more than the breech did. It was practically impossible to reopen the breech of the rifle to reload. This had serious consequences for members of the British Battalion in their very last action, in which I was involved, as I shall mention later on.

We were told that this was one of the reasons for the Treason Trials which had taken place in Russia earlier in the 1930s. But nothing appeared to have been done to remedy the defect in the rifles that we were using. The simplest thing would have been to get fresh bolts made and throw away the old ones. But instead they sent them to the Spanish Republic. I don't know how many men may have lost their lives or how many Fascist attacks may have been successful because of this. Certainly it was a successful Fascist attack that took place on the very last day that the British Battalion were in the line.

Similar faults could not be attributed to at least two other Russian weapons with which I became very familiar. One was the 37mm anti-tank gun, which as I have already said was an absolutely top class weapon, probably the best gun in Europe at the time. Another was the Russian Maxim machine gun. These no matter how old they were, operated with really maximum efficiency. They were a tremendous weapon.

So also was the Russian light machine gun, the Diktorov. Well, it was called a light machine gun but when I eventually came into the British Army and met the Bren machine gun it was several times lighter than the Diktorov. Nevertheless the Diktorov had a marvellously simple lock and was a very reliable weapon under fire. It was a pan-fed machine gun. Nothing simpler than the lock could have been devised, except the final action of the Sten gun, where there was just no lock at all. The Diktorov could be used as an accurate single shot weapon, was well as for rapid firing, and at maximum distances as much as a rifle or the Maxim machine gun.

The Maxim machine guns that the Russians supplied had a heavy armoured metal shield and a water-cooled jacket. The carriage was not a tripod, as it was in the case of British Maxim machine guns, but was a miniature gun carriage which the poor No. 2 on the gun had to carry. And as I was No. 2 on one of these guns for some time, I know exactly what I'm talking about. It was a very heavy beast indeed. It had an extension to the carriage which was a long U-shaped steel tube, which was fixed on to the wheeled part of the carriage by hinges. The wheeled part of the carriage went over your back and the U-tube was hinged down over your shoulders in front. As you marched along over rough ground the wheels of the carriage used to bump up and down on your back, which made fast progress in soft ground not very easy. But in action of course the gun was mounted on the carriage and if you had to move swiftly you just got hold of the end of the U-tube and pulled the gun along. But there again if you were moving through muddy ground, huge tyres of mud developed on the wheels and made it extremely difficult to pull. Then you just had to dismount the gun and pick it up and get going as fast as you could.

After our training at Albacete and Madrigueras the Anti-Tank Battery moved up to the Jarama front. I was observer for the battery and was responsible for the firing of the guns on the Jarama front, which was trench warfare at that time after the main action had taken place three months earlier in the big battle of Jarama.

When the Anti-Tank Battery was on the way up to the front line to take its first part in action, we were visited by a Russian general. His name was not disclosed to us but he spoke to us in Russian and his words were translated to us by another high-up Slav who spoke very good English. The thing that I remember particularly about this talk that we had was that we were told that these guns were extremely good guns, that they were the best in the world, and that it was our duty not only to use them to the best effect, but also to make absolutely certain that in no cirumstances were we to allow them to be captured by the enemy, because the enemy had nothing to compare with them.

We were there on the Jarama front from the end of May or the beginning of June until the offensive at Brunete, which started on July 6th. After we had moved from the Jarama front we had moved round to the north of Madrid and we met up with the XVth Brigade. There the battery was addressed by Jock Cunningham, Chief of Staff of the XVth Brigade, Fred Copeman, Commander of the British Battalion and George Aitken, the political commissar of the Brigade.[99] They told us that we had been having a really cushy time for the last few weeks and that we were going into some real fighting now and that we had to be prepared for the worst that could possibly happen to us. They made no bones about that.

We went into action at Brunete on July 7th. I remember watching the initial action of the British Battalion against the village of Villanueva de la Cañada from the hillside above. Later on that day, after the village had been taken, we went on down the road past the end of the village and then out into the open country. There we were attacked by aircraft and had to jump out of our *camions* and scatter. However , the bombing had no effect on us and as soon as they were past we were back into our *camions*.

We were finally put into position on a hill overlooking the river, beyond which we believed the enemy were situated. I was looking at the enemy positions through my range finder when all of a sudden I saw a black fan opening up out of the earth in front of me some twenty yards or so away. It was the first shell that indicated we had been spotted and were under attack. Then several more shells fell, coming nearer to right and left of me. By that time our three guns, which were on the forward slope of the hill, were starting to be pulled out but not before our first tragic loss took place. A shell passed right over the armour shield of one of the guns and killed Fraser Crombie, a great lad from Kirkcaldy. I think he was a miner. Later on, in the Second World War, when I was in the British Army, I met his nephew, who was in the same squad as I was at Caterham.

I hurriedly picked up my gear and dashed up to the top of the hill, where Malcolm Dunbar, our commander, was viewing the scene from the shelter of a white house. I set up my instruments beside him again. By that time the guns were in safety behind the hill and this short attack was not repeated. But obviously it had had the desired effect as far as the Fascists were concerned. But I am really quite surprised that Malcolm and I were not hit, because we were in full view beside the corner of a white house. All the hills round about there seemed to have a white house on the crest. They were really quite obvious so I think we were quite lucky to get out of that little lot.

It wasn't long before we found out that what Jock Cunningham and the other leaders had told us in their address before the batttle was quite correct. The purpose of the offensive as we were told was to encircle the Fascist troops that were at that time investing the western environs of Madrid. It was intended that we should sweep down behind them and trap them. Unfortunately this didn't happen but it was a significant offensive, because it was the first big offensive that the Republic had been able to mount in which all arms of the armed forces could be used, with artillery and infantry and tanks and aircraft.

The objective was first of all to capture three villages, Villanueva de la Cañada, Brunete and Quijorna. The Brigades managed to capture all three of their objectives but they were then halted and the Fascists managed to get up sufficient reserves to stem our attack. I myself was wounded – I can't·remember the exact date, but probably round about the sixth or seventh day of the offensive – when, along with Lieutenant Black we were carrying ammunition from the ammunition dump down to one of our guns. A decade or so ago I managed to get back to Spain in the last year of Franco's regime and visited the actual scene where I was wounded and found traces of the battle there. The positions could quite clearly be seen by the shape and colour of the vegetation.

Our ammunition dump was behind Brigade headquarters, almost on the roadside, which was protected from the view of the enemy by the crest of the hill on which the Brigade observation post was situated. There was a long trench which unfortunately had been dug in a straight line straight up through the hillside over the edge of the hill. This trench was a death trap because if a shell landed in it then the explosion would be directed along the trench in both directions and any troops in the way would be bound to get killed or severely wounded. That was what happened to me. We came under shell fire as we were moving cases of ammunition up along this trench. We got down flat in the bottom of the trench. Comrade Black was kneeling behind me and there was a Frenchman from the Brigade headquarters who was behind him.

A shell landed on the parapet right beside them. It blew the Frenchman's head off and Comrade Black was blown up in the air and landed down on me. He was killed.[100] I had a splinter of the shell entered my back just above my hip and it travelled up my ribs about halfway up my back, fortunately without damaging any vital part. But I bear the scar to this day.

When I was wounded I was carried off in the ambulance to Madrid, where I was put into a hospital. Before we got to Madrid we were taken to a base hospital, I'm not sure exactly where it was. There I was operated on to have the shell splinter removed from my back. The way the operation was carried out was in retrospect really quite amusing. I was laid face down on a hospital operation couch. A very beautiful blonde Spanish girl was put in front of me and she clasped her hands above my head. The surgeons operated without any anaesthetic. They cut from the opening of the wound up to where the piece of shell splinter was. I didn't feel anything with that. It was just like something tugging away. But when they hit the shell splinter I got a twinge of pain. I gave a yell and jumped up and this beautiful girl very quickly banged my head right down on to the pillow. That's why she was standing there with her hands clasped above my head. That was my first close encounter with Spanish womanhood. After that I went into a Madrid hospital for a few days and then I was transferred to one of two hospitals at a place called Castellejo, which had been a villa I believe which belonged to the Spanish royal family before the war. Not far away, across the valley, was another hospital called Villapaz, which was staffed by British and American doctors.

But the doctor we had in the hospital we were in was a Cuban. The nurses were all girls from round a bout. It was quite extraordinary the number of girls there who had features very like those of the Habsburg family who ruled Spain for so many centuries. It was a coincidence of some kind or other!

But apparently when the Republic took over this place they found in the safe a whole lot of very compromising photographs of members of the Spanish royal family. Apparently the ones who lived there were the ones who were not normally permitted to stay in Spain because their lives were so disreputable, and this was the only part of the country they were allowed to stay in. This was the story that we were told anyway by the Spaniards who were in the place.

One of the nurses there was an extremely beautiful Cuban girl who was married to a Cuban International Brigader, and who in fact I believe was commander of the troops that captured Quijorna. Unfortunately he had allowed himself to get surrounded and he escaped but most of his own troops were captured. He suddenly appeared with his car and stayed with us a few days and then he and this girl disappeared. I heard later on that what had happened was that orders had been issued for his arrest and he was in fact on the run.

He told us about his method of dealing with captured enemy troops. He captured quite a lot at Quijorna. What he did was he shot the officers with his own hand. The other ranks were paraded in front of him and they were made to sign a book in front of him. If they couldn't sign, well, they couldn't read and they were put on one side. If they could sign he looked at their hands to see whether they were hands of workers or whether they were hands of people who weren't workers. He put on the one side those whose hands looked as though they were hands of workers. Then he took the other ones, whom he shot.

I heard later on from Nan Green who had been an administrator at a hospital where this man's wife was working as a nurse that he used to come and visit her when he had any leave.[101] Nan said that he was an absolutely first class shot with a pistol. He used to demonstrate his skill to the people at the hospital with playing cards. He would have an ace card fixed on the bole of a tree and from twenty yards away he would hit this unerringly. What happened to him finally I don't know; whether he managed to get away or whether he was finally captured and executed which would no doubt have happened to him if he had been caught, because not only had he put his unit in a position where it was captured but also he had deserted from the front line himself and then was trying to get out of the country.

Although he was a Cuban he had actually come to Spain from New York. One story was that he was a gunman in New York. His skill with the pistol seems to indicate there was every possibility that that was true, because we really did not have much opportunity in Spain to obtain skill with small arms weapons like pistols. They were in very short supply and the ammunition for them was in very short supply too.

The senior officers of the anti–tank battery and the Battalion were issued with pistols which were German Mausers. They had a wooden holster, which could be clipped on to the butt of the pistol and used as a rifle butt. These were first class little weapons but where they came from I don't know, because at that time Germany was not supplying arms to the Republic: they were suppying them to the other side.

When I was convalescing I was sent back to Albacete. Because I spoke a little bit of French and managed to learn a smattering of Spanish I was put in the office at the guard post in the Guardia Nacional barracks, which was the headquarters of the International Brigade's troops in Albacete. It was very interesting there because I met comrades from all over the world.

One day we had a big parade including a number of Italian prisoners who had been caught by Italian International Brigaders during the big defeat of Mussolini's troops earlier on that year at Guadalajara near Madrid. A number of them had decided to join the International Brigade, and they were paraded in front of us all and welcomed into the Brigade by our German commandant.

One of the other men working there was an old Ukrainian who came from America. He taught me Ukrainian songs. It really was a most interesting experience because anybody who was in transit from one unit to another, or from hospital back to his own unit, came through the Guardia National barracks.

There were a number of characters, not exactly like that Cuban, but colourful characters, shall we say, that one came across. One that comes to mind was an American, a very large American, who obviously, if he didn't come out of the Wild West, meant himself to look as if he did. He was in charge of the incoming English-speaking volunteers who arrived at the Guardia Nacional in Albacete before they were sent out to training bases. He had actually been there at the time of my first stay in the place. He had high boots, riding breeches and two pistols in holsters strapped low down on his thighs. Obviously he meant himself to appear as a very tough character, a very tough character indeed. I had no opportunity to test him out because by the time I had been wounded and got back to the Guardia Nacional this man had disappeared. I heard that he not only was tough but also a criminal and he had been involved in racketering in Albacete. He had been caught and shot, so I was told. What his name was I don't know.

He had been involved in racketeering with foodstuffs. Food was scarce for the ordinary people in Spain. The Guardia Nacional was disposing of large quantities of food for the Brigaders who were coming into the place all the time and being posted out to their units.

So there was obviosly scope there for racketeering on quite a large scale. Tobacco was also very scarce indeed and the troops were issued with regular supplies of tobacco. In fact if you were a non-smoker it was very simple to use cigarettes as a means of barter with the populace. I didn't smoke at all. I used to keep my cigarettes for my pals who did smoke. But on occasion I could buy eggs, which were an unheard-of luxury, and I got a blacksmith to make me a tiny little frying pan with three legs on it which I used to carry around with me. Whenever I could buy any eggs I would fry them up in this pan. It helped to improve the quality of living to a certain extent.

When I left the Guardia Nacional at Albacete I was sent up with a new lot of comrades who had come in to the English-speaking part of the training base of the XVth International Brigade to Tarazona de la Mancha. This of course was the home or reputed home of Don Quixote, although nothing was made of that while we were there. Now of course everywhere you go in Spain you see the souvenir shops, you see little statuettes of Don Quixote and Sancho Panza and their steeds.[102] But at that time the Americans had come in force to Spain, and the English were transferred from Madrigueras to Tarazona.

The base in Tarazona was commanded by an American, Major Johnson, who was a very strick disciplinarian. I believe he had been a Regular officer in the United States Army.[103] His main business was to run the training school that was there, as well as supervising the arrangements for the British, American and Canadian volunteers who were there. I was sent to the officers' training school and I was picked out for that by Lieutenant Willie McDougall, who was Major Johnson's adjutant. Willie McDougall was a Glasgow lad. I didn't see him again until I came back to Glasgow where I met up with him again. He worked for many years for a firm of fish merchants – Uncles, I think, was the name of the firm.

The training school was staffed by one or two instructors who were very interesting chaps. The chief instructor was a Russian known as Captain Ramon, which of course was not his real name, as the Russians were not supposed to be in Spain. They were all supposed to be Mexicans. We of course referred to them as the Mexicanskis. Ramon was a great fellow. He was an officer in the Russian army and had been decorated and wounded quite severly during the Revolution. He used to intersperse his lectures with little homilies on how the Soviet Union treated their war heroes. He was very well liked by us. He gave us instruction in Russian rifles and both kinds of machine guns. I was greatly impressed by the tactics that the Russians had developed for action not only against cavalry but against tanks, even though the subject was really academic for ourselves because none of us were likely to be in the armoured units of the Brigade, who were I think principally staffed by Russians and Spaniards. I don't think there were any International Brigaders in the armoured units of the Spanish Republican Army. The defensive tactics for infantry that they used against tanks were to dig themselves into little pits which would just hold one man. They were so dug that even if the tank tracks went right over you were still safe and snug and you could then throw a grenade underneath the tracks of the tank and immobilise it. Or else they could then fire on the rear of the tanks, which generally were not as heavily armoured there as on the front and sides. This tactic eventually led I think to the tactic of putting infantry actually going into action travelling on the tanks – in the Second World – to deal with enemy troops in these little holes in the ground.

It was easy enough, I suppose, to dig these kinds of defences in that particular type of country because the soil was sandy and easy to get down into. He also showed us how, if you were in a tight spot even armed with only a rifle, you could use it very effectively, by quick firing and quick reloading against a group of men who were more or less within arm's length of you.

All the rifles that we had at this school were the most modern Russian rifles. Some of them were even 1937 models and they were absolutely first class. The Russian rifles are balanced to fire with the bayonet on. The Russian bayonet was quite different from the sword type of bayonet used in the British army. It was much longer than the British bayonet and had a chisel point and was I think, as far as I remember, four-sided. But the sides were heavily grooved and it was like an elongated pyramid in shape, coming to a chisel point. In fact however when we got to the British Battalion we found that nobody had any bayonets at all. Most of the rifles that the Battalion were equipped with were very much older and had that very serious defect that I mentioned earlier on.

I was myself never involved in any bayonet attack because we didn't have any bayonets in the Battalion and in any case I was put on a machine gun team because of my knowledge of the Maxim machine gun and of the Diktorov light machine gun. So I never had any experience of hand-to-hand fighting. There was not a great deal of that so far as I know. The nearest that the British Battalion came to that was on the very last day that we were in the front line, after we crossed the Ebro and the International Brigades were being withdrawn and sent back to their own countries. I'll deal with this later on.

It was in Tarazona de la Mancha that I met another character whom I strongly admired and who I heard later on died a real hero's death. He was an American called Melvin Offsink. He was a young Jewish lawyer from New York. He and I struck up a great friendship. But after we left Tarazona, he to go to the Lincoln Washington Battalion and I to the British Battalion, I didn't hear of him again until during the Second World War when I met an American seaman who came to our house in Glasgow and told me of Melvin's fate.[104]

One of the great characters that I met in Spain was a chap called Barney Shields. He came from Glasgow, I believe. He was quite a bit older than most of us – he might have been forty or older – and he had served a long time as a Regular soldier in the British army, mostly in India as they did in those days before the war. He was a great lad for his vino when he couldn't get whisky or brandy, and in fact we couldn't get much whisky in Spain those days. I never even saw a bottle of whisky in Spain until one day when I was in hospital after we were pulled out of the line in the autumn of 1938 and I walked with a friend from a village called Moya, where the hospital was, to a nearby village. This was away up in the wilds of Catalonia. We went into a small bar there and on the back of the bar was a bottle of White Horse whisky. Naturally we offered to buy it from the barman. But he wasn't selling us the whole bottle. It was the only one he had left. However, he did let us have a drink, and of course it was like nectar compared to what we had had to drink otherwise.

Well, anyway, Barney Shields used to have a great fund of stories about the time he was in India. He used to sing a song which went like this:

     Chin gan goo, gooroo, gooroo vachi
     Chin gan goo gooroo vachi goo

And there were a lot of other things to it, too, which we didn't know what they meant but he obviously got a great deal of enjoyment out of singing it. Well, in the village of Mondejar, where we were in training behind the lines after the offensive at Brunete had been stopped, we were preparing to go up eventually, I think, to the Aragon front. Barney Shields was in the Machine Gun Company along with me and he of course was first-rate in his weaponry. But we had to stand guard one night on Battalion headquarters, which were in a house in the square in Mondejar. Barney Shields came on duty and he was as drunk as a lord. Anyway he was put on the middle watch of the night. He was stationed in the hall of the house. Just on to the hall one of the doors led into Wally Tapsell's bedroom. Now Wally Tapsell was the Battalion commissar. One thing about Barney was that he had a dislike for commissars. He was there to fight, he didn't need any commissars to tell him why he needed to fight. A pet aversion of Barney were the high boots that the commissars all wore. Commissars were probably about the most highly paid people in the Battalion. Once they became a commissar they all seemed to go and get themselves these high laced boots which nobody else seemed to wear. Of course as soon as you saw somebody with high laced boots you figured he was a commissar.

Well, Wally Tapsell unguardedly left his boots outside his door, hoping that somebody would come and polish them up for the morning. Now in the middle reaches of the night Barney was feeling that he needed to go to the lavatory. He also knew that he was supposed to stay on duty. However, he saw those boots, and he thought , "Well, this is an ideal opportunity", first of all to relieve himself and also to indicate what he thought of commissars. So he promptly filled up the boots. And of course next morning when Wally Tapsell came to put his feet into the boots he got a very unpleasant surprise. I wasn't there unfortunately to hear what he said but I am sure they were not the kind of things that a commissar ought to say in public.

Later on Barney showed his true calibre when in the retreat from the Aragon – I think it was in Belchite – he got up in the church tower with his machine gun, and although he had been ordered to retreat he refused to do so. The last that was seen of Barney was him firing his gun at the Fascists who were already in the town. We had moved out but Barney refused to go and he stayed at his post. He must just have been shelled or bombed out.

I don't think Barney Shields was a member of any political party. He was just an anti-Fascist. He had come to Spain because I suppose like a lot of Glasgow fellows he was a fighting man and he wanted to get in and have a fight on the right side. I think the fact that he didn't like commissars was an indication of his non-alignment with any particular political party. The commissars were a creation of the Russian Communists and they no doubt had a role to play in Spain. But Barney didn't feel or seem to feel that he needed any political instruction on what he was there to do. He regarded political commissars – I think rather unfairly – as more or less non-combatant busybodies.

There was quite a feeling among certain of the rank and file against commissars, probably because of their privileges. In fact the boots they wore seemed to excite either the envy or the anger of a lot of people, considering that most of us had to wear just any kind of footgear that we could get hold of.

In my personal experience, and from anything I ever heard said by other members of the International Brigade, there was never any personal friction between those members of the Brigade who, like myself, were there out of a sense of political commitment and those who were there maybe for other motives – like Barney Shields, they liked a fight or at any rate possibly weren't so much politically committed. There was no kind of friction of that sort in the Brigade of any great importance, because you can be pretty sure that if anything like that had turned up that there would have been big political meetings and the whole thing would have been thrashed out in public in front of the whole unit. There is no doubt about that. We would have all been put under pressure to see how wrong our ideas were. And I think possibly Barney was a bit unfair to Wally Tapsell, because Wally, like Barney, died a hero's death in the retreat back from the Aragon in the spring of 1938, when the Battalion suddenly found itself alongside Fascist tanks and half the Battalion, on one side of the road, were killed.[105] I was in hospital at that time myself so I wasn't an eye-witness. But I was told by people who were there what had happened. The only person who tried to create any of this sort of friction was an Irishman named Ryan. He was the only person really that I could honestly say deliberately tried to create friction. In my experience there wasn't any real friction at all.

Ryan arrived in Spain just about the time I was in the Guardia Nacional barracks at Albacete. It's difficult to say how he managed to get into Spain. Certainly when I volunteered for Spain I was vetted by my local Communist Party branch. But with such a large organisation I suppose it was really very difficult to keep out people who were criminals and chancers. In fact, one of the guides we had in Paris was a French-Canadian who had actually been in Spain but had turned up at the headquarters in Paris and was acting as a guide to English-speaking comrades around Paris. It turned out later on that this man was a deserter from Spain. He had got to Spain and found the conditions there not to his liking and he had deserted and managed to get back over the Pyrenees. How he was accepted by the Brigade's organisation in Paris as a reliable person I don't know. As for Ryan, he was a bull of a man, a huge fellow. I'm pretty tall myself but he was as tall as me and about twice as wide. A highly amusing character, a big curly haired fellow, a tremendous drinker – his main aim in life seemed to be to make fun of everything that we were doing. Where he came from I don't know because I didn't see him coming into the Guardia Nacional. I dealt with all the English-speaking comrades who came into the Guardia Nacional and he certainly wasn't in the lot with whom I finally went back up the line, a crowd who had come in from Britain.

But anyway he turned out to be a very good machine gunner. He used to boast that he had a brother who was a colonel on the Fascist side. He himself told me that before he came to Spain he was a gigolo in the South of France. He was in our machine gun team that I was detailed to, on the Teruel front. He was sitting up on the wall of the trench one day delousing his shirt. A sniper's bullet from the other side passed through his chest and tore a big flap of flesh away from his shoulder blade. He was extremely annoyed about this because it left a huge scar on his shoulder blade and spoiled his beauty for the ladies on the beaches of the Mediterranean.

But I and one or two others had very strong suspicions that he was not, as we say in Scotland, the clean tattie. We always thought that his purpose was if not to gather information at least to disrupt things as much as he could. He certainly ended up in the digger at one time.[106] He disliked Copeman, the commander of the Battalion at that time – not only disliked him but hated him. And Copeman thoroughly reciprocated. One time when Ryan was up on a charge for being

drunk and disorderly he annoyed Copeman so much that Copeman
jumped over the Orderly Room table and felled him with a blow to
the jaw. I was on guard on the small cell where Ryan was incarcerated
for a while, and all he could do was nurse his jaw and spit oaths at
Copeman. But later on, in the attack across the Ebro in the summer of
1938, he was in charge of one of the machine guns and he was found
guilty of firing on our own men as they were advancing down a valley
and up towards the crest that the enemy were occupying. I myself was
under that fire and we knew that a gun from our own side was firing
on us but we didn't know which one it was. But he was arrested and
charged in the Battalion and he was sent down to Brigade
headquarters, who sent him to Divisional Headquarters. The Divisional headquarters said, "If we send him down to Barcelona for
trial there are lawyers there whose job it is to try and get these fellows
off."So they sent him back to Brigade with instructions to deal with
him locally, and the Brigade sent him back to the Battalion. I heard
that he was shot by George Fletcher and Sam Wild. Sam Wild was the
Battalion commander at the time and George Fletcher was his
adjutant.[107] And yet the man, although he was such a rogue, was an
extremely likeable rogue. He could be extremely amusing, highly
diverting at times.

Ryan was not a member of any organisation at all. He was totally
anarchistic, if you like. He produced a variant of a song which actually
become quite popular. He started it off, you know, in order to take
the mickey out of the International Brigaders. It went like this as far as
I remember:

> YCLers are we
> Brave members of the I.B.
> Machine guns they rattle
> And cannons they roar.
> We rush at the Fascists
> Just screaming for more.
> YCLers are we

. . . and so on. And of course it had the reverse effect I think to what
he intended because it became very popular.

I first came across Ryan when I was going up to the Battalion after
being in the training school for officers in Tarazona. Harold Horne, a
Londoner with whom I had got very friendly, was also being sent up.
We were with a group of young Spaniards at a place called
Tembleque, an overnight staging point on the way up towards the
front. This chap appeared and there was a parade being carried on
inside this small barracks where we were. Ryan was capering about in
between the ranks. How on earth he escaped the attention of the
Spanish officer in charge, I don't know. But anyway both Harold
Horne and I were utterly scandalised at this. At that time we didn't
hold any rank so we couldn't take any effective action against him, but

Harold said to me, he said "That bloke's a bloody Fascist, John." And I said, "I think you're quite right, Harold." And from then on we kept an eye on him. What happened to him finally just confirmed our original suspicions.

Also in Tarazona at the same time there was a Canadian group, and one of them in fact was a man who came from the Vale of Leven in the West of Scotland, who had been working in Canada and had come across to Spain. His name was Jock McGrandle. I didn't meet Jock again after that because he went off to the Canadian Mackenzie-Papineau Battalion while we went up to the British Battalion. But I met him again when we came back from Spain. He had decided to go back to his home in the Vale of Leven.

In the training school in Tarazona I met up with another Edinburgh lad, Jimmy Rutherford, a member of the Young Communist League. Jimmy had been captured by the Fascists at Jarama in February 1937, and after serving several months in jails in Fascist Spain he along with the rest of the British comrades was repatriated to Britain. But they were warned that if they were to come back to fight again in Spain in the International Brigade and were captured they would be executed as soon as they were discovered. Jimmy was one of these lads who came back. Unfortunately Jimmy was captured and although he had come back to Spain under an assumed name he was recognised by Merry del Val, who was the Spanish Ambassador to Great Britain, I believe, and who examined all the British who were captured by Franco. Jimmy was recognised by him and he was taken out and shot. He was a great lad and a great friend of mine.

In Tarazona they had started to incorporate Spanish troops into the International Brigades. I remember having discussions with a number of them. Initially the Spaniards who were attached to the Battalion didn't come from an Anarchist background. We did now get groups of Anarchists because Anarchist battalions were being broken up because of their unsatisfactory record. This is not to decry the individual bravery of the Anarchists. It was just the fact that they were not prepared to accept military discipline, any kind of military discipline, and it was quite a problem to make them understand this.

We did have a few of these in the Spanish machine gun part of the Battalion and later on they would discuss in quite a friendly way with us reasons why they should accept orders. They were decent enough chaps generally speaking, I would say. These chaps at Tarazona actually had been members of Anarchist formations earlier which had been disbanded by the government and then they were conscripted into the Spanish Republican Army by the government and these ones had been sent to the XVth International Brigade. Some of them were being trained as machine gunners and they went up to the Machine Gun Company which I joined when I got up to the British Battalion.

They were very inclined to question the right of anybody to give them orders, because of their Anarchist beliefs. And we had to try and explain carefully to them why it was essential that in military matters anyway the orders had to be obeyed. The other point that they jibbed about was singing *The Internationale*. They said, "Why do we have to sing *The Internationale*? After all *The Internationale* is not a Spanish song. It is not the Anarchist song. It is the international Communist song. Why should we have to sing it?" The short simple answer to that was, "Well, we're in the International Brigade and it happens to be one of the songs of the International Brigade. And that's why we sing it. Apart from that we consider it's the song of the international working class all over the world." But I don't think they were too well convinced about that. Spaniards are a very individualistic people and the Anarchist philosophy was I think very deep within the Spaniards, basically because I think the Spaniards had lived in pretty isolated communities in the countryside with not a great deal of commerce between the various parts. They were very largely self-sufficient communities, certainly in Catalonia. People grew their own food and grew their own wine. The Anarchist philosophy suited very well the Spanish character as well, because although Spain was oppressed by absentee landlords and so on the actual sort of local affairs were run more or less by the local people themselves. I think that was probably the reason for it.

Another of the instructors in the school was a charming little German fellow, who had been a machine gun officer in the First World War in the German army. He described to us the tactics that the German army used. In fact the methods of defence that were used proved to be extremely effective. They had a one-hill defence and a two-hill defence, I remember, by which curtains of fire were laid down by machine guns which were extremely difficult for infantry to penetrate, because of the way the whole field of battle was covered by this curtain of fire from these strategically placed machine guns. He had been an officer, as I say, in the German army during the First World War and had joined the working class movement and had come out to Spain to do his bit. He described also how he had examined defences which had been captured by the Republic from the Fascists. He said that the way these defences were constructed were obviously the work of German army engineers, because he recognised their handiwork.

After a period of training in the training school I then joined a fresh lot of recruits who had come up from Albacete to the British Battalion, among whom was Harold Horne, with whom I became very friendly. The man that Major Johnson selected to be in charge of this unit was a man from Glasgow from the same Communist Party branch that I had been a member of – Garry McCartney.

After a few weeks of training with the new recruits, instructing them on rifle and machine gun weapons and tactics, the whole lot of us moved up to the British Battalion which at that time was stationed somewhere near Madrid in a village called Mondejar. There it was that I first came across characters like Walter Tapsell, the Battalion commissar, and Fred Copeman. That is strictly not true because I remember seeing Fred Copeman during the battle beyond Brunete, when I was in the anti-tank battery. But I got to know Copeman quite well.

When we got up to the Battalion there was another lad there whose first name was Bunny – I can't remember his second name – at least he was known as Bunny to his pals, but he had also been captured with Jimmy Rutherford. Another of the men who were there at the time was Harry Fry, also from Edinburgh, and a member of the Communist Party. Harry Fry was killed in action later on.

It was while we were at Mondejar that a deputation came from the Labour Party to visit the Spanish Republic. They came and visited us in the British Battalion at Mondejar. It was at a torchlit parade in the square of Mondejar that the First Company of the British Battalion was named the Major Attlee Company, after Clement Attlee, who was the leader of the delegation. I can't remember who the other members of the delegation were but I think one of them was Jennie Lee.[108] We had hoped that this deputation of the Labour Party might have had some effect on the British Government. We had hoped that it might have helped to induce the British Government to change their attitude to the rightful legal Republican Government of Spain. But I am afraid from that point of view we couldn't see any results apart from an increased measure of support generally from people in Britain. But unfortunately it didn't persuade the British Conservative government of the day that it should alter its attitude to the Spanish Republican Government. If it had, no doubt the history of the world would have been different today.

From Mondejar we were sent up north to the Aragon, up to a place called Fuentes del Ebro. We'd been expecting to go into action there but we didn't. We were sleeping out in the open air all the time. The winter was approaching and we eventually made a long march, because of the lack of transport, to what were to prove to be our winter quarters in a town called Mas de las Matas, where we spent our time practising manoeuvres in the hills round about.

It was in Mas de las Matas that J.B.S. Haldane, the British scientist, visited us. I didn't have the pleasure of meeting him at the time but some of my pals apparently had quite a long session with him in one of the bars of the town.

The townspeople there were very friendly to us and we would get invited into their houses. I remember one time seeing a pig being slaughtered in the street. The pig was hauled squealing and struggling out into the street. It was forced on to a low table which was only about eighteen inches above the ground. His legs were tied to the legs of the table, and then a girl came forward with a basin. A man with a huge knife slit the pig's throat and the blood gushed forth and the girl collected the pig's blood in this large basin. When the blood had stopped flowing they cut off the head. Then with a hatchet they chopped right down the spine of the pig, and then they opened it out so that the whole of the entrails of the beast were removed and then various people came forward and they were given different parts. Later on I saw one of the women washing out the entrails of the pig in the stream which ran through the village, through the washing place in the village. This was the main source of drinking water for the whole town.

Before the pig was chopped open women came forward with bowls of boiling water which they poured over the beast. The whole carcase was scrubbed spotlessly clean. And then with a sharp knife the bristles of the pig were removed. Eventually it was obvious that every part of the beast was going to be used except the squeal. The blood was used to make meat balls with. I remember going up to a house later on that day; we were invited in and the woman was stirring the pig's blood in a big cauldron over an open fire. She had pounds and pounds of boiled onions which she was mixing into the blood, and rolling it up into balls. She gave us a number of these to eat, freshly made, and they were absolutely delicious. But they would be presumably stored and kept. The hams would be cured. All the houses had wooden beams in the ceilings and there were hooks on these where they hung their ham. And melons, for instance, were hung up in nets in these houses. It was a totally different type of scenario from that in the houses that we were used to in our own country.

I also remember them killing a steer in the street there. The beast was tied up with a lassoo round its horns. Its forelegs were also caught in ropes, with men straining at the ends of these ropes. The beast tried to back away and the men held on, then a man came up behind the beast with a short special kind of dagger and struck it at the base of the skull until he severed the spinal cord. Then the beast was carted away for butchering elsewhere. It was not actually butchered in the street as far as I can recollect.

The town was built on a hillside and there was running through it a stream coming down from the mountains. This stream was used by all the villagers both as a source for water for drinking, for those who didn't have wells in their houses; and it was used to feed the fountains in the village. But for clothes washing there was a common washing place in the village, which was paved on both sides of the stream, where the women washed the clothes and, as I say, where they washed out the intestines of the animals that had been butchered.

From Mas de las Matas we were eventually brought back from reserve towards the front line. We moved down towards Teruel, which had recently been recaptured by Anarchist troops. During the offensive we were placed in strategic positions on an open front. In one place the Machine Gun Company had its guns situated on either side of a wide valley in case of a Fascist attack. At that place the front was completely open. The villages were more or less abandoned and the only screen in front of us were Republican cavalry patrols, who occasionally skirmished with cavalry patrols from the other side. There was no such thing as a continuous front line, as there had been in the First World War. It was only around places like Madrid and so on where lines of trenches and fortifications had been established. In other parts of the country the front was more or less open. But we were continually supervised by enemy planes and subject to enemy attack. By that time it was getting very cold and the land was largely covered with snow and we dug ourselves into our machine gun posts. We dug our own fortified posts with a slit communication trench running from the post to our dug-out. We just waited there for a few days in case an enemy attack came down the valley. There were several miles between us and the next machine gun post. So if we had been attacked we would have been able to perform no more than a holding action until we were overwhelmed.

While we were there, incidentally, up on the open part of the front unfortunately two of our men deserted. They were both Englishmen. I didn't know them personally at all. I don't think either of these lads were members of any particular political party. And certainly the older man had not a very good reputation in his Company. He was a consistent defaulter. He was, you know, not really the kind of type that we would want out there in any case. How he managed to get out there I don't know. Why he went there in the first place I really have no idea. The other was quite a young lad who was influenced by this older man. The older man had suggested that they should try and get across to the other side. He persuaded this young lad to go with him. Unfortunately for them they were caught by a cavalry patrol and they were brought back to Battalion headquarters. They were sent from Battalion headquarters down to Brigade and from there they were sent to Army headquarters. They were tried and convicted of desertion to the enemy. What happened then was there was a big Battalion meeting at which the whole thing was laid bare to us. General Walter, who was one of the principal International Brigade generals and in charge of our part of the army, came and talked to us.[109] It was agreed that these men should be executed. One or two of my friends were selected to go on the firing party. But in fact only the older man of the two was executed. The other lad, I believe, was sent to a labour battalion and I think he died in action some time later on. Needless to say this was not reported at home. They were both mentioned as having died in action, as it was reported in the *Daily Worker,* which would save their families the shame of knowing what these lads had been doing. These were the only two people to the shame of the British Battalion, that I ever heard of deserting to the enemy. No doubt if there were cases of other nationalities they wouldn't be broadcasting it in any case because everyone would be, I suppose, too ashamed about it. The only other person I have already mentioned in this connection was the Irishman Ryan, who had not deserted but had actually used his machine gun to fire on his own men while they were advancing on Hill 481 across the Ebro. I really can't think of anyone else. I can safely say I have never heard of anything else like that. There were one or two others who deserted and got away, who deserted to the rear. I remember two of them. They were great friends and were in fact friends of mine, who did that while we were across the Ebro. They were caught and they were sent back to the Battalion. They were really good blokes and what made them desert to the rear I really don't know. But they were both thoroughly ashamed. Both of them survived, I'm glad to say, our final days in Spain.

On the other hand I met at least two deserters from the Fascist side. There was one man came across from the Fascist side when the anti-tank battery were loosing off at the Fascists on the Jarama front. This man came across one night and he told us about the havoc we were creating in the opposing trenches, largely I think to my credit because I was the observer and pinpointing the places that had to be fired on.

The other time was when I was in hospital after we finally came out of the line, after we were pulled back from the Ebro. I went into hospital with bad sores on my legs. I met a Spaniard in the hospital there who had deserted from the other side. Originally he had been in the Republican forces and had been captured by the Fascists and had been sent to Salamanca, where he was interrogated. He came from a small village but he very craftily said that he came from Madrid and gave his name as the Spanish equivalent of John Smith. He twigged that they might very well have information about his own political activities in his home village. He decided that discretion was the better part of valour in this case. He had no wish to advertise himself. But, as he said, it was significant that those who told the truth about themselves were taken out and executed. Those who were not executed were forced to join the Spanish Fascist troops. He had originally been in a unit with our German-speaking comrades of the International Brigade. When he was sent up the line by the Fascists he heard German being spoken on the other side so he promptly waited for his opportunity to escape in the night and got back to our side. He had been wounded and that is how I came to meet him in hospital.

Round about the time we were on the open front near Teruel, we were being moved about from place to place. One village we went into I remember rejoiced in the name of Pancrudo. It was absolutely bitterly cold. We moved in there late in the evening. The Machine

Gun Company were given a barn to go into. The Barn was absolutely full of *paja*. *Paja* is the name that Spaniards give to straw which has been chopped up. In those days grain was threshed on threshing floors in the countryside. The way it was done was a heavy wooden sledge was dragged round the threshing floor by a donkey or mule and it was driven by a man who was actually standing on the sledge helping to hold it close to the ground with his weight.

Underneath the sledge there were hundreds and hundreds of little bits of quartzite, little quartz chips with sharp cutting edges, forced into the hard wood of the sledge. Then the harvested grain was laid in sheaves on the threshing floor and the donkey was driven round and round this threshing floor until the whole lot of the grain on the threshing floor was cut up into small bits. And of course the ears of the corn were also split up. There were other workers who were waiting to winnow the grain – they had big flat shovels with which they picked up this threshed grain. They threw it up in the air and the wind drifted the short pieces of straw, the *paja,* to one side and the grain fell to the floor. They continued doing this until they had threshed and winnowed all the grain. The *paja* was then used partly as animal feeding stuff and also for use in the dry lavatories that all the peasants had in their houses. We found that this barn was absolutely full of the stuff. What we did was – it was so bitterly cold – we just dug ourselves into this *paja* and covered ourselves right up to the neck. It was the most marvellous warm experience that I really can ever remember. The feeling of comfort was wonderful, in spite of the scratching of the straw which got down your neck and up your sleeves and up your trousers legs and so on. We had a marvellous rest in that place. Then the next day we had to keep indoors in case of enemy air activity. And because they suspected that the enemy might bomb the village the following night we were moved up on to the plain after dark. We had to dig ourselves small sorts of shelters on the plain. We lay down four men to the bed that we prepared for ourselves. We put two blankets down then we just lay down on the blankets close together and covered ourselves with the rest of our blankets. This was something we had done before but in this case the ground was totally covered by about a foot of snow. As we scraped the snow away we found that the ground underneath us was in fact a frozen marsh. So we had to spend the night lying out on the frozen marsh.

Then one day we were taken to a railway tunnel. We moved quite some distance away. We obviously were being moved down towards Teruel. The place we were going to was going to be our next experience of actual front line. We were moved into this place which was a long railway tunnel. In fact it was a series of railway tunnels, going along the side of a steep valley which had a very high hill on one side. The tunnel was dug through the hill. It was an ideal anti-aircraft shelter. There we were allowed to light our fires and so on. We enjoyed ourselves there for a couple of days and nights before moving on to Teruel.

While we were in reserve down this tunnel and round about there, the Republican forces had started an offensive to recapture Teruel. It was in fact recaptured by fairly newly-formed troops who were men who had been conscripted from the Anarchist militias. They were given the honour of attacking and taking Teruel and they did this. But because of their basic lack of military organisation the International Brigades were put in to hold the line against the inevitable Fascist counter-attack, because it was felt that the Anarchists were not sufficiently reliable troops. They were excellent men for attacking but they did not have sufficient appreciation of military discipline to be trusted with the defence of the town.

So eventually we found ourselves on the way to Teruel, still in the dead of winter. The Battalion was put along the line to the north of the town. The Machine Gun Company guns were spread out along the crest of an escarpment which looked down on a wide valley. At the end opposite from Teruel there was a hill, and the valley moved round both sides of the hill. On the far side of the hill the Major Attlee Company, I believe, was down on the plain in a trench. Other companies were up on the heights above that trench. We were placed there to resist counter-attacks round the sides of the small hill. On the other side of the valley there was a smilar escarpment to the one that we were on. We were told that the Fascists were entrenched along there. Occasionally we suffered harassment by fire from there. Particularly in the daytime there was sniper activity from the other side of the valley. But we spent some time there. We were really not in the front line position. We were there as a stopgap to prevent an enemy breakthrough down the two sides of the valley as it came round the hill in the distance. Beyond that there seemed to be a wide plain where the enemy were moving.

Our stay there was notable for one or two experiences. One night the whole sky was lit up in what must have been the Spanish equivalent of the Aurora Borealis. It was the only time I've ever seen this. It really was a most extraordinary experience, quite a wonderful sight to see.

Where our machine gun post was, a heavily fortified sandbagged post right on the edge of a cliff, we had a communication trench going from that, with dug-outs dug down into the landward side of the trench, where we slept. Just outside the dug-out we had cut out a sort of table on which we kept the dixies for our food. I remember there were quite a number of air battles going on while we were there, and I remember Johnny Hall and I – Johnny Hall was No. 1 on the gun and I was No. 2 – were outside in the sunshine, watching the aerial battle coming along.[110] All of a sudden we heard a tearing sound and we both dived for the foot of the trench. There was a tremendous thump and that was the end of it. We got up and we discovered that an unexploded anti-aircraft shell had fallen down right where our two heads had been leaning over this table. It had dug itself right away down into the soil. We dug the thing out and tossed it over the side. I suppose that was one of the narrow escapes I had during my time in Spain.

Later on one of our favourite occupations was picking the nits out of our shirts. It was here that Ryan, the Irishman whom I've mentioned before, was sitting up on the back of the trench in full view of enemy lines across the road and he was busy delousing his shirt when he was the victim of a sniper's bullet which went through his chest and tore a big slice out of the flesh below his shoulder blade on his back.

While we were up there the Major Attlee Company had found itself in a very exposed position in this trench. They suffered quite a number of casulaties, I believe, from enemy action. They discovered they were being fired on both from front and flank. There was enemy machine gun fire going right down along the trench and quite a number of lads were either killed or wounded there.

Later we were moved out of Teruel and it seemed that the Fascist counter-attack had fizzled out. We were withdrawn and moved down south again, beyond the Teruel salient, back to the countryside where we had been. There a number of us were sent off to a hospital at Valdeganga, more or less for a rest. Valdeganga was a delightful oasis and the administrator there was Nan Green, who was very well known and loved by British International Brigaders. She was for years the secretary in London of the International Brigade Association after we came back. She and her husband George were both administrators, hospital administrators. George actually came up to join the Battalion for its last action and very regrettably he died in that last action. Then we were taken away from Valdeganga. Several of us were kept back because of our physical condition and I was among them. We stayed there for two or three weeks. When I was in Valdeganga I was given the job of acting as labourer to two building workers, an Italian called Pablo, an old experienced building trade worker, and his assistant, a young man from a village in the province of Valencia. He told us his experiences in his village when the revolt originally started in 1936. He was a member of the local Popular Front organisation. When the revolt started up all the members of the Popular Front organisation in the village went round the houses of the local landowners in the district. In one of these houses they found lists of people who were to be shot. So he said, "Well, we also found lists of members of the Fascist organisation. So we just went round to all these people and we gathered them together and shot them. We put their bodies down a well." Apparently this is the sort of thing that was going on all over Spain at the time. But this had been sparked off principally by the revolt of the army in Morocco and the assassination of a left-wing Assault Guards officer in Madrid, which led in turn to the murder of Calvo Sotelo, the leader of the right-wing Spanish Monarchist faction.[111]

It was towards the end of winter that we came out of Teruel. Then when we left Valdeganga we were sent up to Barcelona and we just got across in time. By that time there had been a further Fascist counter-attack, which had taken them right through Teruel. They had recaptured Teruel and they had got down near the sea. We went back up north. All the International Brigades had been transferred up north and had actually taken part in actions up there. When we got to Barcelona I was sent up to a hospital called Moya up in the north of Catalonia. From there I came back to Barcelona and went back up to the Battalion again. I arrived and the Battalion were in reserve – well, not really in reserve, they were strung out along the banks of the Ebro, near Mora del Ebro, quite near the place where we eventually recrossed the Ebro. In the interval the International Brigades had experienced the Fascist counter-attack in the Aragon, and Belchite and these other towns had been recaptured and our troops were driven back across the Ebro.

When I got up to the Battalion again after my stay at the hospital in Moya, I was sent out to one of the posts which was commanded by Paddy O'Daire, an Irish comrade.[112] Our job was to man a machine gun post on a spur of a ridge which could cover quite a considerable part of the banks of the Ebro on the other side. The Battalion was spread out along the Ebro in posts. There could possibly have been a mile or more between each of us. But it was necessary to go a very much longer way round to get to any other outposts of the Battalion, because the intervening ravines were filled with very thick bush. We were along there for some considerable time. I remember we went to visit one of the other posts further down, near the Mora del Ebro. We were visited by a senior officer from some other International Brigade. What he was doing there we didn't know. I was a corporal at that time and I insisted that they stay there until we discovered who in fact they actually were. I may say that he wasn't very pleased about it but there were more of us than him there, and for all we knew he could well have been a spy from the other side. Because in fact we were sending lads across at night. John Peet, a friend of mine, had swum across the Ebro on one or two occasions at night to try and spy out enemy positions on the other side.[113]

During the period while we were there there was more or less a cease fire between the two sides. This was enlivened by one of the Spanish lieutenants in the Battalion. There was a footpath which went along the Banks of the Ebro for several miles. Somehow or other he had got hold of a bicycle and he used to ride along this footpath on his bicycle, wearing a black and white striped football shirt and carrying an open umbrella at the same time. He used to shout across to the opposing side and they used to shout back at him. I'm afraid I can't repeat the sort of things that he shouted across. But they used to shout back at us, 'Coños rojos' – which is not a very nice thing. It means a part of the anatomy that one doesn't normally mention in polite company. His patter was almost as good as the Glasgow patter that I used to hear in the Scots Guards later on. Cypriano, as this Spanish lieutenant was named, was really a tremendous lad and a great favourite among the rest of us. His was a very forthright character and if one of the Spaniards, or an International Brigader for that matter, was speaking to him and he couldn't hear him he used to shout at him: "Habla claro, hombre" – in other words you had to speak up and don't be afraid of what you were trying to say to him. He was a great lad. The last time I saw him was after the International Brigades had been disbanded, and I met him at a transit camp on my way from hospital up to the town where the British Battalion had been taken before it was repatriated. Really, when I saw his face I felt the end was near for the Republic. Because this man, who was one of the bravest and gayest (in the old, not the present meaning) of comrades, was really upset. If many of the other Spaniards were feeling the way he did it really made me – and it still makes me – feel very sad to think about what they were having to look forward to. It would hardly have been surprising if he had said to me, 'Well, you're all right, Jack, you're going home. But we don't really have any future. The International Brigades are going away. It doesn't look very good for the rest of us here in Spain."

Now the food we were getting at that time was fairly basic stuff. But there were a lot of *huertas*, as they are called in Spain – small gardens dotted around the slopes of the hills and from which we could gather fresh peas. They were growing a variety of pea there which was the most delicious pea I have ever tasted. We could cut up the whole pod and eat the pod as well as the pea inside it. These were absolutely delicious fried in a little olive oil. We found one of the Spanish comrades one evening – he actually had been living in France for some considerable time before the war started – with a couple of Frenchmen who were attached to the Battalion at that time and who had found a lot of snails. They were roasting the snails over a small fire. I was fairly good at foraging so I used to quite often go round looking for extra things to sweeten our diet. We discovered that the village of Mora del Ebro was completely evacuated. We used to go down there to see if we could find anything. The first time I went down there we discovered that the peasants who ran the local wine co-operative were siphoning out wine from big vats. They told us they were taking it back down to Barcelona. They told us just to help ourselves. Well, we had no way of getting at this wine, except by lowering our mugs on string down into this vat and bringing it up. It was a slow process but we managed to lift out quite a few mugfuls. Then we went further round the village to see if there were any other wine stores and we found one colossal *bodega* with barrel upon barrel stacked one above another. But there was no way we had of getting into the barrels. Some rascal, an American, I think, had managed to get a bayonet into one of the plugs at the bottom and he had pulled the plug out, and of course there must have been hundreds of gallons from this cask just pouring out on to the ground. There was no possibility of getting the bung back in again because it just wouldn't go back – the force of the wine coming out was too strong. We had no hammers or anything. Anyway I managed to save quite a good bit of this wine and I came out of the place and I was really fairly unsteady on my legs. An officer came along from another nationality in the International Brigade and he was going to arrest me. I just had to brazen it out. I told him in my best Spanish that he couldn't arrest me because I didn't belong to his Battalion and I was a soldier belonging to another International Brigade entirely. If I had been one of his own men, well, it would have been all right. He was a little fellow and of course I'm about six foot three. Although he had one of his other men with him he seemed to see the force of my argument, because I wasn't arrested and I managed to totter back up the hills again to the machine gun post with several water bottles filled with the good wine of Mora del Ebro.

In this happy existence, which was really most enjoyable, we were out in the fresh air and we were sleeping under the open sky. The weather was fairly good and we were getting plenty of exercise and plenty of food. We were drawn away from that when we started our training for the next offensive which was in preparation. That was the offensive of going back across the Ebro. Eventually after moving about to various places we landed in a place known to us as Chabola Valley. It was a long valley leading up to a small village. There were high hills on either side. We were placed in a grove of Spanish hazelnut bushes, which were maybe about six, seven or eight feet high, with wide spreading leafy branches. We could make our shelters underneath them and also against the walls of the terraces. We were very comfortable there and we just spent the time training the new recruits who had moved up, instructing them on the machine guns and particularly the Russian light machine gun, the Diktorov. We had a fair amount of free time there and we used to go up to the village, where there was a large water tank in which we were allowed to go swimming. In the hot weather it was very nice indeed. There was a place also close by which never had the sun's rays shining on it, it was so overhung. There was a stream of absolutely ice-cold water coming out of this. It was very pleasant to sit under that in the hot weather.

We discovered that we were not very far away from the Dombrowski Battalion. They were the Poles. We discovered them when we were out on one of our training exercises on a huge hill right behind us. Looking down from the top of that one day we discovered that the Poles were down there. They were very well organised. They had a small canteen by the wayside. So after our duties were finished I and Harold Horne wandered over the hill to them. We discovered that the Poles wre selling bottles of cognac. So from then on until we left this place Harold and I brought back a bottle of cognac a day each which we shared with our comrades. So far as we knew we were the only folk in the Battalion who had twigged this, so we used to spend very convivial evenings.

While we were there we were visited by, among other people, a group of MPs. Haden Guest, I think, was one of the MPs. His son actually was in the Battalion. It was a happy reunion for him and his father.[114] Then also we were visited by Jawaharlal Nehru, who was a great supporter of the Spanish Republican cause. We laid on demonstrations of our fire power for these people.

We were well camouflaged, having all our *chabolas*, as the Spaniards call the type of rough dwelling that we made under the hazelnut bushes. I don't think we were ever troubled at all by enemy aviation during our stay there. Then came the day when we went to a big meeting in a cutting that was being dug for a new road, at which we were addressed by Johnnny Gates, who was the American political commissar of the XVth International Brigade.[115] We were told that we were going to go across the Ebro. That's what our training was for, and that we were aiming to retake Gandesa on the other side of the Ebro.

We moved up there in stages. First of all we went in trucks and then we started marching through the night. I remember one place we were in. We were in the bottom of a *barranco*. A *barranco* was what we would call a corrie in Scotland, with precipitous sides. There we met up with some of our old friends in the American Lincoln–Washington Battalion and had a cheery evening with them. But that night there was a colossal rainstorm, a thunderstorm. Right above my head, on the top of the cliff, the lightning struck and split an olive tree that was up at the top. Fortunately nobody was hurt.

Later on we were moving up one night towards the banks of the Ebro. We were marching in single file along the side of the road. There were two files, one on each side of the road. The file that I was on was on the right hand side of the road and the hill just fell away steeply below us. Two or three men away from me was Eddie Brown, a friend of mine. Eddie was trudging along when an incident happened which, looking back on it, was highly amusing but at the time was not quite so amusing. We had all been kitted out with the maximum amount of ammunition we could carry. We had also been given a number of hand grenades. These should have been hooked on to our belts by the handle. But Eddie didn't think this was necessary.

The grenades were kept from exploding by a split pin with a ring on the end of it. When you pulled out the split pin and let the handle go the spring forced the handle back and pushed the plunger down to start the fuse. Now Eddie had thought it would be a good idea, rather than stick the uncomfortable handles down inside his belt, if he were to put a piece of string through all the rings and tie this string round his waist. Of course what happened was that as Eddie jogged along, with every thud of his foot the split pin got a little jog and the grenade moved further down the split pin. Fortunately Eddie was on the file where the ground was falling away below him. One of the grenades fell off and rolled down the hill a bit and exploded. And then another one fell off and exploded. And another one fell off and exploded. We thought we were under fire. One or two blokes, I think, were winged slightly by splinters from the grenades. But it caused a great flurry and confusion. One odd queer bloke, a Pole who for some reason or other had been sent to our Battalion, rushed off crying for the ambulance men to come and take him away. There was nothing wrong with him but the sudden explosions had been too much for his poor frayed nerves. Anyway Eddie wasn't very popular with one or two of the blokes for a while after that.

Eventually we got down near the Ebro by daylight. The first attack across the Ebro had succeeded and by the time we got down the crossing was in full swing. We came down towards the Ebro through a dry watercourse with thick reed beds alongside of it. We kept in close to the reedbeds because we were under constant attack from one or two enemy aircraft. They were huge silver beasts and they were swooping down and machine-gunning anywhere they thought we might be. I don't think they were in fact bombing. Perhaps they had got rid of all their bombs before reaching us; but certainly they were machine-gunning the watercourse where we were hiding. I was really quite terrified at the time. Some lads seemed quite unconcerned but maybe these were blokes who had not been in action before. Anyway it was quite a wonderful sight to see because this plane looked like a huge silver fish swimming through the air and then spitting fire at us. It was really quite an extraordinary experience.

Not long after that our own anti-aircraft machine gun batteries started up and the planes were driven off. I don't know whether the machine gun batteries that we had for anti-aircraft were Russian-inspired or whether they had been designed in Spain itself. They were basically three machine guns lined up side by side on a gimbal like contraption. They could swing up and down and round to any point of the compass. All three guns were fired at the same time. So it was really quite a fearsome weapon for a plane to face. They had the effect of driving the enemy planes off. We weren't to come up against them until we were well across the Ebro again.

When we eventually got down to the river bed we discovered that there were a whole lot of small boats and they seemed to be organised by American members of the Lincoln–Washington Battalion. They were in charge of the operation at that part. We got across and eventually all the Battalion was across. Then we moved up on to the road and started advancing into what the day before had been enemy territory.

We marched about five paces apart on either side of the road up towards the line where the fighting was going on. Later on that day another Company of the Battalion obviously had been in action and they had managed to capture a whole lot of Moorish troops. We met them marching back along the road in columns of four led by one or two of our lads. The Moors all seemed to be very happy about the situation. Certainly if they had wanted to break away they could quite easily have done so because there were only two or three of our men guarding them.

Later on we came actually under fire ourselves from the left flank and some of our Company were detailed off to attack against whoever was firing. It turned out they were just two Moorish youngsters who had holed themselves up in a little hut built against a bank, and one of the lads went up on the roof above them and threw a grenade in through the door. When we went back we had a look in this hut and there were two youngsters. They can't have been more than about sixteen, I think. They were both quite dead. The two Moors had been cut off and had opened fire. Actually they had wounded a Cypriot comrade, Michael Economides, the political commissar of our Company, quite badly in the arm.

The rest of us moved further over to see if there was any other opposition to be met in the country round about. The country was hilly there and we were moving along one side of a ridge. Some of us moved up to the top of the ridge, when we were fired on from a parallel ridge. Unfortunately a man whose name I don't know but who was known to the rest of us as Yorkie was shot, a victim of mistaken identity. We were being fired on by a unit of the Listers and it wasn't until we had produced our Republican flag and waved it that the supposed enemies stopped firing and raised their own flag. Each Company had been given a large Spanish Republican banner to carry into attack because of the fact that the Ebro was being crossed on a broad front and there was the obvious danger of firing on our own troops. And this in fact was what had happened. The Listers were a Spanish Communist formation given the name of the man who actually founded them, their leader, Lister. Another famous Republican unit were the Campesinos, who were led by El Campesino. It was just unfortunate that we had not been showing our flag quickly enough to prevent them firing on us. So then we went back to the road and continued our advance up the road, until we came eventually to a position which we knew as Hill 481. It was the last line of hills before we reached Gandesa. There we spent the first couple of days attacking this hill with very little success and losing a lot of men. It was during an early attack on Hill 481 that we were being fired on by one of our own guns, in the hands of the Irishman Ryan.

It was there that Clive was killed. Clive was, I believe, the last male descendant of Clive of India. He was directing the fire of one of my mates against an enemy strong point. By this time the Fascists were well entrenched on this hill and we did take over part of it during the night but we were chased off it again by bombs exploding all around us. Apparently the whole place had been seeded with booby traps and they had fortifications dug into the ground and very well camouflaged and concealed, much better than we had had on the other side. I think possibly with better training and more experience we probably could have taken this ridge.

I can't remember how many days we spent on the opposing hillside. We had to keep down below the skyline during the day. We were attacking across the valley and up the hill on the other side. Their position was very well defended and our attacks were continually being broken up not so much by the fire that they were raining on us but the whole place was littered with grenades and trip wires in the undergrowth. I remember one occasion like that when these explosions started up I threw myself on the ground and I was lifted bodily by the explosion of a grenade just a few feet in front of my nose. I was extremely lucky that I got no other damage apart from some scratches to my legs and ankles. It really was a hellish place to be. I think that was just about the time when I really felt the lowest in all my life. I can't remember a time when I really felt so low.

The weather was good, very good. But this was part of the trouble. The weather was so hot that we were at the mercy of the sun by day. There were a few small scrubby pine trees dotted about the hill on which we were. It was a problem just to try and keep in the shade of these little umbrella pines during the day. We got no food at all during the day because all the food came up last thing at night and first thing before dawn. If the mules carrying our food from the kitchen had been seen moving around during the day we wouldn't have had any mules. We wouldn't have had any food at all because they would have been destroyed by air attack. Air attack was fairly intensive on us round about there. It meant that we got a meal after darkness had fallen. We got a plate of thick soup and a plate of thin soup. It was all made from lentils at that time, which I believe are extremely nourishing. We got one loaf of bread each per day and we had to keep the bread to last us through the hours of daylight. We got a plate of thick soup and a plate of thin soup last thing at night and for our breakfast, the same thing again, a plate of thick soup and a plate of thin soup.

At that time up there at Hill 481 we had no fruit at all. Later on when we were pulled out of there and put back in reserve we were put into a grove which was quite near a village on the Ebro. There was fruit in this grove, largely I think it was fairly unripe but we stripped that fruit. Then George Wheeler and I went down to the gardens in the village and we found fruit trees there with pears. I am afraid we stripped them and brought back haversacks full of them to the Company. We gorged ourselves on those, only to suffer later that night with terrible stomach pains.

There too we found a chicken run that still had some chickens in it. In the grove where we were resting there was a small hut with a couple of old women and an old man in there. We were not able to kill chickens, we weren't experienced at that sort of thing. We brought this chicken up to these old women. They were civilians who had not been, you know, cleared out of the battle zone. We gave it to them, for which they were very grateful.

While we were on Hill 481 we could see in the distance over to our left a huge massif of hills called Sierra Pandols. It was obvious that there was a tremendous fight going on there too. In fact there was a lot of aerial bombardment on the crests of these hills. One night all the brushwood went up in flames. It was a kind of heathery growth on the top of these hills that was set on fire and they burned for several days. We were watching that and thanking our lucky stars that we weren't up there. Little did we know that we were going to go up there!

Losses in the International Brigade in Spain were often very high, but I certainly never came up against any feeling that the Brigade was being used too much for shock troop purposes, and used up too quickly. I think we were all too concerned with defeating Franco. There were individuals who didn't want to go back up and some who got off their marks. But we talked about these blokes who'd done this and if they were ever caught and brought back to the Battalion they were extremely shamefaced individuals, and quite upset about it. As far as being ready to go back into the line, I mean in Spain it was the experience in the International Brigade of people deserting to go back to the front, people who had been in hospital and so on were deserting to go back to the front. This was the main sort of attitude. Whether it developed among any of the officials in charge of the Brigades I don't know but I should think it would be extremely unlikely, knowing the people who were involved, certainly in the British Battalion and among the Americans.

After a spell in reserve we were on the move again. It was then we discovered that we were in fact moving up on to Sierra Pandols. It was a hellish place because by the time we got up there there was nothing but blackened twigs of this heathery plant and just cracked stones. It was a very steep escarpment, the strata had been tilted very steeply. We were ranged along the edge of the escarpment and then up at the top the escarpment turned into a ridge which went off towards the enemy. We discovered that a stone wall had been built up there for protection, because there was no possibility of digging trenches. It was just stone. There were one or two dug-outs further down the slope where some of us spent the night. We had the experience of sitting in these dug-outs and being continually shelled. Because of the steepness of the slope it was very difficult for the enemy artillery to actually fire directly on us. I remember sitting in this dug-out watching the shells just sailing down through the air more or less sort of parallel with the slope and gradually losing altitude and on landing either exploding or tumbling. In one instance we were in the dug-out when one of these shells actually rolled right down into the dug-out – fortunately for us it did not explode. It was there that poor Frank Procter got very badly wounded from rock splinters or a shell explosion, which hit him round the base of the skull and he died before he got into hospital. Frank Procter was one of the original anti-tank men and a well-liked bloke. He was decorated in the earlier campaign. He had been I think one of the gun commanders at one time. A great bloke from Liverpool.

Taffy Evans was killed there too. A mortar shell came over and landed right beside him. He didn't like being in the enclosed space of the kind of trench made up of stones on either side, and he had gone to the back of the trench. The mortar shell actually landed there right beside him and killed him.[116]

We were mostly in defence up there, but one night we made a disastrous night attack. We really didn't know what we were going up against because it was practically impossible to lift your head up to see what there was during the day time because the enemy fire was so intense on us. We made this disastrous night attack and we were driven back. I remember there was a Battalion meeting later on about that at which Sam Wild was not very complimentary to us. And it was there that I saw how effective the enemy anti-aircraft batteries were. They seemed to have an artillery predictor which could lay a barrage of explosive shells high up in the air in front of any plane that tried to get through. I watched one of our planes trying to get through this barrage and everywhere it went it was followed by extremely accurate fire and eventually the pilot could not get through. He was running out of petrol and had to come back to our lines. At that time the British army had no predictor as efficient as that and presumably it must have been German equipment the Fascists were using. I remember after coming back from Spain going on a visit to an army demonstration just prior to the 1939-45 war, on anti-aircraft in the Waverley Market in Edinburgh where they were showing the predictor. I believe it was not very good at all.

So far as the efficiency of the enemy troops was concerned, the only Moors that I came across were those that we captured on the Ebro, and the small group whom we killed. On the front at Jarama where we were the general impression was that the fellows on the other side wanted as little trouble as possible, because a battle would maybe start up at night but nobody came across and the only people who came across from the other side were a few deserters. At Brunete it was different. I think again at Brunete they had the edge over us. But the large mass, I think, of the Spanish army on the other side were not particularly supporters of Franco. They went into the army because they had to go into the army and they deserted when they could do it. Most of the regular Spanish army officers were in fact on his side from the start, you know, and this is where they had the advantage over us, apart from the fact that they had far more material than we had. I think probably in matters of actual military tactics and so on in Spain we lacked trained officers. I think that's true to say that. For instance, the night attack that we made on the Sierra Pandos was an absolute disaster and it was just because we didn't know what the devil we were supposed to be doing. There wasn't you know, a sufficient preparation for the thing beforehand. Well, this experience was similar to one prior to that when we were trying to take a crest at Hill 481 at night and were driven off it because we were unable to see the enemy. You know, the bombs started exploding all around us and it was a most bewildering experience, I can tell you. I was wearing Spanish *alpargatas* and I lost them on this night occasion, and this was when sores started on my feet because I got back to our lines without any footwear at all. And it was the cuts that I had developed from that that finally developed into festering sores that lasted for a long time after I came home.

Eventually we were pulled off the Sierra Pandols and we were sent to another part of the Ebro front, where we were in reserve for a while. It was there that Tommy McGuire and I received our commendations and we were both promoted to the rank of sergeant. Tommy McGuire joined the British Paratroopers in the Second World War and was killed. Funnily enough later on I met an American paratrooper in a pub in Edinburgh who had met Tommy McGuire. I mentioned that I had been in the International Brigade and he thought the International Brigade were the tops and he had met Tommy McGuire. They thought a tremendous lot of him. Tommy McGuire was a great lad, a very courageous, pugnacious young lad from Paisley. It was a great loss indeed that he was killed like so many others in the last war.

It was while we were there that we got some new weapons, Czech weapons. A boatload of of Czech weapons apparently had arrived in Barcelona. Tommy McGuire and I had a light machine gun which was a Czech one, previously we had had Russian weapons but these were Czech. And then we were being attacked by some enemy planes, and Tommy shot this one down. We saw the pilot baling out. He was captured by somebody else. But we went over to the plane and we discovered that the actual ammunition clips on the gun on the plane were exactly the same ammunition clips that we had been using to shoot the thing down. We never got credited for shooting it down. The Americans claimed that they had shot it down. Then we were moved about to various places in reserve in olive groves there, but each time we were under attack from the air. We weren't left in peace very much of the time. We made another attack to take back a small hill that had been captured. We captured it and we were moved back again. Then we got some new reinforcements up, who were relics of an Anarchist group and they were extremely rank-and-file fellows. We already had enough of them, Anarchists in the Spanish Company that was attached to the Battalion. We had to explain to these fellows why they should accept discipline, which to an Anarchist – at least to the Anarchists we met – was a very difficult proposition to understand.

Unfortunately we had been put up overnight on to a hill which had defences already prepared for us by the engineers. But the defences were prepared on the wrong side of the hill. They were prepared on the forward slope of the hill, in full view of the enemy. They should have been prepared on the reverse side of the hill, so that the enemy would have had to come at us over the crest, and where also we would have been immune from machine gun and tank fire. That in fact was the downfall of the Company, because on the very last day that we were in, not long after daylight I was in position on the right flank of the Company and we were strung round this hill in trenches, some of which were only two or three feet deep. They had not been dug nearly deep enough. We had very little cover indeed. It was only myself and another man on the right who managed to get away. Johnny Power and one or two others of the comrades, including some young Spaniards, got away on the left flank of the Company when we were attacked.[117] We were attacked by airplanes, by bombing. A large part of the hill was fairly sandy and dusty and it was very dry and dusty and with the smoke of the bombs and dust and grit that was flying around our visibility was very seriously impaired. And it was only when it had cleared that we discovered that the enemy were advancing up the hill over a brow below us. They had advanced to the foot of the hill in completely dead ground that we couldn't see. They had advanced round to our right, in between us and the nearest Company of the Battalion, which was a Spanish Company commanded by Felix Sais, and they were just moving down on the backs of these poor chaps who were strung in a sort of half moon battery position on a lower slope of the hill. They were just coming down on top of them from the rear. There was nothing we could do about it.

The grit from the atmosphere had filled up the locks of our rifles and I got away three shots before my rifle jammed and even hitting the bolt with a stone I couldn't open it again for re-firing. So I told the blokes. I said, "Get out and down the back of the hill as quickly as you can." But only one of them took the opportunity and by that time we were having grenades thrown at us. So I thought, "Well, I can either stay here and just be captured or killed or I can try and get back to the Battalion and tell them what is happening." I stood up and got out of the trench and was immediately the target for grenades and was hit in the shoulder by one and I stepped over another when it was sizzling at my feet and got down the hill. By the time I had got down to the foot of the hill and was going up the other side of the hill I was being shot at. And our Machine Gun Company were on the brow of the hill behind us. I was absolutely drained of all energy when I was halfway up the hill towards their position. I thought, "Well, I'm not going to get there unless I try a trick." I deliberately waited till the nearest burst of fire came just at my feet, just a second or two after I had made the decision. As soon as that happened I threw myself on the ground and lay there as if I had been hit and killed. After about a quarter of an hour there was no more firing at me and I got up and trotted up to the top of the hill before they started firing at me again. I got back to find the Machine Gun Company just being pulled out. I thought that the whole of the Company had been captured but it turned out that later on when remnants of the Battalion got back together Johnny Power had got away. He was praising up to the skies a young Spaniard who had managed to hold off the enemy with a machine gun. They were on the left flank of the Company and the enemy had not come up in front of them. They were moving along from where they had captured most of the rest of the Company. This young Spaniard had held them off with a machine gun and they managed to get away in short rushes back, firing. But it was their machine gun that had saved them. I didn't tell Johnny Power that this same young Spaniard had come up to me not more than a couple of hours beforehand and told me in confidence – he was a conscript, he wasn't a volunteer. "This is no life for me," he said, "I'm going to get off my mark, and I am going to get away across the frontier as soon as I can." It seemed to me a not untypical example of the kind of bravery that people had when emergency struck, and yet in calmer moments they feel absolutely terrified. What happened to this boy eventually I don't know because we were withdrawn from the line.

One of the bravest men I ever saw was Malcolm Dunbar, who walked about under fire without any compunction at all. He got himself wounded as a result of that. He got shot right through the neck, shortly after I was wounded in the anti-tank battery. There were one or two individuals who were absolutely of outstanding bravery. I always feel that anyone who is not scared must have something lacking in him, you know. He can't be human if he's not scared.

What was left of the Battalion pulled out of the line and we were met by other troops coming up, advancing. We got back to the

Brigade headquarters in dribs and drabs. Then we were taken back down to a village on the other side of the Ebro. We were reformed and I was sent off to hospital with bad sores on my legs which had developed during the past few months out in the country. Then after coming out of hospital I went up to a demobilisation centre in the Pyrenees, from where we finally came home at the end of 1938. Altogether I was in Spain nineteen months.

We felt when we got back that Britain had been watching Spanish affairs with interest, that we were being welcomed back as heroes. We had a tremendous reception in London and again in Glasgow. We had a civic reception in Glasgow, and then we had a much smaller reception for the Edinburgh lads who came back. There weren't so many of the Edinburgh lads left who came back at that time. But I was amazed by the number of friends of mine who I thought wouldn't be at all interested who thought I had done a wonderful thing and were very complimentary to me. I felt rather embarrassed at the sort of respect and adulation that many of us received from enthusiasts because after all we'd only done what millions of people had done before in war. But I was impressed in this way by the number of people who had taken an interest in the War in Spain and saw the significance of it for Europe and the world.

Nan Green playing accordion, her husband George the 'cello. The violinist is a German International Brigader, and the two others Spanish. Somewhere in Spain during the Civil War.

The variety of steel helmets worn by Republican troops [see John Dunlop's comments, above p.134], is illustrated in this photograph which includes Roderick MacFarquhar at top left.

John Londragan was born in 1911 in Aberdeen and brought up there. Before he went to Spain he worked on the railways. During the Second World War he served for six years with the Royal Artillery and reached the rank of sergeant. After the War he returned to work on the railways until his retirement. He still lives in Aberdeen.

JOHN LONDRAGAN

There was a tremendous anti-Fascist feeling in Aberdeen, as there was throughout the whole country. And when the Spanish Civil War broke out in July 1936, we thought it was just going to be precisely that – a Spanish Civil War. But later on, round about December when tales were coming back about the intervention by Hitler and Mussolini in Spain, it ceased to be a Spanish Civil War as we understood it. It was now a war of intervention on their part. And we thought that if we were going to be anti-Fascist in the real sense of the word it was our job to try and help as far as we possibly could. Because at that particular time, round about the end of 1936, the Spanish Republican forces, or what there was of them, were being pushed back and there was a danger that the government could possibly collapse. So committees were formed throughout the country to recruit anybody for Spain. Of course a number of volunteers already had gone over to Spain. They were disorganised in the sense that they were going over individually. There was nothing co-ordinated about it at all. So between December 1936 and February of 1937 committees were set up. With my interest in those committees, and being a member of the Communist Party and being an anti-Fascist I thought it was my duty to go and help the people in Spain. And the fight, whether it be here in Aberdeen against the British Union of Fascists or against Hitler and Mussolini in Spain, was exactly the same fight to me, no difference at all. So as a member of the Communist Party I applied to go to Spain.

And it was in the spring of that year, 1937, that I got word in Aberdeen here that if I wanted to go to Spain I could go down to Glasgow. There was a committee down there who would see me to decide whether I was fit to go to Spain. To my delight I found that Bob Cooney, who was the organiser of the North East Communist Party here in Aberdeen was going too. He had applied too. So both of us went down to Glasgow. But when we arrived at Glasgow poor Bob was turned back because his political duties here in Aberdeen were so great that they couldn't afford to let him leave at that particular time. He was really heartbroken.

So I waved goodbye to Bob and I proceeded, along with another three comrades I picked up in Glasgow, down to London. We went in front of a committee there. There was no medical examination or anything like that, but they had a look at us to see that we looked healthy enough. And they asked us our convictions, our reasons why we wanted to go. They told us, "We don't want adventurers. We want people who are really anti-Fascist, who really want to play a part in the fight against Fascism in Spain." For myself, I had no problems as a member of the Communist Party. They knew exactly where I stood and I passed all right – no trouble at all.

So we stayed in London for about two nights, waiting for word when we were to go. Anyhow word came that we had to congregate at a certain place and that we would be met by a member of the Committee that was sending us over. They gave us tickets for a week-end to Paris. They used to call them 'dirty week-end tickets'. You didn't need a passport or anything at that particular time for a weekend to Paris. Now there was a group of about fourteen of us. There were a few English, some Scots, a couple of Welshmen. We arrived in France then in Paris. We were told to make our way to the trade union headquarters in Paris. We weren't exactly sure where it was. We searched about and we couldn't find the place. We got a little cafe, and I says, "Sit down there, the lot of you." We were too conspicuous because there was a lot of feeling in France for and against what was happening in Spain. We had been told to watch ourselves and not make ourselves too conspicuous. So the others sat down at the cafe and I went on my own. I was searching round one street when I noticed a figure across the road from me and recognised her right away: it was Charlotte Haldane, Professor J.B.S. Haldane's wife. She was our contact but she'd missed us too. So we collected the remainder of the group and proceeded to the trade union headquarters there.

We stayed in Paris for about three days. There were about 300 volunteers there at that particular time. We were boarded out in the different side streets all round about where the headquarters were. And there were groups leaving and groups arriving. Our sixteen went down by train to Lyons. We were met there by a committee member. From Lyons they organised motor cars which took us down to the border.

At this time the border was closed and our only hope to get into Spain was to go over the Pyrenees. So we were handed over to a Spanish guide at the bottom of the Pyrenees. We had about three or four hundred yards to travel before we started climbing into the low foothills. We had to go very, very quietly. Some of our group actually took their shoes off to cross a small narrow bridge to get into the foothills because of the French gendarmes on patrol in the area. Then we started climbing. We were young and we were fit and we didn't have any trouble. Our climb started about six o'clock in the evening and went on until about five o'clock in the following morning. We climbed all the time, with a couple of rests only. The climbing wasn't too difficult but it was very hard work going.

I always remember the sun coming up as we came over the last mountain. Down in the plain below was a white farmyard, the reception centre for all the Brigaders coming over. We got a cup of coffee and something to eat. We left there about ten o'clock in the morning by bus and were taken to Figueras, an old Napoleonic fortress. The time we arrived there it must have been about twelve o'clock and the heat was coming down, it was really warm. Coming from the north we were unaccustomed to this tremendous heat. We arrived in a big square in front of the fortress, and the entry to the fort was through a big cavern. And the moment you went inside the cavern it was as cool as could be.

There were straw palliasses all laid out for us to sleep on. So we got something to eat, then we paraded along with other recruits. There must have been about two or three hundred volunteers there. There were Germans and French and all different nationalities. And there was one captain from Czechoslovakia in charge of organising the volunteers. He could speak every language, I think, under the sun. He went up there on the rostrum to address us. We were all set up in groups – British, Germans, Italians, French. He addressed every group in their own language, telling them what was going to happen next and so forth. In 1928 before I joined the Communist Party, I joined the Territorials as a pal of mine was in the Territorials at the time. And I was in the Territorials until I came out in 1930. As a matter of fact I was a year short of the time I was supposed to stay in the Territorials but I packed it up in 1930. This was just one of the things that the young people used to do in these days, you know.

The Czech captain asked for anybody who had military experience. So I put up my hand. "OK," he said, "you're in charge of the British contingent. Parade them properly. Stand at ease, to attention, and march a few steps." The next day they organised transport to take us down to the International Brigade base at Albacete.

We went by bus down to Barcelona first. There was an air raid on at the time. It was our first intimation of war.

When I came back from Spain I was giving a lecture on air raid precautions and I was asked to tell them something about what bombardment meant to the towns in Spain. And they couldn't understand why it had been necessary to have air raid shelters and things like that, "Because they don't bomb civilians." And I was trying to explain to them that they *do* bomb civilians. War had changed from 1914-18.

In Albacete we were met by the secretary of the South Wales Miners' Federation, Bill Paynter.[118] He was in charge of the organisational side of the International Brigade, the British contingents in Spain. We were formed up in the Bull Ring in Albacete. At this time the International Brigade consisted of five Brigades. There was the XIth, XIIth, XIIIth, XIVth and XVth. The reason for the XVth was to get all the English-speaking people together because they were mixed through the other four Brigades. They were the last Brigade to be formed. All the English-speaking people – this included all the British, the Americans, Canadians, Cubans, Mexicans (they were counted as part of America) made up the XVth International Brigade. So we were allocated to the XVth International Brigade and most of them went into the Battalions. The Americans went to the Lincoln Battalion and the George Washington Battalion; then there was the Mackenzie-Papineau Canadian Battalion, and the British Battalion as another separate unit.

But a group of us, practically all the crowd of sixteen that I came over with personally, with another half-a-dozen or so added to it, were taken away and constituted as an Anti-Tank Unit. This was the first Anti-Tank Unit that had been formed in Spain.

The guns were Russian. But unfortunately their sights and everything were in continental measures, millimetres and so forth, and we didn't know a damn thing about this. So the first thing we had to do was to start conversion, you know, try and convert it down to inches and feet and so forth, something we could understand. It was quite a problem for us for a while. But we managed it at the finish. We hadn't even received the guns at this time, it was only recognised as a unit. And we were sent down to Madrigueras, the training village. There we were met by Lieutenant Malcolm Dunbar, who became the commander of the anti-tank battery until, later on, he was promoted Chief of Staff for the XVth Brigade.

Dunbar was a Scot. He was a University man, a very, very nice fellow. His only military experience was in the Officers' Training Corps in the university. There were very few people in Spain who had previous military experience, very few. A number of them had been in the navy, but I mean you don't call that military experience being in the navy. Very few had fought in actual warfare with the exception of the Germans and a number of the Balkan people.

After a lot of instruction we finally got our anti-tank guns. We practiced on them and went up to one of the ranges. I was No. 1 on my gun and we'd fired and hit the target. It was very pleasing that we'd hit the target about six or seven hundred yards away. Actually the guns could hit a target about five miles away but six or seven hundred yards was quite good for us at that time.

After we'd finished we pulled the guns out. And there was an oldish fellow, stout built, with breeches and a sort of wind-cheater jacket, a beret on his head and the two thick bars of the lieutenant-colonel on his beret. He came over to us, speaking sort of broken English, and an officer from the British Battalion said: "Do you know who this is?" And we said, "No." He says, "This is André Marty, the French revolutionary." André Marty was in charge of the administration of the International Brigades n Madrid, but we didn't know who he was at that particular time.

Anyhow we finished our gun practice and we lay up at one of the villages outside Alabacete for about a week. Then we got instructions to proceed to the Jarama front. So away we goes to the Jarama front. And the Jarama front it was a terrible front, in the sense that it was olive groves and there had been tremendous battles there from January, February into March, you know. And it left its mark on the hillside. There were tunnels, there were trenches, there were shell holes, bomb holes, all over the place. It was just like 1914–18 War landscape.

Jarama is just south-east of Madrid and was acting as a pincer towards Franco's right, to try and stop him from capturing University City in Madrid. We were in Jarama, oh, about a fortnight and we had different missions. One of the big weaknesses we had at that particular time was lack of communication with different units on our left and right. You weren't very sure where the unit was, and if the unit was there whether they were still there the next day. Communication was one of the weaknesses we had at the start, until they were built up later on. So we were reconnoitering round about our own lines to try and get in contact with the different units on our left and right and stay in contact with them.

But the fortnight we had there we spent most of our time taking pot shots at strong points and things like that. The anti-tank gun was very good for dealing with machine gun nests. We could spot them and we used to put up dummies to try and draw their fire and find out where their strong points were, keep an eye on them and wait till a very quiet moment and then let go. Their quiet moment was when we were going to be busy.

One or two skirmishes took place, but they were farther along the line there and we weren't personally involved. But they kept us on our toes. One thing in particular I always remember was one of these thunderstorms. You don't see them in this country. There sheet lightning came down just like that, at night. Total blackness, you just can't see a thing in front of your face, then all at once there is the rumbling of thunder and the sheet lightning starts, you know. And if you had let your imagination take over you could see every tank and enemy advancing towards you. It wasn't long after that that a runner from Battalion headquarters came up and said that I was wanted down below. When we got to the bottom of the hill there was a delegation there – Harry Pollitt, Willie Gallacher, Bill Rust and a few other notable politicians from the British scene, and a number of Spanish politicians.[119] They wanted to have a look round the front. Well, it wasn't my job to do that so I took them back to the anti-tank headquarters and Lieutenant Malcolm Dunbar, the battery commander, took over from me. I wondered at the time why they had come up to the anti-tank unit. Of course I didn't know they were over there because the first Republican offensive was being planned at Brunete and they were over to see everybody before the offensive took place.

So it must have been about two days later that we were withdrawn from Jarama. We spent about four days reorganising ourselves, getting our equipment up to scratch and everything, supplies, the whole thing, collecting trucks. And then word came through we were on the move. This was to Brunete.

So off we went. We arrived at the starting point, where the offensive was going to start, about six o'clock in the morning. And I always remember seeing the British Battalion. It went out first in a flanking movement to one of the villages – I forget the name of it now. The village was captured after about ten hours' fighting. We were used to try and cut out snipers from the church bell tower. It had been used as a lookout post.

Then the Battalion moved off to do their own thing, and we in anti-tank were allocated other duties as we were at the beck and call of all the different battalions who could require us. So we moved off to cover different points along the front. We did the job until we came to the big stumbling block – Mosquito Ridge, just outside Brunete itself. Mosquito Ridge was a very high hill with a commanding view all round it and also commanded the supply road down which our stuff was coming from Madrid. We had to get the Fascists off there otherwise it would mean that if the road was cut we'd be cut off. So after about a couple of weeks fighting round there and attacking different positions and so on, the armaments that we had just weren't good enough against the type of defence that was being mounted on Mosquito Ridge. The result was we had to withdraw to stronger positions to shorten our lines and to get our supplies up intact, without being interfered with by the bombing and the artillery shelling that was going on behind Mosquito Ridge. At this point Malcolm Dunbar was on top of a small hill and saw the Fascists coming over in front of us on the lower level. We canted the guns to try and get at them. Malcolm Dunbar was trying to see exactly where they were when he got wounded. He got a bullet richt through his neck. Luckly it was all right at the finish, but this was our commander gone. We had only one gun in action at this time. The other two were out of action. So we had to pull back and try and reorganise ourselves again.

It was at this point that I got wounded in the leg and the arm. This finished my career as regards the anti-tank. From there they carted me off. We were laid out in a field and the ambulance was a converted van. There were two stretcher cases on either side and I was laid along the aisle, the bottom, which saved me in a way. They bumped across a field on to the main road to take us down to the hospital on the outskirts of Madrid. But the ambulance went off the road and as it went down the embankment it turned over on its side and the people in the sides were crushed. Two of them were dead – I don't know what happened to the other two. I was bruised a bit but other than that I was very, very lucky.

But we finally arrived at the hospital in Madrid. Nobody spoke any English. So you just showed them your wounds and they treated you. They took bits of metal out of you. Then they passed you over to another ambulance to take you down to an English-speaking hospital. As a matter of fact it was an American hospital I was passed down to. So that was the finish of me as being actively involved in the War in Spain.

Later on, when I came out of hospital, I went back to Albacete and assisted Bill Paynter on the organisational side of the Brigade, getting recruits up and that sort of thing. As a matter of fact, there weren't many recruits coming in at the time because there was no need for them. The Spanish Republican army at this time had been built up to a great strength. The one thing that was lacking was armaments. We just didn't have enough armaments, artillery, and particularly aircraft. These were the things which were really missing and really defeated the Spanish Republic at the finish.

So I did my job along with Bill Paynter helping out there until we got recall orders – I think it was in August '38 – to go back to Barcelona. So I proceeded to Barcelona. Bill Paynter went away north to consult with the Battalion about what was happening. But this was the initial order for the withdrawal of the International Brigades from Spain. So I stayed in Barcelona until I received orders to leave. And then all those that were ineffective, including myself, were put off first. So we left Spain at the end of August, I think it was, in 1938. I had been there altogether about a year and a half. When we arrived at Dover we were met by Foreign Office officials and they checked off our names because we had left the country without passports. The Foreign Office officials looked very stern – "Your train's up there." But we didn't bother with that. We just laughed at them, sang our songs and up on to the train and away we went to London. We got a tremendous reception in London and then I came back to Aberdeen – I remember it was a Sunday morning – and I got a tremendous reception because I was the first of the Aberdeen boys to come back.

When we had first arrived in Spain we never had many contacts with the civilian population, because it was such a hurried process of getting organised and into the International Brigade. Even once we were formed into our units we didn't see much of the Spanish people, other than at a distance. It wasn't until after I was wounded and living in the hospital and visiting villages that I got to know the Spanish people a lot better. They were very, very kindly, very helpful. Obviously they had a different culture from my own. There was no animosity. I never heard a word raised against anybody that was in the International Brigade at all.

We would come into the village from the hospital at night and go into one of the little bars they had there and have a drink. And people used to invite us into their homes. I used to be particularly tickled because this was coming on to the winter of 1937-38 and was very cold, just south of Madrid. And they used to take us into their homes and I was always very tickled to see the type of house that they had. The heating was peculiar. There was a circular table with a very heavy damask curtain all round it and about two inches off the floor. Everybody sat round about and it was very, very warm. And I only found out later there was a brazier below the table.

The people were very, very nice. They used to invite us along to concerts. Now and again, being a small village, they were very dependent on the farming community surrounding the village. Once or twice the people on the outside would come back into the village with a pig or something like that. I don't think I saw any cattle at all in Spain, as a matter of fact. There might have been but I never saw any. It was usually pigs that we saw, you know. And they would come in with a pig and kill it and then invite us all to come along and sit down and have a meal with them in the big square. And they had this tremendous social thing about them. It was much like we used to have maybe in the early 1920s, a tremendous sociability between families living in the same blocks. Everybody knew everybody else's business. Well, it was much the same there. All the people used to come together when they ate. They wouldn't go and sit in their little house by themselves. There was this sociability and they used to bring us in with it an' a', you know. Oh, there were no complaints as regards that. The Spanish people, we accepted them and they certainly accepted us, there was no doubt about that, they really did.

The only people I could say might have been a little bit wishy-washy as regards the International Brigade – and it wasn't because of the individuals that we were, but because of the significance of the International Brigade – was a certain section of people in Catalonia who were Anarchists. Catalonia was very nationalistic. They wanted their own independence from Spain and they would do anything to get it. There actually was an incident that took place in Barcelona, in which the Anarchist headquarters had to be raided by the Government troops to bring better order to the province. The Spanish Government – and this is hearsay – had given an order to the military command in Catalonia that the Aragon front had to come alive again to try to take the pressure off the people in Madrid. And they refused to do it, because they said it wasn't their fight. They'd only defend their own border. This was in early 1937. So these sort of things were overcome later on. But this is the sort of thing that happened. And the International Brigade when we used to go through

Catalonian country we always had to watch out for ourselves because we didn't know how we were going to be received at that particular time by the people.

But nothing ever come of it as far as I knew, nothing ever come of it at all. A number of Spaniards served with us in the anti-tank unit. As a matter of fact at the finish of the conflict it was all Spaniards that were in the anti-tank unit because the British were being withdrawn either through wounds or being killed or the fact that the unit was being withdrawn altogether. We got on very well with the Spaniards. They were very childlike. I don't use the word in an insulting way. They were childlike in their innocence and they were very nice to get on with, they'd do anything for you. There's a tale going about, and I quite believe it's true, that in Jarama the Spaniards who used to help the British Battalion used to go back home at night time. They used to leave the line and go back home to their houses and then come back up again in the morning. That was the sort of childishness they had. They had never been involved in war before and had known nothing about it at all. And this was how they treated it, until such time as the central Government had got things organised properly to get a Spanish army organised to take over from the International Brigades and so forth. But we had no trouble with them at all, the Spanish, not a bit of trouble.

As regards the other nationalities we come across, the Germans and all the others, there was a tremendous camaraderie between us, you know. There really was. To be an International Brigader was really something, you know, it was really something.

There were Spaniards came from the enemy side. They were captured, and quite a number of them joined the Republican army. I'm not saying they all did. But quite a number of them joined the Republican army. Of course in most cases they were conscripted into Franco's army in the first place.

Because we were an anti-tank unit it was very difficult to get to close quarters with the enemy as such. You just didn't do it. There was no hand-to-hand fighting. We were fighting certainly at times very close but not so close that you could make out their faces. The only ones that I really met were on the road going up to Brunete, and most of them were either wounded or dead. There were Moors and there were Italians. I never saw any Germans. They were there certainly but they might have been on another part of the front from where we were.

There was bombing of course. They bombed all the time. JU88s were specifically the plane they were using more than anything else, the JU88s.[120] They came over bombing regularly.

So I never had any close conact with the enemy as such other than seeing them dead or wounded. But our job wasn't prisoners, our job was the anti-tank and we were switched from sector to sector to do our job and that. We weren't involved in anything like that.

As for atrocities there could have been atrocities for all I know, possibly on both sides, I don't know. But how can you tell after the event? You can't tell, you have to be there and be an eyewitness. So I can't honestly say that I saw atrocities or anything. I actually never saw any at all myself.

At Jarama the casualties were quite severe, the main reason being of course the poor armaments that they had at that time, because these were the early battles. They were using about four, five different types of rifle and mixed ammunition – sometimes the wrong ammunition with the wrong gun. This was going on and it wasn't until Brunete that the casualty figures started to decrease quite a bit because the organisation of the army was getting better, the organisation of the International Brigade was getting better.

But there were very heavy battles took place later on at Belchite, Quinto and the Ebro. And they took their toll of the Battalion to such an extent that of the 2,300 International Brigaders who went from this country – from Britain – over 500 were killed and 1,200 were injured or wounded. And those were very, very high losses for such a small unit as that.

The official figure was eighteen went from Aberdeen and there were some others possibly had gone from Aberdeen but they didn't give their home address as being Aberdeen so we can't trace these very well. Out of eighteen that went six were killed. And this in itself, a third, is a very high proportion. As a matter of fact it is higher than anything in the rest of the country. There were about four that I know of who were wounded out of that group. One was taken prisoner at Quinto and he died in prison.

All the time I was in Spain I maintained contact with home in Aberdeen very little. All I ever sent was one Christmas card in the winter of 1937. You were sort of living from day to day, concentrating on what you were doing and with your friends round about you. Home seemed far away, you know, you didn't think about it at all. At least I never thought about it at all. It wasn't in my mind. I always remember one night in Brunete. It was the only time my home came back to me, and that was at Brunete. And there was a lovely moon shining. And in Spain moons, like the sun, were far bigger than the ones we see here, you know, a different part of the world when you're looking at it. It was a tremendous moon. I always remember it because when I was at home and used to be coming home about two or three o'clock in the morning after political debates with my friends, I always remember having to look up at a place known as Sinclair Street and walking down, the moon was in front of you. Watching the moon just sort of struck my mind. I always remember that one night in Brunete. This was the nearest I ever got to thinking about home. I was too involved

About the climate in Spain there were two things: the intense heat and the intense cold, depending where you were. For example, down in the plains, round about Albacete and Madrigueras, and all these different places down on the plains the heat was fantastic. It was terrific. It took a lot out of you until you got acclimatised. When we went to Brunete we were right on top of the hill in the anti-tank unit. It was quite warm through the day but at night-time the cold was so intense that even in the little holes you dug for yourself, the blanket you put on was stiff as a board before night was through. I often wonder, looking back, how I survived the cold never mind the War. I was only too glad in a way after I was wounded to come back to hospital down to the plains. You could lap up the heat, but the cold was a dry cold, a frosty cold, it was really terrible.

As regards eating there is a bean they have in Spain like a pork bean. Everybody eats this – at least I assume everybody eats it because that's all I ever got. The only meat we ever got was either mule or horse, mostly mule. There was no fresh meat. I never saw any cows at all in Spain. Maybe the parts of the country where we were there were no cattle. But most of our meat was concentrated on these beans and the mule meat or horse meat as the case may be. We lived on this continually. The only variation we ever got was in the morning. We got a cup of coffee. Coffee was something unusual. We were always accustomed to tea. Well, I didn't go in for wine. I did taste it but it tasted to me like vinegar.

There is one other thing as regards food. They must serve the right food for the climate that you're in because most of the food you got was very greasy, with olive oil in it. And while I was a little sickened with it at the start I acquired a taste for it, and I must say that all the time I was in Spain, other than when I was wounded, I never had an unhealthy day. I felt as healthy as can be, very fit.

Looking back fifty years, there isn't a thing changed since 1936 as regards my views and even as regards historically, what has happened. Fascism is still the same the world over irrespective of how you try and disguise it. I was an anti-Fascist for many years. I went to Spain because I was an anti-Fascist. When I went to Spain I thought I was trying to halt Hitler and Mussolini and their exploitation of Europe. We didn't succeed. Spain was defeated. So we went to war in 1939. I went through the Second World War doing exactly the same job I went to Spain to do. There was absolutely no difference at all. It was an anti-Fascist war. Both were anti-Fascist wars. And looking back fifty years I would do exactly the same again.

It might be a little bit puzzling to say that I'd do exactly the same again because there is a selfishness attached to it. I came out of it. There were a lot of my friends, a lot of my comrades didn't come out of it. They're dead. And to be able to say, you know, that we shouldn't have had it and they'd be alive, is one thing. But the other alternative is somebody had to make a sacrifice. It might have been me. But it wasn't. It was them. But nevertheless I still stick by it. That was the only thing we could do. There is only one way to fight Fascism and that was to defeat it either in Spain or in the Second World War. And I would do exactly the same again if I had energy and ability to do it.

John Londragan (left) and a fellow International Brigader with the two young daughters of a Spanish family they befriended.

Bill Cranston was born in 1911, became an apprentice plater in Leith shipyards but was paid off before completing his apprenticeship and during his occasional spells of employment thereafter worked as a chimney sweep before he went to fight in Spain. During the 1939-45 War he served for five years in the British army in Egypt. After the War he worked for fifteen years as a miner in Newcraighall pit near Edinburgh.

BILL CRANSTON

I belonged to Edinburgh. I met the wife and her brother Donald
Renton. I went out with him two or three times during the week as
well as with my wife, maybe dancing with her pals, and that. And
Donald and I got friendly, pally wi' one another. I used tae go to the
Mound and there we had a' the meetings – they'd go on a' night from
Saturday night tae Sunday morning, they were still arguin' and
discussin' and a' that. Donald would speak on the Mound. Donald
was a member of the Communist Party. And we had talks on various
things, and what was right and what was wrong, and Donald got into
different situations and a' the rest o' it, and finally I got word that he
had gone to Spain.

Donald went to Spain when the war was on two or three month.
Oh, well, no word from him or anything like that, only in the press
that he had been taken prisoner. And it would be about a month after
that that I, along wi' Jimmy Arthur, we decided that we would go as
well. Jimmy actually was an agent for the *Daily Worker*. He collected
the papers and delivered them in Edinburgh. And he wis the coolest
person you ever met in your life. He didn't talk much or nothin'. It
disnae matter what happened Jimmy was jist unconcerned aboot it,
you know – no worries, where other people were scatterin' in half a
panic and all that. I'd like to meet Jimmy again. He was a good friend
o' mine before we went to Spain. He palled about wi' me now and
again.

I didn't belong to any political party at the time I went to Spain and
since I come back I have never been in any party. The only one ah
belong to was the miners' union when I worked in the pits, when ah
come back and ah worked in the pits. And there was only the Union
that I went by. I use my own discretion.

I was anti-Fascist. I felt strongly about that. I had experience of the
Fascists in Edinburgh before I went to Spain. The Fascists had the
Usher Hall and I was there wi' Donald, my mum and dad was there,
and there was a big labourer with us too, Finlay Graham. While the
meeting was on the Fascists recognised Donald. A lot of them were up
from Newcastle in buses and that, and they recognised Donald. And
they laid in at Donald, up in the gallery o' the Usher Hall. And Finlay
Graham, a lad that was pretty to the Left, if it hadnae been for him

Donald would have been over the gallery. Big Finlay got between Donald and them, and Donald in a corner, and he kept them from gettin' a grip o' Donald. But they managed to get Donald pulled out and chucked out into the street.

Anything I didn't like was the Blackshirts, the Fascists here. Because before ye went tae Spain ye were readin' o' the treatment the Jews were gettin' in London and a' the rest o' it, and all over, doesnae matter where they were. There was always a battle. In fact in Edinburgh when there were a busload, up frae Newcastle, it was a fight a' the way for them to get out o' the town again. Their bus got smashed and a' the rest o' it. That's how the people felt then and that was no war on. The only war was between the Fascists and us.

When the Spanish War came, oh, I felt that this was a chance to go there and have a right fight wi' them instead o' getting twelve to one and gettin' hammerins and beatins as they went on wi' some o' them. In fact, in Portobello, there was a businessman there – I cannae mind what kind o' shop he had now – but he had a hatred o' Donald, and Donald had two or three hammerins off him, and this is what it was – because of different ideas. We thought he was a Fascist but ye never saw him goin' about wearing a blackshirt. I was never beaten up myself by Fascists in Edinburgh. I was a good runner! No, Donald got the hammerins, I never got touched. But I mean Donald was a public speaker and all that. They widnae ken who I was, ye know.

As I say, I was married to Donald's sister Isa. And, oh, she was all in agreement with me going to Spain.

Donald was in Spain quite a while before ever I got there. In fact during the time I was going there Donald was gettin' released from prison in exchange for a big shot in the Spanish army. It was an exchange. But he got out on the condition that he would not return to Spain. Well, it so happened that two of his friends, Jimmy Rutherford and Harold Fry, of Newhaven and Edinburgh, they were released. But they went back and Jimmy was executed by the Franco regime. And Fry he was right unfortunate. He was killed the very last day before we were due tae come home. It was the last offensive, ye could say, an' he was killed in that. Harold Fry was a postman and he stayed down Easter Road way.[121] Jimmy Rutherford belonged Newhaven. In fact I worked beside Jimmy's dad, he was a riveter wi' Ramage & Ferguson.[122] But Jimmy and Harold, I didnae agree with them goin' back. They knew when they were goin' back if they got caught they were gettin' shot. So that was the two o' them that returned to Spain that didn't come back home. There were quite a few lads from Edinburgh went to Spain.

Donald and I must ha' passed one another when I was going to Spain and he was comin' back home. Later on when I asked Donald how he went, and he explained how he had gone. It was similar to my experience. We went down to London and we went to the *Daily*

Worker paper. We got tae the Communist Party. So we were told tae go tae such and such a station. Well, we went to the station and there were two or three gathered there. So we were told that there was a boy and he had a white rose in his lapel, and we were told just to follow him. So we done the Newhaven to Dieppe crossing. We got off the boat there and went on to Paris and we followed him. And we were instructed, "He'll stand outside the Co-operative shop and he'll gaze up at the window. He'll stand there for two or three minutes and when he moves youse go forward and right intae the Co-operative." So when he moved we goes into the Co-operative and we were ta'en right down tae the cellars. And we were gettin' glasses o' beer and French soft bread, we were in there for, och, about a week. They were fetchin' in food tae us, and then we got word tae get ready and jump in taxis as they come up. The taxis came. We were a' four or five tae the taxi. And the next one wid follow on. Well, the worst experience I ever had was travellin' in the taxis! They were mad. I thought we werenae gonnae get there across Paris. Well, we were ta'en in these taxis and we were a' gettin' dropped off at different places. We wondered where they were takin' us and here efter they dropped us off we discovered we were in brothels. But it might ha' been it was the only place they could hide us and nae chance o' catchin' us there, or something like that. Only one or two women still there. It wisnae what I'd heard that they were in flat after flat and a' that. Ye'd be in one room wi' maybe another two lads or that. Ye werenae in wi' a woman. Ye were in wi' a couple of lads and then another two or three o' ye all over the building, ye ken. It was a big place, big, oh. Ah wid never ha' dreamt o' gaun in it. It was only to keep us in hiding because we'd been in hiding all the road, and they had to get us somewhere. So they put us in the brothels! We were there just a night. We were away, we were away in the mornin', the whole lot.

Mrs. Charlotte Haldane, the wife of Professor Haldane, was lecturin' us and she says, "Oh, ye'll get pox. Ye'll get VD if you interfere wi' any o' these girls. Stay away from them." I was amused. Ah says, "I never heard a woman talk like that in my life, never."

From Paris we went to Perpignan. We got the train. We were intae this yard and a big bus was in it and we slept in the bus. Well, seemingly we couldn't talk loud. We had to whisper to one another. Seemingly Perpignan was a strong Fascist place, you know. A lot of Fascists there. So we were told to keep our voices down. Well, we were about four or five days there when we were told to get ready for midnight. And we got ready and it was taxis we got there. And they took us to the foot of the Pyrenees. And then we got out and we had to start walkin'. Pitch black. But the guides were there. And the guides took us right over. Now there was one part – we hadnae done that very far – when a' ye got was a hand comin' oot and the hand gie'd ye a sandwich or somethin' like that. An' it was twelve o'clock at night and we arrived at seven o'clock in the mornin'.

Roughly there would be about forty of us crossed the Pyrenees. There was one fellow, Glaser, he was a Jew. And he carried a boy for about three mile at the finish o' the goin' over the Pyrenees. He carried this boy. And the poor guy Glaser he got killed hisself later on at the front. Just a stray shot, too. He was just standin' talkin' when a bullet hit him. There was nae action or anything.[123] The person he carried had just fallen by the wayside and he just picked him up. That was one thing, ah says, "Well, I could never ha' done it, never in my life." I was bad enough doin' the Pyrenees!

We landed in Figueras. We were there for, och, two or three weeks before we moved on. A' we were training wi' was broom handles. Ye know, I hardly seen a rifle in Spain. There wis very few, ken. Ah says, "That's great. Doin' drill and supposed to be firin' a rifle." It was a broom handle. So that's what we had there.

But fae Figueras they got us sorted out, and there was about twenty o' us were ta'en away and here we went tae form the Anti-Tank Unit. And here we got the guns, four guns. And tae be truthful, the hammer and sickle was on them, Russian. And the instructions were, "If anything happens, grab the sights, take the sights off them."

Madrigueras was the name of the wee village where we were. But it was there that Malcolm Dunbar joined us. And I don't know, I had it in my head that Malcolm Dunbar was a son o' Lord and Lady Dunbar. Whether that was right or not, I don't know. But he was a great lad. In fact, I was surprised when I heard about him. When he come home and the War broke out in 1939 he was sent tae the Navy – and he was the Chief o' Operations o' the XVth Brigade, he was the Chief o' Operations and they flung him in the Navy![124] And he died right enough, a good while after the War. I heard some talk that he had maybe committed suicide or something like that. But at Madrigueras nae training there – nae training. Well, we went oot two or three times wi' the guns and firin' intae the hills, ken, practisin'. But nane o' us had a rifle, nothin'. Ye had nae cartridges, nothin'. There was a shortage o' them. The men at the front line were gettin' them. If anything had happened ye had nothin' to fight back wi', bar the gun was there, the anti-tank gun. But when ye were handlin' it they wid smother ye before ye got a chance to do anything!

From Madrigueras we went up tae the Jarama. The Battle of Jarama was finished before we got there, it was a' finished and cleared up. I was in the trenches, in fact, walkin' round them. And here there was a crowd, four or five of them standin'. I didnae know whether they were Moors or what they were. But I carried on. I didnae want tae turn and go back. And here it was Dunbar that wis badly and they sent me to go down to the hospital and fetch up stuff for him. He hadnae been wounded, it was some trouble he had. And while I was up there I was just following about, walking about when I come to where wee

Billy Mason had died. He was an Edinburgh lad. He belonged the West End wey, West End o' Edinburgh, he belonged there. But he was another good wee lad in the Communist Party or the National Unemployed Workers' Movement. I think most of them were in the N.U.W.M. Wee Billy Mason was buried there on the Jarama. No' a gravestone, just a wee cross, and just that he was Billy Mason.[125] And he had a bad death, tae, according to Donald. He was lying burning a' the time. It was somethin' that had got over him. And nane of them could get him off. He just had to lie there until he died.

But they run up against Moors there an' a'. The Moors, well, Donald – and I agreed wi' him – he says that had Spain gave independence to the Moors the Moors would have been on their side. Where Franco he was a big shot in the army and he had the grip o' a' the Moors. That's how they were in the battle. The Republican government made a mistake in not giving home rule to the Moors, then they would ha' been at their back, they would ha' been at the back o' the Spanish people. But the way it turned out Franco more or less had a grip over them a'.

I caught only a glimpse of one Moor. That was the time I went up tae wee Billy's grave. I got a glimpse o' one but I think he had come over tae this side. He was dressed like a Moor anyway, ken, the big white gallabears on and a' that.[126] He mightnae ha' been, he might ha' been a priest, or something like that. But that's the nearest I seen tae a Moor. Oh, they were dangerous buggers them.

Aboot the first offensive we got into actually was Brunete. The first one that got killed wi' us was big Fraser Crombie. We had just placed the guns on a ridge and I couldnae see anybody, we had just placed the guns, and here frae this direction a shell went right over the top o' the gun and hit him. And he was the first casualty, big Fraser. There were only two or three of our crowd, the Anti-Tank crowd, were killed. I wouldnae say there were many o' them.

In the Anti-Tank I think there were only about three that were foreigners. We had Welshmen and Scotsmen and Englishmen. Ye could say there would be about thirty in the Anti-Tank. There were a few of them from Dundee, Arthur Nicoll and his brother and one or two others.[127] There was Miles Tomalin, an English lad. He was a great lad. He kept us goin' wi' the flute thing, ken, one o' yon trumpets. Aw, he was good. He used tae entertain us an' that.

Once we got too far in front o' the line. We were the front line. We had went tae the wrong place. And here we had the guns up in position and here there were nane o' our ain men in front o' us. And here Malcolm Dunbar he was standin' and he had the glasses and he was lookin and he says, "Here they're comin'." The Fascists were makin' the attack. And Dunbar opened up wi' guns on tae them. And they were runnin', runnin'. They were runnin' back because they were gettin' somethin' that they never expected. But Malcolm

Dunbar in fact he got wounded after that. We went over the hill and stayed at the other side and we were sittin' there and Dunbar was talkin' tae us. He was standin' up, and we jist heard the pssstt and the next he was spitting blood oot and down he went. It went in there and oot there, the back o' his windpipe. He was a lucky man. And he was back in aboot three weeks. He was a great man, a good man, aye, an officer, a gentleman, oh, a gentleman. He was a very quiet man. Jist spoke now and again. He wisnae haughty nor nothin' like that. It was jist his style, you know.

I knew Sam Wild. Oh, Sam was a great guy. A comedian, a right comedian. I met Jock Cunningham here in Edinburgh. Jock was just leavin' Spain when I come. Mind the Jarama, he done a good job at Jarama. I knew him efter I came back because he wis home before us. Donald Renton and him were great friends and if he was in Scotland they used to come through for Donald's mother's plate of soup, she made great soup. He stayed mostly down in England.

Fred Copeman was there. I knew Copeman was in a mutiny, the Invergordon Mutiny. He was a good man but I didnae like the way he spoke tae ye – swearin'! I sweer, but if there was a prize – ken, he was so-and-so-so-and-so. I said, "What the devil's this?"

Ye ken this, it was a pleasure wi' the officers, ken, nae bull nor nothin' like that and address them as 'sir' and a' that. That's why when ah go anywhere and I always have now, if I'm passin' a man I'll say, "Aye, sir. Aye, sir." And I made that a habit o' mine. When I was in the army ah says, "If I'm saying 'sir' to them them I'm saying 'sir' to everybody." So even the sergeants, I just used to say 'sir'. In the International Brigade ye were all equal. Maybe one in a position of political commissar, but ye didnae salute him or nothin'. Ye could gie him a salute if ye wanted tae, if ye didnae he didnae pull ye up or anything like that. Ye just carried on. Oh, it was different from the British army in regard tae discipline and everything like that. Ye didnae get marched up on a charge o' bein' drunk or nothin' like that. Ye got a talkin' to, ye had a political commissar there. Tom Murray just spoke away to them nae bother.

Naebody in our unit was sent home for bein' indisciplined. I thought one was a deserter – Winters was his name. And he was No. 1 gunner on the anti-tank gun. And I don't know what happened, but a while efter – nae Winters, ken, I never seen Winters. And it got into my head, "Oh, he's maybe deserted." Now I just thought that and it was only when I was readin' the International Brigade book, here his name was in the list o' killed. Well, I never knew he had got killed. I thought he had just, ken, ta'en a powder. But I didnae say anythin' tae any o' them. It wis only when I read it I says, "And I've been thinking that boy was a deserter," you know.[128]

I was lucky not to be wounded in Spain. I must have been too wee, smaller target! But I did have an attack of dysentery. I think it was something in the swimming water. I was in swimmin' in a pool. Well, somebody telt us, "Ye'd better watch," ken, in the water and that. And the next day it wis big Dunlop took us to the hospital and it wis dysentery that I had right enough. And it wis a job, too. Ye couldnae go tae the toilet. Ye had to go across the road tae get tae the toilets. Sometimes ye had tae stop in amongst the garden 'cause ye couldnae go any further. But I was pretty bad, ken, I was right ill. But it's the only trouble I had.

The last big battle I remember was the Battle of the Ebro in 1938. We were held at the Ebro, we couldn't get across. But we built the bridges across and we got into a place, where we were billeted. But when we crossed the Ebro it was something great. It was a feat, ken. And we were doin' well enough but as I imagined nae plant goin' over for us, nae ammunition, ken, everything was held up. No reserves, no nothin'. They were left to go over, Americans and Australians and a' that. They got over. I think quite a few o' them were lost there because it was jist comin' up tae, they were gettin' tae a standstill. There were no reserves and supplies gettin' across after the advance because the Fascists were bombin' it. They had the planes. We didn't, we didn't. We only had two or three wee fighters, Russian, Chatos. Well, maybe more than that. But regards the material it was nothin', it was only a handful compared tae what they had. They had everything – tanks, every damned thing. I remember once the aircraft bombin' me and George Murray. On this occasion George and I were sittin' in a field and George all of a sudden says, "What's this comin' over?" There were planes comin' over. And he says, "Up and run! Follow me!" And we run across the road intae a field on the other side o' the road and we kept runnin'. The next thing the bombs hit at our back, tae this spot where we had been sittin'. And I don't know yet – I never seen anythin'. He says, "I seen the bombs leavin the plane." Ah says, "Well, I watched them and I've never seen the bombs leavin'." But he was right enough, aye. If we hadnae run some o' us would hae got it. Ah says, "Aw, thank goodness for that!" So that's one thing I had to thank George for.

There was one time I felt really afraid in Spain. It was the time when an officer, Jack Black, and a boy frae Prestonpans, Bill Dickson, were killed. We were lyin' in a slit trench. Ah wis sleepin' at the top end and they two were at the other end and I woke up wi' a bang, and "Oh, what's that?" And I went away tae sleep again. And when I woke up here Dickson and Black were lyin' dead at the other end of the trench, I'd say, och, about twenty feet or thirty feet away from iz. The two o' them were lyin' dead. Shrapnel had just penetrated and if I had been down beside them I would ha' got it an' a', but I was up the other end. Just as usual the wee man was away! So that was Bill, he belonged Prestonpans. I was afraid then when I seen what happened. And Black he was a rare lad, a good lad. They were a' good lads.[129]

There was one day one o' the guns was, well, something happened tae it and we ta'en it tae this big castle. Here it wis the armoury, where they repaired everything. And when we took the gun there for the armoury tae get sorted, we saw another anti-tank gun lyin' there. Oh, Greeks it was, that had it. So we had been up and collected the gun and then we went back again. We says, "There's a gun up there." And we jist went up and says, "Anti-Tank." "Anti-tank?" "Aye, gun, aye." Ken. "Take the gun away." So here the gun was missed. The Greeks, when they went tae get the gun, they had nae gun there. We had it. So here the Russian big shots, they're gaun round about. It wis the only time we seen them. And the gun that we had took we had covered it all up, camouflage. Here they come and they hunted a' round about. Then they found the gun, number on it and that! Right, they admired us. Ken, they appreciated what we'd done. Because it proved that anybody could have went into that castle and got the gun. And Arthur Nicoll was one o' them and Otto, oh, he come frae Holland or somewhere like that. But they never done anything to us as long as they got the gun.

I was in Spain for about eighteen month. During that time the wife was able to write to me in Spain. Oh, the wife could write as many letters as she liked. But I wasnae a writer myself! But she had to manage. I think she got ten shillings a week from the funds the time I was away. It was the funds they had collected, the Party and that collected. It was the Communist Party that actually gied her ten shillings a week. Well, ye ken how much ten shillings is now! I wasnae able to send the wife any money from Spain. We hardly seen the paymaster. A lot of people thought you got paid for it. Well, it worked out at £1. But ye couldnae spend it, you couldnae buy fags. There were nae cigarettes, there was nothin' to buy. Ye couldnae go away to a place for a day or a weekend or that. Ye only got paid when ye found the paymaster. That's it. So the wife had to live on ten shillings a week till I got back home again.

When the International Brigade was withdrawn from Spain I took part in the big final march in Barcelona. Oh, I couldnae explain it. I was wantin' tae cry. We went marchin' doon and the reception we got from the people – women and everything, a' kissin' and huggin' us and all the rest o' it. It's a thing I'll never forget, never.

But oh, we were glad tae be goin' home, naturally, it was a natural thing. And it was just a matter o' gettin' into a train and drivin' on through France. We got to the Dieppe-Newhaven crossing, then we got the reception when we got into the station in London. Donald Renton was workin' in and organisin' in London. He was in some job in London wi' the Party. And he met me when we come off along the platform. Oh, a huge crowd, a big reception we got. We got clothed out and everything. I finished up wi' two suits!

We went on to Glasgow first in buses. But we come by train from

Glasgow to Edinburgh. We got a reception in Glasgow and we got a
big reception in Edinburgh as well. Right down Leith Street to the
Picardy Place Hall. We had the meeting there, ken, all in there, and the
crowd – they didn't all get in. But it was a good reception, a good
reception. And then we went home for our meal, doon tae ma
mother's.

I don't have any regrets about going to Spain. No, no regrets at all.
No regrets at all. I would go back again if I was in the same position. I
think the cause was a worthwhile one. Yes, I do. I do believe it was for
the good because the fact that what we were tellin' them came true
when Hitler started the Second World War. He proved that we were
right in what we said. So it's obvious there is nae argument in it.

*Bill Cranston in Spain (front left), with Tom Jones (back row, extreme right), and Miles
Tomalin (back row left).*

Hugh Sloan was born in 1912 in the miners' 'raws' at Denbeath, Fife, and apart from his time in Spain and a short period in Dundee (when the imposition of the Means Test forced him to live away from his family), he has lived in Fife all his life. He worked as a miner before he went to Spain and after he came back until his colliery, the Michael at East Wemyss, was closed in the later 1960s by a disastrous fire, and he found a job as a school janitor until his retirement a decade ago.

HUGH SLOAN

I remember the outbreak of the Spanish Civil War very well. Ye see, I was politically active in the '30s. The menace of Nazi Germany was beginning to arise. Japan made an act of aggression against Manchuria. Then in 1933, with the coming to power of Hitler and his aggressive intentions in Europe the British and the French governments began to show signs of operating an Appeasement policy, which I regarded as a treacherous policy. So I was concerned with what was happening in Europe.

In 1936, when Franco revolted against the democratically elected Republican Government in Spain, it was like an inspiration to youngsters like me all over the world. I was twenty-three then, in July 1936.

Early in 1937 I decided to go and fight in Spain. I was politically active and I thought over this question quite a lot. I firmly came to the conclusion that it was the logical development of my political ideas and my reaction to what was happening in Spain. I cannae think of any other reason than that.

I had become politically active in the trade union movement and wi' trade union political leaders in the late 1920s. They were members of the Communist Party. At seventeen, I was too young to be a member of the Communist Party but because there was no Young Communist League in these days in the Methil area the political activists made me an honorary member of the Communist Party.

In 1936-37 I was a miner, a face worker, in the Michael pit in East Wemyss, on the north shore of the Firth of Forth. Six miners from this area here in the Methil-Leven area had gone to Spain before me. I wanted to go with them. But the Communist Party decided that I should not go. However, I got a bit angry over this and had a little bit of a row with John McArthur, a leader of the Party and of the miners' trade union in this Fife area.[130] Eventually the Party agreed that I could go. I'm not quite sure why they had been unwilling to let me go in the first place. It would be a piece of conceit on my part to think or say the Party regarded me as too politically valuable locally.

The volunteers who went to Spain toward the end of 1936 and the beginning of 1937 were a sort of spontaneous thing to happen - people who belonged to various walks of life and political affiliations and so on, and some with no political affiliations. So there was a kind of looseness in the way that volunteers went to Spain then. There were intellectuals, there were workers, and there were people representing shades of opinion across the whole gamut of things. I think it was only after the February battle in Jarama, and the development of the situation in Spain with the setting up of the International Brigades, that a serious attempt was made then to send volunteers to Spain. I think that is the reason the Party then relented and allowed me to go.

None of the six miners who had already left for Spain from here in the Methil-Leven area were members of the Communist Party. But they were always regarded as militants in the sense that up to 1936 they were active in the United Mineworkers of Scotland, which was a Union set up for the purpose of unifying the Scottish miners' organisations on a militant basis.[131] So they had some political background in that respect.

Well, after the Party had given me the O.K. to go to Spain I made contact with people in the trade union club in Glasgow. There I met two Glasgow boys, who were going to travel down to London that night. So I went with them. There were no medical exams.

In London I'm not quite sure whom I contacted. I've forgotten about that. But I discovered that there would be a group of about maybe between thirty and forty had collected there. Joe Stevenson, a miner from Ayrshire, was put in charge of the group to travel across. Before we left Dover to cross to Calais a plain clothes policeman said to me: "We know where you're going." I says, "Somebody must have told you." "No, we know where you're going. You'll not get in." I says, "We'll see."

When we landed in Calais the whole group were immediately arrested. We were taken to the police station and we were told that we would be allowed to stay until the following morning. But we were not to leave Calais or we would be arrested. They took our money from us but gave us sufficient to go to the cinema. The following morning we were deported back to England.

When I arrived back at Dover the same policeman in civvy clothes had a bit laugh at me and said, "I told you so. You wouldn't get by." I said, "Because you reported us." He said, "No, honestly I didn't." So the authorities must have known where we were going.

We stayed in London for a week, living in lodging houses, one meal per day, sausage and mash a shilling, and a shilling for our board at night – two shillings. The following week Joey Hughes from Glasgow and myself were separated from the others and we had to cross – now I'm not quite sure about this – but not via Calais. We were then to travel to Paris on the overnight train. Joey and I landed in the Gare du Nord at seven o'clock in the morning. I was to sit there reading *Everybody's*, the weekly paper, and somebody would contact me.[132] Nobody arrived. We sat till about ten o'clock in the morning. I got a bit agitated, and said to Joey, "We're going out to look for somewhere." We went into the streets of Paris and went into a cafe. We knew no French. So I asked for two teas and to my surprise we got two teas.

When we came out the cafe I noticed across the street offices of the Communist Party. I suppose they would be area offices. There was a man standing at the top of the steps at the entrance. I knew it was silly but I went up to him and tried to make him understand what I was after. He just stared at me and ignored me. When I turned to go down the steps again Joey had disappeared. There I was in Paris for the first time in my life, without a clue where I was going or where I could contact anybody.

As I wandered down the street a taxi drew up and Chris Smith from Rutherglen, who was a member of the group, opened the door, and shouted, "Get in, Hughie!" and when I got into the taxi Joey was already there in the back seat.

We then went into the area that was known as the Red Belt area in Paris. There we met Rita. Rita, I discovered later, was Charlotte, the wife of Professor Haldane. She was doing the organising and arranging for the boys who were going to Spain. We stayed in Paris for three days. In fact, the following day was May Day. We were told we could go out and observe the May Day demonstration but not to get involved in it. It was a bit embarrassing during the demonstration, with young people coming up and asking you to take lapel flags and flowers when we were trying to act in a neutral way. However, the demonstration was tremendous and I understand that a million people turned out on the streets of Paris that May Day in 1937. The demonstration was so large that they got to a point where the meeting area was still a mile away and the demonstrators could make no more progress towards it. I wanted to go to the meeting because I wanted to hear Maurice Thorez, the general secretary of the French Communist Party.[133]

We left Paris on the train to Lyons. There would be about perhaps twenty in the group. One of the pleasant surprises I had was that my old comrade, Arthur Nicoll, with whom I co-operated in political activity in Dundee during the Hunger March periods from 1931 to 1934, was in the group. Arthur was one of the most solidly working class people I've ever met in my life. There were absolutely no pretensions in any way in Arthur's behaviour, either during ordinary political work in his home town, such as selling *Daily Workers*, or in Spain dealing with extraordinary incidents during battles. He behaved in every instance as if he were doing an ordinary day's work. No pretensions for a political career or anything, Arthur was Arthur. Arthur is now dead.

There was an incident on the train to Lyons. Five French gendarmes got on the train with us. We didn't want to be arrested again. So every one of the group was afraid to talk in case we gave ourselves away. The strange thing is that the police didn't seem to bother about us and carried on their own conversation, laughing and joking. Jeff Mildwater from Bloomsbury in London, a brickie, was sitting next to me. Facing us were two old maids. The exit door was between us. The two old women tried to get out at this station but they couldn't open the door. Jeff took a hand but he couldn't open the door either. And there we were in a situation like a silent movie, nobody talking but everybody trying to do something. I remember saying to myself, "For Christ's sake, Jeff, open the bloody door before the police interfere." The police in fact just ignored us. Eventually the door was opened. It was an embarrassing little situation, but amusing on hindsight.

When we arrived at Lyons we all got out and the police got out with us. And there was a strange procession, five policemen walking in front casually, Arthur following, and the rest of us walking higgledy-piggledy behind, wondering what in the name of heaven it was all about. The police entered a park, Arthur followed. When we reached the centre of the park Arthur sat down, the police walked on and disappeared through a gate on the opposite side of the park, never to be seen again by us. I could only come to the conclusion that the police had been escorting us on our way.

We followed Arthur Nicoll's instructions. He was in charge. So we sat down at a cafe, had a cup of coffee, and waited. As we waited in the splendid sunshine a man passed by holding his soft hat in his hand. Arthur said, "Let's go, boys." We followed the man with the soft hat up a side street. How Arthur had got the message I don't know but we entered a house and stayed the night.

We stayed in Lyons one night then took the train again southwards. I don't remember the name of the place we stopped at, but we were billeted in a peasant's loft and there we met about forty other volunteers from different parts of the world. There was a little man from Cuba, I forget his name. But we always referred to him as El Cubano. He seemed to dominate all the discussions that were taking place and obviously was a very highly politically motivated person. He told us that the authorities in Cuba had tortured him, twisted his testicles until they were useless. There was also Jack Kent from New Zealand, who had travelled all the way across the world to volunteer in Spain. When we all broke up from this group in the peasant's house and travelled in various ways and manners to get into Spain, Jack was put on a ship – I think it was the *City of Barcelona* – to travel by sea to Barcelona. One of Franco's gunships sank *The City of Barcelona* just offshore, and Jack was lost without ever touching the soil of Spain.

When we were in that peasant's loft a Spanish emissary came up to talk to us. Apparently there was trouble in Barcelona over the P.O.U.M.ist incident. The P.O.U.M.ist Party was an ultra-revolutionary group that had broken away from the Spanish Communist Party, mouthing ultra-revolutionary slogans and causing obstructions to the unification processes that were needed to fight the war. We knew it as a Trotskyist-type party that was open to any kind of provocateur to enter and create situations of difficulty for the Spanish authorities. The incident was referred to as a P.O.U.M.ist uprising, in which the famous novelist George Orwell found himself implicated.[134]

When the emisssary talked to us he put the proposition that if the situation in Barcelona worsened, would we go to the support of the Government to help put an end to that situation in Barcelona? Without exception the whole group agreed that they were prepared to do this.

After our stay in the peasant's loft we then entrained to Perpignan. There we were accommodated in what looked like to me a scrapyard. We stayed there for a number of days. An old peasant lady brought us a meal each day in a basket.

We then left Perpignan in a truck, a little canvas-covered truck. I can't remember how many were in the group, perhaps about a dozen. We travelled through the night, a dark moonlight night, with a guide, in single file. I often wondered how the guide could find his way. At times it seemed to be marshy ground, or perhaps it was only irrigation ditches. Away in the darkness an occasional bark from a dog broke the silence. We never spoke, only following in single file behind each other, with the guide in front.

We began to climb the foothills of the Pyrenees and this went on all night. At one stage in the climbing when we neared the top Joe Hughes' feet began to give way. There was a big fellow in the group, named Ben Glaser, from London, a big Jew. Ben had been one of the original cast in the Unity Theatre's production of *Waiting for Lefty*.[135] Ben picked little Joe up on his back and piggy-backed him to the top of the Pyrenees.

As we reached the summit of the Pyrenees the sun was beginning to rise away across the Mediterranean. We could see away down to the left this vast expanse reflecting the sunshine of the morning, and Port Bou, near the French border. As I looked across my first glimpse of Spain, across the rolling hills, the sun was rising towards a brilliant day. The first sound I heard was, "Cuckoo, cuckoo." That was our welcome into Spanish territory.

We began to descend the Pyrenees on the Spanish side and halfway down we were taken into what must have been a frontier post and given very, very heavy black coffee. It was the first coffee I had ever tasted in my life. We stayed there for about an hour and then we descended down to the ancient fortress town of Figueras. Figueras had the reputation of being one of the strongest forts in Spain, according to what I've read. There we were put under the command of a little captain. I never knew his name, but we addressed him as El Capitan. He was a very nice gentlemanly person. He took care of the young boys during our stay in Figueras. And he gave us advice, and sometimes reprimanded us for taking our drill periods without arms on the square too seriously. But he was a person I began to like very much.

We stayed there for two or three days then travelled by train southwards down the Mediterranean coast to Valencia. On the way the train sometimes stopped or would travel very slowly. And Bill Cranston from Edinburgh sometimes got out, gathered ripe oranges that seemed to be lying around everywhere in heaps, and came into the train with a basketload for everybody to eat. We eventually landed in Valencia and coming from the drab buildings and the drab weather we had been used to in Scotland, the brightness of the buildings and the colour of the windows, the blues and reds, was quite a distinctive visual experience for me. Everything seemed to be bright in the sunlight of Spain.

We only remained a short time at Valencia then proceeded down the coast and inward to Albacete. Albacete, I always understood, was a big town, but the area in which we lived had all the appearance of an old feudal village. That was the then headquarters of the International Brigades. We got some sort of military training but mainly on firing a Maxim machine gun into a sandpit. It was then that three Russian anti-tank guns of a very high modern standard arrived. And an anti-tank crew of about thirty volunteers was set up under the command of Lieutenant Malcolm Dunbar, who came from the Lothians. I understand he belonged to the landed gentry. I often wonder if his ancestor was Black Agnes, who defied the English during the wars between England and Scotland.[136]

Hugh Slater, who had been, I think, reporting for the *Daily Worker,* then joined the International Brigade, was second-in-command. The group was set up into three gun crews of about seven to a gun crew, with sergeants in charge of each gun. The guns were 37mm and fired both armour-penetrating anti-tank and high explosive shells. They were guns that could be used against strong points, machine gun points, as well as against tanks. They had a very high accuracy. They had the telescopic sights on them on which you could pinpoint your target over a visual distance of maybe up to two kilometres even. There was one occasion later on in the Aragon when the British Battalion was ordered to take a hill – I forget the name of the hill – on which the enemy entrenched, overlooking the Ebro. Anyway I was the observer and I pinpointed the enemy movements, and the anti-tank battery fired across this bay opening in the ground across the gap towards the hills and was striking the positions with extreme accuracy. What we found was that the heavier batteries further back were using our explosions as the marking points for sending their own shells in. The guns were easily handled. But on the whole, when travelling any distances, they were loaded on to *camions*. These were trucks that the Russians had supplied the Spanish government, and the guns were carried from place to place on the top of the truck. In a wide-ranging action, where movement was important, that came in handy. These guns were of such a high standard that the American military attachés took a close interest in them.

On one occasion when the anti-tank battery were situated in the hills for a week or so somewhere in the Aragon, time and place not remembered, but before Franco's offensive began, I had an experience involving two inquisitive Americans. As I had been up a good part of the night I was snatching some sleep under an olive tree when I was awakened by Jimmy Arthur, a dour imperturbable Scot from Edinburgh. He was on guard and had his rifle slung over his shoulder. In his typically direct way Jimmy growled, "There's a couple o' bastards up on the trucks examining the guns." "Did you give them permission?" I asked. You just don't allow strangers under any circumstances to mess about with your guns. "No, ah didnae," said Jimmy, "the bastards jist went up on their own." When I looked at the two men on the trucks I immediately recognised Ernest Hemingway, the author, as one of them. I knew him from his photographs. The other man was an American 'lootenant' who was attached to Brigade headquarters and who flaunted his officer's uniform ostentatiously. Being a bit crabbit on being awakened out of my sleep and feeling my proletarian resentment at too much ostentatiousness, I had already formed an antipathy to the lieutenant. I growled back at Jimmy, "Well, order them off and if they don't get off, shoot them!" It was purely an expression of mood, born out of my coal pit expressions, and not an order. But the two men must have heard me for they got down off the truck at once, got into their car and drove off without a word. I remember thinking to myself at the time that a novelist's job was to write about people not things, and here were two dour Scots characters Hemingway might have got some copy from. Many years later Hemingway took his own life. I always had the feeling that Jimmy Arthur was the kind of morose character who might have saved him the bother.

I was made battery secretary, which entailed being paymaster as well, and I also became Malcolm Dunbar's *enlace,* that is, his runner. My job was to carry messages and check up on reports periodically with the guns and every day send reports into the Brigade headquarters of our military equipment, numbers, the types of guns we had and anything else. Wherever Lieutenant Dunbar moved I had to follow him, dog his heels everywhere in case I had to carry messages.

The only training we got in the use of these guns was one day out on the hills, where we fired off one or two shells and the virgin soldiers were instructed on how to use the guns. We then moved up to Jarama some time in early June and we stayed there for three weeks. The battle for the defence of the Valencia road to Madrid had taken place in February. That front had now settled down to static trench warfare. I think the reason we were sent up to Jarama was merely to get us used to the battle atmosphere. It was quite a reasonable pleasant stay, with very little going on except for what I have described myself as 'Jarama nights'.

It was a lovely spring and summer that year, 1937, but there were occasions at night, perhaps around midnight, when the skies seemed to open up with lightning everywhere. Everybody on both sides would get nervous and blast off with everything they had. It was a fantastic sort of experience. After one of these nights I understood there was only one casualty. How we got to know about it I don't know, but I was told that the only fatality was a sergeant in the enemy trenches. A bullet had apparently gone through his sandbagged position and shot him through the head. But everything, the sky, the whole world, seemed to be breaking up during these sorts of nights.

During one of these nights I was wakened round about twelve o'clock. I was rather confused but it turned out that Captain Dunbar was standing over me. He told me to follow him. There was no moonlight but wildfire was ranging across the hills, lightning was exploding and flashing everywhere and the sound seemed to be in a general mayhem. I was confused but I followed Captain Dunbar as he marched up the road towards the trenches.

We approached the communication trench which started from zero and deepened as it went towards the trenches, perhaps about 150 yards distant towards the top of the ridge. It was then that I became aware through the noise and general mayhem that bullets were cracking past us, the whiplash crack of bullets. When the communication trench deepened sufficiently I said to Captain Dunbar, "You'd better get in the trench, comrade." He ignored me completely and marched forward. I said to myself, "Well, I'm going to get into the trench myself, whatever he does." He walked on for about perhaps twenty or thirty yards further before he condescended to get into the trench.

Captain Dunbar, for all the time I knew him, was a very remote, private, uncommunicative person, who always maintained an aloofness and remoteness from the people he associated with. He always remained an enigma to me. I never ever once had any kind of personal talk with him, only through the orders and military requirements he had to give. He kept everybody at their distance. He was a very strange person to me. The only person I could think of whom he had any sort of intimate relationship with was Hugh Slater. I cannot think of anybody else who came close to him, in any kind of way close to him in a personal way. But he was a very, very courageous and dependable soldier, in my opinion probably one of the best of the volunteers that ever went to Spain. He did not to my knowledge have any previous army experience or any military training. But I'm never sure about that.

We stayed at the Jarama for about three weeks and there wasn't much of any sort of battle activity going on except for these 'Jarama nights', which occurred two or three times. So this is my main memory of our stay in Jarama. We were then taken from Jarama and sent to a place I'm sure was Ambite, where we stayed in a little mill with a fast flowing mill stream. There we had a very pleasant fortnight of rest in preparation for our going into the big battle at Brunete later on.

When we were in the mill we had a visit from Professor Haldane. He wore a Durruti cap and a big leather jacket.[137] When he arrived I thought he was a big dock worker from the way he was dressed. He gave us in what Miles Tomalin called the Room of Culture and Rest lectures on what to do in case there should be any gas attack. If we were caught without any gas mask he told us to piss on our hankies and put them over our mouths.

While we were in the mill at Ambite Miles Tomalin, who had been at Cambridge University, set up his 'Assault & Battery' wall newspaper that became famous among all the International Brigaders and the journalists who happened to come by. Miles was a very talented person, a very gentle person, who carved the name of each battle he was in on his musical instrument, the recorder. While doing his ablutions down by the mill stream early in the morning as the sun was rising Miles would play his recorder, which put me in mind of the great god Pan. So I dubbed Miles the Good God Pan, and I drew a cartoon of him with goat's legs down by the reeds in the river. A fortnight before Miles died in 1983 I wrote him and sent him a similar cartoon to remind him. I had described him as "the unlikely warrior". Miles wrote back and said, "Hughie, we were all unlikely warriors." Miles was a very, very talented person, a very lovely person, and I regretted his passing.

From Ambite we proceeded to positions near Madrid. It was clear, and the rumour was strong, that we were about to enter into an action of a major proportion. The battle for Brunete was not only to relieve the pressure on the Basque people in the north[138] but also to cut off a Fascist salient into University City on the west or north-west side of Madrid. So the battle of Brunete began.

In the distance to the north you could see the Guadalajara mountains, where a battle had taken place in March between Mussolini's Italian Fascist forces and Italian volunteer forces in the International Brigade, the Garibaldi Battalion, in which Mussolini's forces received a very serious drubbing.

Our anti-tank battery landed on the side of a road running across a hill from which we looked down on to lower ground. In the distance, perhaps just over a kilometre, lay in the dried up ground the village of Villanueva de la Cañada. As we looked down we could see our troops manoeuvring through the gullies to overcome the final resistance of the Franco troops in the village. It was that morning, I think, in which the incident took place in which George Brown from Manchester, a member of the British Communist Party, was killed. Apparently the Fascists were making an attempt to break out behind the shelter of the villagers. They marched out into the road behind the villagers, showing a white flag. Under this kind of cover George Brown and his company gave them a wave to come on. As they approached George Brown and his Company the Fascists suddenly opened fire, killing George Brown and wounding others including some of the villagers. It was a tragedy because George was one of the very able members of the Communist Party in the Manchester area.[139]

We moved through Brunete towards Quijorna then branched off a side road to the left, alongside a line of woodland. We didn't hear the bombers coming until they were overhead and dropping their bombs. Suddenly flashes of explosions were taking place around our trucks. We always moved with our guns on trucks, our ammunition, our cookhouse, and everything, as one unit. That was the first we had ever experienced bombing from the air. But one of the things you find out in war is that things happen before you know they are going to happen, and the shock is over - you haven't time to suffer fear or anything. You merely react to a situation like that. And of course after it's over you don't concern yourself very much about it then. So fear doesn't really arise unless you are aware what is going to happen: you've to know beforehand. The fear is always beforehand.

We then manoeuvred around till we found a little hillock on which stood an old cottage, surrounded by trees. This would be getting towards evening. Part of my job in the Anti-Tank Battery was to act as an observer. We had a large telescope and also a range finder for the purpose. I got out the telescope and looked through the trees and there I saw some military around an old castle in the far distance. I acquainted Captain Dunbar with what I had seen. He decided that we would do nothing at that stage. It was beginning to get dark. And in any case, as we'd discovered through the night, we had no infantry with us. We were out in a position on our own. Through the night the infantry passed us to take up their positions. This was the first day and the first night of the battle for Brunete.

Early in the morning we got one gun set into position to fire a shot or two into the castle where I had seen the infantry. Everything was in position, with the gun crew ready to fire, when suddenly there was an explosion behind us. As I turned to watch the explosion the gun crew and everybody else withdrew the gun down behind the little hillock. I was sitting in this position behind the cottage with Hugh Slater, when Captain Dunbar came along and said, "Fraser's gone." Both Slater and myself were shocked to hear the news. We hadn't actually seen what had happened. Captain Dunbar himself looked a bit shocked. What had happened was the enemy had spotted us and fired the first shot, one shell. On its way past us it struck Fraser Crombie in the right shoulder, killing him instantly. Fraser was our first fatality. We were caught with our pants down.

I knew Fraser Crombie from away back in the early '30s when the fight was on against the Means Test. The fight against the Means Test away back in '31-32 was on a countrywide scale.[140] Conflicts with the police were taking place in many parts of the country. There were clashes with the police and baton charges in many towns in England and baton charges had taken place even in unlikely places like Kilmarnock. The police were being used to repress the protest against the operation of the Means Test. A demonstration had been called for in Kirkcaldy to put certain demands to the local authorities. The Town Hall, if I remember correctly, was then in the High Street. The High Street is a narrow street. The leader of the demonstration was Pat Devine, who had been arrested in Times Square in America during the protest against the execution of Sacco and Vanzetti.[141] The crowd were gathered in Kirkcaldy just outside the Town Buildings. I had been warned not to go there but I was too curious so I went to watch what happened. A bus came up the High Street and as it passed through the crowd it pushed them into the doorway of the Town Hall, where the police were drawn up in a line. The police immediately reacted, thinking that this was an attempt to break into the Council. They drew their batons and charged the crowd, causing a lot of injuries to many of the demonstrators. After the street had been cleared a little bit I looked from one shop doorway across the street to another shop doorway. I saw a young woman with her mouth bashed in and blood flowing from her injuries. Fraser Crombie was on that demonstration and was one of the thirty-odd people, along with Pat Devine, who were arrested and were eventually given jail sentences. This was the man that died on that little hill in the Battle of Brunete. We picked him up and interred him in a little trench on the top of the hill, and then we left to take up new positions.

We moved through a river - I forget the name of it - a tributary to one of the main rivers. And we went up from the bed of that river, which was beginning to dry up with the warm weather, about three quarters of a mile to Mosquito Crest or Hill. When we arrived there there was a very gory situation. The shell fire at this point was very concentrated. There was nothing but dead men and dead mules rotting in the sun. The smell of death was unbearable. The decapitated body of a man lay with a board on his chest. I looked around but I couldn't find his head. On the board on his chest was the name of a miner from west Scotland.

This little road led up on the crest to a little forward going communication trench. It was there we made our first headquarter position, with the guns being taken forward and slightly down on the other side of the crest, to cover the enemy across the valley there. Down in the valley the British battalion was having a very, very difficult time trying to overcome the resistance. In fact they were never able to overcome it across that stretch. Our headquarters position was continually being shelled very, very strongly the whole time we remained there. One had the impression that the whole war was taking place around that very spot, although, quite obviously, the battle would be just as intense elsewhere. One has always the impression that the war is taking place round about his own person. That's the nature of war.

Willie Dickson from Prestonpans was killed in one of these bombardments the very first day we arrived on that crest. He was our second fatality. I would like to tell about Jack Black, an older, experienced army man, who became a sort of father figure for the young boys, continually keeping them in a happy mood. On one occasion the first, second or third day on that crest, I was sent forward to carry a message from Dunbar to one of the guns. As I was going along the communication trench, the bombardment on the trench opened up in a very intense way. I crashed into a side hole in the trench, along with two Spanish comrades, and waited there while the shells thudded round about us. One shell seemed to hit the top of where we were sheltering, the concussion scattered my brains and for a moment or two I must have felt a bit unconscious. When I recovered the concussion had completely dried my mouth up and I couldn't speak. As I was nestling there in that comparatively sheltered place while the shells were still exploding round about, Sergeant Jack Black appeared above me on the other side of the trench. He was looking backward, and apparently was very concerned about something. Then he disappeared forward again towards his guns and almost immediately another shell exploded very close to that area. Again I was slightly concussed with the explosion and remained in that position for I don't know how long.

When the shelling had eased off I decided to get out and carry on with my message. I climbed out of the trench and was moving forward when I noticed a number of bodies lying in the trench that obviously had been caught in that last close explosion. One of them was lying on his back in the trench and wearing puttees. Jack Black was the only soldier I ever saw wearing British type puttees. I recognised the puttees. It was Jack, lying on his back, gazing up unseeingly into a very blue sky. Jack was dead. I immediately went back and told Captain Dunbar and Hugh Slater. They were very shocked because Jack was regarded as one of the more stable persons in the anti-tank battery. We all treated him with immense respect. When each time we went into battle we would receive some American cigarettes, he coined the phrase, in order to quieten his brood, "When in trouble, smoke a Lucky!" - a Lucky Strike cigarette. We knew each time we were given an issue of Lucky Strike cigarettes we were in for trouble. I carry on this expression even today, out of an immense respect I have for Jack. Jack was a Scotsman who was a member of the Dover Labour Party. I don't know about his life. He's just one of the men I met in Spain.

I think we would be on the Mosquito Hill position for a few days. I must confess that there was a complete difference between being initiated at Jarama, which was quiet and settled, with just odd outbreaks of firing, and this battle. This was the real stuff we were in for the first time. The experience was very traumatic for young people like myself. I still had a certain timidity about war and I had to break through and harden myself up.

On one occasion Captain Dunbar ordered me to go towards the left and carry a message to the commander of the American Lincoln Battalion. I made to go straight along the ledge but Dunbar ordered me to go down the gully and come up the other gully. But a shell was occasionally passing over and landing at the bottom of this gully that I would have to travel. So I said to him, "But Comrade Dunbar, there's a shell dropping there." And Comrade Dunbar ordered this little *enlace*, "That way - get on your bloody way!" So I had to travel past the hazard of shells continually falling in that direction. I was a bit apprehensive but I then went along a lateral gully, where I met two wounded British members. One was obviously dying, the other was wounded in the knee. I was aware that they were lying in a gully that might not be visited for a very long time. I could do nothing for either of them but I promised them I would report where they were, and had to leave them.

I then climbed up one of the gullies again towards where I thought I would find the Lincoln Battalion. At the top I came across an American soldier lying in a little scrape facing forward. There was a spattering of trees around. I asked him, "Where is your commanding officer?" He waved his hand vaguely toward the right but said nothing. He seemed to be staring at me with some disapprobation. Then I realised we were in view of the enemy and that bullets were splattering around, which I had hitherto been unaware of. I must have been attracting the fire. I had innocently got into a situation that the American boys in their scrapes in the ground resented. I immediately moved further to the right in the direction he indicated, searched around but couldn't find the command post. I returned along the ridge towards our own position, feeling very ashamed of myself because I hadn't fulfilled the job I had had to do. Through the whole time I was in Spain with this kind of job as an *enlace* carrying messages I continually found I couldn't make contact with the ones I had to carry messages to, got lost in the gullies, and returned with a sense of futility and shame because I hadn't completed my job. It was very awkward for me, something that still bothers me.

Well, the fighting went on and the concentration at Mosquito Point, this particular little area where we had our command post, went on for two or three days. There was one incident in which I was utterly amazed at the behaviour of some of my comrades. Bill Cranston from Edinburgh, who was in charge of our ammunition supplies, had dumped his boxes of shells just immediatly behind the communication trench. It was the centre target of the barrage against us. I had a little *chabola*, that's just a little hole in the ground where you took shelter if the situation got too heavy. On this occasion during a heavy barrage I looked up to discover our ammunition dump was on fire and shells were exploding from the heat. You could see torn cartridges spinning in the air all round about. But the thing that amazed me was that Arthur Nicoll, Otto Estenson[142] and one or two others were moving about separating the boxes that were on fire from the rest of the dump. It was something I did not feel like doing myself. I was astounded by their behaviour. I had the feeling that Arthur Nicoll in particular believed he was only doing another emergency job that had to be done. But believe me it took a lot of self-confidence and control to move in amongst exploding shells and separate the fire from the shell dump.

We then moved further left to a position just slightly below the ridge, with our guns withdrawn from firing positions. Obviously we were there to reinforce if need be a position that was regarded as weak. We gathered our comrades of the battery around a largish tree, once the position became dangerous in front of us. Some of the younger boys in Spanish units had broken and an emergency arose. They had just been drafted in and had no experience of any battles before. Obviously their inexperience caused some concern. Anyway we had to shoo them back into position. I don't think I should say very much about that.

There was a comical incident involving Bill Cranston and an American. In shooing the young Spanish boys back Bill and the American had lifted hand grenades to try and encourage the youngsters to go back. And when they went back the American comrade discovered that he had pulled the pin on his hand grenade and said to Bill, "What the bloody hell am I going to do with this? I've pulled the pin." And Bill in his typical direct way says, "Throw the bastard thing away."

We then went back to the position near the tree to discover it had suffered a direct hit, was split and broken down the middle, and that all our personal possessions and some of our trucks had been damaged. It was only then that we also discovered that Malcolm Dunbar had received a serious wound during the fracas where the young Spanish boys had broken for a time. Malcolm had received a bullet wound through the neck and had been taken off to hospital. I wasn't present when he received the wound through the neck or saw him after it. But a bullet going sideways through your neck seems to be a very serious thing. So we had a lot of concern about Malcolm. That left Hugh Slater in charge.

So the fighting went on at Brunete for about three weeks. By this time, with the weakened position of the Basque people, the enemy were able to withdraw forces from the north and concentrate them in this battle at Brunete. We were then forced to give up certain positions.

At Brunete I experienced for the first time the kind of person that Jock Cunningham was. Towards the end of the battle of Brunete I was sent as *enlace* or runner to Brigade headquarters at twelve o'clock one night to await an order, when we were to withdraw and where. I was sitting outside the Brigade command post, waiting for an order to come through. On the ground a Spaniard was lying moaning, "Oh, mucho malo." He was gripping his belly and I came to the conclusion that the pains he felt in his belly arose from extreme fear. Jock Cunningham, who was a major in the XVth Brigade at the time, emerged from the Brigade headquarters. Jock was a very, very aggressive working class person. He turned to the Spaniard lying on the ground and he says, "What the fucking hell is wrong wi' you?" The Spaniard lifted up pleading eyes and said, "O, camarada, mucho malo, mucho malo." Jock immediately grabbed him by the scruff of the neck, lifted him physically off the ground – and Jock was not a big man, perhaps about five feet six or perhaps maybe seven – booted him in the arse, and sent him spinning forward, saying, "I'll mucho malo you, you bastard, I'll mucho malo you."

Jock Cunningham was a rough hewn working class type of person, very aggressive out of the nature of the conditions in which he grew up no doubt. He became a major in a People's Army, and when you compare him with the polished professional officer that Major George Nathan was, it bcomes an extraordinary situation.[143] Nowhere else could anything like that have happened, except in such a situation as the Spanish Civil War that arose when the army was taken under the control of Franco and rebelled against the elected democratic Government and left the Spanish people without any defence to oppose it. The people sprang to the need of the situation and developed their own officers out of the struggle. Jock Cunningham was one of these people who were thrown up out of the battle. He played a very, very important part at the battle of Jarama, when he rallied the British boys to go back and face the Moors.

A few years back Bob Cooney of Aberdeen and I had a talk about things and we talked about Jock Cunningham. Bob says, "I only met him once, Hughie, after that. I was addressing a meeting in Aberdeen when Jock appeared in the audience. Apparently he was doing what he had been doing for most of his life – wandering around the country. And Jock shouted at me: "Are ye still at that game yet? Ye'll never get anywhere." The thing that struck me about Jock Cunningham, if ye take that incident, it is amazing that out of the nowhere situation in the early' 30s arose a person like that and then he subsided and disappeared back into anonymity again. He was a member of the Communist Party. He was withdrawn from Spain by the Communist Party after the Brunete battle. There was an enquiry into what happened at the Battle of Brunete in which the British Battalion suffered grievous losses. And Jock Cunningham along with others was withdrawn. He never returned to Spain after that. But he had something in his head about how the Communist Party was dealing with volunteers. There was an incident about his talks with Harry Pollitt, the secretary of the British Communist Party. And I understand that Harry Pollitt had to have a bodyguard or something present. Now I could understand that because Jock was a very aggressive, belligerent person. But I think he must have left the Comunist Party after that, because he accused Harry Pollitt of sending young men to be killed in Spain for political reasons. Well, I went to Spain but not because Harry Pollitt sent me. I can't think of anybody who was compelled to go to Spain. That is just too ridiculous. Everybody went as a result of their political experiences leading up to the Spanish Civil War.

I wasn't in too close or too personal an association with Jock Cunningham in Spain, but there were occasions when I was able to make some kind of judgements on the man. For instance, after the battle of Brunete we in the anti-tank battery were lying at Ambite in the little mill. Professor Haldane paid us a visit there and gave us lectures in the room of culture and rest that Miles Tomalin had set up. On another occasion we invited Jock Cunningham to come up and we in the anti-tank battery were going to entertain him. And I remember Jock talked in a cryptic kind of a way, the words just rushed out. I had the distinct impression that he had a not too rational way of thinking. Jock Cunningham was a man who expressed himself by his actions, not by his political or analytical powers. I think the asset about Jock Cunningham was his tremendous energy and his tremendous aggressiveness that were needed in these kinds of aggressive conditions. That brought the man out and made him a very distinctive person. On his judgements, I don't know. Jock Cunningham was continually on the go, travelling all over the area under his command. There was one occasion when I was present. He had discovered a number of wounded in an area that was difficult to have them evacuated from. And on the occasion I was present a big German doctor was in charge and obviously was being overworked. And Jock was telling him about these men who needed to be evacuated. But Jock always did things in his own way, in his own style. And he told the German doctor: "If you don't get these men out I'll fucking well shoot you." In these conditions he was a very dominant person.

I rather liked Jock Cunningham because he was of my people, the kind of working class people that I was brought up with in the miners' raws. I didn't like Fred Copeman. Copeman was a garrulous person. I remember during the time we were on Mosquito Hill one of the English boys coming up and saying to me, "That bastard down there is going off his nut. He's sitting there and he's throwing his pistol around and mumping to hisself." This was Copeman. So in the very casual way that I knew Copeman I didn't form any affection for him.

I remember later on when the Brigade were evacuated and we came back to England I met Freda Devine, the wife of Pat Devine, a political activist who had been thrown out of America for his political activity around the execution of Sacco and Vanzetti in which he got an eleven years' jail sentence. Freda was blazing, cursing Copeman for his domineering behaviour. That was when they were making arrangements for the return to our own home towns. So I never had any great affection for Copeman. And I don't think, if the Battalion member who spoke to me is to be believed, that he was any great kind of a commander. It indicated to me a weakness in his character that he should submit to this kind of mood in the middle of a battle.

There is utterly no reason to believe that any commander, including Jock Cunningham and Fred Copeman, used his pistol against any member of the Brigade. But when you get to understand what war is all about I wouldn't be surprised, because there were occasions when I threatened to use a pistol, and I'm not a homicidal character by any means. I'm a very timid person actually, who was just behaving according to his convictions and his philosophy. I never heard anyone saying anything against Jock Cunningham. I came to the conclusion that all the comrades in the Battalion had a tremendous respect for him. That was my impression.

When Malcolm Dunbar was wounded and Hugh Slater took over after the battle of Brunete we returned to our little home of culture and rest in the old mill. Hugh Slater expected me to act as a batman who would clean his dishes and look after his personal requirements. And I made it quite plain that that was not on for me. I did have some kind of relationship with Hugh Slater on a personal basis, but sometimes we were a little bit antagonistic.

I mentioned in passing George Nathan, who was killed towards the end of the battle of Brunete. I never spoke to George Nathan but he was there to be seen. To working class people like me he was an experience just to see – well dressed up in military fashion, with his walking stick, and presenting a figure of British officer type phlegmatic calm. I don't know if he was a Regular British Army officer. But he certainly behaved in the way that we've learned from the cinema and books, this typical British army officer, an upper class type who behaves under all circumstances with cool and calmness.

That's the impression I got from him but I never spoke to Nathan in any personal capacity. I saw him on one occasion during the bombing just previous to the one in which he was mortally wounded. He was strolling around, but when he was in the company of Steve Nelson, a leading American International Brigader,[144] one of the bombs came too close and mortally wounded Nathan. Steve couldn't find a doctor or an ambulance so he went up to a commander of, I think it was a French commander in charge of French volunteers, and at the point of his gun confiscated an ambulance to take Nathan to hospital. And Steve was on the verge of being court martialled for this action. I never heard of Nathan addressing the men in the Brigade when he was ordering them to charge, as "My ladies". He obviously was a very, very extraordinary sort of person. These are the kind of people that you never meet among the working class. But you've always to make allowances for the behaviour of these kind of middle class types. But I never heard anything even suggesting any kind of perversion in Nathan.[145]

We had been withdrawn to that position because the situation at Brunete had got a wee bit chaotic. And as an indication of this disarray that we found ourselves in in the anti-tank battery after Malcolm Dunbar had been wounded, Hugh Slater brought us into a position where we were not sure if we were going to regroup and go into action or move further back into a reserve position. But in the affray we had lost many comrades. So that we had a gun that had lost almost its whole personnel. In that position on this particular day nobody had a clue what was happening and we were merely lying there awaiting some kind of contact with the command to put things into order, when there was a little bit of hysteria. I think it was among the Campesinos, the Spanish soldiers led by El Campesino, a legendary Spanish commander. The Campesinos were moving past us backwards. We had enough men as withdraw two of our guns since our *camions* – that is the trucks that carried our guns - were not in position, were away on other work. We were left with a gun that we couldn't handle. And we had the feeling that we should retreat a bit further back, with the Campesinos going past us. So we asked a group of Campesinos to take this gun that we didnae have the manpower to handle, two kilometres back the road, and there we would pick it up. Unfortunately the Campesinos took the gun all the way, appropriated it and claimed that possession was nine-tenths of the law. So they stuck to the gun.

Now the guns were new guns given by the Russians and the Russians naturally had a supervisory control on them. So one day, about a day or two days after that, we were lying back in a reserve position two kilometres behind the battle area. A little Russian came up who couldn't speak very good English and demanded an explanation from Hugh Slater, who was in charge of the anti-tank battery, of what had happened. And apparently there was some kind of misunderstanding of the language that was being interpreted by an American Pole. The Russian supervisor had got the impression that we had lost our gun through cowardice and he accused Slater of cowardice. As the conversation got more and more confused and angry the Russian drew his pistol and placed it at Hugh Slater's belly.

Now I myself being the commander's runner always carried a big what we called Peter the Painter pistol.[146] You took it out of its holster and you butted the wooden holster and extended the gun and it carried a full clip. Anyway I had this in my possession. So I drew the Peter the Painter pistol, a large German pistol and I pointed it at the Russian's belly. So the situation was a real comedy. The Russian replaced his pistol and I took mine away from him. That ended the matter. The Russian went off. I don't know if I would have used my pistol. Anyway I had to make a gesture in defence of my commanding officer.

There was always a tremendous shortage of artillery on the Republican side. You could understand that the Russian interests were very concerned about the guns. Eventually with a little enterprise by the members of our battery we were able to retrieve the gun and therefore salvaged our reputation. The allegation that we had lost the gun through treachery or weakness wasn't persisted with.

So after the battle of Brunete we went back to the little mill near Ambite where the British Battalion was sheltered. And we were about half a mile away in a mill with a fast flowing mill stream. We took it up as our abode of rest. That's where Miles Tomalin, our very cultured member of the battery, set up his famous room of culture and rest, in which we entertained people like Jock Cunningham as I've mentioned and Professor Haldane and others. We stayed there for a fortnight.

It's strange how immediately an action stops you become completely involved in what you're doing at the moment and disengaged from what has passed. That fortnight on the mill was a lovely period. But I had to travel with a report every day a kilometre or so back to Ambite, where Brigade headquarters were in a larger mill. And this day I discovered that Major Attlee, the Labour leader, was to visit the Brigade headquarters. I decided to stay as long as I could at headquarters to see Major Atlee making his appearance.

The emergence from the grounds of the mill took a sharp turn away to the left. So we couldn't see who was approaching. Word was given to the Brigade headquarters that Major Attlee was on his way. So the whole headquarters staff, including all the commanders, were drawn up to salute to his appearance. I was sitting on the gate waiting on Major Attlee coming and could also see the Headquarters staff drawn up outside the mill, when suddenly round the bend came Segundo. He was a little comical character who was treated with a lot of deference and humour by everyone including the staff. They had I think as a joke made him a corporal. And the corporal's stripes were a big inverted red v-sign the whole length of the arm. On a big bike rocking from side to side that was meant for a six foot person Segundo, who was a very little person, about five feet two or three, rode up. Somebody must have carried the joke just a wee bit too far and told the staff that Attlee was on his way. But the staff drawn up and expecting Major Attlee, appreciated the humour in the situation.

It was a lovely period at the mill and we spent most of the time playing in the fast flowing mill stream because the weather was really terrific. That was the first official rest we had been given since leaving Albacete where the anti-tank battery was set up.

IN THE ARAGON

After a fortnight's very pleasant stay at the mill which stands out in my memory we took our trucks and moved down the road to Valencia on the Mediterranean coast. There we stayed a night, then entrained in boxcars on a journey into the Aragon alongside the Ebro, in northern Spain – a trip that took us about two days, the train was so slow moving. We landed at Hijar, which became the base for the International Brigade headquarters during the rest of our stay in the Aragon. I think we landed on my birthday the 21st of August because I have a photograph there that proves that, with Otto Estenson, Chris Smith, Arthur Nicoll, Bill Cranston and a big boy, who was eventually killed at Belchite, from London, big Brewer – I forget whether it was Drewer or Brewer.[147]

There we carried out an action against Quinto. The second day we went into action which because of my position I didn't have the opportunity to witness. But after the battle Jimmy Arthur from Edinburgh, who was a gun member, a very dour, imperturbable kind of Scotsman, and I decided to walk over the ground where the battle had taken place. It centred over a graveyard just lying above the Ebro and looking down into Quinto. The enemy had obviously improved trench work through the graveyard and bones and tibias and all sorts of human remains were lying all over the place. This is where the battle took place. We came to a machine gun post. Our anti-tank guns had obviously struck it and two bodies were lying. One was obviously an officer. In these days fountain pens particularly Blackbird American fountain pens were a kind of prize. I confess that I removed the Blackbird fountain pen from the officer's breast pocket and appropriated it. I didn't indulge in looting. I don't regard that as looting. It was a lovely fountain pen and a fountain pen was always a prize kind of article for me. So I was very proud of it. But Bill Alexander, who didn't smoke, saved up his cigarette rations and offered them to me for the pen. Reluctantly, because of my weakness for smoking I succumbed.

From Quinto, I'm not sure of the order of events at this stage, but basically we moved towards Fuentes del Ebro and positioned ourselves in a situation where the enemy was strongly entrenched at the entrance to a valley that led from the Ebro right up to Saragossa. The intention was to carry out an action that would make a breakthrough and we would move towards and attempt to take Saragossa. The positions held by the enemy were short, with rising hills on either side, in front of a little town that I don't remember the name of now. But we were in a position perhaps less than a kilometre facing these enemy positions. We could see the very strongly built up enemy trench work and it meant that any attack could not take place on a broad scale. It had to be confined to an open charge across the ground towards the enemy positions.

One morning when I think Hugh Slater had turned ill, and Bill Alexander was left in command of the anti-tank battery, I counted forty seven Republican tanks, drawn up in battle line about half a kilometre behind us. This was the greatest display of tank forces that I had witnessed. It was clear that these tanks were going to make a frontal assault on the defensive positions at Fuentes del Ebro.

All the morning passed. The tanks, although revved up and roaring and apparent for even the enemy to see in open display, remained in their positions for the whole morning. Eventually towards midday or the afternoon, the time I don't remember, the tanks began to move forward. Then we were told that they would pick up infantry and charge through and over the enemy positions.

The tanks in my opinion made the mistake of going at full speed and leaving the infantry who were to follow too far behind, so that they became exposed. It was another thought in my head that the speed of their attack did not leave the enemy time to panic or retreat. The result was that they lay down in their trenches until the tanks came overhead. The speed of the tanks was throwing the men who were riding on them off on to the ground over the bumpy way they had to travel. Then things all seemed to be going wrong. Tanks were being crippled and set on fire. We could see everything quite plainly across the enemy trench work. The tanks were being knocked out and destroyed and set on fire. The enemy obviously had decided to play possum or lie low until engagement at close quarters became possible. A disaster was unfolding and this became utterly clear to us.

I was standing with Bill Alexander, who was then in charge of the anti-tank guns because of Hugh Slater's absence due to illness, when Captain Smirka, a Czechoslovak who was in charge of the Brigade scouts, came rushing out towards Bill and myself in a panic, screaming, "Advance!" It was an utterly ridiculous order and we couldn't believe what we were hearing. I looked at Bill and Bill looked at me and we were so amazed that we didn't say anything. But Smirka kept repeating , "Advance with your guns!" And immediately the picture came into my mind of three anti-tank guns moving over harassed ground with the enemy still in their positions and the advanced tanks isolated or destroyed. It was too utterly ridiculous for me to accept when forty seven tanks had failed to do the work. But Bill, being a good officer, said nothing. He turned to me and he said, "Come on, Hughie." And immediately I retorted, "Not on your bloody life."

Bill Alexander wasn't ordering me. In my position as *enlace* I had to accompany the commander everywhere he went and therefore it was a legitimate instruction he gave me. I wouldn't say it was an order that we should go and look for positions. That's the best we could do at the time. But it meant the two of us moving into open ground to look for a position where we could put our anti-tank guns. If that was the intention then it wasn't necessary for our guns were already in position over open sights to command the strong points of the enemy. So the idea of attacking with the three anti-tank guns was utterly ridiculous.

When I told Bill, "Not on your bloody life," he said nothing but turned to a young boy who had just joined us and whose first battle experience this was and said, "Follow me." And as the two of them disappeared over the ridge that gave our positions comparative safety I felt utterly disgusted with myself. I remember quite clearly saying to myself, "Hughie, you're a rotten little bastard. You have allowed that young boy to go who's never had any battle experience. It's his first time in action." So immediately I ran after them and started shouting at them. But in the noise they couldn't hear me.

We were going through long, waist high yellow grass when I was shouting at them. Suddenly a machine gun opened up on us. As I flopped to the ground I saw Bill and the young boy flopping to the ground as well. The machine gun kept on us for quite a period. When it stopped I decided to move forwards to where I thought Bill and this young comrade were. I knew I was well past the position and came to the conclusion that I had lost them. But I still moved forward until I came to a little ditch running across the open ground. It was about twenty inches deep. And I came across two members of the British Battalion who had obviously been attempting to follow up the tanks in their attack but had been pinned down. One was groaning about his ribs. The other one said one of the tanks had come over on top of him in the ditch and crushed his ribs. I said, "Well, there's nothing I can do for you for the moment. I'm looking for my commanding officer." So I moved along this shallow trench towards the right, never meeting anybody.

As I went I came across an irrigation ditch. There I saw a tank half submerged in one of the irrigation canals and the driver or person in control standing by, obviously waiting on help coming to get him out. I had the impression that he might be a Russian but I never spoke to him and he never spoke to me and we just stared at each other.

I decided I would go back the way I came and passed again the injured comrade and his mate and went towards the extremity of the left where the ditch began to rise to the high rocks on the left. I travelled up through that until I eventually came to a Canadian machine gun post. There we could see the extent of the disaster from our height. We could see tanks burning. The Canadians were very concerned about what had happened.

But my job was to find Bill Alexander and I had got myself lost in trying to do so. As a runner or message carrier I found myself getting into these situations quite often, where I became detached and concerned about what was happening. I then decided to retrace my steps and crawled over the open ground again back to our first position where we had received the order. There I found that the young boy had received a bullet wound in the knee with the machine gun bursts that we first suffered, and that Jeff Mildwater, who was second in command but was also in charge of one of the guns, on the instruction to move forward had taken his gun down the road, and in searching for a position to place his gun had also received a bullet in the knee. These were our two casualties as a result of what I considered to be a very stupid order. We never got one gun into position where it could be used against the enemy.

The following day the disaster became worse. Harold Fry from Edinburgh, the commander of the British Battalion, who had been made a prisoner of war at Jarama but had been returned to Britain then volunteered to come back to Spain again, was killed. The political commissar Whalley, whom I didn't know but who I understand was a very fine comrade, was also killed.[148] The following day Bill Paynter, who was in Spain keeping a watching brief and looking after the interests of the British lads, came up to visit us. Bill, a member of the Communist Party, eventually became the general secretary of the National Union of Mineworkers after the Second World War when the pits were nationalised. Bill and I had a talk and I told him what had happened as far as I could see. Bill seemed a bit gloomy, I thought, at what I was describing and as he left he merely said, "Look after yourself, Hughie."

To me the tank attack was a disaster that should never have happened. In my opinion the attack was poorly conceived. There was no preparatory bombardment by guns. In fact we of the anti-tank guns were ordered not to take part in the attack, to withhold our fire. There should have been bombing since the Fascists were strongly entrenched in positions that we had to attack over a short line. Nothing like that happened. Instead there was that ridiculous charge like the charge of the Light Brigade – a gallant effort but a stupid effort.

The objective of that attack had been to move up the Ebro and through the valley it flowed through towards Saragossa and capture Saragossa. That disaster put an end to that intention.

After that disastrous attack we moved over to Belchite. That was part of the Aragon offensive. Belchite, we understood, was a town that Napoleon's armies failed to capture. It was said to be a legend during the Peninsular War. Anyway we were told that, whether it means anything or not.

But the XVth International Brigade pushed into Belchite and surrounded the town. The town itself was a fortress-like feudal town in the Spanish manner, compact, enclosed and ancient. I was along with one of the guns, up on a hill overlooking the town. We could see the back ends of the church and other important buildings. We could actually see any movement inside the houses. On the top of this little hill where our gun was was a threshing ground. There was a small primitive building of which the end had been knocked out and our gun was placed nosing through this opening, facing the positions that the enemy were holding. Their command had fortified their positions right in the centre of the town and were obviously ordered to hold out to the last. Extremely close house to house fighting took place in which the American Lincoln-Washington Battalion were involved. They had, under very difficult circumstances, to break through walls to capture the next house, and were suffering quite a lot of casualties. In this kind of close fighting – our first experience of it – our guns were placed in position to fire down the narrow streets against enemy strong points.

In crossing the threshing floor on top of our hill we were exposed to a machine gun that opened up on us every time we moved to the gun position on the top of that hill. But that didn't last very long. In fact, I'm quite sure that we put an end to that with a couple of shell bursts.

I was observing through a gap in the wall when I saw movement through a window in a certain building. There was only Jimmy Arthur and I present on that occasion and I told Jimmy, who was in charge of the gun. I pinpointed the position and the next time we saw movement he fired off two shells through the windows. From then on there was no question of any return harassment by machine gun fire. So our access to the gun position became safe.

In that position we remained while the fighting was going on through the streets and houses of the town. And it was during that fighting and breaking through walls that Steve Nelson received the wound that nearly killed him. He had to be taken back. Steve Nelson was the famous working class activist who became the commissar and political 'daddy' of the American comrades fighting in Spain. He was a tremendous personality and everybody respected him as a kind of father image in the fighting. Anyway the fighting continued and had to be resolved bitterly at great cost in that kind of way.

Belchite was a particular kind of battle at close quarters. You were seeing the person you were killing. That's a different thing from killing people at a distance. In that respect it was a very bitter battle. Towards the end of fighting in Belchite there were dramatic moments. The political commissar of the XVth International Brigade after Steve Nelson had been taken to hospital – I forget his name though I knew him very well – made a dramatic broadcast over the loudhailer about twelve o'clock at night.[149] He called on the beleaguered remains of the Fascist garrison in the town to give in immediately, to come forward without their arms or they would be completely destroyed. He put the message forward in strong American language that at twelve o'clock midnight was really dramatic.

Almost immediately there was some excitement and action taking place in the middle of the town. It was utterly dark, no moonlight, and we didn't know what was happening. But we all grabbed for our rifles and guns and stood to in case we should be involved. The story that came to us was that after the commissar's broadcast there had been an attempt by some of the beleaguered garrison in the centre of the town to give themselves up, but that their commanding officer was using arms against them. Anyway things settled down. The following day the last of the garrison had been wiped out. Belchite was completely in our hands.

I remember walking up what you could call the main street, rather an enclosed narrow way, and I couldn't bear the smell of death. Some of our people were digging large holes into which all sorts of remains of living things, human but also pigs and goats, were being thrown. We came to the square or plaza. There a very large heap of dead human beings was piled up. And in the very hot weather the smell was completely unbearable.

We passed a hospital where the wounded, the dying and the dead were still enclosed. Again the smell was utterly unbearable. I had to cover my nose. I had never smelled anything like it. It was decided that in the circumstances the best thing to do was to throw petrol over the dead bodies and burn them. So they were set alight. I went through the town with others and observed all this before I left. The fighting was over. Now I hate to have to describe these horrors because I want to talk about the positive features of things in Spain.

Shortly after Belchite had fallen, a book was published in Spain in English giving little stories of volunteers' experiences during the War so far. One appeared under the name of M.D. concerning me. I could only think M.D. stood for Malcolm Dunbar. But as Malcolm Dunbar was not present during the incident concerned but Hugh Slater was I held Hugh Slater responsible for the little sally into literary frivolity. What happened was that before the enemy had been completely overcome Jimmy Arthur and I were at the gun position on the little hill inside this little closed crude building, when Major Merriman appeared. He was an American who had come to Spain as part of his university studies. I understood he was a lecturer at university, I'm not sure. But he came to Spain with his wife in connection with his studies and joined up in the International Brigade. He was a very splendid big blonde man with spectacles and a very fresh complexion. He had a prisoner with him.[150] He brought the prisoner up to us so he would show where the remains of the enemy garrison was trapped. And the prisoner pointed out their positions. Major Merriman left and we were discussing the positions indicated to us by the prisoner when in walked the prisoner and plaintively pleaded he didn't know what to do. Merriman had gone off, forgotten about his prisoner and left him wandering about on the threshing floor. I immediately grabbed a gun and started pulling the prisoner by the shoulder across the threshing floor. Suddenly there was derisive laughter back at the building. I looked back and Hugh Slater and the others were calling me, reprimanding me for not making the prisoner walk in front of me. I had the clear impression that the prisoner had made up his mind I was taking him out to shoot him. Actually I was taking him to the edge of the threshing floor so that I could shout down towards Major Merriman, which I did. I shouted down to Majòr Merriman, "Comrade Merriman – the prisoner!" Merriman merely beckoned the prisoner to come running down towards him and walked on.

But the story by M.D. in the book published and issued to every volunteer distorted the whole thing in a frivolous way which I resented. It said something about how the first one to cross an exposed area under fire has the advantage, and that I had therefore decided to allow the prisoner to go first and gallantly came behind. So later on when I met Dunbar and Hugh Slater together and they were giggling about it, I blew my top with them. I just went haywire and blew my top. "If that's the best way you could entertain yourselves then you're too bloody frivolous."

After the battle of Belchite, our next main experience was the battle of Teruel. That was towards the end of 1937, at the turn of the year. What I remember about Teruel is on the last day of the year 1937, Auld Year's Night, we went into the hills in the dark. A blizzard, one of the most violent blizzards I've ever experienced, came on. We didnae know where the enemy was but we were up in the hills. It was decided it was an impossible situation. So we decided to march down into one of the villages below. We went down into a village and into a farm building where we buried ourselves among the straw and slept the cold Auld Year's Night through. In the morning everything was covered with snow. Out of nowhere, I don't know how he managed it, Arthur Nicoll of Dundee produced porage oats. There was no milk, there was no sugar and there was no salt but we decided to have porage for our New Year's Day. So Arthur made porage and of course we ate it up, the taste wasn't important. Immediately we finished three enemy aeroplanes came across and bombed us in the snow. That was how we brought in New Year's Day 1938.

We settled round Teruel with our guns perhaps about a kilometre to the north or north east, I'm not quite sure, of the town. Joe Stevenson, a miner from Ayrshire, who had been in charge of us when we had left England to go to Paris, turned very ill and I had to take him along this road to Teruel to the *sanidad*, the first aid. It was a lovely, sunny, quiet morning when we went out but the road lay along the breast of a hill that was completely exposed to the enemy. The British Battalion was on the lower ground further down. The *sanidad* was in a doctor's house in the plaza, and there I left Joe. I had something to eat and in looking at the place found in a cupboard or wee recess a gold watch that must have been overlooked. Well, what do you do with a gold watch? Do you hand it over, who do you hand it to? The obvious and sensible thing was to keep it. So I kept it.

That winter was the first winter I think we had failed to have sanitary conditions of living and I think Joe had contracted typhoid. Anyway, poor Joe, to go to Spain to die that way.

I then had to travel back along that road towards our gun positions. On the way back the enemy opened up with everything they had. They seemed to be concentrating on that road – I don't know why, because I was the only person on it. To get refuge there was a hole that penetrated the cut through part of the road section and went through and opened up into a huge excavation. I could only have imagined it was dug for a gun position but there were no guns there and no troops, nobody – just me. So I decided to shelter there till the barrage was over. And by the time I got back it was beginning to get dark.

About Teruel: even on our memorial visit in 1981, I looked at it and it was a very sad place. Teruel is a place isolated in the mountains and has possibly existed since the days of the Moors. Although a big new road has recently been opened up from Valencia into Teruel it still remains a very sad place. On our visit to it we met two men who had been in jail during the Franco regime. One, who had fought in the International Brigade, had spent twenty-two years in a Franco jail. They told us that when the Moors and other Franco forces occupied Teruel after we were driven out at the beginning of January 1938, they lined up 5,000 of the townspeople in the plaza and executed them. After Franco had died the people took the remains of the victims and buried them about three kilometres out from the town in a piece of open ground. Their intention was to build a memorial. That was in 1981. Teruel still seemed then an isolated, very sad place that belonged out of time. And that was the impression we had during the fighting as well, a place out of time.

The battle of Teruel was an extremely cold, hard one. For one thing, there was that Auld Year's Night I've just described. The other effect it had on us was that we didn't have any sanitary conditions. It was the only time I grew a beard for one thing, and quite frankly my beard was lousy. This was the kind of situation we were in. It wasn't after that blizzard, I would say, extremely cold but it was a cold period, a very cold period, particularly after the extremely warm blazing sun of the 1937 days.

I said I was the paymaster of the anti-tank battery. And after Teruel, about March, just before the big Franco offensive on a fifty mile front started, I had gone back to Hijar, which entailed a couple of days' journey, hitch hiking with anything that was going in my direction, to lift three months' back pay for the battery members, which amounted to 21,000 pesetas.

I don't remember the exchange rate in sterling. But in value it was worth practically nothing in Spain because there was nothing you could buy. You could buy a fountain pen. You could buy wine, which we didn't have access to and which didn't concern me in any case. Things like that. If you were an officer and wanted to deck yourself up, you could make special efforts to have officers' clothing. However, these things didn't concern us. So I had allowed the 21,000 pesetas to drift back because we never had occasion to use money, we weren't in a position to use it and in any case what could you buy? So money wasn't important. Actually all the troops were paid ten pesetas a day, which extended to the civilian work as well. The standard wage was ten pesetas. So money was a meaningless symbol. Anyway after travelling all night, hitch hiking my way back, I found that the anti-tank battery had located itself three kilometres outside Belchite. I arrived back about nine o'clock in the morning. The anti-tank battery was lying by the side of the road in a field. I decided to have whatever kind of meal I could and then have a sleep. About eleven o'clock in the morning I was just beginning to think about resting when an American came running by and told us that we had better get off our mark quick as the enemy had broken through. We heard the firing begin in the hills. We just had time to load our trucks with our guns and go the three kilometres back to Belchite under intense artillery and what at times I thought was aerial fire, because as we were passing through Belchite, somebody, – Bill Cranston, I think it was – remarked, "Jesus Christ, they're firing anti-aircraft guns at us." A shell would explode in the air and you would see shrapnel splashing off the buildings all round about us. There on the other side of the town we decided that a number of us would wait back on the higher ground on the other side, the ground from which we had originally taken Belchite and on which fortifications remained. We left the guns then to go a devious route from that position. I was attached to a group that Major Merriman had rallied round about himself on the south side of Belchite. We gathered ourselves together. I still had the 21,000 pesetas.

We were towards the extreme end of these fortifications facing southwards where there was a long plateau with hills and trees on either side. Merriman came to me and he said, " Come with me, Smithie." My name was Hugh Smith Sloan, but I used the name Smith then. "Come with me, Smithie, I'm going back to have a look at the town and see what the situation is."

Well, by that time we discovered that the enemy had occupied the town lying immediately below us 200 or 300 metres and had installed a machine gun in the church tower. And also we found that the enemy was firing anti-tank guns on the left of us, towards one of our tanks that had been set on fire and was blazing away. They kept poking their anti-tank shells as if they were just playing themselves. Soldiers have their own sense of humour. There was nothing else to fire at.

We learned that the enemy had then gone to the right of us and had us practically surrounded except for this long plateau. Merriman says, "The only thing we can do is to run for it across that open ground." So when I came back, in the maze of trenches I couldn't find the briefcase with the 21,000 pesetas in. I came hurriedly to the conclusion that the money wasn't important in any case. Actually in the same skirmishing that took place over the next day we lost the Brigade paymaster, captured and shot, and the British Battalion paymaster, captured and shot. So they lost between them I don't know how many pesetas. I know that the British Battalion paymaster lost there 120-odd thousand pesetas. But money wasn't important. The thing was to get out of this very difficult situation.

Anyway Major Merriman then decided that we would run off in groups of twelve. So the first group was sent off. As they ran the machine guns opened fire and you could see the bullets spraying amongst them. But fortunately I never saw anybody falter or being struck. But the Fascists were still firing anti-tank shells at the burning tank on the right. The next group of twelve went and the machine guns opened up again until they got out of distance – and again fortunately I never saw anybody being struck. But you could see the bullets splattering the ground around them. I was kept to the last with Major Merriman. By this time I had made up my mind I was going to do something very odd. My idea was to cause the enemy, who were obviously watching us, to wonder what the hell I was up to. I started but instead of running forward with the last group, at which the machine guns opened up again, I ran at an angle towards the burning tank. I reckoned that the enemy would be curious to see what I was up to. Secondly, that they wouldn't divert their fire from the main group to me. So I started running on a diagonal line towards the tank, but when I had got to 200 metres from it I decided to swerve back towards the main group who were still running ahead. I don't know if they were still being machine gunned but by that time we were all getting out of range anyway. It was beginning to get dark. When I caught up with the main group I met an old comrade of mine from Dundee,

Micky Sullivan, who is still living but is now in a home. He was trailing the bogie of a Maxim machine gun, somebody else had the jacket or the gun. So I decided to help him trail the heavy bogie. We walked on through the complete darkness. There was no moonlight. We walked on and on it seemed for hours, until eventually we came to a river. We then decided that we couldnae get the bogie across the river as it was pretty heavy, but we would hide it so that the enemy couldnae get it. So we hid it by the side of the river. We then crossed the river.

There was quite a group of us by then. We came immediately in the darkness into a town where other members of the International Brigade had collected themselves together and decided to doss for the night. We discovered that many of them were in a baker's shop. We went in there. They were in the process of trying to bake themselves some bread from the dough that was left on the machine. So we tried it, but I don't think we actually succeeded in making bread. We allowed the fires to cool and then some of the boys got into the ovens and slept the night there. I met Arthur Nicoll and Micky from Dundee again and we slept in the hen coop for the rest of the night.

The following morning the members of the anti-tank gun battery went on the road and we came to a road junction where we had to take immediate cover in a culvert. These culverts exist on all the roads in Spain because of the drainage system there. Planes came across and we were bombed. There would be about half a dozen of us, all belonging to the anti-tank battery, trying to get back to our unit which had gone the other road.

We then went towards a village, whose name I forget, but we stayed the night in it. We started walking back towards the front to meet up with the improvised defences that were set up, when down the road came one of our guns with its rubber tyre burned off. The gun crew and myself were told then to take it back to Hijar, where our Brigade headquarters was. An incendiary bomb had burned the rubber from the gun. We had to go by winding roads over the hills to Hijar. It was a distance maybe of about thirty kilometres. As we were winding round the hill a *camion* or truck came up full of new fresh troops who were being sent in, dressed in green new uniforms, obviously a new army unit that had been set up. I had a wee Mauser rifle, a short rifle but I didnae have any ammunition for it. So when the truck came up the hill road I jumped oot in front of it and held up the unloaded wee Mauser rifle and pointed towards the truck and stopped them. I said to the driver, "We need your truck to take our gun back to Hijar for repair." He said I would need to take the troops to their destination first. So I says, "Right, but I'm getting in with you." So I accompanied them back and delivered them to their unit in the hills and then brocht the truck back. That driver stayed with us for months efter that because he got fed and looked efter.

Anyway we got the truck, loaded the gun on, landed back at Hijar and reported to old Major Galliano, an old Italian-American with a big dark square beard. And he says, "Don't unload your gun. We are going to evacuate the base. It's under threat." That came as a shock to us. We didnae know the extent o' the damage that had been done wi' the Franco breakthrough. So we loaded some of the commissariat stuff on to the truck and we used it to evacuate the gun across the Ebro further down.

One of the things you do learn living this kind of life is that – and this must have been through a' the eternities – soldiers improvise and, in the American sense of the word that we got to learn in Spain, 'organise'. Organising means looking efter yoursel' and gettin' your own thingmie. The Americans put a new meaning on it when they talked about organising, get yoursel' organised. Well, you learn a' the tricks. In evacuating the base the second assistant commissar was a wee boy named Mark from New York, I think. And he says, "There's a box there. Will you take that wi' ye?" "What's in it?" He says, "Cigarettes and chocolates." I says, "No, we havenae room for it." So we moved into another room to get the commissariat papers and I gave Bill Cranston a wink. So we landed up wi' the crate o' cigarettes and chocolates on our truck!

We eventually landed down on the road on the north side of the Ebro. We saw the camp fires in the fields and got off the tank trucks that we were hitching on and went across and here it turned out to be our whole company, anti-tank battery – guns and everything. And there we settled down, had a meal, and spent a couple o' days gettin' oursel' pulled thegether. We had been away from the rest of the company several days.

Anyway we found ourselves in a situation where we didn't know where our unit was and things like that. The Russians were racin' tanks oot in their tank carriers. I presume they were Russian, it was Russian equipment anyway, tanks loaded on their tank carriers. They were rushing round yon roads and they were obviously in a hurry because they were getting out of a difficult situation, maybe to face some other kind o' situation. We had the humiliating experience though, during that evacuation when wee Willie Moses and I was thegether, of watching the flight of hundreds o' people who had lived for centuries within their ain wee provincial set-up. Possibly they had never moved oot their village in their lives, because that was the nature of the conditions that existed for the Spanish people, living in the villages in feudal conditions. The road was filled wi' them, evacuatin', carryin' their beddin', and the auld grey haired women on donkeys and burros or maybe in donkey carts and things like that. One peasant stopped his cairt and he said to me, "Are you English?" And ah says, "Aye." He says, "England's a democratic country?" No answer. "Why is it they don't come to oor help?" And he was very angry and almost blamin' us, Willie Moses and me, for it. I had no answers. Watching the people streamin' oot leavin' their villages for the first time in their lives, I felt really humiliated. It is something I always remember, something disgusting that people should be subjected to these conditions. Well, people obviously through the whole of history have been subjected to these conditions with the wars that have been carried on. And they still happen on a greater scale. But nevertheless that was my personal experience o' a situation that was humiliatin'.

After we had left Hijar and eventually caught up wi' our unit and our field kitchen, which was most important, and had a meal, the following day a' oor Spanish boys attached to our unit – and we had taken many on by that time because o' oor losses – were a' happy smokin' cigarettes. We had caught up wi' our mail and the Woodbines that my father posted on to me in one of those long envelopes, six packets of Woodbines, had arrived as well. We also had that crate from the base that we said we hadnae room for. Everybody, cooks were busily, merrily in the sunshine makin' a meal and puffin' cigarettes everywhere when wee Mark the assistant commissar came up and he says to me, "Hughie, you are a dirty bastard." I said, "I dinnae ken what you're talkin' aboot, Mark." Ah says, "Oor mail has just arrived frae England wi' cigarettes. Are you wantin' twenty Woodbine?" And I handed him twenty Woodbines. The crate was full o' Lucky Strike! Ach, well, I'm telling you in a war you have tae be organised. This is something that normally you would object in principle to or your scruples wouldnae allow ye tae dae. But in war you have to descend to that level. There were things that I found I couldnae do because o' my scruples. You're never basically destroyed but you have to learn, as the Americans say, to organise yourself. All's fair in love and war, as they say.

The Franco offensive in the spring of '38 took place on a fifty mile kilometre long front that involved every resource o' the Republican forces tae try and maintain. Actually, there was a general fighting retreat in which we had to hold positions and in which the whole organisation of the Republican forces became disjointed and in cases broken up, and where individuals had to find their own way back in various ways across the hills, hidin' and things like that. Some o' them were found and killed but many o' them began to gather down the Ebro a bit – I forget the name o' the place, on the north side o' the Ebro.

THE EBRO

Well, up to that point where we were chased across the Ebro by Franco's offensive I had a clear idea of events and of what happened before. But from the Franco offensive everything became confused and it's more difficult to recall incidents and times. After the whole

International Brigade, and the XVth Brigade in particular, had regrouped and rebuilt its organisation we made a forced march one night up the Ebro towards a point where we intended to recross and carry out a minor offensive action against Franco's march to the Mediterranean. Up to that time I had kept diaries and notes which clearly helped me to remember my actions in Spain. Now it became more difficult, and one of the reasons for it was in this forced march up the Ebro we were forced to march light and discard all unnecessary possessions. I was forced to leave my diaries. I don't know where, we had to discard them at the moment. I never got these diaries again, so that made it more difficult for me to recall all the details of the actions in the Aragon and the later recrossing of the Ebro.

However, I remember well the recrossing of the Ebro because it was a very, very dramatic moment in time for everybody. The point at which we crossed the Ebro was enclosed very tightly by the hills on either side. There was a tremendous concentration of troops, guns and actions in that one spot. The Franco aeroplanes were coming down the river, bombing and attacking us continually before we got across. Our anti-aircraft guns were blazing at them and there was a tremendous buzzing of splinters from the shells buzzing through the air as if we had been invaded by an extraordinary mass of bumbees. Occasionally there would be a plop near you when an anti-aircraft nosecap would plummet into the ground. With the guns going off, the bombing, the buzzing of these shell splinters and the plop of the nosecaps one was tempted to try and seek shelter wherever he could. But there was no shelter. I remember looking at a small drainage ditch about eighteen inches high, a ditch with a cover across it and wondering if I could crawl into it to get away from this continual assault by everything that could be thrown at us.

Troops were crossing the river on an old primitive rope suspension bridge, the kind you would see in countries where primitive people lived. Big Peter Kerrigan was there that morning we were crossing the river. He was in Spain looking after the interests of the British boys and British volunteers, a sort of administration job. He didn't belong to any particular part of the military organisation as such. He was merely looking after the British interests. Peter was a very powerful swimmer. On occasions in the past before the Spanish War such as the Fife miners' gala, Johnny Boyle[151] and I and big Peter would go out swimming. It was one of Peter's favourite pastimes. Well, Peter took off his clothes and handed them to one of the British boys crossing the Ebro and swam across the river under these hostile conditions. I don't know why but Peter so enjoyed swimming. Now the Ebro is a broad river at that point, perhaps 150 yards across, and reasonably fast flowing.

After an hour or two we were ordered to advance with our guns down to the river. At that point huge reeds about seven feet high lined the banks of the river, and as I said the bombing was continuous. It was said that the peasants further down the river were plucking the dead and stunned salmon from the river as a result of the bombing. As we reached the reeds towards the barge that was to take our guns across, which were still mounted on trucks, there was a bout of bombing from the air. And many of the units had been caught in that particular vicious part of the bombing and many men were injured and I suppose many were killed. As we neared the river to get on to the barge that was to take us across, pulled by ropes, men came screaming out of the rushes and tall grasses. Men came rushing out, many of them with blood flowing from their faces and bodies, in a state of hysteria because of the assault that had been launched against them. They were trying to get away from this hell they had been caught in. I was standing on the top of the truck as we were mounting on to the barges as they were streaming past us. One man with blood all over his face and his eyes wide open with what could only be described as terror stared at me. I stared back. The horror and hysteria in his large dark eyes has left a picture in my mind. However, we crossed the river on the barges at a moment when the bombing from the air had ceased. We then proceeded inland towards the higher ground that had already been occupied by our troops perhaps an hour or two hours before that.

The rope suspension bridge wouldnae be any more than a yard wide and it was crossed single file by the infantry. I didn't see any boats being used. So I presumed at that point that the bridge was the only way of crossing the river. But half a kilometre further up there was a broad barge pulled back and forth by ropes with men on either side pulling it back again to carry the trucks and guns across the river. So it took some time to cross single file over the rope bridge. The rope bridge ran from the higher rocks across the river but it was clear enough in the centre, well above the water level.

For three days after we'd crossed the Ebro no food supplies were coming in, which meant that the boys who were doing the fighting to try to reach Gandesa and round about that area were very hungry indeed. My job was to continually carry reports back and forth to Brigade headquarters. Three days after we had crossed the Ebro I was sent to headquarters with a message. On returning across the river, perhaps about a kilometre on the south side, I came to a village that had been evacuated. Now our units were perhaps another kilometre or two further on. When I reached this evacuated village in the hills I was surprised to find dumped at the gable end of the very first building into the village a stack of loaves of bread and wooden boxes which on examination turned out to be tins of sardines. I had learned to contend with hunger so I was delighted to find this. I gathered as many loaves of bread and sardine tins as I could carry and took them to the anti-tank unit, where the boys appreciated them very, very much. This had been perhaps their third day without eating anything, other than any rations they had about their person. I call this a minor miracle, the minor miracle of the loaves and fishes.

It is very difficult from that time onwards for me to find a sequence. I can only remember incidents and little unrelated experiences I had. One of my problems is smoking. There was an occasion when we were isolated in the hills in the Aragon for three weeks without contact with any of our own units never mind the enemy. No supplies were coming up. Bill Alexander and Paddy Ryan were in charge of the Brigade supplies.[152] Bill Alexander – I don't know about Paddy Ryan – never smoked in his life. I said to Bill, "Are there any cigarettes in the store?" He said, "Hughie, there are no cigarettes in the store." I was very annoyed and illogical in my response. I accused Bill of smoking all the cigarettes himself, fully knowing that he had never smoked in his life. This is one of the minor annoyances I have to suffer, this compulsive need in me to have a cigarette.

When I was eighteen years old I had suddenly become addicted to smoking but the same cannot be said about drinking. While I like occasionally a pint of beer I have never been compelled to take alcohol merely to dizzy my mind up or anything like that. But there was an occasion well on into the Aragon battles in which the anti-tank unit was broken up and we were attached in a temporary way to various other units. In my case I found myself attached to Jack Cooper, an American comrade who was in charge of the machine gun group. We were in a narrow valley facing hills where we expected the enemy to attack from. In fact there was a rumour that a German Panzer division was lying behind the hills ready to make a break-through. So the defence of this road was very important. The machine gun post was safe enough in general except perhaps for a direct hit. But because I had no experience in guns or machine guns I was used merely as a messenger by Jack between his unit and Brigade headquarters. So I had to do a lot of running back and forward over one ridge, across a vinefield, over another ridge and down towards Brigade headquarters. I would do this at least once a day. There was a lot of shelling continually going on from the enemy positions beyond the hills and there were times when I would rather have stayed in the comparative safety and shelter of the machine gun post than carry these messages. I remember one occasion when I had to carry a message back. It was a very warm day. Going over the first ridge towards the Brigade headquarters I was passing three Spanish boys when suddenly the ground started spurting up around us as a machine gun opened up from higher ground from the enemy's positions. We all scrambled into a little slot in the ground, a *chabola*. It was meant for two people but the four of us scrambled in on top of each other. We were only aware that the machine gun was firing at us. You could hear the thud of the bullets as they spurted round about us. Suddenly there was a louder thud in the trench itself. One of the Spanish boys started shouting out, "I'm hit! I'm hit!" We examined his foot where he indicated he was hit. Sure enough he had been hit but only in the heel of his boot or shoe and the bullet had done him no physical damage. The Spanish comrades didn't say anything at that particular time, but I would guess they would kid him on a bit later as the man who was wounded in the heel of his shoe.

When everything quietened down again I got out of the excavation and carried on with my message down to the Brigade headquarters, across the vinefield and over another ridge. On my way some shelling began to open up. With the heat of the day and the excitement of things, I was sweating profusely. Water is very important but it was very difficult to get water in the hills. Anyway I landed at Brigade headquarters which was in an excavation on the side of rocks and handed the message over to a young Spanish political commissar who was in charge. When I was about to leave the shelling became very, very heavy and I hesitated to make my way back to the machine gun post. The young commissar must have noticed my hesitation because he handed me a bottle of cognac and asked, "Caro beber?" – "Would you like a drink?" Not being particularly fond of drinking any kind of alcoholic stuff and in the mood I was in, I just said, "No, fuck your cognac." I looked out the exit to the barrage of explosions that was taking place outside. Then suddenly I turned back, grabbed the bottle of cognac from his hand, threw my head back and let the golden juice of the vine flow down my throat. There was an immediate electrifying transformation in my attitude. It was something I had never experienced before. I suddenly felt my fist tightening aggressively. Suddenly I set out from Brigade headquarters into the mayhem outside. I brandished my fist and howled at the top of my voice, "You bastards, I'll punch you." I proceeded on my way without any thought for what was happening all around me. I could hear what I thought were the shells approaching me, but actually they would be past me. I carried on with the courage of the vine in me, ready to do battle with every projectile that was coming my way. I passed over the first ridge going back to the machine gun company post and was crossing the vinefield when I met a man trying to crawl his way into the ground. He was whimpering in sheer terror, making little animal noises. I stood over him and looked at him arrogantly. He lifted his face and merely whimpered. For a moment I felt like kicking him in the ribs to get him out of the funk he was in. After all, he had only about 200 metres to go to the next ridge, where he would have found comparative shelter with others who were sheltering there. Then in disgust and arrogance I turned away and left him still trying to crawl hissel' into the ground. I call this experience the Courage of the Vine.

Towards the end of our commitment on the Aragon, I think it would be about September 1938, stories began to arise about withdrawing the Internationals. There was a grapevine, a sort of unofficial rumour that was going round about. The anti-tank battery had been disbanded by then and we were attached to various units according to the circumstances we were in. We were withdrawn from the front for a short period about that time and we lazed around for a day or two. We were quite aware that our fate as members of the Republican Army was in the balance. And lying around in the sun – it was still very hot – among the olive trees, we ruminated a bit, discussed things a lot and began to show signs of a desire to go home. I think it was because we had reached the point where a certain tiredness had crept into us. There was also among us a realisation that the fighting in Spain was fast reaching a critical point since Franco had several months earlier broken through from Teruel to the Mediterranean shore, and was beginning to push against the defenders of Barcelona. So we talked a bit and became a wee bit sentimentalised on home.

Well, the rumours were also backed up by the decision to send home some comrades. We knew that some were being sent home but we didn't know who. Chris Smith told me later on that his name was considered. We were speculating on that and perhaps that contributed to the little bit of depression. When you're in a battle you haven't the time to philosophise or sentimentalise in any way. You're committed to the actual experience of the moment. For this moment we were left detached from the action and perhaps these things generated this mood. This was the first time I ever felt slightly depressed. I wasn't exactly depressed but moody – that would be the better term. This was the only occasion that I felt this sort of mood and the others were perhaps feeling it much stronger.

What helped to generate this kind of desire to go home was the fact that George Baker, a Welsh boy, was selected – the only one selected in our group – to be sent back to Britain. George was one of the very fine comrades who made up the anti-tank battery. In the heat and the killing of Brunete there was a moment when George, as a result of the close shelling, became shell-shocked. He developed a little bit of hysteria, without control of himself and we had literally to hold him down. So George went to hospital. When he had recovered he came back and went through all the fighting from Brunete up to this point in the Aragon, without ever batting an eyelid. George was a very splendid comrade. Well, George going home perhaps reawakened our own desire to go home. Actually even then I had arrived at the conclusion that I would never leave Spain, that perhaps I would die in Spain.

But it was a moment in isolation, with nothing else to think about, when these thoughts of ours arose. We were sitting around, just musing in the sun, shaded by the olive trees. Big Ben Glaser, who used to be a bit of an actor, I think, in the early '30s, – he had appeared in Clifford Odets' play *Waiting for Lefty*[153] produced by the Unity Theatre – was talking away casually to himself, half aloud, "Red and green lights on the main masthead." Chris Smith, who was sitting on his left, said "Apropos of what?" "Oh, I'm just recalling some of the lines from plays I've appeared in," Ben said apologetically. But it was clear that Ben was feeling a bit depressed. I understand from what Chris told me later on that Ben wasn't keeping very well physically.

As I've already said, after our retreat across the Ebro everything became confused and we were continually finding ourselves in one situation after another without continuity. So my recollection of these later events after all these years is a bit hazy. But after being attached to Jack Cooper's machine gun crew during the counter offensive we carried across the Ebro, I was taken to Brigade headquarters to work mainly on the production of the *The Volunteer*, the Brigade paper. There mainly I was to do cartoon and illustration work as well as help with the general production of the paper. I discovered being attached to Brigade headquarters meant that I was beginning to receive food and things like that in a way that I hadn't experienced for a long, long time. I appreciated very much indeed their food service with their splendid big American cook. Dave Gordon, the American political commissar – the Americans had now taken over almost totally the control of the XVth Brigade headquarters – was responsible for bringing me in to do this work. One night about the end of September 1938 Dave came for me about twelve midnight on a moonless night and informed me that the treachery of the Munich Pact had just taken place. He then asked me to accompany him to where he was to hold an emergency meeting. I'm not quite sure what the meeting was all about but I believe it was to consider the future of the British volunteers. But on the way we discussed the Munich betrayal and we came to the conclusion that the Spanish Republican Government was going to be defeated. Secondly, we came to the firm conclusion that the Second World War was now inevitable. They were both depressing conclusions.

The question of the evacuation of the International Brigaders or volunteers from Republican Spain arose out of the critical necessity for the Republican Government to maintain some sort of base in Spain. It had been hoped that by making the gesture of allowing the International Brigaders to leave that there would be reciprocal action on the Fascist side. Unfortunately it was like all the other hypocritcal conditions that had been imposed on Republican Spain but not on the Fascists during the whole period - reciprocal action on the other side didn't take place. But it was then made known that Dr. Negrin, the prime minister of Republican Spain, was discussing with the League of Nations the possibility of withdrawing all Internationals from Spain.[154] It was then all the volunteers were gathered in Ripoll, near to the Pyrenees, ready to be evacuated through France.

Now evacuating the Internationals was an immense task, as many
of the volunteers had come from either Fascist controlled countries or
very anti-democratic countries, and what would happen to them?
Well, we lay around, passing the time in Ripoll. The negotiations with
the League of Nations dragged on and dragged on through the latter
part of 1938 before a final decision was made.

One incident that happened in Ripoll involved my foster brother
George and others also. We were lying around in Ripoll waiting to be
evacuated and with nothing much to do, and getting bored, when
suddenly George disappeared. For a whole fortnight I searched and
asked around but couldn't find a trace of him.

I had been given the job, just to have something to do, of taking
charge of his stores by Captain Hookey Walker. He had always been
in charge, right through the whole history of the British Battalion, of
the field kitchens. During that period I found that there was tea and
condensed milk in the stores and the first thing I did was to brew me
up a cup of tea with sugar and condensed milk. This was the first tea
I'd ever tasted in Spain. Actually the coffee that we had been getting
over the latter end of the period was not real coffee. It was toasted
corn. This was the kind of beverage we had to drink and it had very
little stimulative quality. On drinking my first cup of tea I felt welling
up in me a tremendous sense of well being. The sweat began to pour
off me and I felt tremendously stimulated. It was a tremendous
experience. So each time I returned to a cup of tea I had a similar
experience of this access of well being – but in diminishing degrees
until my body got used to drinking the tea and the euphoria more or
less disappeared.

I put in the rest of my time, just for something to do, looking after
Hookey's kitchen and his store rooms. About a fortnight later my
foster brother George suddenly turned up from nowhere. George
looked very sheepish when I told him that I had been very concerned
about him and had been searching everywhere for him. He said,
"Hughie, I started thinking about these poor Spanish boys and the
trouble they're in. And I couldn't help it. I went back to live with
them in the trenches." So George was a soldier who deserted to the
front.

There really isn't very much to say about that period other than we
felt bored in Ripoll and tried to find something to do. There was one
lovely moment that I remember when Chris Smith and I, wandering
about the town, came across a lovely big cherry tree in a woman's
garden. It was a fine sunny December day. We asked the woman if we
could sit up on the tree and eat the cherries and she agreed. Chris paid
her back with some butter. He must have had it sent from home. So
Chris and I through that lovely sunny day sat up on the tree, picking
cherries and tasting their succulence, and just passing the time
blethering about things. That memory remains with me. It was such a

pleasant moment in time. The worries of the war were now beginning to drop away and we were getting more into a mood where we could return to a civilised way of behaving.

It was during this period in Ripoll when we were waiting to be evacuated that we were driven south to Barcelona to be given the tremendous accolade and thanks from the people who turned out in what appeared to be millions to watch us parade through the city. The people cheered us for miles along the main street. I don't remember the name of the street. I never heard any speeches. It was impossible. There was too big a crowd and what anybody said or did didnae arise. In any case I don't even remember getting anywhere near where speeches were made. The women would come running out of the crowd and embracing the volunteers as they passed through. It was like a victory parade. But actually we were quite well aware that behind this enthusiasm was really an unfolding tragedy. I couldn't help but think of the possibility of the enemy bombing this march past. If they had, tens of thousands of people could have been slaughtered. The enemy must have known that any interference with the parade would only have resulted in an adverse reaction throughout the world. So they let us alone. And we went back to Ripoll to await our evacuation.

GOING HOME

After that we began the journey home. The precise memory of these things is very vague to me now but we entrained, I think, at Ripoll and went across the border into France. Quite clearly the French government didn't want us to receive any sort of political or any other kind of accolade in any way. So the train was made to travel practically sealed off right through France to Calais, except for one short stop at Versailles. It was there that Major Malcolm Dunbar disappeared from the train. It was a typical thing for Malcolm to do because he had the feeling that he was going to be involved in a public way that he wished to avoid. So Malcolm disappeared off the train. But this was typical of Malcolm. You couldn't say that he was an anti-social person. But he was an intensely private person and he communicated nothing of his feelings. But he expressed everything in his behaviour. Whether he was aware of it or not his ability to deal with all situations, including the times when he was wounded, in a calm, quiet way commanded respect from everybody. I remember he was wounded in a bombing raid up in the Aragon when he was Major in command of operations, and an American comrade said to me, "That is some man that Dunbar. He's sitting there smoking his cigarette in a long holder, having his wounds dressed and dealing with the military matters he has to deal with." Malcolm always smoked a cigarette at the end of a long holder, a typical upper class image. He was really unique. He was always an enigma to me, a person I could never understand. His motivation in going to Spain was, well, this is difficult as well, because he obviously had a political philosophy that he never even indicated, except that in one conversation I heard him engaged in with Hugh Slater, they were talking about Socrates' dialogues. They were making fun in, I thought, a rather middle class frivolous way of how workers understand these things. From my working class attitude I rather resented the offtaking way they referred to workers' understanding of these things.

I think he was a member of the Communist Party but I'm not sure of that. I think he was. You'll understand that there were many middle class people who understood maybe better than a lot of working class politicans the period of time they were going through, and were looking at life and their commitment to life in that sense. With the rise of Fascism the Civil War gave them an opportunity to make a choice. And therefore it was visualised that with the disaster that might follow with a Second World War, world revolution could possibly be the outcome. So it was a period for thinking people to choose which side are you on. And I think Malcolm Dunbar, Hugh Slater and all the others at that period of time chose the Communist Party. I also don't know for sure if Malcolm had any military training. I would think that he did.

So he disappeared from our train at Versailles and I was never to see Malcolm Dunbar again. I understand now that he was drowned on the south side of the Forth many, many years later. The circumstances I know nothing about.[155]

So apart from that short stop at Versailles we went right through and on to the boat at Calais and into London that night. We received a tremendous welcome, both at Dover and in London. We were entertained to a great reception, I think it was in a Co-operative hall, where various speakers came along to welcome us back. But I don't remember very much about that either.

The only incident I do remember clearly is when I was going up on the lift to the reception hall a man's voice behind me asked, "Does anyone know Ben Glaser?" I said I did. "What happened to Ben Glaser?" And I told him, then I discovered the man was Ben Glaser's brother. I didn't wish to explain all the circumstances of how Ben died. So I was as short as possible in my answers and decided not to explain too harrowing experiences to his brother.

We stayed for a short period in London where we were given private accommodation by people who wished to help us, before getting the bus back to Glasgow. There we were given another reception in the St. Andrews Hall, with Sir Hugh Roberton and the Orpheus Choir in attendance.[156] Sir Hugh gave us a personal welcome back and we were entertained by the Orpheus Choir. That was another tremendous reception. Then I travelled home to Fife.

There were people came to Kirkcaldy Station to greet us, my father, relatives and others, and photographers. We were given a brief welcome at Kirkcaldy Station, got on the bus, with some friends accompanying us, and landed home. I'm not quite sure now how many from the Brigade landed at Kirkcaldy. In East Fife there are now only two volunteers left, Tommy Bloomfield and myself. And I can't remember how many came back to Kirkcaldy station. But the attention seemed to be focused on Tommy Bloomfield, George and myself. So I don't think there were any or many more than us three.

In this small area of Buckhaven, Methil and Leven, seven local men had gone to Spain. Three of the seven were older married men, and were re-shipped home shortly after arriving because of family obligations. That left four of us in Spain. One – Jimmy Donald from Methilhill – was killed in the Ebro battles. The ones that remained to come home after the League of Nations decided to evacuate the Internationals were George Smith, my foster brother, who died in 1985, Malcolm Sneddon, whom I knew before he went to Spain, who last time I heard of him was living in the Nuneaton area, and then myself. There were other comrades who had left from Kirkcaldy. I cannot tell you how many but there is one left there, Tommy Bloomfield. There were others in West Fife but I have no knowledge of many of them. There was John McCormack. I don't know if John is living yet or not. There was John Penman, who was still kept a prisoner after the evacuation, came home with an incurable disease and died.[157] I cannot think of any other Fifers who went to Spain. I did get a communication recently from an East Fife merchant navy man who was operating in the Mediterranean ports of the Republican Government, carrying in supplies from various areas. I didn't know this person myself.

Anyway in Methil, my home town, we were given a reception by the then Provost of Buckhaven and Methil Burgh. Unfortunately a snowstorm raged that night and only a handful of people turned up. The theatre wasn't heated up. It was very cold sitting on the platform and I'm afraid that I couldn't get myself going to say anything about our experiences in Spain and I folded up very quickly, while others wondered what had happened to me. Actually, talking in such conditions to about a dozen people I felt a lack of conviction in anything I said and I just folded up and sat down.

After I came back from Spain I started immediately in the pit, the Michael pit in East Wemyss. I went to the pit official, and his comment was – he called me Smithie, my middle name, which I used in Spain – "What the bloody hell did ye gaun tae Spain for, Smithie? Could ye no' get enough fightin' tae dae here?"

When I returned I found that I couldn't bear to talk about Spain and the sense of loss that I felt about it. The sense of loss was equal to the contribution that you felt you had made and that was tremendous. And you felt you couldn't bear to talk about it. I didn't talk or even think about Spain for years after that.

But I became active again, starting in the pit, and became a member of the Miners' Union Committee. You know that the miners were held in a reserved occupation. Well, I was in no mood to volunteer for any fighting in the Second World War at that stage. But as the War progressed I got involved in the political needs of the War. When the Russians became involved in the War in 1941 I organised a big meeting in one of the cinemas, in which I managed to get the M.P.s, trade unionists and other notables to speak from the platform, calling for the opening of the Second Front. Tom Kennedy, who had been the Labour M.P. for Kirkcaldy Burghs since the early '20s, was one of the main speakers.[158] So we carried out work of that kind. The other work was concerned with the normal trade union activities.

Looking back fifty years later my conclusions about my experiences in Spain have obviously got to be generalised. And the first conclusion ye come tae, that is while the Spanish Civil War arose out o' Spanish conditions the War itself was aggravated through and carried on by, and the defeat o' the Republican Government arose oot o', the political and other events that were taking place in Europe. With the rise of Fascism and Hitler's threat that the German Reich would dominate for a thousand years it became necessary in the early part of the '30s to arouse people to the danger of Fascism. But that only arose because of the treachery of the British and French Governments in particular. It was because of the failure of the British and French Governments to give support to the Republican cause in Spain and, on the other hand, the intervention, even as far back as 1934, of Mussolini, in which he gave money support to the Fascist elements – we'll lump all Francoists as Fascist elements in this respect – giving financial support, promising military intervention. The appeasement policy generated by the French and British Governments which even withheld the money and interest, financial interest abroad, from the Republican Government at a time when they needed that money to sustain the struggle against Franco's insurrection, was sheer treachery. I cannot accept the excuses made by apologists that the uncertainties in any political action taken by the British Government would only have made the Second World War more certain. I cannot accept that as an apology. It is merely a bloody excuse for the treachery of the Chamberlain Government and the Daladiers and the others in France.[159] The tragedy of Spain is that in the beginning the people had to take action on their own in resistance to the Franco insurrection. The army was taken over by the military and also by the Church. And the intervention of Germany and the Italians, supplying tanks, planes, guns, troops and military specialists on the Franco side shows that Non-Intervention was as it had always meant to be – a dead duck that was merely to prevent any victory for the Republican Government in Spain. The reason for the British Government's failure to support the

Republican Government was because inherently it involved a revolutionary change in the whole set up of Spanish society. The changes that were required, the bringing of the peasants and the whole economy into a modern economy away from feudalism, involved inherently a revolutionary change. But it was not the aim of the defenders of the Republican Government to create a revolutionary change. Of course there were elements that demanded revolutionary change. In fact, the P.O.U.M.ists, calling themselves a Marxist Revolutionary Party, a breakaway group from the Spanish Communist Party which had hitherto been a smallish party, raised such slogans as, To Win the War is to Lose the Revolution. These were all divisive, confusing slogans to raise at a time when the Republic was fighting for its life.

Now it was a tremendous feat by the Republicans and the forces uniting behind the Republican effort to create an army of any kind. And the support that was given to them by the volunteers from fifty-odd countries throughout the world showed that there was tremendous support for the fight against Fascism and for the Spanish people in the fight for democracy and peace. The volunteers that came from these countries played an important part in building up a people's army from the ordinary loose mass of workers and peasants in Spain. It could only have happened because the mood of the people was aroused to the point where they were prepared to fight and die rather than give in to the insurrection. It would be wrong to say that the volunteers played a decisive part. The Spanish people played the decisive part. But the volunteers gave them an inspirational factor as well as expert advice. So when the army had been treacherously taken away from the support of the Government by the Francoists, the International Brigaders played an important part in building up the people's army from scratch. That was a tremendous fact. There are many things to be learned from the Spanish struggle. That is one – the unity in action of the Spanish people, despite historical differences both in its geography and in its political set up.

Appeasers who betrayed the whole situation in the 1930s to the inevitability of the Second World War in which sixty million people died, should be recalled and thought about by the present generation of people, to learn the lessons of the Spanish struggle. If the British and French Governments had been truly democratic governments, the opportunity was given to them again and again by the Soviet Union to create a situation in which the Second World War would not have been necessary and the Spanish Civil War would not have been necessary. If these two western Governments had co-operated to the full and in good faith with the offers made by the Soviet Union I feel that neither of these two events could have happened and that the defeat of Hitler could have been brought about. He was beginning to run into economic troubles as a result of his policies and only sustained his position through the so-called victories that he was allowed to attain in expanding in Europe. I could say all that arose from very ambivalent strategic considerations that had been operating from 1917 onwards when the Russian Revolution took place, because it was the main consideration in all capitalist countries to bring about the destruction of a country that seemed to indicate the end of the capitalist system of society. But these are loose generalisations I'm making.

As for the impact on me personally of the Spanish War, well, I've said I couldn't bear to speak about the war until some years after I had returned from Spain. But that didnae change my attitude to things. No, no, that didnae change my attitude. In fact, looking back over my life I have the clear conviction in myself that it has been a continuous developing political situation for me, a continuity and confirmation of all my beliefs. My attitude is essentially political. I have never for one moment felt that in any way I have been side-tracked from that continuity of things. For instance, when I was in Spain I heard one British International Brigader early on discussing why volunteers went to Spain, saying in a rather facetious or funny way that perhaps some of them wanted to get away from family troubles, their wives and so on. Well, my political attitude in going to Spain arose out of a compulsive need for me to act according to my political involvement and convictions. It seemed to be a logical progression of my political development. And I felt a little bit disgusted at that kind of remark even although it was just in a frivolous kind of conversation. I was almost puritanical in these convictions about things. So I don't think that there was any interruption or digression in my political, or in the development of my philosophical or my emotional development, even although I was a bit put out after the defeat of the Republican Government. I feel that my personal development has been continuous and more and more am I convinced of the correctness of these convictions that I developed through all the periods of my life. The Spanish Civil War was the central experience of my life.

Garry McCartney was born in Glasgow in 1909. As an apprentice he took part in the 1926 General Strike. Apart from some periods of unemployment and his time in Spain he worked all his life as a blacksmith. He died early in 1985, a few months after these recollections were recorded.

GARRY McCARTNEY

In the summer of 1936 Bill Donaldson and I were up in Skye climbing the Cuillins. We had been up there since the beginning of the Glasgow Fair right on. We hadn't read a paper during this fortnight, and when we came back down from the hills we learned that there was a war raging in Spain.

Now Bill and I were both in the Communist Party. It didn't take us very long to come to a decision that rather than just speak about being anti-Fascist, here was an opportunity of doing something much more tangible. We agreed that we should consider seriously the whole question of getting to Spain to play our part.

We were already politically motivated, as were many, many thousands of people up and down the country, because we had seen the advent of Fascism in Germany in 1933, when Hitler got in power. We had seen Mussolini flexing his muscles in the Abyssinian war. So Fascism was on the march in Europe. And in Britain Mosley, who had made attempts to form his New Party by coming to the St. Andrews Halls in Glasgow for a meeting became a member of the British Union of Fascists – actually he was the Party. And we had the experiences of the anti-Fascist struggles in Cable Street, London, and suchlike episodes up and down the country.[160] So that we were not taken by surprise that we were suddenly embroiled in an anti-Fascist struggle because this was part and parcel of what was happening in Europe and attempts were being made by Mosley and company to bring about a similar situation in Britain.

The working class movement in Glasgow was very much informed and very much involved in the anti-Fascist struggle. Glasgow at the weekend was a forum of meetings, all over the city, at street corners, and in the centre of the city. We had the tramp preachers, we had the Y.C.L., we had the Independent Labour Party, we had the Labour Party, we had the Communist Party. It was a whole seabed of discussions, all aiming in the one direction: how do we get socialism? What do we have to do to win socialism?

So Bill Donaldson and I were part of all this and we were fully committed. But it wasn't until Phil Gillan, who had gone to Spain very early on in the war, was badly wounded in the neck, repatriated home, and did a series of meetings, speaking about what was

241

happening in Spain and suchlike, what the struggle was all about, that if Bill and I had had any doubts about the need for us to go to Spain, towards the end of 1936 we were fully convinced that this is what we should be doing.

Bill and I were both working and we made overtures to the Party to get to Spain. Now this was done in January 1937. I don't know what happened. I think perhaps they looked into the background of our families, or they may have thought about the work we were doing already within the Young Communist League and the Party. But it wasn't until June of 1937 that Bill and I were told, "Do you still wish to go to Spain? The opportunity is there now." So we grabbed it. And along with another Glasgow lad, John Riley, we left Glasgow towards the end of the first week in July 1937.[161]

Now I had written a letter to my mother. I didn't tell her where I was going other than that Bill and I were going to do some climbing in the Pyrenees. We knew at least that much, that's the way we'd be going in to Spain. And I took the letter up to my brother Andy who worked in the *Daily Record* office in Hope Street. I said, "Andy, give this to mother when you see her in the morning after your night shift. I'm going away to Spain. Don't tell anyone because if I'm caught leaving the country there is the question of a jail sentence under the Foreign Enlistment Act."[162] Bill had left a similar message for his folks. And we were on our way to Spain.

We went down to London, to King Street. Now the three of us, Bill, John Riley and myself were interviewed in King Street about our status politically and why we wanted to go to Spain. It must have been satisfactory because I was given the cash to get tickets from the station in London to Paris. It had already been decided in Glasgow that I was going to be in charge of whatever was necessary, meeting people and suchlike.

On the ferry we met Val Sherman and Tommy Moore.[163] Val Sherman came from London, Tommy Moore from Manchester. They had been in King Street at the same time as we were, although it was only later when we were introduced to them. And again they knew that I was the so-called group leader. There were no problems about getting to Paris because we didn't require passports. At that time there was a big exhibition in Paris and all that was required was the purchase of a weekend ticket that got one into France and out again without passports.

So we had to go to the House of Syndicates in Paris and I made the contacts with whoever was in charge. We were directed to the area called Combat in Paris. We were there for about ten days. We thought we would just be moving in and moving out, but that wasn't the position. There must obviously have been a whole organisation dealing with volunteers. We were about ten days in Paris before we made our next move, to Lyons. I was told how to ask for five tickets to Lyons. We would be met – "Don't worry and we'll take it from Lyons for the rest of your journey."

The one thing that was emphasised was that no drink was to be taken. There was to be no drinking at all because people might speak through drink and reveal who we were and that we were going to Spain and why we were going. I can remember in the carriage Val Sherman said, "Garry, look what I've got." And he had two bottles of liquor. He had bought them. I don't remember whether Val was in the Communist Party or not. But he didn't have, I think from memory, the same attitude towards going to Spain as I had. So I said to him, "Listen, Val. You heard me quite clearly about no drinking. There was no drink to be taken. These were my instructions to be given to all of us." And I said, "Give me the two bottles." So I received the two bottles and dropped them out of the carriage window. On reflection I think it was a waste of good drink.

We went to Lyons and had an overnight stay. The people who had met us then arranged for us to continue our journey the following morning to some place before we got to Perpignan. I can't remember the name of the town. But we had the same procedures. We were met, then a night's overstay, then on to Perpignan. So we were about roughly two weeks already in France by the time we got to Perpignan.

There we met Sam Russell.[164] Sam had already been in Spain and was the liaison officer for comrades going and coming back. I remember Sam looking at the clothes Bill and myself were wearing. We were pretty well geared up, you know, young men about town, both of us working and with good wages in those days. We had nice overcoats, which would not be necessary in Spain. We had nice jackets, which again would not be necessary. So we just decided, "We'll leave these things." And as far as money was concerned I think we had between us about £40 in English currency. And we gave this to Sam for whatever cause it would be – the *Daily Worker* fund or perhaps the Dependants' Aid Fund or whatever.[165] I can't remember if it was stipulated. But I'm quite sure it was given to the proper source. Sam was that kind of person.

We were at Perpignan for one night and then we were moved in a group of about fifty people, who had gathered just on the outskirts of Perpignan. We were taken to a farmhouse. There we stayed until well into the night and then all of us had to leave. Our rations were handed to us as we came out the door. All of us had *alpargatas*, rope-sole sandals. Now these were obviously for doing the climbing, where the ordinary leather footwear would not have been suitable. We had left our own footwear for comrades who were returning from Spain.

We did sixteen hours of climbing and got into Spain. And coming across that top hill that separated France from Spain there were two guards, two members of the Spanish Republican Army, and they rushed forward, cheering us and welcoming us. And it was downhill of course to a village, where we were put in coaches and taken to Figueras. In this contingent of around fifty volunteers, there were three of us from Glasgow and Val Sherman and Tommy Moore. But the rest were from all the countries, I think, in Europe, not least Germany. Now these lads were escaping from a Fascist country to come to Spain to do what they felt they should do, continue the anti-Fascist struggle where it was being fought.

It would be the following day, after we had washed and rested ourselves the comrade in charge of the fort at Figueras called us together. He was a member of the International Brigade, speaking good English. I don't know his nationality. But he wasn't English. He asked us, "Are you quite sure now, even at this eleventh hour, that you want to continue going into Spain, being part of the International Brigades?" And he painted what war was all about. He painted a word picture that didn't sound very happy at all. And I mention this in order to show that there was no question of us being mercenaries in the way that we would understand the word. We were volunteers. If perhaps in a fit of enthusiasm we had said we wanted to go to Spain, the offer was now being made that, "If you wish to go back nothing will be said. We won't have any recriminations of any kind. You've just been too enthusiastic and now you know when you see the kind of picture as it has been painted to you, you've got other ideas. Nothing will be said if you wish to go back." But none of us did. To my knowledge this was the *modus operandi* for all the volunteers. Now I've heard volunteers saying that they never had this opportunity that was given to us. Perhaps they were there before we went. It may have been a different comrade in charge of the fort. I don't know. But this was certainly said to us.

Now we went a train journey from Figueras down to Barcelona. We spent two days there and then we were taken on to Albacete, which was the base for the Internationals. I think we had already signed on in Figueras, if that's the term to use of voluntarily becoming members of the International Brigades. But anyway we did further signings in Albacete and then it was a relatively short journey from there to Tarazona, which was the English-speaking training base for the volunteers.

There were quite a number of English comrades already in Tarazona. But there were also the Americans and the Canadians billeted in Tarazona. So this was the base, the township, for the volunteers going to do a period of training before moving up to their respective battalions.

Shortly after going in to Tarazona I was sent to a place called Pozorrubio, to take a course for officer training. I became quite expert with the rifle. We were under the tuition of a Russian comrade, an adviser. I was to be a sniper. I never was a sniper. I never got the opportunity of putting into practice what I had been taught. I became a machine gunner.

When we came back to Tarazona there were lads who had been at the school with me. We were also in a class, I shall call it a classroom, getting further training as officers.

Now this didn't suit me at all. I felt disturbed about all this. It wasn't at my asking. This was being shall I say imposed on me. George Fletcher, who was an officer in the British Battalion, was taking a group of some thirty comrades to reinforce the Battalion going into Quinto, where there was a battle. I decided that the lads with whom I had gone into Spain, Bill Donaldson, Tommy Moore, Val and John Riley and other comrades with whom I had made friends – these were the people that I wanted to be with, not, with all respect due to them, the other comrades who were at this officers' training school. So I said, "George, I take it as long as you've got thirty people in there you won't mind an extra member?" He said, "I've nothing to do with it. My eyes are closed." So I decided to stow away. And we went to Albacete. I jumped into the van and I was on my way to Albacete – "Goodbye, officers' training school, I'm now part of what I wanted to be, part of the Battalion." And in the early morning this American comrade, Johnson, who was the officer in charge of the base suddenly appeared at the base of Albacete. This would be around three or four in the morning. And George Fletcher was asked, "Have you a Garry McCartney here?" Of course, there was a Garry McCartney there. And feeling very sheepish I was called out and brought back. "Now you've committed a crime, McCartney. You've deserted. Right enough you're deserting to the front but nevertheless you are a deserter from the base. And we don't take decisions lightly about having classes and schools and suchlike. People in these places are expected to obey the rules and regulations and accept the responsibility, and you haven't. You decided to run away and join your mates." Or words to that effect.

So as I said I was rather sheepish about the whole affair and I was brought back to Tarazona. And there I was kept for another three or four weeks before finally joining the Battalion. The officers' training in the main was technical classes. Could one say the art of learning warfare? How to deploy one's forces and take cover, adopt camouflage – these kind of things, and day to day lessons on the Maxim gun. Now the Maxim gun is a heavy machine gun, water cooled. It wasn't always water, incidentally, that was used to cool it. Sometimes it was urine, when we didn't have the water. And we had to learn the five stoppages that gun has. We had to dismantle the lock and if perchance we had to do this at any time during a battle or at night time we had to be able to dismantle the lock, take it down blind-folded and put it back up again. So day to day training and tuition on this most important part of the gun, the lock, was very good and I think that all of us passed our tests quite successfully. The officers were taught how to get the range of fire. There were three guns in the Battalion, at least with the Spanish machine gunners. Now I had to draw, say, No. 1 gun. I would put it on the swivel and push it its maximum to the left and take a note of where the extreme left of range of fire was that I had in my gun. It may have been a house, a tree or a footpath or something, and I would make a sketch, turn it completely to the right, and take the same reading. Now I had to make sure the field of fire of No. 2 gun at least met up with that of the No. 1 gun, in order that there could be criss-cross fire to ensure that there was no space left whereby the enemy might come in. And the same with the No. 3 gun. So there was a range of lessons and knowledge required that was most helpful to anyone being in the position that I was put.

This was now well into the autumn or the fall of the year. Quinto had already been won by the Republican forces. There was a big tank battle there, that we used to get lectures on. I was put in charge, incidentally, of the Spanish Machine Gun Company. We had three guns, as I've said, Maxim guns. I had already a smattering of Spanish because at this officers' training school we were given Spanish lessons. And I was picking it up quite well, I think – although that wasn't the reason why I was given this job. I don't know why I was given that job. I was put in along with the Spanish machine gunners – "And you are in charge."

The first action we were in was Perales upon the Aragon front. And that was the baptism of fire. Bill Donaldson was with me, near me, anyway. We weren't together in the actual battle but Bill Donaldson – the lad with whom I went to Spain, an engineer by vocation and a great anti-Fascist comrade, a Glasgow man, came from Dennistoun – Bill said, "Now, Garry, I've already been under fire at Quinto. It's nothing to be alarmed about." He said, "Those bastards over there, the only reason why they fire is because they're frightened that they're going to be fired on." Almost within about ten minutes or so the firing started. We were in fairly good sheltered positions. But one can be in a good position, relatively safe, shall I say, but when one hears gunfire and even heavier stuff, one never knows how one's going to react until you are put to the test. And it's rather shattering, it's rather nerve-racking to know that what you're hearing are things full of lead. It's the ones that you don't hear of course that do the damage. They've already penetrated the body. So that was a baptism. To be honest, I was a little bit afraid listening to the fire coming towards us. But one gets so interested in the job in hand, and with the responsibility that one has and the discipline that goes with that, and the anti-Fascist conviction above all else, then already you're on fairly secure grounds that you'll do your very best to ensure that the things for which you went to Spain will come to bear.

Next was Teruel, where the big battle took place. And so on into 1938. Teruel was captured by Spanish Republican soldiers some time in late December 1937. There was great jubilation on the part of the Republican forces when this took place because Teruel was a key point. To have inflicted such a defeat on the Fascists was really a red letter day for the whole of the Republic. And it says something that again should always be remembered, that we International Brigaders went to Spain principally as a gesture of international solidarity. We didn't go to Spain to teach or show the Spanish people how to fight or the Spanish army how it should be done, bcause they were the first to take up arms in defence of this democracy and we were only privileged to take part as an integral part of the Spanish Republican army. We were members of the Spanish Republican army and it was only incidental, you know, that we were fighting alongside Spaniards.

Our ranks were augmented by sometimes two and three companies of Spaniards. So that as I say we ought not to think that we went to Spain and we won all the battles. It was the other way around. They had our assistance but they were the ones who were doing the job.

Now that apart we took over from the Spanish brigades. There were the Canadians, the Americans, and the British in different sectors of the Teruel front. And it would be towards the middle of January when the Fascists were reinforcing themselves to make an onslaught and recapture Teruel. Now the battle of which I am going to speak is the one that saw the deaths of some twenty-odd British comrades at Teruel. The machine gun positions were placed as they had been since we had taken over from the Spanish companies. Bill Alexander was the commander of the Battalion at that time. And No. 1 company, which was called the Major Attlee Company, went down into the valley, over the river on the way to Concud. And shortly afterwards the Fascists pinpointed the position where our comrades had gone. They landed shells marking a square of quite large dimensions and then saturated that square not only with shell fire and machine gun fire, but they sent across their aircraft to bomb it. So that there were tremendous casualties, not only down in the valley. The shelling was most accurate and caused havoc on the positions. The trenches which we had built and taken over from the Spaniards were also saturated with heavy shelling. It was quite a remarkable day from very early morning right on till late at night. And we had to count our losses, I'm afraid, rather sadly.

The Fascists entrenched themselves in the territory which thcy had won, which wasn't so very far away from our heights up in Teruel – perhaps about three or four hundred metres. And there was a quietness on the front for the next three or four days. If the Fascists had continued they had nothing to meet them really. There were whole stretches of trench lines empty of Republican soldiers, and they could have marched into Teruel. But we were withdrawn some time towards the end of January and the Spanish brigades took over from us. I'm afraid, because of the situation prevailing and the amount of material which Franco had, and used, Teruel went to Franco towards the end of January. And that was the beginning of his big push in the Aragon. We were in a position whereby we were in the main fighting during the day and going back north east at night time. It was a dreadful position in the Aragon for almost two months. That was the two months following our withdrawal from Teruel towards the end of January. It was not a happy period for the Republican High Command.

One of the reasons was the different types of rifles and ammunition that we had. Now an army can't fight a successful battle if they have Mauser rifles and ammunition that only fits the Maxim machine gun. We don't go very far that way, successfully anyway. And this is what was happening. All because the Committee of Non-Intervention, which was formed at the beginning of September or end of August 1936 at the behest of the British and French Governments. Now this Committee of Non-Intervention had taken a decision that they would not interfere in any way whatsoever with the War in Spain. They called it a civil war, with warring factions, one side against the other, purely Spanish – which wasn't the case, because the Fascist powers in the shape of Hitler and Mussolini had already had a pact with Franco and were putting it into operation. And where Franco was getting all the assistance in men and materials that he required to try and overthrow the democratically elected Republican Government, the Republican Government on the other hand was denied its right to buy the arms it sorely required to defend its democracy.

I think there were eight or nine countries forming that Committee of Non-Intervention, and the Soviet Union was also a party to that particular agreement. But it should be remembered that Professor Maisky, who was the Soviet representative on that Committee, made it abundantly clear that the Soviet Union would only recognise the terms of the Non-Intervention Pact in so far as they were recognised by other powers.[166] And if other powers were supporting one side, the Soviet Union could take it upon itself to say, "The Pact is not being observed and we reserve the right to help where we can and if we wish."

So the Soviet Government did help the Republican Government to the best of its ability in quite substantial terms on these occasions with material. Unfortunately the frontier was closed between France and Spain and the French Government certainly put into operation in a very, very forceful way the pact, and did not allow the free transit of materials. It was only ships that could make the long journey from the Soviet Union into Republican ports that helped out the Spanish Government, although when one looks at the geography and the distances that had to be travelled this was something that really could have been overcome more easily had the Western Powers taken a decision to support a democratically elected Government. So that they weren't playing the game in which they were supposed to be all for democracy. They were definitely leaning towards the side of Franco and hoping that he would win that particular war. That's one reason, and a very important one, I think, why the Republican Government found great difficulty in getting the means to defend itself.

Sam Wild and myself it so happened had been the longest serving members of the Battalion, I think, other than Hookey Walker, who was the commandante of the kitchen staff – a great person. But Sam and I were given leave of absence to go to a place called Valdeganga, where Nan Green was in charge of this rest camp. And we were going to have a few days in Valdeganga, Sam and I, and then on to Madrid. Now this was a great thing, you know. I had never been to Madrid and was looking forward to it. Sam had already been to Madrid but he also was looking forward to the leave and the rest. But about 3 a.m. or 4 a.m. word came, "McCartney and Wild are required at Battalion. We're moving and going into action." So the leave never happened to me, you know. I think I had two or three hours' sleep. I had a hot bath right enough, which was very nice, I remember that. But we were back and joined the Battalion.

So it was action all the way from there until the morning I was captured at a place called Calaceite. This was on the 31st March, 1938. That was the beginning of almost a year in one of Franco's camps of concentration. We were taken to the Academy in Saragossa, about three days or so after we had been taken prisoner and had given our declarations to those who had captured us, as to why we had gone to Spain and from where and suchlike. The Battalion had been reinforced by new recruits just prior to going into that particular battle at Calaceite. Consequently there were many comrades who were prisoners that did not know each other. And being prisoners we were rather cautious as to what we were saying and to whom we were speaking. I can remember being in close contact with Willie Collins from Govan, and Donald Carson, also from Govan, a member of the Amalgamated Society of Woodcutting-Machinists who had worked formerly in the bookshop in High Street for the Communist Party, and another comrade whose name I forget the now – I knew him to be a Party member. Now we were a group of four people and we were taking decisions arising from our close conversations as to how we should react under certain circumstances. We felt that a discussion and maybe decisions would be useful. And if we thought this a correct decision we should try and get other comrades who had been taken prisoner to act in a like manner.

Another group including Danny Gibbons and Maurice Levine, was doing the same thing. They were comrades that I didn't know, but they were members of the Party and taking decisions such as we were taking. Danny Gibbons came from the Vale of Leven, but had been resident in London. He had already been in Spain, had been repatriated some time after Jarama, had done a propaganda tour and had gone back again.[167]

The military academy at Saragossa was where Franco had learned his soldiering. And this academy was the scene for a whole lot of the European press who had been forewarned that British prisoners were coming. There were maybe 120 of us that were captured at Calaceite, among whom was Frank Ryan, a great Irish patriot. Now we were told that being prisoners of Franco we would have to conform to the rules and regulations of the prison camp and it would mean, of course, giving the Fascist salute when required to do so. And this would be done forthwith.

Now this was obviously for the benefit of the press that had gathered. We were lined up in a single file. But Frank Ryan gave us a very good lead when he said, "Don't give the Fascist salute, comrades. We're British. And we have rights under the edict of the League of Nations in respect to what they may or may not do to us. And I would think that we are on safe grounds not to give the Fascist salute." It was along these lines that Frank was speaking.

There was a lad there called Maxie Parker, who was an American who had been captured. He came from the Bronx. He spoke quite a bit of Spanish and he was acting as interpreter. So we asked for a meeting to discuss this question of having to give the Fascist salute and this was granted to us. So there was a number of us met, not as an elected committee but merely as people who were interested in not complying with the order of the Fascists. We came to this decision: we'd make a compromise. On the command to give the Fascist salute we would raise our hand and give the British salute, raise our hand slightly and then back again to the forehead and down. This was the compromise. Now you've never seen such a shambles. When the order was given it was like seeing a hundred tick-tack men at a racecourse, all waving their arms about in different directions. We knew that the press were obviously not getting the satisfaction that possibly they thought they would get from seeing some hundred-odd men giving Fascist salutes on command some two or three days after being taken prisoner. So the question of a salute fell by the wayside at that time.

While we were at the military academy Merry del Val appeared. He was a member of the former Spanish government on the justiciary side and had been Spanish consul in Britain. He spoke very, very good English as one can imagine. We were lined up, and Jimmy Rutherford, who was beside me at the time, was a lad who had been repatriated earlier after being taken prisoner at Jarama and came back home to Edinburgh. All of the prisoners captured were repatriated home to Britain. Jimmy after doing a propaganda tour had gone back to Spain and was captured for the second time. League of Nations' legislation was passed that if persons were repatriated after having been taken prisoner the government of that person's country would ensure that he did not take part in the War again. Now Jimmy had broken a promise that was legally binding on prisoners of war as far as the League of Nations was concerned. So that when Merry del Val passed along the ranks Jimmy says, "This was the lad who was in the courtroom, and he'll probably remember me."

Jimmy wasn't known as Jimmy Rutherford when he was taken prisoner. He had given his name as Jimmy Smith. But Merry del Val, passing up the ranks, had just passed Jimmy two or three steps when he returned and said: "I've seen you before." Now obviously he recognised Jimmy as one of the prisoners that had been repatriated in 1937 and he was going to do something about it.

We were transferred from the military academy in a railway truck journey to a place that was to be our home for eleven months San Pedro de Cardenas near Burgos. And Jimmy was taken from our midst about three weeks after we had gone to San Pedro. He was taken to Burgos and word was conveyed to us by Colonel Martin. He was the representative of the British Government in Burgos.[168] He came to the prison camp and told us that in view of the fact that Jimmy had broken his faith going back to Spain to the War he had been shot. And of course the people in Edinburgh held a memorial service for the memory of Jimmy and all that he had stood for.

Frank Ryan was also taken from our ranks in San Pedro de Cardenas. He was kept a prisoner of war in Burgos for many, many months even after the War in Spain was finished. Later he was transferred to Germany. And it was claimed that he was assisting the Nazi chiefs of staff in making broadcasts over the radio to Irish patriots and suchlike as to how it was much better to be under the rule of Hitler than under the rule of a British democracy and suchlike. Now anyone who knew Frank Ryan would know the integrity of the man, how staunch he was for the cause of the working class in its struggle to achieve socialism, and could not but come to a conclusion that what was being put out about Frank Ryan was just a tissue of lies. He was supposed to have agreed to make a journey in a German two-man submarine to Ireland and then work on behalf of the German Government in whatever way they had asked him to do. Now to our knowledge there was some credence given to that story but he never arrived in Ireland and was back in Germany. We can only assume, knowing the man Frank Ryan, that if Frank agreed to go to Ireland it would not be for the purposes of Hitler but Frank would be making contact as soon as possible with his former freedom fighting comrades in the cause for which he always stood. But whether that was factual or otherwise none of us knows. But at Loughborough College, where some thirty International Brigadiers had a meeting about four or five years ago we had a seminar one afternoon, discussing Frank Ryan, and all of us came to the conclusion that Frank was such a person that anything written about his Fascist sympathies was derogatory and not in keeping with the true facts of the situation.

Frank Ryan died in Germany and his grave was in Dresden, East Germany. I was a guest of the East German anti-Fascist Committees about six years ago, visited the grave and photographed it. It was only within the past few years that the Irish patriots asked through the Irish Government to make contact with the East German Government, whereby the body of Frank could be returned to his native Ireland. This was done and Frank was reburied in some place in South Ireland.

Conditions at the concentration camp near Burgos were dreadful, dreadful. We never dreamt that guards could be so brutal to other human beings, because these guards were not human beings in many, many respects. The camp was controlled by the Gestapo, of whom there were at least three members. We made declarations to them quite regularly in which we gave them our name and home address. We had to answer why we had gone to Spain, did we have a rifle, and suchlike.

We had formed the semblance of a Committee in the camp, comprising Danny Gibbons, Jack Jones,[169] myself, an American comrade, a German comrade – all members of the Communist Party. To the best of our ability we met regularly and discussed situations that had arisen and might arise, in order that we could give whatever guidance and leadership we could to some 400 prisoners already in that camp, all Internationals. There were three to five thousand Spaniards also in the camp as prisoners, used as reinforcements to labour battalions and suchlike. It was an old convent in which we were incarcerated, but the Internationals were separated from the Spaniards, from one side of the place to the other. We occupied two floors in this old convent, San Pedro. As I say the conditions were abominable. For example, when we were taken down for food there were two huge bins of soup or something akin to soup, and we were told: "Help yourself." No queues. And hungry men, not knowing how to speak to each other, going forward, putting in a cup or a plate and pulling it out, with the Fascist guards standing by with their riding crops and sticks beating us in order that we did not linger over taking what was within the bins. This was the kind of treatment. Now we couldn't continue in a situation like that. And we, the British, through the committee, organised a queue. We decided that we should get away from the camp as mentally and physically fit as possible. So we suggested through the committee to the various Internationals they should follow the lead of the British.

And we went out first on the following day or so and we lined up in file in order to move forward to get the food. The rest of the prisoners followed behind the two files that we had made, thereby denying the opportunities of the Fascists to say, "This was only a rabble, we'll have to beat them to get some sense into them." And this was a good tactic that we started off. The queue became part and parcel of our daily routine. It didn't matter who was first or whatever. But we followed in a queue, rather than going up in a charging mob to grab the food that the Fascists would have loved to see us continue to do, so they would have the opportunity of beating us indiscriminately.

I am in no doubt that the Fascists did this as a means of deliberately humiliating the prisoners. No question about it. It wasn't just a question of inefficiency on their part. They did this quite deliberately.

Again we had to take part in Mass every Sunday. No matter what our religion was this was given as an order. We protested to the commandante of the camp that not all of us were of the Catholic faith. And we felt that the rules and regulations of prisoners of war, as laid down by the League of Nations, surely gave the right of prisoners to observe freedom of religion. We asked that an understanding on this question should be given to the Internationals. This was refused to us. We were told we would require to take part in the service every Sunday.

Now we had a meeting about it. There is part of the Catholic service in which one goes down on one's knee though I am not just quite sure what part of the service that is.[170] We were in a huge quadrangle that accepted these numbers of perhaps three or four thousand men. We, the Internationals, were right at the back and all the Spaniards were out in front of us. And when the service was being performed by the padre conducting the mass he came to that part of the service that indicated that we observed this. Now we had already discussed the question and some of the Internationals stood and some got down on their knees. There was nothing sort of regular about what was happening on that particular Sunday. But when we saw our German comrades getting beaten up we decided that something should be done. Again we asked the commandante of the camp to observe the regulations on the rights of prisoners of war. Again he refused. So we protested and made further protests to the British Government that this was happening when we contacted Colonel Martin, the British Government's representative. We decided that we would, under protest, take part in the service and comply with what they wanted. But it didn't mean we accepted what they wanted us to believe, that religion was a way of expressing freedom of speech, because they were denying us the right to have our own kind of worship if we so desired.

The German comrades had been beaten because they refused to go down on their knees. We explained to the German comrades and to others that we would treat this the same way as we did the Fascist salute. We wanted out of the camp as physically and mentally fit as possible and that bending the knee at mass didn't mean anything because we knew that the anti-Fascist feelings of the vast majority of the International prisoners of war were as solid and sincere as ever. No one was demeaning himself by observing these rules under duress.

We had to my knowledge four visits from Colonel Martin. The first time he came was to see the prisoners. This was perhaps about four or five weeks after we had been in San Pedro. He got names and addresses and suchlike and we were asking for the right and permission to be able to write home to our people, because quite a number of us had already been listed as killed in action. Our people at home didn't know we were prisoners of war and didn't know whether we were alive or dead. For example take George Drever, an Edinburgh man captured at Belchite towards the middle of March. It was reported that George had been seen as a corpse, and this was conveyed back to Britain. A memorial service was held for him in Edinburgh but when George went home some time towards the end of 1938 after his period of incarceration in the two camps he was in, he went to the *Edinburgh Evening News* and told them that the report of his death had been greatly exaggerated.

At San Pedro we were housed on two floors. When I say two floors I mean that literally. If you were lucky enough to have a blanket that was all right, perhaps you were a wee bit warmer than many of us who had no blankets or no utensils, cups or plates, whatever. We had to try and organise and get these things, not always successfully.

Up in the front lines on the Republican side we all had lice. But that was nothing to the millions of lice and fleas that were part and parcel of every hour that we were in that prison camp. It was dreadful.

We had five closets for over 400 men – dry closets, I'm talking about. We organised ourselves into groups to take part in the cleaning of these dry closets.

There were four washhand basins, so-called, down on the floor, on the first floor and the only thing on the top floor where I was was a pipe with cold water gushing out continuously. To try and have a modicum of cleanliness Willie Collins from Govan and myself – he and I had been captured at the same time – used to go along about two or three o'clock in the morning and have a cold shower and dry ourselves with our hands then back to sleep on the floor, on the floor, with no blanket, no mattress.

It's very, very cold in Burgos in the winter time and I can tell you it took a lot of courage and fortitude to really withstand these conditions and maintain a semblance of manhood. Conditions were really dreadful. We were cold and in need of nourishment. There were two meals a day, or so-called meals, consisting of that soup I told you about at midday and in the evening two small loaves with a plate of little fish like sardines, cooked in a grease and a concoction of olive oil and something else, served up head, tails, scales and guts. But you're hungry, so you eat what's in front of you, and happy to get it. There was a gruel given at breakfast but not everyone could even look at that and only a few of us could swallow that horrible first course.

There were three or four comrades died during that period while I was a prisoner. The same coffin was used for all of them. The body was put into a box, not a coffin shaped as such but merely a box, taken down and up-ended into a hole that had been dug by the Spaniards. The box was then taken away again, with the priest giving the last rites, whether the dead person had wanted them or not, and with perhaps a dozen or so prisoners observing the memory of the comrade who had passed on.

I wouldn't know what these men died of. I think it must have been undernourishment or whatever. The fact that we were herded so close together on two floors meant it couldn't be anything else but a hotbed for diseases and suchlike things to take over on a person who was the least bit ill-equipped to fight against them.

Dysentery was very, very rife. You know we had this kind of treatment where dysentery was such a common feature, and to see lads perhaps not being able to be continent, and the need to go to the toilet while they were out on the courtyard and suchlike and not being allowed in the sense that the toilets were, as I said, upstairs. But we were supposed to conform and do all the things that nature requires to be done but in which not everyone could conform because of the physical situation in which they found themselves.

We didn't have any doctors among the prisoners of war, and none of the prisoners to my knowledge were themselves skilled in medical aid. But we did have a part of the prison camp in which the Sisters of Mercy had a small hospital that possibly held about twenty beds. These were used at times. For example, my comrade Willie Collins took quite ill from just weakness and ill-nourishment in the winter time. And he was in the hospital for a little over a week. Now the Sisters of Mercy, let me say, did what they possibly could to ease the discomfort and help the patients but I would imagine that their sources of revenue were such that they could have done much, much more if only they had had the funds and the proper food and the milk to make it easier for such people within their care.

We always knew or felt by virtue of the fact that we had the British Government's representative Colonel Martin seeing us on a few occasions, that the British people would be making agitation and calling for our repatriation. We always felt that we at some time would be repatriated. But the comrades from Central Europe, particularly the German comrades, they had no chance, because they had escaped from Nazi Germany to go into Spain to fight Fascism. And one could only conjure up what happened to these comrades after we left the camp. Despite the fact that all of us had the sticks over our backs at some time or other, we were a restraining influence, I think, on the Gestapo and on the Fascist guards from really going to town on prisoners. But when we left who else was there to speak? There were no visitors coming on behalf of the prisoners that remained from any of the Fascist countries, Hungary, Poland, Yugoslavia, Italy, Germany – there was nobody coming to speak on their behalf or to do what they could for prisoners. And we can only imagine what happened to them after they were sent back to their various countries that Hitler was in complete control of.

I remember there were three Germans escaped while I was at San Pedro. Two of them were brought back. I don't know what happened to the third one. These two Germans were isolated when they were brought back by being put in the dungeons. These were right at the basement of the prison. It was shortly before we were repatriated they were put there and they were still there when we left, several weeks later.

There was another occasion when attempts to escape were unsuccessful. This was during the summer time and we used to be allowed out, principally to delouse ourselves. It wasn't a question of a grandiose gesture on the part of the Fascists – "Go out and enjoy yourselves." Delousing was the reason for it. We were in the quadrangle and the little bit beyond, but the guards were around to ensure that nobody took it on the lam, that is, got off his mark. Now we tried to form ourselves into social activity, and the Americans challenged the British to a game of rounders, or baseball as they called it. And on such days, perhaps, there was a little bit of light entertainment, even in these conditions, and we had this kind of friendly game taking place among certain members who were prisoners. Now during these proceedings there were two German comrades who decided to practice for the cross-country race and they hid in the bushes until we were all taken back into our quarters. It was discovered later at roll call, that two prisoners were not present who should have been. This roll call was taken very early in the morning just as daylight was coming when we were called to form up ranks. And at night time, last thing at night before the Fascist guards finally left the premises the count would be made. Now they appointed the prisoners during the night to stand guard over their fellow prisoners to ensure that no escapes were contemplated or perpetrated.

Well, the two escapers were recaptured and brought back in chains. We were taken out to see them in this condition. They were beaten with the sticks. They were in a different quarter from us. We were up on the top floor, they were down below. But we did learn that they had been on the run for about two or three days. But unlike the persons who were put in the dungeons they were allowed to still mix with their fellow prisoners. Of course the Gestapo were in control of the situation. They knew that some time in the future all their anti-Fascist Germans would be sent back to Germany. We think that the worst possible things must have happened to the International Brigaders from Fascist countries and from those countries occupied by the Germans once the 1939 war began.

There was never anyone executed at San Pedro camp. The only thing that we heard was that Jimmy Rutherford had been shot after being taken away from our ranks. There were not even any executions among the Spanish nationals. Six or seven of them used to come across to us once every three weeks to give us a haircut. They took the number one clipper from the forehead right back the way. But we didn't mind this. It helped to keep the lice down. And they shaved us. So they clipped our heads and shaved our faces once every three weeks. It helped a little bit.

Beatings though were a regular part of our existence at San Pedro. For example, when we were out saluting the *bandera*, the flag, in the evening one prisoner would maybe take the opportunity of speaking to his neighbour. If he was seen by one of the guards speaking during the ceremony his name would be taken. Sometimes it happened during the Mass when going down on one knee with heads bowed there was an opportunity to say something to your next door neighbour, or make an observation or give some sign that you were talking. If you were seen by the guards this is what would happen as far as the International Brigaders were concerned. About midnight or one in the morning the prisoner who had misbehaved earlier in the day would be taken downstairs to the courtyard and made to face the wall – as close to the wall as possible – to stand all night, all night. Now if he tried to ease himself and make himself comfortable the loaded riding crop would suddenly be whipped over his back to make him again stand at attention.

When any Spanish prisoner was seen talking what happened to him – and this was visible to us, when we looked out of our cell windows, in the summer time particularly – was that he would be taken out and forced to kneel in front of the cross at the plinth all day in the sunshine without moving. Now it must have been very, very hot in the summer time. It must have been around the high '90s. But again, in the winter time, really very, very cold up there.

I don't think there were any of the prisoners that didn't experience the beatings at some time or other. On one occasion I had experience of being put against the wall – but not for very long, not for very long. I didn't suffer this all night but only for two or three hours. And it wasn't nice, it wasn't nice. Once the loaded riding crop came over my back.

The *bandera* was the flag. We were taken down every night to salute the flag. And the officer of the day or whoever it was that was conducting that ceremony would give the Fascist calls. He would say, "Espana!" And all the voices in the courtyard would say: "Uno!" "Espana!" – "Grande!" and "Espana!" – "Libre!" Now we kept quiet with the first two, One Spain, a Grand Spain. But when it came to the third one suddenly the 400 voices of the Internationals would shout out "Libre!", meaning "A free Spain!" It was like a Hampden roar.

And this didn't go down too well with the officer in charge or the Fascist guards.

We had taken the earlier decision that we would only conform to giving Fascist salutes. You were only supposed to give Fascist salutes if you passed an officer and suchlike. We just didn't see the officer – intentionally, in order that we wouldn't be doing these things, you know.

I remember we were going down for a meal one day. And this person in front of me – I thought he was a prisoner – was saying "Salud!" or "Arriba!", "Arriba, Espana!" you know, to an officer or guard on his way down for the food.[171] And I said "Camerad: no es necessario – Arriba Espana, no es necessario!" And then I realised that I was talking to a soldier. Christ, McCartney. Nurmi couldnae give me ten yards of a start in a 200 yard dash and catch me, I can tell you that.[172] McCartney was amongst the prisoners like a flash of lightning and burying himself. Because the lad turned round and looked at me, as if to say, "What the ...?" "What's happening here?" I was busy telling him, "It's no' necessary to salute. Forget the salute!"

The three Gestapo men I mentioned earlier as being at San Pedro and who took the declarations from us, were in civilian clothes. All of the Internationals were taken down at some time or other to make these declarations. On one occasion all of us were taken down individually, made the declaration, and were given an intelligence test. I was asked two questions: Which eye did Nelson lose in the French wars? And name one of the longest rivers in the United States of America. I mentioned the Mississippi as one of the longer rivers. I didn't know which eye Nelson lost, though I did know he had lost one.[173]

The purpose of these questions I wouldn't even begin to understand. But there was one lad, he was an English comrade, he was asked a question about the planets. This was his pet subject. Not only did he answer the question that was put to him but he made a further technical observation that must have mesmerised his questioners.

What the object was of the Gestapo men asking these questions I don't know. We thought it was possibly they were trying to establish whether or not we were an inferior race of people. I mean they were always asking us, "Who are the Jews among the prisoners? Do you know the Communists in there?" And of course we didn't know of any. They were trying to ferret us out. There was an Austrian person who joined our ranks some months after we had been prisoners. Now he had obviously been planted to join us and find out what he could. And he wanted to learn English. Tommy Booth, a comrade from Paisley, took it on himself to teach this Austrian some English, pidgin English. Tommy would say to him, "I'm going along the Sweeney Toad (the road) to go up to my Uncle Ned (Bed) and go to Little Bo-peep (sleep)". So the Austrian learned his English. Tommy egged him on. "Yes, you're doing well. This is good English," and suchlike. The Austrian was trying to find things out of course about who was who within the prison camp, particularly who were the persons in the leadership of the camp.

It's maybe speculation but perhaps the purpose of the Gestapo's questions was to try and find out who was knowledgeable, like our friend of the planets, so they might find out the leaders or potential leaders.

The first batch of prisoners had been repatriated, George Drever among them, in the month of July 1938. There were about 132 of us Britishers at this time. Colonel Martin came and said that 100 Britishers were being repatriated forthwith. And as he called the names out these persons would step over and clearly identify themselves.

Now you can imagine the feelings. There's 132 of us, and there's 100 to be repatriated. McCartney and Collins were part of the 32 remaining. And we were counting, as well as everyone else. When the names were being read out we knew, you know, "Now 90 over there, there's ten to go, and there's forty people left." And of course the lads who were told that they would be repatriated were quite jubilant and I think we were happy for them. At least we knew comrades were going to go home and they would be raising questions quite sharply about those who had been left behind.

These 100 people were sent from Burgos, from San Pedro, to Palencia, run by the Italians. And the treatment there, we learned later, was much, much better that these 100 comrades received – better food, and not so stringent rules and regulations of the camp, certainly no beatings and no whippings. And then I think another two months elapsed before they were finally repatriated some time towards the end of October 1938. Those thirty or so of us British left at San Pedro didn't get home until towards the end of February 1939.

When at last we left San Pedro de Cardenas at the end of January we were taken to San Sebastian to the central jail. We spent almost three weeks there prior to us crossing over the international bridge at Irun and into France at Hendaye. When we crossed the bridge some of the comrades struck up *It's a Long Way to Tipperaray*. And we were giving clenched fist salutes to the French people and they in return were giving us it back, when we crossed into France. We were met by the French on the bridge and by the British representatives once we crossed the bridge. We signed a declaration form indicating that we would repay our repatriation fare. It came to about £6 or something, I think. But to my knowledge not one of us ever repaid that money.

Anyway we were greeted and welcomed very, very much by the French people, given a hot shower – and that was the first hot shower we had had for a long, long time – and then home by way of the Channel port.

I would look back on the Spanish war this way. Some 2,100 volunteers went from Britain. 540 were killed. Now as far as Scotland's concerned 476 volunteers went from Scotland. Of that 540 who were killed, 134 were Scotsmen. And 65 of those came from Glasgow.

Now I think I would be summing up the feelings of most of the Brigaders when I say that we came back from Spain still very devout anti-Fascists. And I think that the years since that War have reinforced tenfold our beliefs, our dedication and the things for which we felt we were fighting. We didn't go to Spain to usher in socialism or communism or anything like that. We went to Spain to continue the fight for the freedom of a people to put a cross on a ballot paper and elect its kind of government. We were already in the main devout anti-Fascists and the comrades who were repatriated, along with the main body of International Brigaders who were withdrawn from Spain in the fall of the year 1938, gave a pledge to the Spanish people that only the fronts would change, that when they got back home they would continue that fight. And on behalf of the memory of all the comrades who died in Spain I would think that we who are fortunate enough still to be alive and to continue that stuggle, have vindicated ourselves by the very fact that Communist Parties, Socialist Parties, and the trade unions that were made illegal under Franco are now legal. The Spanish people have elected a socialist form of government, tentative as it may be. It is a tremendous step forward for the Spanish people and we think that we made just a little contribution towards that end.

and we think that we made just a little contribution towards that end.

Flag Day collecting for Spain in Aberdeen 1937.

Food supplies leave Aberdeen for Republican Spain 1937.

David Stirrat was born in Glasgow in 1915 and was brought up there. His boyhood memories include street picketing scenes in the 1926 General Strike and shouting impertinent remarks at unemployed men on one of the Hunger Marches through Glasgow. David Stirrat himself became unemployed for several years after leaving school. On his return from the Spanish War he was soon directed to war work in factories during the Second World War when he also served in the Home Guard.

DAVID STIRRAT

I had been a member of the Young Communist League in Glasgow for several years when the Spanish War broke out. I was engaged in a whole lot of activity with an organisation called the Spanish Aid Committee.[174] I was familiar with the political events that led up to the outbreak of the Spanish War. I knew people who were fellow members of the Y.C.L. who went to Spain quite early on in the War. One particular friend of mine was a chap called Tommy Flynn, who had gone to Spain early on and been killed. He was killed shortly after he went.[175] He had given me part of his library before he went away, political books and that sort of thing. So I had some emotional involvement in that sense that I knew people who had taken this action. I also had an uncle in Spain who was later killed at Jarama. I actually volunteered to go to Spain some time in 1936. I don't know dates, you know, I don't recall dates.. I haven't written anything down or anything like that but between the beginning of the War in July and the end of the year at some time or other I knew that volunteers were going and I had heard talks by Phil Gillan and David MacKenzie, another volunteer who had returned, and Johnny Lochore, people like that.[176] These fellows had been to Spain and come back wounded or whatever. I had a great admiration for these people because I understood why they had gone and they had the courage to go.

But as I say I volunteered to go. I met this uncle of mine just about this time down in the library in Bridgeton. I lived in Bridgeton at this time. He was a chap called Bill Crawford and he was a man whom I liked very much. He wasn't a great political theorist or anything like that but a genuine type of man and he had been in the First World War. He was much older than me of course and was a manly man, put it that way. He told me he was going to Spain. So I said, "Oh, aye, I've decided to go as well." And he said, "Well, I wouldn't attempt to stop you. But what I'm going to tell you is when you get there number one is the important person." And this sort of coloured my attitude afterwards, you know. I understood what he was talking about. Bill got killed himself at Jarama. But there are I know from my own experience circumstances where it doesn't matter what you do you're going to get killed or injured. Anyway this was Bill's attitude.

I also got offered a job. I was unemployed. I'm not quite sure whether it was Johnny Lochore or not, but anyway the guy that was driving the *Daily Worker* van came to my house and offered me this job, because I was in the Y.C.L. He told me, "I'm going to Spain." I said, "I can't take the job because I'm going as well." Which I thought at that time I was, you know. But apparently I was too young – that's what I was told anyway, I was too young. I was twenty, and they told me that twenty-one was the age. Now whether that was true or not I don't know but anyway they said I wasn't going and I was put off the list for the bus that left Ingram Street in Glasgow with all the boys who eventually went to Jarama. I can remember those days and I often recall them when I get the smell of fruit because the Communist Party rooms were near the Fruit Market and this is where all these sort of things took place.

I got stopped from going anyway but I took part, as I say, in a lot of activity down Rothesay Dock, where some of the Spanish merchant navy boats used to come in, meeting the crews, entertaining them and that sort of thing, and showing them Glasgow. And I used to go out and collect food round the doors with a bag – bags of sugar and tins of milk. I just asked people if they would like to donate and they did. We would cart this stuff down and, you know, make a contribution to foodships.[177] This was going on all over Britain, of course, and it was that kind of activity. I was really involved more of less all the time with that kind of work and also going to meetings, which I had been doing for years in the '30s, and listening to speakers like Tom Mann, and Willie Gallacher, Harry Pollitt, Finlay Hart [178] and a lot of people that were proficient speakers and were brought out by the protest movements of the time.

But as I say I got knocked back by the Glasgow Party I got on my bike, as Norman Tebbit would say, and I went to London. I was in London about a year or less. But on my twenty-first birthday I left. I joined up in London and went to France. That was in the middle of September 1937.

I went over to France on a weekend ticket. I had a passport for France but I didn't have to use it. I went over with a party of nine men. One fellow was the leader, a chap called Joe Norman.[179] So I didn't have anything to do with the arrangements about tickets. He looked after that sort of thing.

We went on the cross-Channel train, through Dieppe to Paris. We were in Paris for some time. We went to the International Exhibition that was on, a trade exhibition, with different countries exhibiting their wares. And from there we went down by train to Béziers in the south of France. We just followed instructions. We stayed in a hotel until taxis came for us and took us into the foothills of the Pyrenees. We stayed on a farm there for some time and all this time we were gathering more men. I got the impression that it was a big crowd but I couldn't give you a figure on it. Eventually one night a bus arrived and we all got into this bus. There were six guides to take us across the Pyrenees. The guides had side arms and this was the first time I had seen a gun.

So we set out at night and started to climb the Pyrenees. The bits I remember about it, it was pretty hard going all the time. I remember running past French sentries on the roads. When the sentry came to the end of his beat a half-a-dozen of us would nip across the road before he turned and came back. And crawling through people's gardens, things like that.

Eventually we got into the real mountains and it took about ten hours to get over altogether. We had two stops, about ten minutes or a quarter of an hour each time, and that was the lot. The rest of the time we were going pretty fast, you know, walking. It wasn't difficult climbing or anything like that but it was quite dark and you had to keep going. It was a fairly arduous business.

My first recollection of Spain is dropping on the ground and all these lizards and little animals crawling all over me, insects and things that were quite strange to me. I am definitely a city-bred type of guy, you know.

I went down to Figueras and we were there for a few days. Figueras was a big fort. It had been built by the Moors as far as I was informed. It was maybe about 600 years old. It certainly smelt as though it were pretty ancient. Because while these places might look picturesque from a distance, when you're inside them they seem to accumulate all the smells of the years that have passed.

From there we went down to Barcelona and began to see something of the kind of organisational side of the army. There were trucks flying along the road with banners flying and the different unions and political parties represented by these banners. Catalonia was quite a strong Anarchist stronghold. They had a great leader called Durruti who got shot. And the P.O.U.M. was quite strong. That was the sort of I.L.P. of the Spanish political situation. But there were quite a lot of different factions and unions. And just about this time it happens that the army was really being formed. It wasn't like an established army. It started off in the early days just with people, trade union branches, being issued with arms. It gradually began to get organised.

We went down on the train to Valencia from there. From Valencia we went to Albacete. That's where I joined the army proper, in Albacete. That was on the 8th October 1937. We were in military barracks there and gradually began to get issued with clothing. All this was completely strange to me because we got jodhpurs and puttees to put on. Not very many people knew how to put puttees on. The ones who did know were trying to help the other ones who didn't know. I soon got rid of mine and bagged a pair of trousers because they were a lot easier: you just pulled them on and that was it. After Albacete I went to a little village, Tarazona, which was a training base for the

British Battalion. We began to get military training.

This process of integration into the Spanish army was just taking place at that time, because when I arrived at Tarazona we used to drill and form fours like the British army. Just at that time thay changed it to the continental column of threes and all the orders were issued in Spanish. Spaniards were introduced into the British Battalion in greater numbers. This was to unify the army and make it more efficient. It was really an emerging army, it was just in the process of being formed actually.

We got training with wooden rifles. They were cut and shaped like rifles, you know. They didn't have enough real rifles to practise with. The rifles were all needed at the front. For people who didn't know how to carry rifles this was quite effective. And we got the drill movements and that sort of thing. So it meant you were carrying something.

We got what's called triangulation training. There was a little target that a guy held in front of a paper. And we had a rifle to use on this occasion. You lined it up and fired. When you fired he marked the spot. The idea was to get a small triangle on to the paper where he had marked it. So there was that kind of thing, and forced marching, you know, marching up and down. A lot of people didnae even know how to march. That kind of training.

Then they asked one day for people who had actually fired a rifle to come. I volunteered for this, although I didnae know how to put the bullets in. But the fellow next to me showed me what to do and I got five rounds to fire. The first one nearly broke my jaw because I was no' experienced with it. But I managed to get five of them fired off anyway. I don't know whether I hit the target or not. But that was me a rifleman.

We had a couple of machine guns, light guns. And we had two Russian instructors who were very efficient, and taught us quite a bit of unarmed combat and things like that, and invited us to try and spear them with a bayonet and really have a go at it, you know. They would take a shovel and defend themselves. All I knew about these Russians was that they were instructors. One of them was called Ramon, I forget the name of the other guy. The Ramon fellow he did all this unarmed combat stuff. The other chap did the light machine gun instruction. They were characters, you know, very strong characters, and helpful. They had a lot of good ideas. I took the attitude that I wanted to learn this business because it meant survival to me and I realised that I was a back marker. I knew nothing about it.

But I got sent after some time back to Albacete. This was really a machine gun school but it had anti-aircraft guns mounted on the roof, and that's where most of the instruction was given, on this flat roof. It actually was quite a pleasant situation because we were pretty well looked after in this barracks. It was certainly not uncomfortable.

The instructor was an ex-officer in the French Foreign Legion. He seemed to me to be quite an efficient guy. Some days we would go into the country in a truck and take various machine guns with us and fire at strip targets, strip the guns down and reassemble them blindfold, and learn all the stoppages. We got all this for the various types of guns that were used in Spain.

The principal machine gun was a Russian Maxim gun, mounted on a small gun carriage with wheels, and two light guns – a Tokharov and a Diktorov. There were many other types of guns, Spanish Hotchkiss, and French St. Etienne, and Chauchats, even British Lewis guns, First World War guns. I think it was just a question of they'd take guns from anywhere, wherever they could be found. But the Soviet Union seemed to be the main supplier of anything that was reasonably modern.

There was a big outbreak of fighting in the north. This was at the time of Teruel. By this time it was the middle of winter between '37 and '38. We all got bundled on to a train and on to lorries at different stages. I'm not quite sure where we were but we were travelling for quite a bit of time. I was in a train for about three days. Of course these trains would only move a few yards then stop. We were in a box-car. It was like a refrigerator. Conditions began to get a lot worse from the purely physical point of view. But when we left the train I saw a little notice. It said: Teruel. I knew about Teruel, I knew where I was then. The ground was covered with snow and conditions were quite bad there.

By the time we got there the Battalion who had been fighting at Teruel had been moved away to another place and so we got back on to lorries again and we were actually looking of the Battalion. It seemed to take quite a long time. We were stuck on the lorries for I don't know how long but it seemed to me to be weeks on end. One night we were travelling and we were unarmed, we didn't have any arms. We were stuck in the back of the lorries. Eventually the lorries made a sudden about-turn and there was an outbreak of fighting in olive-groves on either side of the road and men were running and climbing on to the lorries. We were going like the clappers back down the road again. We almost got captured. This was at Caspe. That's where I joined the front line Battalion. The Fascists were attacking all the time. There was a big retreat really. They were trying to get the Battalion re-formed. This is how things went. We were maybe stopping in fields and they'd issue arms and take them back in again. There were all sorts of problems. But eventually we got issued with good arms. New rifles came in wooden crates. They had to be de-greased. I got one of these new guns, a Maxim machine gun.

We were sort of re-grouped. By this time it was into March 1938. The weather had eased off a bit. We had experienced a lot of sudden rain. We had got used to living in the open and surviving under extreme conditions. Lots of little dodges that you learn from other people.

We were going to the front and marching along a road very early in the morning, just about sunrise, when we encountered a column of tanks. The first thing I knew we were getting machine gunned from a tank that was sitting in the middle of the road. It was only about 100 yards away from me. Apparently the column had marched right past these tanks. There was a general melee.

I set up my gun, a heavy machine gun, on the right hand side of the road, and another gun was set up on the left hand side of the road. We started to fire at the tank. We could only see one tank at first. But it kept coming down the road, coming at us. We didn't have any anti-tank ammunition or anything, just an ordinary belt of ammunition. But the tank went on fire anyway, whether a shot got through one of the slots. The crew jumped out on to the road and ran up the road. I don't think they survived the journey, put it that way.

By this time some of our fellows had been getting wounded. We were getting attacked from the right flank. When I looked round the other machine gun had completely disappeared. Groups of prisoners were beginning to appear in front of us under the guard of Fascists. They obviously had us surrounded and our fellows were getting captured.

Another tank appeared on the road and we fired at the tank and it retreated. I don't know whether it was damaged or not but it seemed to pull into the side of the road. There might have been about two hours of this sort of thing. This attack that was coming to us from our right flank seemed to have petered out. I fired quite a number of shots in that direction, and whether it was snipers or not it seemed to cool them off and we didn't get any problem from them again. But the next thing that happened was an aeroplane appeared and started to strafe us. We pulled away from the road and away towards our right flank. And this of course cleared the road and the tanks poured through in a column. There were tanks and armoured cars just swept right past us. That was the first indication I had of the strength of the opposition. I believe that it was Italian Black Arrows, Mussolini's Black Arrows, whom we were fighting at the time. They were Mussolini's crack troops. But I mean at the particular time when this was happening I didn't know who they were because they were just people running at us with guns.

There were maybe about thirty of us left in this group by this time. No officers or nobody in command. I was the only one that had this gun. The situation was hopeless. So we discussed what to do. I decided that the only possibility of anybody getting out was to split up and every man to attend to himself. One guy wanted to make a last stand. Other people wanted to surrender. But the option I chose was to go my own way. I didnae really want to surrender because I had left a bag with my personal papers in it and there were quite a lot of political books, things like that, in it and also my birth lines. I wasnae very keen on surrendering at all. So I thought I would have a go at trying to get out of it.

I had heard stories about what prisoners were subjected to by the Fascists. Some of the stories I had heard were that there were Moorish troops in opposition, and they believed that when they died they went to heaven, and heaven was inhabited by virgins and were there for their pleasure, you know. They believed it was a great honour to die in battle and to kill the enemy and also to deprive them of their wedding tackle before they went. This is the impression I had – castration. Some of the stories I had heard were about that. I don't know whether that's true or not. But it was certainly worthwhile making an effort to avoid getting into that situation. And this was the line that I decided to adopt anyway.

So I took the lock out of my gun. That's the principal part of the mechanism, and I took it with me. I went away on my own. I had a rifle by this time and I had a pocketful of ammunition. Shortly after, I was going down a track and I heard footsteps behind me. One of the other lads was behind me. He was carrying a huge axe. Where he had got that, I don't know. All sorts of things appear on battlefields, you know. But anyway he had this bloody big axe. We teamed up together. He was a fellow called Donald Weston. He came from Sheffield and he had been a Scots Guardsman prior to going to Spain.

Well, the next thing that happened was we met four Spaniards from the Listers. That was another army unit, a Spanish army unit, who had been on our right flank and had collapsed. We teamed up with them. They were more familiar with the landscape. We tried to keep up with them but they were going at a terrible pace. There were little groups of people trying to escape from this encirclement and we were just one of the wee groups. Then we met two civilians, two peasants. They told us to stay there and they would go for help for us. But the Lister boys let them go out of sight and then buzzed off, because they thought they were going to inform the Fascists.

But we couldn't keep up with the four Listers. It was getting dark by this time. And Donald and I climbed a little hill and decided to settle down there for the night. We could hear the gunfire of the Fascist army advancing and we knew the general direction which we had to go. Our idea was to follow the Fascist army and try to get through the front line from the one to the other.

But during the night a troup of cavalry camped round the base of the hill we were on. We could hear them singing these flamenco songs. They were either Moors or Spanish Fascists. Anyway they were definitely Fascists. By this time the gunfire was too far away for them to be otherwise. We could hear the horses, you know. They were a big group. We had to wait until they cleared away in the morning.

We tried travelling at night but we found this was much too difficult. While the Fascists couldn't see us, we couldn't see them. And also we couldn't see where we were going. It's not an easy thing to go across a strange country at night time, especially in Spain because the fields are set in hills and they are all little walls like steps. You have to jump up and down these things. It's quite difficult to cross at night time, especially under the hostile conditions where there were cavalry patrols about.

All this time of course we didn't have any food. The first three days we had nothing to eat whatsoever. People talk about living off the land but the land that we were crossing was absolute stone. They call it the Aragon desert, stony land, stony desert. We began to get quite hungry. After three days we decided to approach some of the peasants. Previously we had passed them because we didn't know what the attitude was going to be.

The first place we approached I'll never forget. There was a big tall stout woman dressed in a white smock, sort of kitchen apron thing. She was an immaculate clean woman and couldn't have been more helpful. She gave us fried eggs and she gave us information about the Fascist patrols. There were groups of cavalry scouring the hills looking for people like us. She told us where to go and where not to go. She directed us round this hill and was very helpful.

We set off and now we weren't afraid to approach people. But we had quite a lot of near misses. We found it difficult. I mean I'm a city chap and I think Donald was too. Donald must have had some training in soldiering but living off the land was difficult. For example, the first time we caught a rabbit. Now that's your dinner but what do you do with it? It's kicking about and it's got fur on. And how do you get it into a pot? These were the sort of problems. Donald said he knew how to skin a rabbit but the first thing he did he cut through the skin down the stomach, took the gut as well, and it was one hell of a mess. I carried a little hatchet in my belt and we used that for chopping the head off. Things like that, it's a question of learning how to survive.

We tried eating grass, cutting off the little roots and frying it in some olive oil that we found. That made me violently sick. It just couldn't lie on my stomach. Then we were breaking into houses. It was terribly cold at night time. By this time we didn't have any extra clothes other than a blanket each. We decided to disguise ourselves as Spaniards so we got two big straw hats and stuck them on our heads, and a blanket over the shoulder, and just walked past the Fascists in the daytime. This was the only way we could make any headway at all.

In the morning we would fix a point north-east, say, a mountain top, and we would head in that direction. Sometimes we had to divert, maybe come from a main road, or get over a main road, or if we could see a group of Fascists we would take a circular road. But we always knew the general direction we were going. This is how we sort of managed along.

We broke into a house one night. One of the things that was extremely uncomfortable was always being lousy. You couldn't get a sleep, apart from one of us having to sleep with one eye open and being on the alert. Sleep was very difficult with lice crawling about your body all the time. Anyway we went into this particular house and we were sleeping with our clothes off. The clothes were hanging on a beam. The bed was about six feet above the floor with a ladder up to it. It was pitch dark. The door opened and a guy came in and dumped a rifle on the floor. We had made stew with this rabbit I was telling you about. We heard him drinking the stew. And of course we didn't know who it was. But he started to say "Campesino" – peasant – and climb this wee ladder up to the bed. I was trying to figure out how to get at my clothes and how to get past him and out the door. But I asked him what nationality he was and he said, "American." I said, "Shut the door and come in," you know. His name was Maurice, but I don't know his second name. He was just known as Maurice.

We eventually came to the banks of the Ebro. We didn't know who was on the other side but we thought that the river was probably the front line and we succeeded in crawling through the Fascist lines and into the water. We did this in daylight, maybe about ten in the morning. But the water was extremely turbulent. There were whirlpools. The three of us went in and unfortunately Maurice was swept away. He didn't survive. He got drowned. And there was not much we could do about it because it took us all our time to come out. And we had to come out on the Fascist side again.

Maurice had the only gun. He had a wee revolver and he had a hand grenade. And he had all the tobacco. I remember thinking when I saw hime swept away, "Well, that's Maurice away. And he's got the tobacco and he's got the gun." I'm afraid these are the kind of practical things that you think, the sort of brutalising effects that these experiences have on you. Maurice was just swept away. I got confirmation of that later on. They had got his body on the other side. It had been swept over, you know. In any case we had to crawl back through the Fascist lines again and make a big detour, and try again to cross the Ebro.

The next people we met were two Germans. We approached a house that we had been in before where the woman had given us wine and nuts and things. And when we approached the door this second visit, I thought it was two boys who had run in. I went up to the door and hammered on it. And I'm telling them in my best Spanish we were friends and to open the door, thinking it was two boys. When the door opened there was a guy in a khaki uniform and just inside the door there were steps going up to a top floor and up there was another fellow covering us with a rifle. They were two anti-Fascist Germans from the Thaelmann Battalion. So we were now four strong. One of the Germans and Donald went away foraging and they came back with nine rabbits. And that's where I got instructed on how to skin a rabbit. They showed us how to hang them up by their hind legs and strip the skin off like a jersey, you know. We were quite successful at it and we cooked the whole lot of them and found some flour and made pancakes. We were there for a few days.

We set off at night time this time and we came again to the Ebro. There's a railway runs on the south bank of the Ebro and we went through three tunnels while marching along this railway. We didn't know if we would encounter anybody in these. But eventually somebody fired on us from the other side of the river and that's when we knew that was the side we wanted to go to.

So we got down into the water and swam across and got to the other side. But in his excitement one of the Germans started speaking out loud and of course he was talking in German. So we got attacked with rifles and grenades. These were our own people who were attacking us. They thought we were a patrol coming from the Fascist side. One of the Germans dived back into the river but the other three of us went up the bank and were taken prisoner by this patrol. They took us into a hut. But when we convinced them that we were from the XVth Brigade they produced a bottle of cognac and we scoffed it. And that was it. Our journey from behind the Fascist lines had taken three weeks altogether.

We weren't very far from our own battalion as it happened. We had come about forty miles across country and landed within a few hundred yards of the British Battalion, who were occupying a series of trenches on the north bank of the Ebro. The Ebro was the sort of dividing line between the two sides. We were taken in the morning to the British Battalion and up to Brigade headquarters or some higher command anyway. We got interrogated by, well, I'm not sure who it was but I think it might have been Copic.[180] He was a foreigner anyway. He might have been Russian. But he wanted all the military data, what we had seen. He was interested in the tunnels, any boats in the tunnels, things like that, and the estimated strength of the troops we had seen and the arms they had. We had seen huge units of Fascist machine gun companies with the machine guns packed on to mules. We had seen things that might have been of interest to a military man. But these people wanted to know all this anyway.

Then we were sent back to occupy trenches. I was in these trenches for two days. By this time we were pretty well exhausted. The first night Donald started to swim on dry land. He began to get a bit unbalanced and he was taken out and sent to hospital. This was the result of his escape. I had noticed prior to us coming over the Ebro he was beginning to become a bit confused.

I had been injured by one of the hand grenades that had exploded on the bank when we had got back to our side and it had caused a sort of gravel rash down my left leg and in the small of my back. These sores began to fester and I got sent to the hospital and met Donald there, down at Cambrils on the Mediterranean coast near Tarragona. But Donald got sent home and from there he became very vague and couldn't make his mind up even about having a haircut. He used to say to me, "I'm thinking of having a haircut. Do you think I should?" The last thing he said to me was, "They want me to go to a panel." This was a committee that decided what was going to happen to you. He said, "Do you think I should go?" I said, "I think so." And I never saw Donald again.

I was in the hospital for eight days. The first night I was there it got bombed. So it wasn't a sort of restful place. I went back to the front anyway from there. When I was leaving the hospital I had a blanket round me, and when I got to the door the nurse wanted the blanket back, which left me with nothing. And I told her this. So she directed me round to the back of the hospital where there was an outhouse. All the uniforms were in there that had been cut off other people coming in, blood-soaked. She said, "Get something in there." And that was what I had to do. That was the equipment situation.

It's a long story really from there. I went back up to the Ebro and we were there for I don't know how long, a few weeks anyway. But I was on constant nightshift more or less there because we had to go in and repair guns and bring out broken rifles. You couldn't move in the daytime. It was all night time work. These were more or less my activities while we were there.

I can remember some of the incidents that took place there. There was a bit of shouting over with the Fascists because the Ebro was just about the width of the Clyde down there and you could shout across at night. The Fascists used to shout on one of the Spaniards called Cypriano, who was an officer, and a great character he was. I was quite friendly with him. They used to shout on him at night and they knew him by name. He would take a trumpet down with him and make rude noises at them. And they would invite him to come over and tell him all the good things they had, you know. But that was put a stop to.

This was at a wee town called Garcia and it had been a wine store. There were huge barrels of wine and after we had done what we were supposed to do, we used to bring out some samples of this wine. But we moved out of there and went up to Lerida. This was a big action, more military activity that I had seen in the past. There were aeroplanes going over for three days and nights – ours, for a change – bombing the Fascists.

On the road up to Lerida I had to take a lorry load of ammunition to the front. And while I was standing at the side of the road there were huge columns of men marching up and a lot of French artillery, the old '75 millimetre French artillery getting trundled up there. And I met the two Germans who had swum over the Ebro with us, you know. They had rejoined their battalion and this was them back into action. We had a great reunion at the side of the road. But the thing fizzled out. The British never even got into action in that particular place. We came back and it was moving about and getting built up to strength again, you know.

By this time I was in pretty poor fettle. I was all broken out in sores. I had lumps under my arms. My glands were swollen in my thighs. I began to get left looking after ammunition and things like that. More or less that was the story of my life until I came home. I wasn't really engaged in any action after that.

My condition was deteriorating pretty badly. I was in hospital again. They would get the skin thing under control and it would break out again. Very often I was all bandaged up, you know. They seemed to try different ointments. One sort of medical station I was in it seemed to be people with these kind of ailments. There are a lot of uncomfortable things happening to you when you are living like that. You get piles, very painful, you know. Things like that, and outbreaks of skin rashes and blood disorders. This particular place seemed to be devoted to dealing with these things. It was a kind of walking wounded place and I was in there for quite a while until eventually we went to Ripoll. I was in Ripoll for about a month waiting on the British consul. By this time we were all coming home. There were probably about 300 men left. I came home with that crowd in December 1938. I came home by train from Ripoll right through France and on to the ferry and landed at Victoria. There were about 30,000 people there to welcome the Brigaders' return. People were very hospitable, inviting us in to pubs. And then we went to the Co-operative halls in the East End and there was a reception there. And the same thing when we in the Glasgow contingent came back to Glasgow. I think it was in the City Halls there was a big meeting and reception.

Spain has always been a part of my life, you know, but not to the same extent as a guy like Garry McCartney, who made it more or less all of his life. It seemed to be his sort of reason for living, as it were.

It's difficult to say if you'd do the same thing again because you're talking about individuals and individual attitudes. At the time I felt I had a duty to go and do something about it. But how I look at it: if it was right then it's right now. There are so many parallels today – Chile, for example, where the same thing has happened, where the Allende government was by no means Communist and yet it was overthrown by brute force and people murdered. You know I think the same protest is due, the same sort of reaction is due.

I'm not particularly keen on being a soldier because I think it is alien to my nature. Some people like that kind of thing, you know, but it's not the kind of thing I would choose to do. But sometimes we do things that we think we ought to do.

When the Second World War came I got called up, had a medical and I passed the medical Grade I. But at that time these marks on my back and my legs were quite fresh and they were rather peculiar looking because they were splattered all over, right down to my ankle. They asked me what they were and I said it was a hand grenade, I was in the Spanish War. So they sent me upstairs to an officer – I'm not sure what rank the guy was – but he was obviously interested in matters like that and he asked me in great detail about what had been happening to me, you know. I never ever got taken into the forces.

George Drever was born in 1910, the eldest in a family of eleven children. His father, who was often unemployed, was a shipyard labourer in Leith. Despite his early life of hardship and poverty George Drever went from school to Edinburgh University where he studied chemistry and gained two degrees. After returning from the Spanish Civil War he eventually found employment as a metallurgist in Sheffield. He now lives in Glasgow.

GEORGE DREVER

There were two reasons why I became involved in the Spanish Civil War. One, of course, which was of prime importance, was that I wanted to help the people in Spain in their struggle against Franco and the German and Italian Fascists. At the same time I also wanted to get some experience of military arms. And the reason for that is that for several years before '36, I was very active in the working class movement. And being a Marxist-Leninist, of course, I recognised at that time, and I still believe, that the working class will never be able to achieve its aims without fierce opposition from the ruling classes whoever they are, and of course there will be military struggles. Now normally one would say, well, that's all very well, wait until that time comes. Or you could go of course into the army. But I couldn't go into the army because I've got a spinal curvature. I wouldn't be accepted. But I would be accepted in the Spanish Republican army of course because they would accept anyone.

Before I went to Spain – it must have been about 1935, when Mussolini went into Abyssinia, I felt so annoyed about it – not annoyed in a selfish way – I wrote to the Abyssinian ambassador in London, offering my services in the battle against Mussolini and his Fascists as a volunteer. Oh, I knew I wouldn't be paid! But I got a reply. They said, "No." They thanked me very much for my offer, they said, but they wouldn't be able to make use of any services I had.

I was 26 when the Spanish War broke out, and 27 when I went to Spain in the beginning of 1938. Before that I had been working for Imperial Chemical Industries in Manchester, at Blakely, in the Dyestuffs Research Group. I was a chemist at that time. I had a B.Sc. First Class Honours in Chemistry from Edinburgh University, and a Ph.D., after doing two years' research. I had been taken on by I.C.I. for what was known then as a year's probation because they let you work for a year to see how you were getting on. On the last day of my year the Director of Research – a man called Barraclough I think he was – asked me to come up to see him. He said, "We want you to resign." I said, "Tell me why?" He said, "We don't think you come up to our standard." So I laughed at that. And he said, "Don't you think our standard is high?" I said, "Your standard may be high. I'm not really very sure about it. But it's certainly one that I can easily attain

277

and have attained," He said, "No." I said, "You're getting rid of me of course because I am in the Communist Party." I used to speak to laboratory boys, also to my co-equals, chemists, research chemists and so on – they didn't pay very much attention. But I said, "No, I'm not going to resign." And of course if it were the case that I hadn't been any good at research they would have put me in charge of some of the works operations, which was normal. They just wanted rid of me. So I got the sack.

That was in Manchester. I went along then to see Bill Rust, who was the Communist Party organiser in Manchester at that time, and I told him what happened. I said to him, "I think what I'll do is go to Spain. Can you make arrangements for that?" He said, "Oh no, you won't do that." He said, "You'll go back to Edinburgh and get a job."

So I went back to Edinburgh and I didn't get a job and I was still carrying on my political activities. I used to be a tutor in the National Council of Labour Colleges, under Charlie Gibbons.[181] And also I was doing some classes for the Communist Party among the young people there.

And I remember, I think it must have been in December of '37, at one of the Party meetings, Fred Douglas, who was organiser then,[182] said: "We've got a letter from the centre," he said, "that things are very difficult in Spain and we want our best comrades to go." I was single, I wasn't married at that time. So I went along and I said, "Right-o, Fred," I said, "put my name down." He says, "Why do you want to go?" I said, "You've just told us that they want the best comrades to go. I consider myself one of the best comrades." So he said, "Right-o."

Before I went I went along to see the doctor in Edinburgh, Julius Lipetz.[183] I had known him of course from seeing him at meetings and so on. So he gave me a check. He saw that I had spinal curvature of course but there was nothing wrong with having spinal curvature and being able to do work in the usual way.

So in a few days I had got my railway ticket, they gave you a railway ticket. I hadn't told my mother or father what I was doing and I didn't tell the girl who liked me because she heard it from somebody in the Party. So I went down in the train with Cecil Thomson, who was going to take on the job of Young Communist League organiser or some job with the Y.C.L. in London, and with another man, John – John who now? – I've forgotten his name, who came from Mid Calder somewhere. He was a miner, had been a miner, a young man, probably about my age, but I haven't been able to contact him since then. These are the people I remember going down to London with.

So I remember in the Waverley Station when I was leaving my comrades from the Plebs Club[184] and Communist Party and Labour Party, trade union people, they came along to say cheerio to me as we went off. And I remember one of them gave me a mouth organ, I used to play the mouth organ. Another lad gave me £1 – £1 was quite a lot in these days. And so I had these with me when I got down. I also remember another man who was – I forget his name – in the Communist Party, and he said, "Och, don't you worry," he said, "when you get out there, when they know . . ." – what he meant, what a clever lad I was, see, "you won't have to carry a knapsack." I just looked at him and I thought, "A bloody strange sort of Communist that, to give advice like that."

When we got to London we must have gone to King Street, the centre of the Communist Party of Great Britain at that time, though I can't remember us at King Street. Eventually I found myself at the station. It must have been Victoria Station going down to whatever port it was – I don't know – across on the ferry and eventually getting to Paris. But I can't remember anything of that, although I recognised some of the boys whom I met later in Spain who were on that train.

We must have left Edinburgh some time about the 3rd or 4th of January. When I got to Paris of course I sent a postcard to my mother saying, "Dear mother, I'm on my way south. Don't worry." But she did of course.

I don't think we did anything in Paris at all, except that when we were in Paris we were certainly examined medically by somebody. Up to that time I was sweating with anxiety in case the doctor would say, "Right, you can't go." But of course he didn't. He just said, "Right." Because they would take anyone.

From Paris down through France, various places; stayed in some village near the frontier. Then we were taken by bus to the Pyrenees. And up over the Pyrenees. It wasn't a difficult climb for me at all. I was quite tired. But I was fit. One incident I do remember. There was a man in front of me, a young man, a Londoner. We went up more or less in Indian file, single file. It wasn't a moonlight night, naturally. I think the moon came up later on when we were on the other side. But this young man in front of me kept on getting lost at first. So I said to him, "Right, you go on, keep behind me," and I put him several places down below.

I remember going to Figueras and the great welcome there from the Spanish Republican soldiers. There must have been some International Brigade men there, too. A great welcome. The first thing of course they were asking was, "Any cigarettes?" Well, I don't think we had any cigarettes. Some of us must have had cigarettes but I didn't take any cigarettes with me. I took soap with me. We were told there was a great shortage of soap in Spain. But the soap I bought, which I bought in Paris was all toilet soap. When I gave it to the women washing our clothes in the river they just threw it away.

Another thing at Figueras were the wee ones that asked for "Da me pan" – "Give me bread." They didn't look as if they were absolutely starving. But they were still begging for the bread.

From there we must have been put on the train and journeyed fairly rapidly on to the south, through Barcelona and Valencia. I think we got off at Valencia or it might have been a place further down, I forget now, although I've been there often since I came back from the Spanish War. We went through Albacete and on to Tarazona, which is not far.

It was very cold. I used to sleep with my clothes on. During the day we were getting our drill, wooden rifles, learning the orders, left and right, forward, *adelante* and so on. We ate the old bean soup, with little bits of donkey meat, burro meat, dry bread. Although you weren't able to buy bread in the shops because it was rationed, if you were lucky you might be able to get into some Spanish house where they would serve you up a fried egg with some newer bread and a drink of wine. For that we used to pay ten pesetas. We were paid ten pesetas a day. But there was no way in which we could spend those ten pesetas. There was a canteen which had a very limited supply of wines and cognac. In those days I didn't drink, or I didn't drink because I wasn't going to drink there in any case.

We were given rifles and fired – I forget how many shots, very few shots, just firing the rifle, because they didn't have any live ammunition because of the operation of the Non-Intervention. But no army ever has enough ammunition, no matter how well they're supplied. In the Republican Spain there was a chronic shortage of everything.

We must have been at Tarazona about six weeks or so, because it must have been towards the end of February when we started moving to go up to where the Battalion was. And I forget exactly where it was when we came across them. But it was up in the Aragon front, near Belchite. And by that time the commander was Sam Wild. Bob Cooney was the political commissar of the Company there. I had met him earlier when he was down in Edinburgh for a spell. He came from Aberdeen and was a very fine fellow.

A few days after that we started moving around from place to place, I forget where we were. But for the next day or two we moved about from position to position, not in any trenches or anything like that. We were just moving. Then they said, "Right-o, get up, get on." Probably because they hadn't decided of course what was happening, because – I know now of course – the front must have been in a hell of a state of disorder at that time. And we eventually went up then through Belchite.

I remember marching through Belchite. Now Belchite was a town which had been captured by the Republican forces in the previous summer. The whole place of course was just in ruins, complete ruins. And it was quite shocking to see this. You had seen these things in pictures of course and so on but it was even more shocking to see it in reality. Since then of course I've been back and seen it and that town is still in ruins, exactly as old Franco left it because he left it as a monument to that.

Anyway we marched through Belchite and we took up positions. It must have been to the west of Belchite. In front of us there were some fairly high hills. I went out with Jimmy Rutherford to more or less scout. He was an officer at that time. There was Jimmy Rutherford and somebody else and he asked me, or somebody said to me, "You go with them." And I think that Jimmy was told because he could speak Spanish of course that there were Spaniards to the left of them, Spaniards to the right of them. And when I got back eventually we got some breakfast. And while we were eating our breakfast the Fascists started a shelling barrage. This went on for a considerable time then airplanes came across. We hadn't done anything much. They said, "Right-o, take your positions." And we sat there or lay there with our rifles, saw men in the distance, fired at them, and so on. And then tanks were coming and I think that we were told to retreat but I didn't retreat. There were three fellows with me and I said "Right-o." The tanks were more or less on top of us. Now what I said was, "Right," I says, "just lie down in this ditch and let the tanks pass over." But then there were infantry – Moors, in this particular place where I was. So we were obviously cut off.

And we were cut off for three days. The first night, when it was dark, we were trying to get back. We were creeping up and one of the lads there, John Goldstein, who came from Northumberland somewhere, he could speak Spanish. We could hear voices and he was listening to them. "Oh no," he said, "they're Moors." So we wandered about a bit and of course I had no sense of direction – I've still got no sense of direction at all. We spent that night in some hut that we came across. It was the most beautiful sleep and rest I ever had. When I woke up in the morning what a bloody shock it was to find out where we were!

Well, we moved about, trying to get back for three days. And then one morning when we woke up there was a posse of Spanish cavalrymen outside. And that was the end of us. And that was the end of my experiences fighting in Spain. There must have been about ten men in this group, I heard them saying to one another, "Son rojos" – "They're Reds." They took us then towards where the front was. We were a good bit behind the front now because they had moved so rapidly. They must have handed us over to some superior officer. I remember the officer saying so-and-so so-and-so so-and-so, and pointed over there, see. Now I had heard of course that Franco of course wasn't very concerned about prisoners. So that I really thought at that time when he was pointing over there that we were gonnae be bumped off. When I thought that I didn't feel afraid. I just thought that. I was saying, "Well, it'll be a shame. But that's that because you know what it's about." The other two lads were John Goldstein and another lad from the north-east coast. He was a bit nervous, this lad. "Och," he said, "I didn't like yesterday at all. The day before when the battle was on, it was nothing like that in Shanghai." He had been a British soldier in Shanghai. I said, "You were bullying the Chinese, the Fascists are now bullying you."

They had tied our hands by this time and when we were going down we saw masses of guns that Franco had gathered together for this offensive. There was a fellow coming down, an Italian officer. And he saw us of course. He must have known in some way that we were English or British and he said, "Oh, hallo, hallo, you chaps." He said, "I'd like to have a word with you." Well, he just knew English of course. He said "I'll come back and have a word," but he didn't come back.

We were taken to what must have been their staff centre which was on the top of this hill. And from this hill you could see everything. In other words they saw everything that was going on before we got there. There were Germans there who spoke English, young German officers, Spaniards as well. They saw everything that was going on. I said, "We want to eat and drink because we've had nothing to eat." They said, "After you talk, see." I said, "But we need this now." But they didn't of course try to force you to do anything because they probably thought we were so stupid – as we were, of course, to be perfectly fair about it.

We were then taken as prisoners to some station somewhere. I don't know which town it was, and we were put in a train to Valladolid. That's where we ended up. There were the three of us on that train, myself, John Goldstein, and the other lad. And I think we got a tin of tuna fish and a piece of bread and some fresh figs.

We were in these closed cattle trucks. When the train stopped (and it stopped many times) there were always women at the various places with cans of water to give us water to drink. We met tremendous sympathy from these women – you always get this of course from women. It was very touching to think that this was what was supposed to be enemy territory but these women were there.

I remember of couse there were some very poor cases among the other prisoners on the train. There were Spaniards there and there must have been some other International Brigaders, because there were a number of Poles in the truck that we were in. And there were some poor fellows who were – I don't think they were wounded – just very disordered. I suppose they were feeling sorry for themselves and would be hungry too of course and thirsty.

I remember there was one big Pole, he was a very big lad, a very handsome chap, beautiful moustaches and so on, and he was always at the window to get the water and drink it. So I spoke to him and made him to understand that he should pass the water out to these other people who were there. He paid no attention. So the next time I got up and I tried to speak to him again – in English, he knew some words in English. I said, "If you don't pass this water out," I said, "I'll kick you in the balls." And I gave the motions of that, see. And of course he could have just squashed me but he wouldn't of course because he was a bully. So when next time we came to the watering hole he got some water and he did take it across to some of the other men. There were things like that, ordinary things, every aspect of life.

Eventually we got to the camp in Valladolid, which was a shed in which there were hundreds of prisoners. There was only some chaff lying on the floor of the shed. It was dark when we got there but in the morning when we awoke and were assembled outside we noticed there were quite a number of Spaniards with all their packs and bread and chocolate and cigarettes and everything. Of course there were deserters as in every war and they had just come across with their equipment and rations.

Of course there were no cigarettes to be got there, and we used to be looking for them. We used to sometimes get a couple of ends that somebody had thrown away and roll them into a cigarette.

We were very miserable in that camp. I think we must have been there for about a month. The English people there became very, very despondent. And there were all sorts of tales got around. We used to call them shit-house rumours – as they called them, I think, in any army – that we were gonnae be released next week. Not only were we gonnae be released but we were gonnae be given suits of clothes and £5! So I realised of course what was happening. I said, "This is just absolute bloody rubbish." I said, "Stop thinking like that. Concentrate on where we are, how we've got to live here, what we've got to do." Some of these people became really poorly just thinking about these rumours.

In the morning we lined up for breakfast. And we got – you know those bars of chocolate, you used to get eight pieces in a bar, Cadbury's chocolate? We got one of these small squares of chocolate, handed out – well, we queued up for it. We got that. And we got some coffee, very watery coffee. That was our breakfast.

At midday we got one roll of bread about eight inches long. I don't know what the weight would be. And that had to do us for the day. We queued up to get the roll, got the roll, then went back in the queue again to have bean soup, just beans boiled up in water. We were so hungry in that place that we used always to say to ourselves, "Right-o, I'll just eat half of this bread now and I'll keep the other half for evening." But none of us were ever able to do that, we were so hungry we just ate it before then. So when evening came of course you just got these beans.

And every day in the morning one of the guards would come along and he would say, "Right," he said, "todos los extranjeros, aqui!" – "All the foreigners here!" And of course we had to start digging up the latrines, which were just open slit trenches. And there were so many people there that there was little ground that hadn't already been dug. That was a really filthy job. But of course we didn't worry too much about that under these conditions.

We were lousy. First of all when you got up in the morning you were so cold that you had to keep on walking about to warm yourself up. Then when the sun came out of course you could take off your clothes, take off your jacket, pick off what you could see, look at the seam, delouse it, put it down, take off your shirt, your trousers, do them. By the time you came up to put them on again of course the young ones had developed into good blood-sucking lice.

Oh yes, I remember on one occasion when one of the lads I got friendly with there became ill. He had got sunstroke. He was taken to the hospital. Well, the hospital was another shed some distance away from the first one in which the man just lay with a blanket. They gave him a blanket. And I think in his case he actually got some milk as well now and then. But we collected his bread for him and went up to give it to him. But he didn't want it, so we ate it. So John Goldstein and I had a good bit of bread that night. On another occasion when I went to see him when he was lying in the so-called hospital one of the guards came and grabbed me together with some Spaniards and he said, "Right, come with me," and he took us somewhere to take a man who was sick to hospital. He was in a sort of covered stretcher. And I remember that time. There were actually two men at the front of the stretcher – I think there were six men altogether – two at the front, two in the middle, and two of us at the rear. We walked then through the streets of Valladolid to the hospital. It was a very strange experience walking to the hospital through lighted streets where people were living a normal life. I can remember I was certainly very tired carrying only the sixth part of this stretcher before we got the man to the hospital.

When we got to the hospital we took him into a ward. The nurses were nuns. They put him in the bed. And some of the Spaniards of course said who I was, "an extranjero." And I remember the nuns saying "Povro chico – poor boy."

There was a blanket on this man, see, and it was a sort of tartan affair like a horse cloth. It was covered with all sorts of bits of vomit or something like that. It was just absolutely manky. I said to the doctor, "Let me have it." So I took this back with me and of course we used it – stretched it over us to keep ourselves warm. It was absolutely stinking but it was warm, it was warm.

I think we left the prison camp at Valladolid after about three weeks or so. We were then taken to another camp at Burgos. The Burgos camp was a very big camp. And the food there wasn't very great. The guards weren't too kind if you were not able to move fast enough, if they said, "Do this," or "Do that." As far as I was concerned it was only a case of course when you were going in, of "Hurry up!" and they would give you a bash with their stick.

When we were in the camp at Burgos there were people from the Gestapo came along and took our photographs, front and side view. By this time of course we had our heads shaven, which was probably a good thing for health reasons. And as the Gestapo man came up somebody was picking out a number of different people from among the prisoners who were there. I saw of course that they were picking out boys who were typically Jewish looking, and boys who were coloured – there were boys from Malaya there, some negro boys, people like that. I remember saying to Jimmy Heath as they came up, "I'll bet you anything you like he picks me." He did. And when we had been picked out they gave us two oranges, see. We were supposed to be having our meal outside with a tin of beans and the two oranges, see. So I said to Jimmy Heath and John Goldstein: "By the way, don't leave your oranges to the last. Eat them now and then you've got them." And we did that, see. Then we ate our beans. But the other boys ate their beans first. They didn't have time to eat their oranges – the Gestapo man and his assistants took them away from them. Well, I can't be sure of course these were Gestapo men. But they were certainly Germans. They weren't in uniform. Well, I'm not sure about this. They might have been in uniform but I can't recall that they were in uniform. But they were Germans.

I have already mentioned Jimmy Rutherford, who was a New-haven, Edinburgh, man. He had been in Spain before this particular time we are discussing and he had been taken prisoner. He had been released, with the proviso of course that he did not return. But he did return. And he was there at the time that I was there, in this camp at Burgos. I remember him saying to me, "George," he said, "I don't know what's happening but I think that they know." And he just said that. Jimmy was a fair bit younger than I was. And then one morning he came along and he told me, "I think that I am going to be taken away." And he was and he was executed. This was shortly before we went to another camp for prisoners at Palencia. Well, what I did that time when we went to Palencia was we were given paper to write on. So I wrote a letter to Fred Douglas, who was the Communist Party organiser then in Edinburgh and I put in the letter of course about Jimmy Rutherford. I didn't mention his name, because he had already taken another name, but mentioned him in such a way that Fred should know that there was something going on. I said, "We haven't seen him for some time." And Fred should have known what I meant. Whether he understood or not, I don't know.

That was the only case of people who were shot in that way outright. I also remember of course when we were discussing these things a few years ago in a seminar at Loughborough, some of the people, ex-International Brigade men, said the Communist Party should not have sent Rutherford out once again. Now I disagreed with that. I didn't disagree during the debate but afterwards when we were discussing it with the man who was interviewing me. It is true of course we are concerned about what the orders of the Communist Party are. But I would have gone back again after being released from the prisoner-of-war camps. And the reason for that is that this business of being a prisoner, of being out of the battle so quickly, which is a ridiculous conception now of course when I am so old because it doesn't matter whether you're in a battle for one hour, half a day, ten days or that – something is going to happen to you in the end. And that was the reason of course why I said I would have gone back again. And at the same time when Fred Douglas said, "The Communist Party wants our best comrades to go out to join the people in Spain," and I went, at that time I knew from what I was reading that the War was lost. I knew it was lost. But that didn't make any difference because it wasn't lost until right at the very end.

I can't really say very much more about Jimmy Rutherford. He must have been only twenty-one I think when he was executed and at that time I'd be twenty-eight. But I remember him because he was a boy who came from Newhaven and he was in the Labour League of Youth. Two or three years before I joined the Communist Party I was in the Labour Party and came across him there. But he was just a boy to me. Seven years of difference when you're young is a very big difference. But he was a very fine fellow. We know he was because of what he did. But that's all I can say about him.

I was there at Burgos for perhaps six weeks. I was then sent to the prisoner-of-war camp at Palencia. About 100 English-speaking men were taken there. It was Italian soldiers who were in charge there. There were Scotsmen there and of the two Scotsmen I knew who were there one was Donald McGregor, a Clydebank man. These men are now dead that I'm talking about. We were fairly well treated there, fairly well treated, we got good reasonable food, we also got ten cigarettes each week. The very first thing that happened with these cigarettes was that people started gambling for them.

I wasn't beaten or otherwise ill-treated at Palencia. I think in the main of course that the people didn't have very much to grumble about. Well, they think about other things happening in the world of course. We were there for some time then we were sent home. I was a prisoner from March 1938 until November that year, when I came home.

We were repatriated before the other prisoners of war. The men from the British Battalion came back after the prisoners, because I remember I was organising a meeting of welcome for the men who were coming back to Edinburgh and the Lothians. And Tom Murray was there. Tom Murray was a great lad for making a show about that, see. It was in the Free Gardeners' Hall in Picardy Place. I remember writing an article to be published in the *Evening News,* called 'Scots in Spain'.

While I was in Spain I was reported dead, I was reported killed. I didn't know anything about this until I got home. But my mother got a notice – I suppose it would be from Fred Douglas' wife, that was the job she had, to tell the parents or the wives of men who had died. The report was that I had been killed on the Aragon front. So she got that on my birthday. I have the death certificate still, signed by Copic, who was the chief of the army group at that time. My mother collected £10 off the death insurance from Pearl Assurance Company. But some notice must have got through to the papers that I was not dead, it was a false alarm. Of course she didn't pay the money back.

I had to pay back to the government the £5 or £10 or £20 that they had asked me for the fare home from Spain. Lots of the other prisoners of course never paid and I wouldn't have paid it back either but by this time I was working in the English Steel Corporation in Sheffield at the beginning of the war and they'd already begun asking questions about this man Drever. So I decided to pay the money.

Before I went to Spain I had worked as a chemist with I.C.I. and naturally when I came back I was looking for a job as a chemist. There were quite a number of chemical firms in Edinburgh. There was the Rubber Mill at Fountainbridge, there were paint works, dye works out at Granton and there was S.A.I. of course.[185] That of course was again I.C.I., although perhaps my name hadn't percolated up here. But the number of places to which I wrote looking for work! And I got interviewed of course at every one of them. But the lads who interviewed me of course they had known – because of this publicity about being dead – where I'd been. They didn't offer me a job.

Looking back half a century on the Spanish War I have no regrets whatever, none at all. The way I thought then about the world, people in the world, I still think that way and still act and behave in such a way that I can forward the struggle of the people, mainly of course the working class people.

Steve Fullarton was born in Glasgow in 1920 and was brought up in Shettleston. During the Second World War he served in the Royal Air Force. After that War he returned to his trade as an engineer. He now lives in West Lothian.

STEVE FULLARTON

I don't think I could truthfully say that any individual or even organisation influenced me to go to Spain. Actually it was just a case of knowing the situation. To have grown up where I grew up, in Elvan Street, in Shettleston, Glasgow, now on one side of the street there were five what we call closes. And from these five closes, let me see, there was Jimmy Reid, Willie Gauntlett, Willie Dougan, myself – that's four anyway from five closes who went to Spain.

So that's only a reflection of the kind of feeling that there was in the particular area where I grew up. And as I say it wasn't so much that anybody specially recruited you or anything like that. You just read the papers or listened to topics of conversation and you had feelings. And it was as simple as that. And you were reading about the bombing of civilians by German and Italian planes and all the terrible things that the Fascists did in Spain. Guernica was just part and parcel of the whole. Guernica become sort of symbolic more or less later.

As I say, you get feelings and I had had these feelings for a wee while. And knowing that there was such a thing as an International Brigade it happened that one night I was at a dance – a Communist Party dance. I saw George Campbell, the organiser of the Communist Party, in Shettleston there that night and told him that I was interested in going to Spain. He questioned me about my age my family circumstances and one thing and another. To cut a long story short he said he would come down and see my mother, who was a widow, on Sunday morning. He did, and my mother's attitude, which was predictable, was, "Well, if that's what Steve wants to do there's no way I can stop him." I was eighteen then. I wasn't married. So that was that. By this time on the Saturday night, I had told my pal Willie Gauntlett that I was going. "Oh," he said, "I'll go too." Well, I know that he didn't have any political leanings although I did.

I wasn't a member of any party at all. It was just feelings. And as I say, it was a political area. I can go back a few years before the Spanish War and tell you about parading the street with all the other kids, "Vote, Vote for John Wheatley!" at the election. I don't know what election but it's one of my memories.[186] But as I say it was that kind of area in which politics was important. I don't think they had anything else to do because there were very many unemployed and in fact I

289

think to be employed was the exception. I was employed myself. I worked in Boyd's in Shettleston, engineering.

Campbell, who was the organiser then, went into Ingram Street on the next day, on the Monday, saw somebody. I think actually Isa Alexander was in there and I think Bill Cowe was there. Anyway he went in and saw them and he took us with him. Campbell said to Willie Gauntlett and me, "Before I go in here," he says, "you better say you're 19." "O.K., I'll be 19 if they ask." They did ask. They told me, I think it was the Thursday, "You'll be going down to London now and they'll see you in London and you better tell them ye're 20 because 19 sounds a bit young." "Aye, O.K., I'll be 20." Well, when I went to London my age increased from 20 to 21: "You better say you're 21." And when I got to Paris that was me 21.

When we went from London a fellow named Smith from Kirkcaldy who had been in Spain before was put in charge, given the money to buy the tickets and so on and so forth. Smith was given the instructions and I just followed the instructions. He was the one who knew what it was all about. This was him going back for his second time.

I think it was six of us went from London and Tom Murray made seven when we got to Paris. Tom Murray was a Labour Councillor in Edinburgh – I think for Liberton Ward. But as I say we six arrived in Paris under our own steam which on reflection I found was a bit amusing, too. Because there we were six people only one of whom had been outside the country before. And there were we travelling from London to Newhaven by boat train. Newhaven to Dieppe by boat, and train to Paris. I think the fare was 28s. 6d. for a weekend ticket from a Friday night to a Tuesday morning. In Paris we found our way to where we were supposed to go, the Place de Combat, I think, found the people that we were supposed to meet and were put up in sort of private residences.

We spent at least a couple of nights in Paris. And we got the first medical there and I think there were at least three doctors. And it was in Paris – I think the first morning – that Tom Murray turned up. That was the first time I had met Tom and I was very impressed. Tom had travelled under his own steam because he had his own passport, one of the rich, you know! Because it wasn't normal for working people to go abroad in these days. Anyway, Tom had apparently been put in charge of us and was given the instructions what to do on I think the Monday or Tuesday night. I think it must have been the Tuesday because we were warned about being inconspicuous when we got to the station in Paris, when we were leaving Paris to go to Cerbère in the South of France. We were told to meet but not in a group, just to keep in sight of each other at, I think, six o'clock at night or something, and well warned about the 24 hour clock in the railway station. And that was it. We got the right train and off to Cerbère and got out at the right place. There were taxis outside at Cerbère, a lovely sunny morning, and it was a case of, well, just get in the taxi. I never heard anybody give any directions but we arrived at this hotel. And that was it. We arrived at the right place and were shown to our rooms.

We were at Cerbère for a few days. And then we were told one day to get ready after our evening meal and we'd be taken to some place. A taxi turned up for us and we were taken to a farmhouse. There were, I think, about fifty men of other nationalities there. And we hung around there for a while, had coffee, and then later on we were all put in a bus, or I'm not sure if it was two buses, with the lights out, and travelled to the border and then disembarked. At that farmhouse we had been issued with *alpargatas,* rope-soled sandshoes, and this was to keep us quiet going across the border. So when we came off the bus ready for our climb in the Pyrenees we had to change into our *alpargatas* and shoes, tie our boots, as in my case, round our necks with the laces and that was us. Off we went follow-my-leader over the Pyrenees. This would be the end of March 1938.

Tom Murray then had the job of practically carrying the boy Smithie, who had been in Spain before. Smithie had been wounded in the legs and his legs gave out on him. His heart was big but his legs couldn't match his heart. So Tom performed the task of more or less carrying Smithie over the mountains. I can't remember an awful lot about climbing the mountains except that it was very tiring. Every now and then we'd stop for a five minutes' break. But we were well warned, "No smoking" and "No talking," and that was that. In fact after a long time of this climb we passed over a wooden bridge of some sort. It was lit up and there was a sort of guardhouse there. I thought this was us had arrived because there were lights on, and, "Oh, we've arrived!" Little did I know this was one of the French frontier guards' posts. I was careless and was stomping away across this bridge and the others are all saying "Ssshhhh! Ssshhhh!" I didn't realise I was still in the French territory.

It was cold. I actually had an overcoat on. It was my good overcoat, in fact it was the only overcoat I ever owned. That went through with me right until we left for the Ebro months later. However, we carried on and eventually it was over and we got to the other side and we started coming downwards. So that was a blessing. There was a halt. We had coffee somewhere, a big cave-like place on the Spanish side. Then we went on to Figueras. It's referred to as Figueras by everyone but I never saw any town. It was just in this sort of school, convent or something like that. But I was never outside it really. So as for seeing any town of Figueras that they talk about, I don't know. It is the only place that I knew in that area.

There were no dropouts. No, just Smithie and I think actually when we got to what they call Figueras Smithie was sent home from there.

That was the end of his second trip to Spain. Tom Murray was the other breakaway. Once we had arrived at Figueras he moved off rapidly to join the British Battalion right away. We stayed there for maybe a week, maybe a fortnight. It must have been more than a week because I had been there for a week when Jimmy Reid turned up. Jimmy Reid stayed in the next close to me in Elvan Street. I was quite surprised to see Jimmy there. He was another man who was much older than me – well, they were all older than me actually. Going over the Pyrenees, as I say, it was cold. But when we got to Figueras it wasn't so cold because Jimmy Reid – this is the bit that sticks in my mind – fell asleep with his hand on his chest and got more or less burned, but it left the white mark of his hand on his chest. So it was warm enough to do that.

We were there at Figueras maybe a couple of weeks doing a bit of training under an American instructor. He was a lieutenant in the Spanish army. It was just rifle training. But when I say rifle training it was wooden rifles like the Home Guard had in 1939, just imitation rifles. So we practised with these.

We moved from there to another place the name of which I don't know but it was a mixed International place, a small place, not many of us there, say fifty, sixty people. And we were there maybe a couple of weeks, I'm not sure. But the next thing we were moved from there to go and join the British Battalion. Although I didn't know it at the time this was when the big retreat was on from Belchite. And obviously they couldn't take us raw recruits into the Battalion because we would have had to run along with the rest. There was no profit in that. And presumably that's why we were held back for these few weeks. But eventually we were taken to join the British Battalion in the XVth Brigade. So we joined them at a place – I don't know the name of that either, because I just drifted through, to be honest with you. Well, we were taken on a lorry and we arrived there. You could see all the big crowd, and they were British – British mainly anyway – and of course they were so anxious to meet somebody from home, "Oh, what's all the latest news from home?" kind of thing, which we did appreciate. However, we milled among them but while this was going on there was a shout, "Get the hell out of there!" kind of thing, "Don't you break ranks without my order!" So, what the hell's this? This was Paddy O'Sullivan. Paddy, an Irishman, I think he was southern Irish, a strong disciplinarian, was a lieutenant in charge of No. 1 Company. Well, this was Paddy, and of course he did scare us. "Oh, what the hell's this?" because it was the nearest approach to discipline with any serious intent.

Then we were split up. Those of us who were British Battalion – "You there, and you there." Me, I went to Paddy O'Sullivan's lot. I thought, "I've got problems here!" However, just listening to the boys who were there, "Oh, no, Paddy O'Sullivan's all right, Paddy

O'Sullivan's all right when you're in action. He's a good man to be with," and you know, "All right, he's strict and he gives you a hard time before you get there, but when you're there you'll be thankful for him." So I accepted that kind of advice from old–timers, and although as I say I was always apprehensive of Paddy I always did what I was told. I came to think, "I wish to hell I could get out of here." One of the lads that I had sort of palled up with was Tommy McColl, who came out in that second batch with Jimmy Reid. Tommy McColl had been posted to the machine gunners. He came over to me one day when we were in Chabola Valley. "Hey, Steve," he says, "there's a chance they're needing somebody over here in the machine gunners, a runner or something. How do you fancy coming?" And I thought and thought it over but by this time I had become used to Paddy O'Sullivan. I had always wanted a chance to get away from Paddy O'Sullivan but when I had got the chance I realised – "No." I had got to know him a bit better then and I realised that his attitude was the right attitude. So I said, "No – I'll stay with Paddy O'Sullivan." And I have no regrets about that.

When we moved from there we were in a train for about two days. I know the area of the country was such that you couldn't travel two days anywhere but we must have been going up and down on the same line. I don't know but to me it was two days. We travelled overnight and it seemed like two days. And we arrived at some place, a biggish kind of place. I'm not sure if it was a town called Vich or not. But we arrived at this place maybe about twelve o'clock in the day. Starving of course, because before we had set off we had been given a wee tin of bully beef or something and one loaf of bread and naturally enough that perished on the first day! So we were all starving this particular day. We were waiting and waiting for something to eat, "Oh, it's coming at 2 o'clock . . . 3 o'clock . . . 4 o'clock . . . 8 o'clock." And in the meantime Paddy O'Sullivan had got us marching up and down on the road! I suppose it was his idea of keeping you from moaning and groaning and getting depressed or demoralised. He gave us a hard time, and especially when our tongues were hanging out. But as I say I've since learned that he was right, you know. I had heard it said, but it was only hearsay, that he had been in the Irish Guards. He carried himself like a Guardsman, always wore his hat down over his eyes like a Guardsman. But again these things are all just hearsay and there is nobody sort of challenges you on anything like that, and I couldn't vouch for the authenticity of that. The man in charge of the whole company was Paddy O'Daire. Paddy O'Daire, another man from Southern Ireland, was in charge of three companies I think it was. We were No. 1 Company, the Major Attlee Company. Arthur Nicoll, a Dundee man, was in charge of No. 2 Company, and No. 3 I'm no' sure, I cannae remember, maybe a Spaniard. Paddy O'Daire and Paddy O'Sullivan were good pals and they sort of hit it off.

But the nearest approach to a real friend that I saw Paddy O'Sullivan had was Michael O'Riordan.[187] I think he used to come over from the machine guns area and I used to see Paddy O'Sullivan and him in long conversations together. They appeared to be good friends.

But we didn't stay long at that place where we didn't get anything to eat. We were only a few days there and then we moved on to Chabola Valley. In Chabola Valley it was a case of, "Well, stop here." We'd been instructed, "Wherever you stop, start digging a foxhole." That was always it, "Dig a foxhole," no matter whether you're going to be there for ten minutes or ten days. This was against aerial attack mainly because the Fascist planes just roamed the skies at will. Only at an odd time we'd see one of our Moscas or Chatos. It was a rare occasion when one of them would fly past.

Being in No. 1 Company I was associating with Dusty Miller from Alexandria, Benny Richardson from the North of England, Jimmy Glavin from Glasgow, who hadn't been in the same gang as me going out, Peter Cassidy and another man – I think he was from Dundee. I forget his name, what I would call then an elderly man, he may have been in the forty range, like Jimmy Glavin at that time. Now right away Dusty decided, "Right, off and cut down a tree!" And I thought, "What the hell?" He cut down a tree and then used the branches as well. Well, he got us all involved in this and made such a structure that I think it's still there! It was almost a bomb-proof shelter he made, you know. We had set up this den against a *barranco*, which is a sort of step in the land, and covered it with earth. It was definitely a good dug-out, it stood up to all the rain or whatever, you know.

So in Chabola Valley it was a case of training, marching or rifle practice – aiming and one thing and another, practising crossing a river, and that kind of thing. Chabola Valley is near the Ebro. We were behind the Ebro training for when we were going to cross it back again after the retreat from Belchite. By this time Franco's forces had broken through in their attempt to get to Valencia but they only just got to the sea, the Mediterranean. They didn't actually capture Valencia. But they broke through about 100 miles south of Barcelona, say sixty miles south of Tarragona. And we were in the north part. So that was us. At Chabola Valley we had rifle practice, actual rifle practice. I only fired five rounds, because you couldn't afford to use ammunition. Tom Murray said, "Right, we're going to be firing today and the best shots will get a day out at Tarragona." Tom Murray was one of the people that got the day out to Tarragona! I never got any day out to Tarragona. I remained confined within the length of Chabola Valley, between the two wee villages – I forget their names to be honest. No matter, that was the extent of Chabola Valley, between the two villages.

After a wee while Paddy O'Sullivan made me corporal in No. 1 Company. I was very proud of that. I got on fine with Paddy O'Sullivan by this time and as I say I really liked him. They were organising a corporal's school in one of the villages and he sent me to go and get training as a corporal in this school, which I enjoyed very much. It was very instructive. The man in charge there was a Russian. I presume he couldnae speak any other language than Russian because he always had an interpreter. The interpreter sounded like he had been of Russian extraction, born in Canada. His English was perfect. I always remember that part of the Russian's instruction was how we were going to cross the river. "And where you have to cross," he said, "there's a loop so that you can attack each side of the loop, cut off the sort of peninsula part of the loop, cut them off and you've got a base to operate from and you can spread out from there." I can always remember him describing this and drawing it on the blackboard. And that is exactly what took place when we did cross the river. We crossed at that kind of place.

However one day or evening at the corporals' school we got word, "Right, pack up. Everybody back to your own companies. Report back." Of course I didn't know what was happening. Things were a wee bit chaotic, people coming and going and running and shouting. Off I set to get back where I had come from but when I got there, oh, there were hundreds all on the move. I went down to our dug-out – nobody there. "Where's. . . ?" "Oh, they've all gone. They're away. No. 1 Company's away in front." So I had to set off and practically run – and it was dark of course – practically run along the length of all these troops until eventually I did catch up with our crowd. And that was me back with the Battalion.

That takes me back to the overcoat I had worn since we'd climbed the Pyrenees. That's what happened to my overcoat in the chaos. I had left in the dug-out any stuff which I did have, which wasn't very much anyway. But my overcoat was among it. I remember getting on to Dusty, "What did you do about my overcoat?" "Oh, tae hell, we never bothered about your overcoat." And I was a wee bit disappointed that nobody had thought to bring my overcoat. But that was silly, you know. It had been important to me but on reflection I realised it wasn't so important at all. That was it. I never saw my overcoat again.

So off we went and we marched all night. Come daylight we rested among trees somewhere. And then the next night we marched again. The next night we set off again and marched for some long time again and we arrived at the river's edge. And, "O.K., we're crossing the river. They've got a pontoon bridge up. We're going to cross on the pontoon." Some had crossed by boat and other means. But just as we got to the pontoon a Fascist plane came along and circled very low, taking good sights on what was going on. And of course we naturally had to hide and get among the reeds. But then he dropped his bombs and that was the first angry bombs I had heard. It was a frightening experience. You just got your head down. All you hear is the bang, bang, bang. However he was trying to get the pontoon bridge actually which was just submerged below the surface of the water. I don't know if he actually saw it or not or was just a bad aimer or whatever, I don't know. But he dropped his bombs. I don't know about any casualties but once he had flown off it was just a case of, "Right! Quick! Everybody across the bridge!"

And off we went across the bridge to the other side. And on we went. We just kept going, some shooting and one thing and another. The main encounter was at a crossroads – I don't know where – and of course it was a case of, "Down! Take Cover!", because there were a lot of Fascist planes appeared just at that point when we reached the crossroads. And we just put the head down because we'd been taught, "Always keep your face down because your face shows up white to them." But because we were no threat to them they flew low enough to be able to see us in any case. So they bombed away. And once again that was really a frightening one because of the screaming of those bombs coming down. I can't tell you anything about any insignias on the planes. They were just Fascist planes, because as I say when you saw them you got your head down – well, I did anyway! As I say, that was part of my training. And one thing I did do was to try to carry out my instructions. It was face down and just hope that they would go away, or if they dropped their bombs that they dropped them on somebody else, no' me!

Anyway at this crossroads, oh, they dropped a hell of a load there but funny enough it was only mules and horses that were killed. I never saw any people killed.

So we moved on. There were snipers in different places and we were shooting back at them and one thing and another. I remember Dusty Miller found some old bread in a house and it was very welcome because we were starving. Supplies of food and ammunition were very poor. We got a meal on the night before we crossed the Ebro. And I think we got coffee in the morning and that was it! Ye're away to dae your fighting on a cup o' coffee, a can of coffee actually.

In fact that was one of the first things you had to do when you arrived in Spain, to find yourself a tin can, which was your billy can, and it was for everything. And even a spoon was hard to come by. We weren't provided with cutlery. Oh, you were provided with nothing like that. You had to, as we said, 'organise' that for yourself. But somehow or another we managed. A lot of them had formed wooden spoons. This is how desperate we were for supplies of any sort. But a lot of them had wooden spoons that they had shaped out of pieces of wood. I'm not sure what I had. I may have had a metal spoon, I'm not sure. But it was something we might have been instructed to carry with us before we had gone out, you know, but that's with hindsight. It wasn't the kind of thing that anybody returning from Spain would say: "Well, send out spoons for the boys." It was more important you got food and other things there. We were very much an army that marched on our stomachs – empty stomachs! Food was always a topic. It was the biggest topic always. We were always hungry. Always starving, always. Whenever there was a lull in conversation about anything important food cropped up, and that was it. Hookey Walker was the cook. He did marvels in the normal way. On high days and holidays sometimes – when I was with the Battalion – Hookey Walker managed to rustle up some meat and made rissoles. He did the best he could in very difficult circumstances. But when you are on the move like that it is difficult and especially for us.

So we were detached from the main body to go and sort out the snipers. The snipers had been attacking the traffic coming to and fro where our forward troops were. So we were attacking them in one way or another until it became dark and then it was a case of, "Well, get the head down till morning." Well, we got up in the morning and we were just hanging about waiting for further instructions and some shooting started. Now we were on top of a sort of knoll, a small hill. And it was a case of, "Dive down, lie flat," you know. And these shots were just cutting across. There must have been somebody on the same level as us amongst some trees across a sort of valley. He must have been watching us and then picked his moment, and he wounded quite a number. There were two boys called Bennett in the machine gunners, two brothers. The machine guns they had were these heavy Maxim type things where you had a heavy cast iron tripod that one carried on his shoulder and the other one carried the gun mounting. Anyway it happened that in trying to deal with this sniper or snipers the machine gunners had been called on to provide a machine gun because we couldn't see. We could tell where the sniping was coming from but you couldn't actually see who was doing it. So the best thing was to rake the area with a machine gun. Anyway this big fellow, a big Irishman again by the way, Ryan, I think his name was, he got on top of the knoll and wandered about there.[188] Now we had been getting shot at right, left and centre and he stood about there and said, "Right, then, we'll have the gun over there," and came back down again. And I marvelled at this. "How the hell? The snipers must be away." Well, the boy Bennett started to climb over this sort of banking but he only got probably up to chest high and he got shot – killed outright, like that. And as I say, big Ryan had got away with wandering about. Whether the snipers were reloading their gun or whatever happened I don't know. But there was Bennett killed right in front of me, and of his brother too, because his brother was carrying the gun.[189]

There was a lighter side just prior to that when Ginger Benson, a

Yorkshireman was wounded in the foot and he was shouting for somebody to come and give him a hand. And he was lying there, shouting, "Give us a bloody hand here," you know. "They've shot me in the bloody foot." Charlie Framp, who was the sergeant of our company, Charlie Framp shouts, "Ginger, be quiet," he says, "you'll give your position away!" Ginger Benson, quick as a flash, says "Well, if I haven't already given my position away some bastard's told them where I am!" I've never forgotten that and I thought that was great, you know. I'm lying here and didn't dare move and I'm listening to all this, and I thought, "Christ, Ginger, on the ball." But eventually I managed to slide back and get to the safe side of this knoll. And so also did Ginger Benson.

Eventually that was all sorted out and we moved off from there and then we joined up with the main Battalion and we were posted to the forward position for Hill 481. Eventually it came to the point where we had to do a frontal attack on this Hill 481. That was suicidal really, on reflection, but – O.K., get over and attack.

By this time, funny enough, I don't know if this was one of Paddy O'Sullivan's means of protecting me but I always had a rifle until we got to the action and then I was sort of promoted to the Russian Diktorov light machine gun, which was a better weapon. It had a round pan. It was more like a Bren gun than a Lewis gun, but instead of the magazine loading from the top in that segment of a circle as in the Bren, it was a complete circle but it lay flat on top as in the Lewis gun. It was on a spring like a gramophone spring, and this is how the bullets were rotated as you fired. It held forty-nine rounds. Well, in addition to the one on top you carried a can with three other disks of ammunition in it. But it was bloody heavy tae carry. And I think this was Paddy O'Sullivan looking after me! He didnae want me to carry the thing but once it came to action then, "Right, Steve, you're on the machine gun!" I didnae mind, you know, it was all right.

But anyway as I say by this time I was on the Diktorov. We were put in a forward position at Hill 481, which was within sight of Gandesa, which was the main target anyway. Gandesa had loomed large in memories of the Brigade, having retreated from there some short time before. But by this time the Fascists had picked out the best spot for a defensive position and they worked hard on it. On two nights I was out with the patrols and you could hear them working. Unfortunately from our position their hill was almost sheer. To attack it you had to go down a slight drop, up again to higher ground, then really down low and then you were almost perpendicular up to where they were. And they had their machine guns fortified up there. In fact, we could see them working during the day, you know. We would fire at them but somehow or other they obviously got their work done irrespective of any damage that we might have done. But if we'd been able to call on artillery we could have demolished these positions quite easily and it would have made a big difference to our attack.

Funny enough on the day that we attacked that Hill 481 frontal on during daylight I think there were seven tanks appeared from well over on our right. They just appeared and stopped and fired some shots and then they just withdrew.

We were supposed to get aircraft support. I think there were a few aircraft flew over but the aid they gave us was nil. But we didn't have equipment, you know. Had we had the equipment to do anything worthwhile we would have got it. But we just didn't have the planes. I now realise that our position was really hopeless, in the sense that we were matching manpower and rifles against heavy artillery. I've just mentioned that I was out on patrol, two nights prior to our attack. During these patrols what would seem like some accidental firing would start and in no time all hell would be let loose. The Fascists were throwing in everything – their artillery, mortars, the lot. And I was thankful that I was right out in the forward position, because they were shooting over our heads. I thought, "At least it's only if they drop their sights a wee bit or make any mistakes that they'll be firing on our position here." In terms of actual real fire power we had nothing to match them. Had we had anything of that nature I'm quite sure that Gandesa would have been ours. But that was our main stumbling block. If we could have shifted that defensive position on Hill 481 that they had built up I think we could have gone straight to Gandesa at that time. Although, to be honest, I think that in the long run it wouldn't have mattered. The end result would still have been the same, because we still had nothing to back up our forces, due to the disastrous policy from our point of view of Non-Intervention. As is well known the Chamberlain Government sponsored Non-Intervention, backed up by the French Government. And everybody was well aware that Non-Intervention was just a farce, and it was just another means of strangling the Republican Government.

Anyway, as I say, it was a case of, "Stand to, and get ready to attack Hill 481." And eventually after some long time – we were supposed to wait for this artillery bombardment which never materialised – it was a case of, "Well, right, lads, on we go!" and off we went to make a frontal attack on Hill 481.

Having run as hard as we could to get as near as possible to the Fascists and then found it was practically a sheer rise in front of us our attack came to a halt at various stages. In fact many of our lads came to a halt long before they got as far as where I'd gone because they had been either wounded or killed.

I ran out of ammunition for the Diktorov, firing up at these machine gun posts. One that was right down on my right hand side was having a field day shooting up the way. There was one shooting down and one shooting up and they had us in a very sticky position. However, I was shouting for anybody who had any ammunition for the Diktorov and somebody from my left, on the higher side of me, threw down a can with another three drums for the Diktorov in it. So I fired these off and then that was me run out of ammunition.

But by this time the attack was completely petered out and there was nothing more happening. All around anybody that I could either see or hear was either dead or wounded. And that was that. I realised there was not much more I could do with this Diktorov, firing with it anyway. So I started to attend to the people who had been wounded round about me. One in particular that I can name is Kelly from, I think, Dumbarton.[190] I was attending him. he had been wounded in the forearm by a dum–dum bullet. Using these dum–dum bullets was contrary to the Geneva Convention. A dum–dum is a bullet that just leaves a small hole as it enters but as it comes through it either explodes or expands or bursts on impact and it tears its way out instead of, you know, just going straight through as a normal bullet would do. So that Kelly's forearm from the wrist to the elbow was just a gaping hole. He also had a wound on his neck, on the right side under his chin.

While I was attending to Kelly – he was lying sort of feet downhill, on his back, and I was feet uphill, lying head to head with him – a shell exploded just about his feet. Of course I got quite a shower of grit, but that's all I got, no shrapnel. And when we'd sort of come to I said to Kelly, "How did you get on?" He raised his head and looked down, because I didn't know – I was keeping as low as possible – he raised his head and looked down and he said, "Oh," he said, "my legs." So I thought he was in a bad way right enough. This wound under his chin worried me. I thought, "Well, that must be in his head somewhere." However, having attended to him I attended to two or three Spaniards and then Paddy O'Sullivan called me and I went up to him. He was wounded in the right leg and left arm. He asked me to put a tourniquet on his leg and his arm. I did that and checked that he could release it to suit himself. I said, "Are you all right otherwise?" He said he was all right. Oh, aye, he was fine, he was quite sensible, and talking away. So he says, "Well, find some cover somewhere," he says, "and come back for me when it's dark." Says I, "O.K." And just as I was taking off, he says, "But wait." Paddy O'Sullivan, being the good soldier that he was, he reminded me, he says, "Check where I am before you leave." I thought, "Aye, right enough," because it was so easy to forget where you were. And I had a look round about. There was a tree that had been cut in two, and where the upper part had dropped down it was pointing directly to where he was. And I said to myself, "Och, aye, easy enough to remember where he is." But just as I was getting into a hole which was probably a shell hole, I was just on the very edge of it, I got wounded right in the abdomen, the right side. I fell flat right into the hole. I lay still. I thought whoever shot at me – because the shooting was over by this time –

must have deliberately shot at me, having seen me quite clearly. So I lay still for some time just letting him think I was dead if he could still see me. But eventually I moved my hand down to feel what had happened. I could feel where it was. And here a hand round the back and I thought I couldn't feel anything and I thought, "It must be still there." I lay there until it was getting dust and then I heard a man I knew was Pollock, Jim Pollock, I think it was. He came out and he was shouting for Paddy O'Sullivan. So I shouted to him to come over. I said, "Paddy O'Sullivan's up there." And I told him about this broken tree that was pointing right to him. "O.K.," he said, "Have you got any bombs?" I said, "Oh, aye, I've got two." That was hand grenades. It was part of your normal issue. You were issued with 300 rounds of ammunition, bullets, and two hand grenades – one shrapnel and one percussion. And I still had these two because I had never been near enough to throw them at anybody. So I debated with him whether to give him any. I said, "I've still got to get back." However, he finally persuaded me to part with one and I gave him one. And I left him at that, thinking he was going for Paddy O'Sullivan. However, it's only since the war's over I know what happened. I met Pollock after the war and asked him why he did not get to Paddy O'Sullivan, because I gave him precise instructions where he was. "Ah," he said, "I collected bombs on my way up there," he said, "and I went up to the top side of the hill where there was a machine gun post." He went up there and he off-loaded all these bombs or hand grenades, one after another, against the machine gun post, and then ran for his life. And that was it. He never went near Paddy O'Sullivan nor anyone else, apart from collecting hand grenades.

Paddy O'Sullivan is listed as being killed in that action, when in fact he was only wounded and not fatally wounded. And if Paddy O'Sullivan died it must have been only as a result of what happened to him after the action. When the Moors counter-attacked they must have killed him, as well as Kelly, because he's also listed as killed in that same action. There were no prisoners reported from that action, which was ridiculous because some were just ordinary wounds, which I know from my own personal experience. But, as I say, there were no prisoners taken there. It would appear to be very common for the wounded to be killed. It would appear that that must have been normal for the Fascists to do by that time, though in early days they had taken some prisoners. But now in these days there was no question of them taking prisoners. They just killed them and that was it.

Well, I managed to get back to where we had started from then I was taken to a sort of dressing station at the rear. I spent the night there then was taken back to the river, across the river and then to a cave. I spent a couple of days in that cave and then was evacuated by train to hospital in Tarragona. From Tarragona I went to hospital in

Gerona. Actually the hospital in Gerona was a Spanish hospital and there were only two of us who were British in the whole hospital. I was sixteen days there and any Spanish that I did learn to speak was during my sixteen days in there because I was forced to! In fact, I got somebody to buy me a dictionary, which I still have. It was a Spanish-English dictionary, it wasn't an English-Spanish dictionary. But it didn't matter – it was better than nothing.

After that I was at various places which were reported as being convalescent places. Certainly it was an improvement on what had been before but it was certainly rough and the food, as usual, was very scarce. There was no variety. It was either beans, lentils or sometimes rice, with fish or meat in it. At that stage all our thoughts were always on food and what we would do when we would get free! From then on I was never back to the Battalion. They were later in action at Hill 666, at which the lad I mentioned earlier, my pal Gauntlett, was killed, or at least just disappeared. And that was that.

But as I say I was never back to the Battalion and I shifted from place to place after that, until eventually I finished up at a beautiful place on the coast of Spain, San Feliu de Guixols. It was a series of fifteen villas which had been owned by foreigners to Spain but they had been taken over as a convalescent place. It was a lovely place, beautiful. Of course the food was no better but nevertheless the conditions were superior, in fact marvellous. And we had beds in there, iron beds. Normally you just had your blanket and you flopped down on the floor, or the ground, wherever you were, and that was your bed normally. So that to be sleeping in an iron bed with sheets as well was real luxury.

It was from there that I was invalided back home. It was actually after the Battalion had come home that I managed to get home. I came home 23rd December 1938 and I think they had come home at the beginning of December. But being sort of isolated, there were four of us who came home together. One was Dusty Miller – I had met up with Dusty at Barcelona. He had been wounded somewhere in his forearm, had injured the tendons in his fingers and couldn't close his hand properly. The others were a man from Cambuslang – I forget his name – Jimmy Reid, and myself. We were sent on a hospital train to Port Bou, on the Spanish side of the frontier. We were given 200 francs, French francs, and our pay book was stamped, "Authorised to take 200 French francs out of the country".

We had to go to a railway station on the French side, and I remember being in the buffet and buying chocolate, Swiss chocolate. Well, this was real luxury. We just went daft, actually. You know, seeing things that you could buy to eat. It was really marvellous. So we bought this chocolate and ate it. And on the train we had a meal and of course when the waiter came with the bill I remember telling him: "Just charge it to Lord Halifax," who was the Foreign Secretary for Britain at that time.[191] I just signed the bill and that was it.

When we arrived in Paris we went to the station hotel for breakfast. I'd had the foresight to ask a Swiss nurse who spoke English when I was in this convalescent place at San Feliu, "How do you say 'ham and eggs' in French?" Because this was our dream. And I remember her telling me, she says, "Jambon and oeufs." And I was struggling with this "'n oeufs". So when we got to this station hotel the waiter came up and I says, "Right then, 'n oeufs." So the waiter brought a big platter of ham and eggs – there were four of us at our table and of course I became so popular with all the others. So that was another case of "Sign the bill and charge it to Lord Halifax." But coming over the Channel on the boat we were all really violently sick. And I think it was just reaction. We'd never been used to decent food. I spent the trip back in the toilet, being sick all the way. All of us did actually.

However, we got to London and we reported to wherever we had to report, I forget where or what. We were taken and kitted out with a new suit and a greatcoat by the Royal Arsenal Co-op. Apparently we had been given tickets to get from London to Glasgow and we were told the train would be so-and-so and so-and-so. We were to spend a night in a hotel. Well, I went straight to bed, I was really tired. But they must have sent word to Glasgow and said that we were arriving. But having slept overnight, Jimmy Reid had gone out for a pint to a pub and he had met somebody and had said that I was there too. So he made arrangements that we would see these people the next night, rather than get the train in the day as we were supposed to do. So we decided to miss that train and get this next one. But apparently there was a reception committee in Glasgow waiting, I think it was at Glasgow Central Station. So that caused a bit of a stir when we didn't turn up. But we knew nothing about this. We travelled up that same night and arrived in the morning and that was it. The reception we had to go to was there right enough; unfortunately we missed it! Of course I would not have wanted this fuss and carry-on anyway.

The Spanish War made a considerable impression on me politically. My politics have always been more instinctive than theoretical or dogmatic. When I'd gone to Spain I wasn't a member of any political party. While I was in Spain Paddy O'Sullivan asked me to join the Spanish Communist Party, of which he was a member himself, because everybody who was a member of the Communist Party then anyway joined the Spanish Communist Party. So I joined the Spanish Communist Party, although this was in name only because in fact we only associated in any way at all, which was very infrequent, among ourselves. So it wasn't a case of sort of integrating with Spaniards in the sense of here we were all Communists, Spaniards, French or whatever. It was just a case of our own grouping under a different name. Then I joined the Y.C.L., the Young Communist League, in Shettleston, after I came back home. And later I joined the

Communist Party. And that was more or less it. After I came back from Spain I attended classes run by Willie Joss, who was then a well known Communist lecturer.[192] And I was very much impressed with what Willie Joss had to say and how he explained it. And I think in that way he sort of consolidated any views – I never had any doubts as to my leanings politically regardless of parties. I mean my leanings were always straightforward working class, usually of a militant character, and that was all there was to it. But later on I just sort of drifted away from the Party after I got married and one thing and another.

After I came back home I wanted to continue the fight against Fascism. Because everyone with any common sense at all could foresee that the Second War was coming. There was no doubt about that. This was really why many of us went to Spain in the first place – to stop Fascism in Spain, rather than have it come to Britain. But as you know we lost and War did come to Britain. In July or August 1939 I applied to join the Royal Air Force and though they wouldn't take me then, I did get in very soon after.

Looking back on the Spanish Civil War, fifty years after it began, I have no regrets, no regrets that I tried to do something. There was that one occasion I've already referred to when we'd been marching and mucking about at a time when I thought we should have been getting fed and we hadn't been fed for a couple of days and so on. And my morale was a wee bit on the low side and I used to always tell myself when things were going bad that, "Well, I volunteered. And whatever happens it's my own fault." But that one particular time I did say to myself, "Oh, I think I'm sorry I came." But it only lasted briefly. It was hunger that was at the root of that. But only on that one occasion did I think to myself, "I'm sorry I came." It was only a brief, fleeting thought. As soon as I got fed that night it was gone and I was back in business again!

Oh, there is no doubt that the Spanish War was a tragedy but as I say it was engineered by international Fascism to which Chamberlain was friendly at least. He certainly wasn't antagonistic to international Fascism as spearheaded by Nazi Germany and Mussolini's Italy.

Born in Aberdeenshire in 1900, grandson of a Free Church of Scotland minister and son of a small tenant farmer, Tom Murray himself became a farmworker. The 1914-18 War was one of the great formative influences of his life, profoundly affected as he was by the sight of hospital trains with wounded from the Western Front often passing up the railway line near which he lived in North East Scotland. He was successively from 1919 a member of the Independent Labour Party, the Labour Party, and (clandestinely) the Communist Party before the Spanish War, when he also became a Labour Town Councillor in Edinburgh. Tom Murray remained politically active until his death early in 1983, a few months after these recollections were recorded.

TOM MURRAY

My interest in the Spanish War, of course, was aroused by the circumstances in which a democratically elected government was attacked by a junta of military officers, led by among others Mola and Franco, Franco being the ultimate leader of the campaign against the Republic.

It should be emphasised that those of us who were closely identified with the struggle in Spain, and were members of the International Brigade, do not regard the War as having been a Civil War, except for the first two months or so, because actually Franco was defeated in the first two months in his efforts to get to the French frontier. And indeed he would have been completely routed by the Republic if it had not been for the fact that he immediately brought over hordes of Moorish mercenaries supported by ample supplies of arms from Italy in the first place and Germany ultimately.

My first immediate contact with this struggle in Spain occurred in Brussels, where I was attending the International Peace Conference, and where I was introduced to Dolores Ibarurri, better known as La Pasionaria, a woman who led the Republican movement, especially in Barcelona, and who made the famous observation that it was better to die on your feet than be a suppliant on your knees. So she emphasised how serious the War situation was. And the outcome was that my family, all of whom were already greatly concerned and interested, took an intense interest in the developments in Spain. I happened to be going on holiday with my wife to Oban, and when I was in Oban my sister Ann phoned me to say that she was so impressed with the necessity of helping the Spaniards that she was prepared to volunteer as a fully qualified nurse. She asked my opinion. I said, "If you have those feelings then I would not stand in your way, and indeed would encourage you to go." She went in 1936, one of the first people to participate in the struggle, and long before the International Brigades were formed. She served right through the war in various hospitals and had many narrow escapes with bombings and so forth, but emerged physically unscathed and retreated over the Pyrenees when the Republic was finally defeated, and came up through France back to this country.

Later on, in 1937, my brother George, who also was much

impressed by the importance of the Spanish struggle, volunteered to go and went with a number of comrades from Glasgow and the west of Scotland and various other parts to participate in the War. He was at various times an anti-tank gunner, a security man, and a person who handled various specialised aspects of the organisation of the International Brigades.

I volunteered at the same time as my brother – in fact I volunteered, I think, earlier. But the Communist Party, of which I was a member then, told me that I wasn't to go. I was a Councillor in the city of Ediburgh, and they regarded my function as more important here, especially having a sister and a brother out in Spain. Well, the circumstances which led to my going were rather unusual. Early in 1938 the situation in Spain was desperately serious because of the intervention of the Italian and German forces. The Republic was being pressed seriously by the enemy, and indeed they had practically divided Spain into two parts by that time. So a local official of the Communist Party asked me again if I was prepared to go, and I said, "If it's the view of the Party that I should go then I'll go."

I went to Spain early in 1938. I should perhaps mention that before going I travelled up and down Scotland interviewing people who had expressed an interest in the possibility of serving in the International Brigades. And I recruited twelve comrades, who went with me.

We all set off to London and we bought return tickets to Paris from London, after having been interviewed by – oh, the name has slipped me – at Lichfield Street, which was the recruiting centre for the British Battalion of the International Brigade.[193] We had a medical examination and so forth in London, then we found our way to Paris, where we went to a centre – a very clandestine place, because the French Government was hostile – in the Combat district. There we had another medical examination and we were either passed fit for Spain or we were rejected. Most of my lot, in fact, all of them if I remember correctly, were accepted, including myself, of course.

We now set off down through France to a place called Béziers and in Béziers we were accommodated, also surreptitiously because the French authorities were very bad at that time, in a kind of farmhouse. I fortunately had a passport. None of the others had passports and the result was that whilst I could trip around Béziers with a passport, as though I were a tourist, the other poor blighters had to be confined in this room all the time for several days before we set off for the Pyrenees.

It was rather amusing that every time I went back to be with them there was a multitude of questions about what I had found, what I had seen, what I was doing, and so forth. They were frustrated by being confined there like prisoners in a cage. The great opportunity arose of course when we were told that we were going on the move. So we loaded into buses and set off for the frontier, which was a mountainous part of the Pyrenees. We had to travel in the dark of course because we were liable to be caught and taken back by the French and imprisoned. But what we did find was that the French gendarmes of the district seemed to be sympathetic because they were always absent any time that we thought that we would be liable to see them.

We walked across what we learned later was the narrow ledge of a deep dam of some kind of hydro-electric reservoir or at least a reservoir of some kind. We went in single file across this in the dark and I remember there was a village where a brilliant light was shining, and we had to sprint across a certain part because our shadows showed up on the gable ends of a building. However, we got across and we took off our shoes or our boots and we got *alpargatas*, which were rope-soled shoes. And we put these *alpargatas* on because you couldn't climb very easily over the rocks in ordinary footwear.

One of the lads – I forget his name for the moment – from Kirkcaldy who had already been in Spain and was wounded, was going back again with us.[194] But his legs were in a bad state and I had to carry him practically the whole way over the mountains on my back. I must have been very robust at that time because it didn't seem to bother me very much. There was no question of any kind of lights, smoking or any other light. We were told we must not talk. We must follow guides who took us over – I think they were French guides who knew the paths over the mountains. There were roads over the mountains into Spain, but we had to avoid the roads. Hence the necessity for climbing over these blessed rocks.

Well, we got over there silently, taking a rest now and again, and arrived at a rendezvous on the Spanish side where we were welcomed with great cordiality by our Spanish friends. They had great quantities of coffee all ready for us to help us on our way. From there we went to a place called Fortienel, where there was a centre that had been used as a girls' school, a large building with a great many offices of one kind and another, including a large loft which could sleep several hundred people. We went there and I met Mick Economides, a Cypriot. Mick Economides and I were asked by the person in charge of the reception place at Fortienel if we would take charge of the guard organisation, which we did.

Some amusing things happened. The first night we were all lying in this big place – about six or seven different nationalities at least all sleeping there – when there was an alert and we all had to get up and go down into slit trenches. That was the first breath of war that we experienced. We stayed at Fortienel for a litle bit and we had to put up guards to guard places that were used as prisons because there were people we couldn't identify – there were Fascists, there were all kinds of people. These were closed in there until they could be investigated. And we had to provide guards. One of my jobs was to act as the supervisor of this business of providing guards one or two nights.

There was an amusing incident happened. There was a young boy from Glasgow who swindled his age – he said he was eighteen but we discovered afterwards he was only sixteen, and far too immature to be mixed up in a business like that. Anyway he was put on guard duty and I was sound alseep when I was awakened by somebody coming clattering along the floor of this long building. This was about three o'clock in the morning. He came right up to me. He was holding a rifle. It was the young boy from Glasgow, who incidentally had been leading a sing-song the night before of all the various nationalities with great enthusiasm. I said to him, "What the devil are you doing here? You're supposed to be down there." "Oh," he says, "I can't stand it any longer." His nerve was gone. These locked up people had been telling him that if they got out they would screw his neck and so forth – terrible threats were being thrown at him. So you can imagine the state of mind of a young boy like that, who was physically big enough but far too young to be in charge doing a job like that. So I went back down with him and overcame the difficulty. I told them if they didn't cut it out there would be trouble. There was no more trouble that night.

We found that there were about two or three people who had volunteered to come to Spain who had taken cold feet. Mick Economides and I decided that all the English-speaking volunteers would be lined up one morning and we'd put it to them that at three o'clock that afternoon there would be a show of hands of those who didn't want to go any further. We had made up our minds that we would be sending this young Glasgow boy back home in any case.

Including this boy, at three o'clock in the afternoon there were five held up their hands – sheepishly, and in fact very sadly in some respects because it was a painful experience. You see, we told them that this was not a picnic they'd come to. One of them said he thought he was to be in the ambulance. We knew damned fine that he had never had any illusions about being in the ambulance. So we decided to send them home. But these were the only ones that we had any trouble with. We were very glad to do that because to take these people with us would have been a mistake – they would probably have been deserting or somthing like that. So we sent them home.

By the way, shortly after I came to Spain Peter Kerrigan, who represented the Communist Party and the *Daily Worker* at that time – he had been in the fighting ranks before that – came to me one day and said: "Look here, you've got to go back home to Britain." "Well," I said, "how does this come about?" "Oh," he said, "a mistake has been made. There's been a fearful row about you being allowed to go to Spain in view of the fact that you had a brother and sister here. And you've got to go home." And I said to Peter, "For the first time in my experience as a member of the Communist Party I refuse. I will not do such a damned foolish thing as to go away back. What kind of a picture would I present, taking twelve people out there, having a look at Spain, not near the danger zone at all, and away back home? No, no," I said, "it's no use, Peter, I am just refusing." And then I transferred my membership from the Communist Party of Great Britain and I became a member of the Communist Party of Spain, a card-holding member, instigated, I think, by this incident to some extent, although I felt it was my duty to be a Spanish Communist Party member, more than anything else.

My wife and I had had a lot of disucssions about my going to Spain. She was not sure about me going, as a matter of fact, and she and Fred Douglas' wife kicked up a row about my being there at all. They realised that it was a mistake, I shouldn't have been away to Spain at all. Well, in any case, my wife raised enormous sums of money for Spanish Relief. She always appeared, you see, as the wife of an International Brigader and naturally that created a little bit of a response. There was one occasion, for instance, in the Usher Hall, Edinburgh, I think they collected about £600 or £700 at one go. I was away in Spain at that time of course. She was active in a number of other organisations. She was a member of the Communist Party and so on.

Well, getting back to Fortienel, we went from there then to the town of Figueras. Fortienel wasn't far from Figueras, and Figueras was the bigger town. We went there but I can't just remember all that happened to us at Figueras – we must have been accommodated somewhere. But we did do a certain amount of training – square-bashing sort of training. I had had some military experience of course because I was in the British army for three weeks right at the end of the 1914-18 War, and in fact before that I had been in the Local Defence Volunteers in Scotland. So that we did a bit of training at Figueras. It had started at Fortienel as a matter of fact, once we got over the initial difficulties and the enrolment and so forth. We had to enrol everybody and we had to find out exactly who they were and where they came from and so on.

Well, at any rate we went from Figueras to a place called Los Presos, Now Los Presos was a village beside a dried up river bed, a *barranco*, and we were all distributed in this *barranco*. This was our first real training place. We were stationed there for quite a while, the purpose being of course to prepare for, to get training for the Ebro offensive. I was still a private, as it were, up to that time and did a little bit of ordinary work, such as being a sentry and so forth – and it was an eerie sort of business being a sentry in a strange land. But very soon afterwards, when the machine gun company was being formed the Commissariat of what became the essence of the new Battalion decided to create a number of commissars, as well as officers. And I was asked because of my political knowledge and political understanding to become a commissar of the machine guns. So I became a commissar, and a very interesting job it was.

Before discussing the functions of a commissar I'd like to say how we lived there in this *barranco*, this dried up river at Los Presos. We just slept on the stones but we also, if we wanted to – and we did of course – make some kind of shelter, *chabolas*. We made our own *chabolas*. These were just made with branches of trees and leaves over them.

Then we found that we had brought along with us recruits from Spain itself so that when the Battalion was reformed and reorganised with us in it there were Spaniards as well. We were about half-and-half Spaniards. One of the jobs of a commissar was to provide educational facilities, especially for illiterates. And we trained a number of Spaniards in the elements of reading and writing and so forth.

I vividly recall two Spaniards, Ors and Linaris, both of whom I am sorry to say were killed later on. These two had a *chabola* and I used to listen to them in the evening laboriously trying to read Spanish. I thought to myself what splendid fellows they were, making an effort like that because they had been denied education earlier in life.

Well, we did a lot of training there and I became a machine gun commissar and of course I had to study the technique of the machine guns. We had machine guns that were called Mexicanskis but we knew that that was a pseudonym for Soviet machine guns, heavy machine guns, water-cooled. We had to learn the nine major stoppages of a machine gun, and how to correct them quickly. Well, in any case my job was confined of course principally to the administration of the Machine Gun Company.

The role of the commissar of course is an extremely interesting one and a valuable aspect of a popular army. You see, in the days of Cromwell and the Roundheads, they had what was similar to commissars, but they weren't called commissars – they were really religious to some extent. [195] But it's noteworthy that the commissar in the Spanish army had a dual role. He had an equal military status with the commander of the unit to which we was attached as commissar. But he never interfered with the commander unless he felt that something required to be corrected. All the time I was a commissar Jack Nalty, an Irishman, was our company commander, and a very capable man he was. Unfortunately, he was killed in the last stages of the War. [196] Jack Nalty and I of course ran this organisation of the Company and only on one occasion did I exercise my authority as a commissar against him. He was dead beat and we were marching along a road with the machine guns and I was becoming more and more conscious of the feeling that we were going in the wrong direction. I said to him, "Well now, don't you think you should halt the Company and let us think about it?" Oh, he wasn't in favour. He says, "We're all right." "Well," I says, "I'm afraid that I've got to exercise my authority as commissar," and I halted the Company. A runner from the British Battalion, whose commissar was Bob Cooney, had been sent down in fact to see where we were. And right enough, if we'd gone round another corner we'd have been bang into a group of Fascists with machine guns. That was the only occasion on which I exercised my authority to supersede the function of the commander of the company. But it illustrates the high responsibility which rested on the shoulders of the commissar.

The commissar was the master of all trades, as it were. Our job was to look after the welfare of the personnel, their clothing, their recreation, their food, the distribution of food, and the general military efficiency. The military efficiency of course was the primary consideration over-shadowing everything else, and we had the job of dealing with any people who were browned off or who had been there maybe for a long time and had come back into the company from the front, from the earlier actions before the rest of us were there at all. And some of them of course were exhausted, mentally and physically exhausted and we had to get them back to a normal state by whatever form of special treatment that was desirable.

For example, I remember later on at the time of the Ebro offensive, I think it was Johnny Lobban was the quartermaster. Then there was Sergeant David Cornwall. These were the lads who were with us at the time. Johnny Lobban was a lad. I think it was Johnny who was quartermaster and he got fed up dishing out the food and he was giving the first lot out of a big dish of stew – we were everlastingly getting stew – which was very good on the whole because it was a mixture of vegetables and meat and so forth. The poor blighters in the rear tried to give us something that was good for us at the front. One of my jobs, you see, as a commissar was to make sure that everybody got a fair deal with the food. And one day, it must have been Johnny Lobban, he was fed up, he was tired and he was this, that and the next. I says, "Christ almighty, Johnny, if ye give all that big helpings to the front lads the blokes at the other end of the queue are going to get nothing." "Oh," he says, "to hell, you do it then." And I said, "I'll do it." I reduced the rations, otherwise there would have been none left. But that's the little kind of incidents that happened and it was no reflection on them at all because they were really tired out some of them. And some of them who had been at the front before and had been wounded and were back again, their morale was far better when we were actually fighting at the front, these chaps. Some of them that we thought were hellish characters to deal with when we were in training base, when we were at the front they were completely transformed, very good.

The commissar also had to pay particular attention to important political questions, international, national and local. One of the jobs I had to do was to study the national question of the Iberian peninsula. One of my jobs in that connection was to distribute the press, to make sure that all the members who wanted to could get copies of the Spanish press. And I had to be careful that *Las Noticias* and other papers of a Catalan quality had to be given to the Catalans.[197] The Catalans didn't like to be called Spaniards and we had to be very careful becuase they were touchy about that, some of them. They were Catalans, they weren't Spaniards, they said. And we had them all together of course. But we distributed the press, the Spanish press and the Catalan press. And that was one of my responsibilities – to make sure that that was done properly.

Then another job that the commissar had to do was to create a wall newspaper. And we had wall newspapers with all kinds of press cuttings and contributions from various people who were writing up little stories and so on, and writing up reminiscences and their observations and so on. And the wall newspaper was always a popular rendezvous for people to meet and discuss things.

My wife sent me a cartoon by Low, who was the cartoonist for the *Manchester Guardian*, I think it was at that time. And Low's cartoon, I'll never forget it, was a picture of the whole of Europe and right over the Ural Mountains. And there was a Red Army soldier lying on his belly looking at a whole lot of little figurtes with tile hats and frock-coats, rushing about from Paris to Vienna, from Vienna to Berlin, from Berlin to London, rushing about. And he had one eye closed, and the caption Low put on it was: "'The Watching Eye." And I thought it was a prophetic thing. It was just the kind of thing we put on the wall newspaper.[198]

Now one of the main jobs of the commissar of course was to maintain morale as far as you could physically, usefully do it. You had to oppose erroneous ideas, such as rumours. The most fantastic rumours spread around. On one occasion the rumour-mongering got so serious – this was before the Ebro offensive began – that we had to take some steps to deal with it. The Battalion separated the Spaniards from the British elements, and we had a meeting of the British elements. We knew that some of them had longingly hoped for the repatriation which was alleged to be on the way. The deputy Battalion commissar took Bob Cooney's place because Bob Cooney, the commissar, was ill. He had some kind of stomach trouble or something. And this deputy chappie was a Welshman – I won't mention his name. But he was given the task of making a statement to strengthen the feelings and the morale of those people who had been constantly talking about going home. He made such a hell of a mess of it that I intervened, because the statement was made that we wanted to hear the point of view of the members of the Battalion who were British. Well, I made a statement in which I said – and I can almost remember word for word the speech I made – "Look here, we're soldiers of the Spanish Army. The Government, Dr. Negrin's Government, has a 13-point programme to which all of us have subscribed.[199] We are the disciplined soldiers of the Spanish army. We are not here to speculate about whether we're going to the front or going home. We're the servants of the Government and the Government will decide our policy. Meantime we know that we are preparing for an offensive against the Fascists, and therefore the only question before us is how efficiently we can prepare." And I got a resounding response, a resounding response. There was a sequel to it which I won't discuss at any great length but it was a fantastic business. The effect of my speeech I am convinced countered the rather heavy, lugubrious type of speech that this Welsh chap had offered.

So we had all these troubles, you see. We had the waiting business and so on. We had extraordinary experiences with the weather, for example, because at that early part of the year – in March, I think it must have been – there was torrential rainfall. And of course we were sleeping out in the open. And I remember we were taken from one point to another in *camions*, that is, trucks; and we were told to dismount in the dark, in the middle of the night, maybe about three o'clock in the morning. And it was pouring rain. We were told we had arrived. When daylight came we were in a sea of mud, an absolute sea of mud. I had an old raincoat that I had brought with me from this country and it was soaked through, soaked through. The only redeeming feature about the weather was that the sun got so hot during the day that it dried us up. But down in the *barranco* I used to lie among the rocks – there was no proper way to sleep otherwise – and the little lizards used to come tripping along and walk across our faces sometimes: tiny little lizards, they were harmless creatures. But I was really fond of reading and we had reading material. I got some glow-worms to crawl on the page and I could actually read with the glow-worms. The blighters wouldn't stay in the right place, though, you had always to push them back. But that's just an indication of the kind of life we lived.

We had enough food but it was very so-so, you know. There was a little rice sometimes. We got plenty of stew at that stage. But this stew was made sometimes of horse meat and sometimes of goat meat. The great merit of the goat meat was that you could chew it all day and it was still there! And we got what was called *mermelada*. It was great blocks of stuff like jam, you know, and they had to be cut up in bits.

We got a certain amount of fruit, although it wasn't the best time of the year for fruit. Later on at the front I used to take grapes off the vines ready for eating, and other kinds of fruit. We didn't have so many oranges, they are much later in the year. We had a few rather scruffy figs. But we had good peaches and plenty grapes. In fact, we ate far too many grapes at times. There were a lot of stomach upsets as a result.

But we had enough food, you know, and my health was remarkably good. There was only one occasion on which I had a touch of stomach trouble but nothing much, it only lasted a day or something like that. I had really no trouble at all. And of course I could sleep. I could sleep anywhere at the front, anywhere. I could just make up my mind that the time had come to sleep and sleep I would do. And I think it was a saving factor.

As for drinking, well, there was a certain amount of wine. We got rations of wine. But, oh, I tasted the stuff and it was terrible. It was like vinegar. Not that I drank it, because I didn't drink. Some of them of course were so desperate to get it. There was plenty of water behind the front, but when we got to the front it was a different story.

Also we got rations of cigarettes, and being a non-smoker I held on to my packet of cigarettes until the men were nearly all mad with desperation to get a smoke. And they used to come sidling up to me and say, "Have ye any makings?" This was maybe half of a cigarette that we rubbed down. I used to say, "I've no bloody makings. Wait until you're all finished and ye'll get what I have." Well, the Company was about ninety or a hundred or so strong, and there were exactly eighty who smoked. The rest didn't smoke. And what I did I used to line up all the smokers, when they were all exhausted. And my one packet of twenty cigarettes was left, and I says, "Now four of you can have one cigarette and you can all smoke it turn about. Or I'll chop it up into four bits and give you a bit each. Ye can please yourselves. I'm not interested in the blooming thing." However, there it was. These were the things you had to do.

Well, we had then to move on to the preparations for the crossing of the Ebro. This was the real test of our morale. And it was very good. There was great enthusiasm. Everybody was up to sky-high, heights of enthusiasm for the crossing of the Ebro.

We were all down on the banks of the Ebro during the night. The pontoons had been put across. And it should be mentioned that we got messages across every night by the *campesinos*, the peasants. Some of them were in the Franco forces but they were supporters of ours. They were up at the Ebro and they used to swim across with messages about the situation. The Battalion and Brigade knew all the forces that Franco had at the other side, and the names of the units, and even names of commanders and so on.

The peasants all over were very much in sympathy with us, of course. We got great receptions from them. As a matter of fact, on one occasion we were taken to a hall for a concert that was being given by Spanish men and women. We were all sitting there listening to the singing and so on when suddenly we were called out. This was before we had actually been in action. We were called out as the Fascists had threatened a breakthrough up at Balaguer or some of those places.

Well, in any case, we marched away and the local village people were crying because we were away to the front, but at the same time they were cheering us on and one thing and another. And then the order was cancelled and back we went to finish the concert!

The crossing of the Ebro at night was a remarkable performance. The pontoons consisted of narrow buoyant sections tied together and men would sit straddled across the junctions of these sections to hold them firm, because the Ebro was a very fast-flowing river. And then others went across in boats. The mules were swum across. We went across the pontoons carrying our weapons, our machine guns. We had light machine guns as well as the heavy ones. We had five machine gun groups in our Company. No two people had to be on one section at the same time. We got across all right, lined up and marched up to the top of the hill.

The Fascists got scared stiff. They had been about to celebrate Mass, some of them, down in the valley, and there were tons, great streams of white muslin, which had been part of the preparation for this mass. We used them as mosquito nets, as a matter of fact, later on.

But we crossed the Ebro and made a rapid advance towards Gandesa. The real fighting then began, because the Nazi German planes were sent back and they bombed us like the devil. However we got our machine guns set up and we defended ourselves. I think we maybe made a tactical mistake in not rushing down right past and round Gandesa to prevent the Fascists fortifying it, which they did next day.

Well, in any case, there was a real battle there and we were winning. Undoubtedly we were winning. It was a very exhilarating experience. It was a bit of an experience for those of us who had never been in action before. Bullets were coming whizzing past us and all the rest of it. But at the same time we scared them. The crossing of the Ebro is now regarded in military circles as one of the most brilliantly operated military operations in the history of war.

But of course we had no backing. We had no reserves. We were just a front line capable of this operation, but with no reserves. And no equipment to make up for losses. And what we did know and which was very annoying and was one of the factors in creating a little bit of difficulty in the days I've mentioned when I was making the speech to bolster the morale of our comrades – we knew that vast quantities of arms destined for the Spanish Republic were held up by the French Government north of the Pyrenees. There were always rumours coming round that the French were going to release them. And if they had released these great quantities of arms that were held up and that had accumulated over a year or two, we would have made a much better job of it.

Now a commissar was equivalent to the rank of a captain or a major in the British army, although we didn't regard it as being of any significance in that connection. In fact I have some contempt for those people, ex-British army people, who hang on to titles like captain and lieutenant and major after a war when it means nothing. But for the purpose of comparison of the lack of weapons, if I had been a captain or a major I would have been well armed. Well, as a commissar I was many times without any arms at all. I would sometimes have a rifle, sometimes I would have a pistol, and sometimes I would have a hand grenade. And I would hand these over to people who were more likely to use them effectively. And on one occasion up at the front, on Hill 481, I think it was, when we were attacking there – I think it was there, you know you forget some of these places – but in any case I got completely cut off from the rest of the Battalion. And I discovered that I was in what might be termed no-man's-land. And I thought to myself, "By God, if they catch me with this commissar's badge sticking in my cap I'm in for it." So I was preparing to throw that away if there was any danger of being seen. Because when commissars were identified, they were just shot. Oh, there was any number of them just shot if they had been captured by the enemy. But in any case I ultimately got back to the ranks.

We were on Hill 666 or 481 – I don't remember which – at any rate we had our machine guns established at the top of the hill, and on one occasion there were three of my Scots comrades killed by an anti-tank gun that had been firing from the valley down below up to the top of this hill, and it just got them. I was down the hill a little bit when Paddy Duff, an Irishman, who was the adjutant of our Company, came running down the hill. There was a great lump of flesh out of his arm, just as though a dog had bitten it. Paddy says, "Christ almighty, you'd better go away up to the top of the hill. There's some dead." I tore off his shirt and made a kind of tourniquet for his arm, and I says: "Now, Paddy, don't faint until you get to the first-aid point." I said, "You faint here and there'll be nobody to carry you down." So, I says, "Off you go and I'll go up to the top of the hill." And up to the top of the hill I went. You had to bob down as there were shells bursting and all sorts of things. It was a nasty situation. Well, I got up and here I found George Jackson lying stretched out. George Jackson came from Cowdenbeath and I think he was one of the recruits that I got to go with me when we went out there. Charlie McLeod of Aberdeen was lying with his head on Geroge Jackson's chest. And Malcolm Smith of Dundee was lying about a yard or so away. All were dead by the blast of this anti-tank shell.

One of the jobs of the commissar when people were killed was to take their personal effects off their bodies and send them home to their people. Also our job was to bury the dead. And as a matter of fact, up on these sierras or mountains, Sierra Pandols, you could scarcely get enough earth to cover them. It was a most difficult job finding ways and means of covering the dead bodies. As a matter of fact, in order to get the utmost protection when I lay down to sleep I lay in a slight declivity, just a very few inches deep. And just above where my head was was the dead body of a Fascist. And all that I did with that dead body – you can imagine in the hot weather the smell was terrible – was to leave it there and scrape dust over it every day, because it was a little bit of a protection if a shell had burst nearby.

At that time on that hill I remember sitting when there was a quiet spell. I had some writing paper and I started off to write an essay on sights, sounds and smells of a battlefield. But, alas, the silence of the guns didn't last so very long and in fact we had to change our positions a little bit and consequently my essay was unwritten.

But there were other things happened. I remember when we were first going up the hill after we crossed the Ebro we went in single file and a lad who was walking with me said: "Don't pay much attention on the right hand side." I said, "What's wrong?" He said, "Oh, there's dead bodies there." "Good God," I said, "there'll be a lot more dead bodies before the day ends." However, we came to a place where there was a slightly deep ravine, maybe about ten feet deep, which had been a water course when there was a flood of water on the hills but it had dried up. This was before the incident I have referred to with the three Scots lads being killed. We were marching up there and we were going into action, and there was a Fascist machine gun firing up this ravine. The only way to get safely across in these circumstances was to string a blanket across so that they never saw you passing. You could race across and by the time they fired you were across. Well, they couldn't just keep the machine gun going all the time. Well, we came there and I had half the company and the company commander had the other half. They were a wee bit further along. "Now," I said, "we've got to cross here and we've no blankets. We'll just take a chance." And they'd never been in action before, you see, and neither had I for that matter. And I said to them, "Now, you better start off." And I said to one fellow, "You're the person who has to jump across there first." This felow hesitated and hesitated and hesitated. I can't remember who it was. And they were all hesitating because he was creating a bad impression. "Well," I says, "we've got to go. So I'll just have to do it myself." So I jumped across. Brrrrtt – a burst of machine gun. But it was too late, you see, I was across. We got all across and we hadn't been hit, and away up the hill. These were little incidents I recall from that battle.

But up on the hill in the Pandols we had some rather odd experiences, too. For example, the water supply. Well, it was a heck of a job. You see, you are away up on these mountain tops, there was no water at all, it had all to be carted up from down below. We sent one or two comrades down with sixteen water bottles, down to the valley. Shells burst amongst them, killed them and peppered every one of those water bottles so that it wouldn't hold water. What a job we had. There was one fellow – I forget his name now, who was from Glasgow. His tongue swelled up, and his lips were swollen from lack of water. And it was making him cry almost, tears were running down his cheeks. But we had to wait until night, when the coffee came up.

Now on one occasion we were sitting on the side of the hill and we saw the *mulero* fellow with a mule and panniers, one with coffee and one with stew. And he wasn't coming. The mule was standing and there were a lot of shells coming over and landing in the valley, and he wasn't moving up. I sent a runner – you see, we had runners, people who ran messages from place to place. I had two and the company commander had two. I sent one of the runners. I said, "Go and see what's holding him up. He's sitting on the ground or lying on the ground." He went down and he found that this was a shell-shocked bloke who had been given the job of leading a mule and he was refusing to go. Incidentally, in the middle of an action, you don't go holding the mule by the head, you've a long string, so that if you're killed the mule isn't killed. And if the mule is killed you're not killed, you see. So there was this long string – a great length of a string, maybe about ten yards, twenty yards long. So this runner came back and he says, "He's not prepared to come up." he says, "he is just refusing to come up with the mule." And of course I says, "Good God, we're all desperate for food." This was just before dark and we knew it would be dark in no time as it turns suddenly dark. Well, in any case, I thought the best thing was just to go down and get a hold of the mule myself. So I just went down and got this mule and got it up. We dished out the food and of course they were desperate for food and especially for the one mug of coffee they got, a mug of maybe less than a pint of coffee.

Well, there was a machine gun set out on a promontory, a very narrow promontory just a few feet wide and down each side was about 300 feet of a sheer drop. It was just like a peninsula with an island at the end of it, as it were. And we had a machine gun out there. And we had to think, "How on earth, we've got to get food across to these people." We had no proper utensils. However, we had a thing for holding coffee. And the lid of the pannier – we filled it up with their share of the stew. And I crawled along, pushing this lid in front of me, and carrying this bucket of stuff. Crawled along there on my hands and knees, pushing this thing along becuase there was nobody else to do it. I had to see that they got fed. That was one of the situations. Well, it was a hair-raising experience, too, you see, apart from the shooting that went on. In fact, you didn't feel so scared at the shooting as you did at the danger of tumbling over one of these blooming precipices.

Being a teetotaller I was in charge of cognac. The cognac was given out in small dollops every second day or so. And I hid this jar of cognac. But one of our members, who was the sort of commissariat man, he looked after food and one thing and another, he twigged me. He was an awful boozer. And by God, I found him rolling, roaring drunk one day. He had seen where I hid this jar and had gone and had a good swig out of it and put it back again. I won't mention his name bcause it was really a disgraceful episode. And we're up on the side of this sierra and there was a sheer drop down which a mule had fallen, about 200 feet or 300 feet, a sheer drop. In fact when the mule had fallen down there our kitchen staff immediately rushed down and took slabs off this mule's body to cook for us for food. However, this Johnny – we'll call him Johnny – and I were rolling about in my efforts to quieten him down, near the edge of this damned precipice. He was throwing pieces of paper up in the air – this was during the day – and he says, "Those bloody Fascists, let the whole bloody lot of the bastards come here." I says, "Good God, there are spotter planes up there." So we rolled about together, the two of us, until I got him quietened down. It was a more alarming experience than shells bursting.

There was another occasion when my brother George went missing. You see my brother George and I were up at the front. He was in Company 2, he was an observer at that stage. Well, No. 2 Company went on a night attack. Most of them came back but my brother wasn't seen by anybody. I went up to the Battalion commander, Sam Wild, and I said to Sam: "Have you seen my brother, George?" "No," he said, "I haven't seen him." Sam was standing with his hand up against a rock and a blooming shrapnel shell burst just then and there was a wee bit went right through his hand. I never heard language like it, neither before nor since, when Sam got this wee bit of shell, a tiny little splinter, in the back of his hand! But he hadn't seen George, so I wandered about, asking everybody if they had seen my brother. Yes, they had seen him when they went into action but they hadn't seen him since. I thought, "Well, that's him done in." Meantime my sister Ann was the nurse in charge of a hospital train in a tunnel, through which train all the wounded from the British Battalion passed. Every time a stretcher came in of course Ann ran to see if it was George or me. She heard that I was killed, she heard my brother was missing and vice versa and so forth and so on. It was a gruelling experience for her too. Well, I had given up George for dead. I said, "Oh, he's had it." So I was walking up and, of course, in these sierras the rocks peel out and there's a great deep sort of v-shaped bit with bushes and all the rest of it growing in it. And I was coming up and here I saw my brother and another bloke lying sound asleep down in one of those crevices! The bit was almost falling over but it had been like that for donkey's years, you see, there was no danger of it falling over. But that's what like it was. So I found my brother George there to my great relief.

Before this, George of course at some of the other battles that were fought was shot through the chest. The bullet went in at the front and went out at the back and shifted his heart. And he was at death's door for months. But he recovered and went back to the front.

Well, in any case, we carried on this struggle as long as we possibly could but the situation was getting more and more desperate. We used to see clouds, flocks of German bombers coming in the distance and we used to watch the bombs falling from them. We used to wish to God that the bombs would fall a bit further on and miss us. We were bombed and we were machine gunned and we were shelled. We were marching along a road one time and we had to lie in the ditch and German planes were coming down and strafing us on the road. One or two of the mules got hit and they stampeded. The Germans were not only machine gunning us but also they were throwing hand grenades out, they were coming swooping down and throwing a shower of hand grenades out. And you know lying in these circumstances you never thought you'd be hit on the head or the feet. You always thought you'd be hit in the small of the back. Strange. Others had the same experience.

Well, we had that kind of experience and we had nothing to put up against them. This was one of the terrible aspects of that struggle on the Ebro offensive – we had nothing to put against them. We had hardly any planes. An occasional Republican plane would come along, but one against scores – scores of German planes and Italian planes, but principally German planes, the ones that bombed Guernica.

That reminds me of an experience I had before we came across the Ebro. I was at this village near Los Presos and one evening another comrade and I – I forgot who it was – were walking along just having a stroll, and we saw a lot of children playing. And we thought we would go along and see the kids. We went along and there was a little girl sitting on the dyke. She couldn't play because she had a leg off and an arm off. And these were the victims of Guernica. There were one or two of them with little crutches. It was a pathetic sight that, and of course it made us more vicious and angry with the Fascists than anything because it was a terrible thing these children being bombed. And my sister had a similar experience. When she was working at a hospital in Barcelona there were children brought in with their hands blown off. And what the Fascists did was to drop what appeared to be packets of chocolate. And when the kids picked them up they exploded and blew their hands off. My sister had a lot of experiences of that kind.

She'd also had another experience she told us about. One time a Moor was brought in with his leg shattered. He was a prisoner. And he was holding on to a parcel like grim death. They couldn't get him to let this parcel go. Eventually they just pulled it from him and took his clothes off. He was bleeding to death if they hadn't got at his leg and dealt with it quickly. Well, they opened up the parcel, and what did they find? His wages as a soldier, consisting of obsolete 1914–20 German mark notes. They were of no value. And yet this poor blighter thought he was wealthy. That was one of the kind of things that Franco did to his Moorish mercenaries.

The Moors got terribly slaughtered, of course. You see the Fascists were sending them in in impossible situations, just grinding them down because they were Moors and press ganged more or less or intrigued in as mercenaries. Up on Hill 481, I think it was, there was this attack by us and there were thirty five dead Moors lying scattered around more or less in a heap. We took their blankets off them. I don't know who buried them. I had nothing to do with burying these people. I don't know who buried them but they must have been buried somehow. But there were thirty five of them, we counted thirty five dead bodies. These Moors had been killed in the fighting. They weren't killed as prisoners. Oh no, we didn't shoot anybody, oh no. The Fascists did, though. But these dead Moors were just a heap of humanity thrown into a war that they certainly didn't understand the slightest thing about.

We didn't handle prisoners of war at all, especially in my case, I was a machine gun man. The other four companies, they handled prisoners. And the like of this Moor that I referred to, he was captured – he had his leg all shot off. We captured numbers of them, you see, surrounded them and captured them. But of course they were just taken to the rear and put in concentration. Some of them of course were innocents abroad, a few Spaniards that were in Franco's forces. But we saw very few Spaniards at all, it was mostly Italians. And the Germans of course were mostly in the artillery and the air force. The Italians were the people who were mostly in the infantry.

We might have shot some bad characters, you know. Well, there was one bad character. When we were up at the front there was a member in my Company. I won't mention his name. He was Irish, he came from the Free State, he came from the south. And he was quite a capable bloke, too. It was an unsavoury business. But we decided on a certain move, and he resisted it. He was in charge of one of the machine gun crews, and he resisted it. And we couldn't understand why on earth he was resisting it. And he wanted to place the machine gun and his crew in a situation which we thought was extremely vulnerable. I said to him, "Look here now, you are going to do what you're told." I says, "We're at the blooming front, we're not playing around at the rear, we're at the front. The enemy is over the dyke more or less." And he said, "To hell with you, I'll so-and-so so-and-so." He picked up a hand grenade and was about to throw it at me. I jumped out of the way and we took him to the rear. However, we were sure that there was something radically wrong before he was taken back and quizzed. And of course he was boiling with hostility by this time because we had dragged him back from the front, from the front line and demoted him, as it were. He would be a *cabo* or a *sargento* or something like that, you see, in rank.[200] And we dragged him back and of course he was very angry with us. There wasn't much of a court martial but there was established information, and his conduct of course was reprehensible at the front, his carry-on, you see. You couldn't stand for that sort of thing. It would have been chaos. It just would have been anarchy. You had to be very disciplined at the front. I won't tell you who did it. I didn't do it and I won't tell you who did it. But there was a decision taken to get rid of him because of what we discovered about him. We were suspicious of this customer. Just as we had of course infiltrators on the other side they had infiltrators on our side. Well, at any rate, it was decided to let him have it, as we had discovered that he had a brother in the Fascist ranks. He had a very strong anti-Soviet background and anti-Socialist background. At any rate he was got rid of, just shot in the back of the neck.

On the subject of the motivation of those who went to Spain to fight: the reasons were quite clear and logical. It was the view of everybody who went to Spain to fight for the Republic that if Franco were defeated Mussolini would collapse. And if Mussolini collapsed it would undermine Hitler and probably destroy the danger of a Second World War. That was our view. It would create a major international crisis if we had been able to defeat the invasion of Spain. Because, as I've said earlier on, it was only a civil war for a short period and then it became a question of repelling the invasion of foreign elements such as the Italians and the Germans. As a matter of fact we never saw Spaniards at all on the other side. The people whom we were fighting were Italians, Italian conscripts sent by Mussolini. And the opposition that we had to contend with at home was that there was a widespread feeling that, "It can't happen here in Britain." But it did happen here, and we said it would happen here if we didn't defeat Franco. This aspect of the attitude of the people who went to Spain to fight should be clearly understood by everybody. It was an extremely important sentiment and conviction that the prospect of a Second World War would have been changed, if it ever occurred at all, if Mussolini had been defeated as a result of the collapse of Franco. But of course the so-called Non-Intervention policy was intervention in favour of Franco. The Republic of Spain was a properly constituted Government recognised internationally as being the legitimate Government of the Spanish people. And to prevent them from getting arms, purchasing arms, which they were prepared to do and pay for them, was of course simply part of the sabotage of the oppositon to Franco and bolstering up the Franco regime. This is an important aspect of the struggle in Spain that we must never forget, that this blighter Franco would never have existed for any length of time, and certainly would not have become a dictator, a Fascist dictator, if the so-called Non-Intervention policy, supported by the British and the French and the American Governments, hadn't occurred.

The Spaniards were just as enthusiastic as the British volunteers and we had no difficulty in associating with the Spaniards and co-operating with them. We were on very good terms, and we were on very good terms with the civilian population. The civilian population was obviously supporting the cause of the Republic. One thing that struck me was a discovery that schools had been established by the Republic throughout Catalonia, where we were fighting. We saw evidences of schoolrooms having been destroyed in the War, and school books and exercise books scattered all over the place. Down near Gandesa, for example, I came across several exercise books. And this was one of the great triumphs of the Republic, that they established schools that hadn't existed in the past under the old monarchist regime.

Another thing was that you had electrical developments in Catalonia – I don't know what happened in other parts of Spain. But in Catalonia you had a hydro-electric scheme every bit as advanced and extensive as our later Highland hydro-electric scheme in Scotland. These pylons and the wires were all smashed of course by the War, but the pylons stretched all across the countryside.

Prospects for the future of the Republic were quite good as a sort of a liberal progressive administration. Nobody could call it anything other than that. It wasn't a Government of Socialists. The Republican Government was a Government more or less of Liberals, with Socialists and supporting Communists and so on. And the terrible crime of the P.O.U.M. in my view was that they tried to foster the idea that this was a revolutionary war. It wasn't a revolutionary war. It never had any signs of a revolutionary war. The people of Spain were not revolutionary in the sense of the Bolshevik Revolution of 1917. They were people concerned to expel the Italians and the Germans from their territory, which was a revolt against an invasion by foreigners into their territory, a foreign invasion which was sponsored by the handful of generals led by Franco. I think it was a great tragedy that at a certain period in the struggle there was fighting behind the lines, instigated in my view by those who believed that it was a revolutionary struggle. And this has got to be clearly understood: it wasn't a revolutionary struggle. It had none of the elements of a revolutionary struggle. It was a struggle for the expulsion of foreign invaders. But the lack of unity ensuing created a terrible handicap.

For example, the Anarchists were very strong in Spain, although it should be noted also that the first Marxist study groups known to exist anywhere were in Spain, even when Karl Marx himself was alive, I believe. I'm not certain about that. But at any rate there were groups in Spain studying the teachings of Marx and Engels before any other country possessed such groups.[201]

Now the Anarchists, who were very strong, were the people who thought there was a short cut to socialism and anarchism. My view is that there was no indication that there was any short cut in Spain or anywhere else. It's a hard gruelling struggle to get a change from imperialism and capitalism to socialism. It should be borne in mind that there is no such thing as Communism in practice anywhere in the world even today, but there is socialism.

And the struggle in Spain was handicapped greatly in the early days by the failure to unite all the elements who were genuinely opposed to Franco, and that of course included some of the P.O.U.M. people. They were genuinely opposed to Franco. But their motives were different. When I was in Spain I was well aware of these differences. But by that time there was unity under the Negrin government, which as I have already indicated had a thirteen-point programme which we were called upon to support and we as loyal members of the Spanish army were obliged to uphold.

The personalities that one came across during the course of the War were a mixed variety of people. There were of course a number of distinguished visitors to our training base at Los Presos and the other localities that we were training in. For example, Nehru, the Indian leader, was there and we spoke to him and in fact he signed his autograph in my book and we had quite an interesting time with him. He spent quite a bit of time with the British Battalion. He was very sympathetic to the Republican government. And he expressed concern about the Non-Intervention policy. I remember that. And we gave him a good reception too.

We also had visitors like Harry Pollitt, the secretary of the Communist Party, who came out there quite often. And then we had people like Peter Kerrigan, of course – I've already mentioned him. We had a visit from Charlotte Haldane and we had a visit from Professor Haldane, if I remember, I'm not sure about him, but Charlotte Haldane was out. Gallacher was out several times but not when I was there actually. And I remember Bill Rust, the editor of the *Daily Worker*, was there. The British Battalion had a meeting with him, kind of listened to him on the international situation. Jack Jones, later general secretary of the Transport and General Workers' Union, of course was in the International Brigade in Spain at the same time as I was but he wasn't so well known in this country in those days as he is now. In fact, I think I met him there. There are two Joneses and I think it was Jack Jones that I remember meeting one time.[202] Fred Copeman was away by that time. He wasn't there, he wasn't on the Ebro. Jock Cunningham wasn't on the Ebro either. Well, there is nothing much more that I could say about individuals if I could remember who they were. Clement Broadbent was from London, was a councillor in Dewsbury and he and I were very friendly out there. He was a Labour Party member, and he was accidentaly shot by a stray bullet. But he had been wounded earlier and was on his way back, I think, to the front when this happened. I can't just remember precisely. But there was also another comrade from London who confided in me that he was very frightened. This chap said he was really scared. We were going up in open file up the hillside and there were a lot of shells coming over. When a shell is falling you go in open file to avoid a lot of people being killed by one shell. So I was good bit behind going up this hill and I saw him dropping. And I went up to see him and he was lying there dead. I discovered that a piece of shrapnel had entered his heart. There was hardly any mark at all, just a cut on his chest. So he died in a manner that he would be least expecting. He would expect to be injured but he was killed going up that hillside.

We also had a number of distinguished people whose names I forget, French, Polish, and a number of Germans. We had a number of these people came to visit us but I can't remember their names and I don't think I have notes of them. We certainly had General Walter, we knew him. And incidentally I should mention that immediately after the last war in 1945 the International Brigade was invited to send a delegation to Warsaw. The people who were sent were Nan Green, secretary of the International Brigade Association, and myself. And we spent several weeks in Warsaw at that time. We had meetings with the veterans of the Dombrowski Battalion, which was the Polish Battalion in the Spanish War. There were a lot of Poles in the Spanish War.

Next door to us on the front, on the Ebro offensive – I'm jumping about a little bit – were the Italian Garibaldies of the International Brigade. And the Garibaldis had in their ranks Mehmet Sheku. Mehmet Sheku later on became the prime minister of Albania and I got to know him very well because I was twice in Albania after the Second World War and toured the country and I met him several times. His English was very good. Unknown to each other we had been almost cheek by jowl in the attack of Gandesa. He was a rather pleasant individual, a rather nice person to know.[203] Wherever I've gone abroad, whenever it became known that I had been in the International Brigade it sparked off an extraordinary amount of interest. I remember being at a conference in Lisbon, an abortive kind of a conference, some years ago. It had nothing to do with the International Brigade but when it was known by some of those present that I had been in the Spanish War, great interest was expressed and I was told about certain people in that conference who had been in the resistance movement during the Franco period, had been over the border helping the resistance to Franco.

Casualty rates in the Spanish War were terrible. You see, I didn't realise it was such a bloody affair till I came home and began to reflect and began to compare the destruction of life. It was terrible, you see. There was a tremendous lot of our people killed or wounded, even on the Ebro offensive. Well, I told you about those three; there were others wounded, like Paddy Duff, as I've mentioned, who came from Ireland. Paddy got his left arm all palsied, you see. He couldn't do anything with it. The casualty rate was so high because we hadn't the equipment. We hadn't even spades to dig trenches if there had been any scope for trenches. We had nothing and we were blasted by shells. Good gracious, the shells were coming showering over us like peas over the hill. They were terrible. I don't know how some of us survived. There was one occasion, for example, there was one shell after another was coming over and the most disquieting, the most almost terrifying experience, was the nose caps coming whizzing past after the shell had burst. The shell was quicker than the nose cap, you see. The blooming thing burst and the nose cap came whizzing along. You were always feeling that if that blooming thing gets you you're cut up to pieces. The number of wounded that we had was very high but it was largely bombing, a little machine gunning, but nearly all artillery, artillery shells.

I was very fortunate that I was never really seriously touched. I remember once a small piece of hot shrapnel went down my neck, and I thought, "My God, that's right into my heart." I was looking for the blood, but there was no blood. It was a superficial injury but it was roasting hot, you see. The only other thing I suffered was one time I was lying on the hill when the shells were coming over and there was a shell cut a mule's head just clean off like that, and the poor brute just fell over. They were extraordinary characters, the mules. A shell burst and they just gave their lugs a wag and that was it. Well, I was leaning on my elbow with my right hand on my ear and talking to somebody and a shell burst, oh, just a few yards away and it affected my left ear. I can only swim now by putting a plug of some kind into my ear.

The International Brigade had artillery but not nearly enough and then a lot of it was lost in the retreats that occurred. Yes, our anti-tanks were short of equipment, although the anti-tank gunners were very successful in dealing with the Fascist tanks, which were largely German tanks and Italian tanks, of course.

The International Brigade, I would say, had no tanks. We had nothing in the way of motorised equipment worth speaking about. Nearly everything was carried – boxes of ammunition and so forth were carried on our backs. For example, light machine guns had to be carried. We dismantled the heavy machine guns, and one person would carry a wheel, another would carry the carriage part of it. And up these mountains we had to climb carrying these bits and pieces and ammunition. Of course it was heavy ammunition, too, great boxes of ammunition, and so on.

Talking about carrying things and overloading I remember one time we were marching up during the night at the other side of the Ebro before we crossed the Ebro, just preparing for the crossing. We were marching up a road during the night, because you didn't go marching during the day. Suddenly a blooming bomb went off. And this was Eddie Brown, who was overloaded with belts of ammunition, carrying a light machine gun on his shoulder or something like that, and he had several hand grenades laced on to his belt. And he had laced one of them by the loop of the safety pin, and walking up there the blooming thing came out and dropped down and exploded. There were about thirteen men injured. I was coming up a good distance back, helping a bloke who had got bad feet, and I was going to get him into a truck, the one truck that came up with us that time. Then came this explosion. Some of them came running down and I says, "Where the hell are you running to?" "Oh, the bloody Fascists are..." I says, "Fascists? We're at the wrong side of the Ebro for the Fascists." I says, "It's some of our own people. It's a lot of nonsense. There's been an accident of some kind." But Eddie Brown, you see, he walked on, he walked straight on, and this blooming thing was sizzling behind him and he was clear of the danger. Eddie Brown's still alive of course, and we laugh often about that incident.

I was in Spain from about March to the end of September 1938, shortly before the International Brigades were broken up. Dr. Negrin's Government decided on that as a gesture, in the hope, oh, it was a foolish hope in a sense, that Franco would get rid of the Germans and Italians. That hope was a lot of nonsense since without them he was sunk, even at that late stage, because there were uprisings and clandestine activity against Franco all over Spain at that time. But of course he had the whip hand with the military power he achieved.

The reason why I came away from Spain a little bit before the Government had disbanded all the Internationals, although by that time the Government had taken the decision to disband them and I knew it, was that I was being rushed home to attend a Labour Party conference. It was being held in Edinburgh, and at it I was to make an appeal, a desperate appeal, for Spain.[204] I got back – I had some fun getting back, but I got back – and I was appalled at the indifference of the delegates at that conference to the Spanish struggle, and appalled at the preoccupation with the trivia, as I saw it. Those of us who had been in that bloody struggle felt that it was very important thing. For example, the second or third day after I came back from Spain, I was walking along Princes Street and I met somebody whom I knew and the first thing they said was, "Wasn't that a terrible murder at Murrayfield?" Somebody had been murdered at Murrayfield. "Good God," I said, "A week or two ago I saw thirty five dead Moors. A murder in Murrayfield!" I said.

Well, I came back from Spain as I indicated, hurriedly, pushed over the frontier to get back quickly. It's quite a story. I was taken to the frontier near Port Bou, much further and nearer the sea than when we crossed over earlier and I was told to keep a white building and a depression in the top of a hill in line. And if I would go there on my own during the night I would hit a road in France. Well, I went down through the vines during the night and I reached the road at a bridge and lo and behold there were two French gendarmes leaning over the bridge chatting away. It would be really difficult for them to see me in the dark, but I lowered myself very slowly down until I was flat on the ground, hoping that they would go in the direction of the Spanish frontier instead of the other way...[205]

SPANISH FIESTA AND FAIR

FRIDAY, 16th and SATURDAY, 17th December 1938
11.30 a.m.—9 p.m.
CENTRAL HALL, Tollcross, Edinburgh

to be opened by

His Excellency, DON PABLO de AZCARATE

SPANISH AMBASSADOR, LONDON

Her Grace The DUCHESS OF ATHOLL will preside

Mr Alfred Barnes, M.P. says:—
"The most immediate and urgent need, with Winter approaching, is a terrific flow of food stuffs for the starving Spanish Population."

"9,000 Cows had been slaughtered in the Suburbs of Barcelona for lack of Cattle food."

Dr. Audrey Russell, working with the International Commission in Spain for feeding Child refugees, says that "Relief Work is only touching the fringe of the problem. Rickets had formerly been unknown in Spain, but signs of it were now becoming evident. It cost £1,000 per month to feed 10,000 Children of all ages, and to save the Children under two years of age in Barcelona alone would cost £3,000."

"EDINBURGH AND DISTRICT JOINT COMMITTEE FOR SPANISH RELIEF" aim to raise at least £1,000 by 17th December 1938.

This is a matter of almost desperate urgency. This is an appeal for exceptional effort on the part of all friends of the heroic Spanish People. This is to urge that your Church, Trade Union, Political Party, Co-operative or other Society shall organise a levy, subscription drive, or other special effort in support of the Fiesta, and appoint immediately a Representative to serve on the Fiesta Committee, but—it is also a Special Appeal to "YOU" to offer your personal services.

Kindly complete the appended Form and return (½d. Stamp) to Councillor Thomas Murray, Fiesta Organiser, c/o Peace Council, 85 Hanover Street, Edinburgh, 2. ('Phone: 26573.)

To SPANISH FIESTA AND FAIR COMMITTEE, EDINBURGH.

Please enrol me as a Worker for the Fair. I shall endeavour to interest the organisations with which I am associated and also individual friends.

Name, ...

Address, ...

....

Date, ...

WARWICK & SONS LTD., EDINBURGH.

Leaflet advertising a Spanish Fiesta and Fair in Edinburgh organised by Tom Murray, 17th December 1938, in aid of Spanish Relief.

The anti-tank battery of the XVth International Brigade.

Bob Cooney (hatless, in brown jacket, and facing to centre of men) leads cheering at a XVth International Brigade meeting just before the crossing of the Ebro in the Republican offensive in July 1938.

Notes

1. Peter Kerrigan (1899-1977), a Glasgow engineer, member of the Executive Committee, Communist Party of Great Britain, 1927-9 and 1931-65, leader of Hunger Marches from Glasgow to London, 1934 and 1936, successively Scottish Secretary, National Organiser and Industrial Organiser of the Communist Party, himself took part in the Spanish War.

2. The formation of special military units of foreign volunteers to assist the Spanish Republic was considered by the Spanish Communist Party within two or three weeks of the outbreak of the military and right wing rebellion in July 1936. The idea was taken up by the Executive Committee of the Communist International and approved by Stalin. Formation of the International Brigades was formally authorised by the Spanish Republican Government in October. By that time the earliest foreign volunteers to arrive had already formed units like those named after Tom Mann (1856-1941), the veteran British trade union and Communist Party leader, and Ernst Thaelmann (1886-1944), German Communist Party leader murdered later by the Nazis.

3. Six International Brigades, about 35,000 men in aggregate, were formed in the course of the War, on a basis of language spoken: XIth (German), XIIth (Italian), XIIIth (Eastern European), XIVth (French), XVth (English), 129th (Central European). A seventh Brigade, the 150th (Central European) existed for a time in 1937.

4. General Emilio Mola (1887-1937), a leading organiser of the Fascist rebellion.

5. About 75,000 Moors were enrolled in Franco's forces in the course of the War. See Hugh Thomas, *The Spanish Civil War* (London, 1977), 980.

6. Denis Sefton Delmer (1904-79), War correspondent 1936-8.

7. Esmond Romilly's book was *Boadilla* (London, 1937). See also Jessica Mitford, *Hons and Rebels* (London, 1960).

8. The Committee, set up in August-September 1936 as a result of the agreement on Non-Intervention in the Spanish War by Britain, France, Germany, Italy, Portugal and the Soviet Union, and on which virtually all the states of Europe became represented, began a scheme of enforcement from April 1937 in which the borders and coasts of Spain were to be watched or patrolled and merchant ships bound for Spain belonging to states that were signatories to the Non-Intervention Agreement were to take observers on board. Non-Intervention, a policy inspired by the British Government which yoked to it the Popular Front French Government led by the Socialist Leon Blum and which indeed appeared publicly to take the lead in proposing the policy, proved a dangerous farce. Italy and Germany continued to

333

pour supplies and armed forces in to assist Franco and successfully blocked or evaded attempts to reduce the supplies or secure withdrawal of the troops. The Governments of Britain and France, apparently moved by fear of being drawn into the War lest it develop into a general European conflict, but particularly in the British Government's case because of an unwillingness to do anything that might help the Spanish Republic which they regarded as 'Red', followed a policy that contributed to the eventual defeat of the Republic, the creation of a Fascist state in Spain and hence the removal of a friendly one from France's southern border, and to strengthening the conviction of Hitler that the two Western Powers would not act decisively to oppose the expansion of Nazi Germany. Non-Intervention deprived the legitimate Government of Spain of its right under international law to buy arms abroad for its defence. The Soviet Union declared in October 1936 that unless violations of Non-Intervention by the Fascist powers ceased it would send help to Republican Spain – and did so, as did to a much lesser extent the Mexican Government.

9. Thomas H. Wintringham (1898-1949) served with the Flying Corps and R.A.F. in France in the 1914-18 War and commanded the British Battalion of the International Brigade in February 1937. He helped found Osterley Park Training School for the Home Guard in 1940 and was author of *English Captain* (London, 1939) and other books mainly on war.

10. John Cornford (1915-36) and Ralph Fox (1900-36), poets, were among the first British volunteers to fight in the War.

11. The revolt or mutiny was in 1920. After his return home from Spain after the battle of Brunete in summer 1937, Cunningham left the Communist Party and seems to have wandered about Britain for many years as a casual labourer or tramp. He turned up in 1951 at a meeting in Aberdeen, but no one seems to know the date or place of his death. Thomas, 723, 956; and private information.

12. Chapiev or Chapayev, a Cossack leader made a general in the Civil War and War of Intervention in Russia, was killed aged 35 in September 1919.

13. The Popular Front was the electoral alliance of parties – Republican Union, Left Republican, Esquerra or Catalan Left, Socialist, Communist, P.O.U.M. (Partido Obrero de Unificacion Marxista), and some others – that had won the general election in Spain in February 1936. Although the Anarchists did not join this electoral alliance many of their members voted for it at the election. The Republican Government consequently formed, although it contained no Social-ists, Communists, P.O.U.M. or Anarchists, was the one against which General Franco and his army colleagues and the monarchical and Fascist parties rebelled.

14. James Prendergast (1914-74), an active member of the Communist Party of Ireland, had studied at the Lenin International School in Moscow, served as a rear-gunner with the R.A.F. in the 1939-45 War, and afterwards became a leading figure in the National Union of Railwaymen. Frank Ryan (1902-44), a member of the Irish Republican Army in the Anglo-Irish War, 1918-20, had fought with the Anti-Treaty forces in the Irish Civil War, 1922-3, was a founder of the Dublin Branch of the National Union of Journalists, and was leader of the first group of volunteers from the Communist Party of Ireland to go in December 1936 to fight in Spain. Ryan was taken prisoner by Franco's forces in 1938 and spent the remainder of his life in captivity first in Spain then in Nazi Germany where he died. His remains were re-buried in Ireland in 1979. The Irish Republican Congress, formed in 1934, was a grouping of Left Republicans, Tenants' and Unemployed Associations, and others. Michael O'Riordan, *Connolly Column: The*

story of the Irishmen who fought for the Spanish Republic 1936-39 (Dublin, 1979), 25, 56, 57, 58, 132, 139, 140, 157; Bill Alexander, *British Volunteers for Liberty: Spain 1936-39* (London, 1982), 194.

15. Colonel Sigismundo Casado (1893-1968), commander of one of the Republican armies, attempted early in 1939 in alliance with some anti-Communist sections, to negotiate peace with Franco and carry out a coup against the Republican Government.

16. The sign Donald Renton refers to is not certain. John Dunlop believes it may have been that of a rifle being aimed.

17. Philip Pembroke Stephens, aged 34, son of a barrister, was killed by Japanese machine gun bullets while watching fighting between Chinese and Japanese at Nantao on 12 November 1937. After leaving Cambridge University he had entered the film industry, then became an official of the League of Nations secretariat before entering journalism about 1928. Before joining the *Daily Telegraph* he had been *Daily Express* correspondent in Vienna for four years, then Paris and in 1933-4 Berlin. He was arrested and expelled from Germany in May 1934 apparently after making enquiries about 'building activities in a wood'. He spent a year in Spain attached as *Daily Telegraph* correspondent to Franco's armies, about which attachment a question was asked in the House of Commons. He had been in China about three months. See *The Times*, 12 November 1937. In October 1936 Nazi Germany and Fascist Italy agreed to co-operate on a number of issues, including Spain, and this agreement became known as the Berlin-Rome Axis. It became a formal alliance, the 'Pact of Steel' in May 1939. In November 1936 Hitler made the Anti-Comintern Pact with Japan and it was joined by Italy a year later. In 1940 a formal Tripartite Pact was made between the three states.

18. Julio Alvarez del Vayo (1891-1974), Socialist, Foreign Minister of the Republican Government, 1936-7 and 1938, Spanish representative at the League of Nations, 1937-9.

19. Marquis de Merry del Val (1864-1943), born in London, son of a Spanish diplomat, entered Spanish diplomatic service in 1882 and was Spanish ambassador in London, 1913-31. He was created Marquis by royal decree in 1925 and was at various times a private secretary and chamberlain to the King of Spain. Merry del Val held honorary degrees from four English universities.

20. Sir Oswald Mosley (1896-1980), Labour M.P. 1924 and 1926-31, founded 1932 and led the British Union of Fascists. Mosley was imprisoned under Regulation 18B during the 1939-45 War.

21. The Potsdam conference between Britain, U.S.A. and U.S.S.R. met from 17 July to 2 August 1945. The Declaration of Potsdam issued on 3 August declared *inter alia*: "The three Governments feel bound to make it clear that they for their part would not favour any application for membership [of the United Nations] put forward by the present Spanish Government which, having been founded with the support of the Axis Powers [Germany and Italy], does not, in view of its origin, its nature, its record, and its close association with the aggressor States, possess the qualifications necessary to justify such membership." Spain remained excluded from membership of the United Nations until December 1955.

22. *Workers' Weekly*, 1923-7, was the official organ of the Communist Party of Great Britain. The paper changed its title in 1927 to *Workers' life*.

23. Joyce (1906-46), Mosley's former lieutenant, went to Germany in 1939, became a naturalised German and throughout the War broadcast over Nazi radio to Britain, where he acquired his nickname. He was hanged for treason after the War.

24. I.e., to the police station there.

25. Juan March (1884-1962).

26. At its annual conference in early October 1936 the Labour Party, by 1,836,000 votes to 519,000, approved Non-Intervention, provided it was made effective on both sides. A year later the Party conference unanimously passed a resolution demanding that the Conservative Government abandon Non-Intervention and restore to the Spanish Republican Government its right under international law to buy arms.

27. Wilfred F.R. McCartney or Macartney, a left-wing journalist and author of *Walls have Mouths: a Record of Ten Years' Penal Servitude* (London, 1936), was wounded when Peter Kerrigan was demonstrating the mechanism of a firearm. Alexander, op.cit., 91.

28. It was Jock Gilmour who died. George Watters' other friend from Prestonpans, Jimmy Kempton, survived the Spanish War, worked in Prestongrange Colliery, East Lothian, after his return and died in the 1970s.

29. For Dickinson, see also below, p. 48.

30. Tito (pseud. of Josip Broz) (1892-1980), fought with the Red Army, 1917-20, became Croatian labour leader on his return to Yugoslavia, was imprisoned for five years for Communist activities, recruited Yugoslavs for service with the International Brigades in Spain, 1936-7, became General Secretary of the Yugoslav Communist Party in 1937, was leader of Yugoslav resistance to Nazi occupation in the Second World War, and was successively Marshal, Prime Minister and President of Yugoslavia from 1943 until his death. There has been some disagreement about whether Tito was ever in Spain during the Civil War, see, e.g., Thomas, op.cit., 454.

31. John Burdon Sanderson Haldane (1892-1964), F.R.S., Professor of Genetics, 1933-7, and of Biometry, 1937-57, at London University, Chairman, 1940-9, of the Editorial Board of the *Daily Worker*. Harry Pollitt (1890-1960), General Secretary, 1929-56, and Chairman, 1956-60, of the Communist Party of Great Britain.

32. *Comida* – meals or dinners.

33. William Gallacher (1881-1965), Communist M.P. for West Fife, 1935-50.

34. Founded in the mid-19th century as a special armed and strictly disciplined constabulary, the Civil Guard, some 30,000 strong, were stationed in villages and towns throughout Spain. Carefully segregated in barracks from the local population and always moving around in pairs, the Civil Guards' relations with peasants and workers were generally very hostile. About half the Civil Guard supported the Fascist rebellion in 1936.

35. Woodbine – a popular brand of cigarette.

36. James Duffy, Glasgow, was killed in April 1938 on the Ebro. Alexander, op.cit., 266.

37. Jack Grahl (1912-79).

38. Winston Churchill's nephew was Esmond Romilly – see above, p. 18. David Guest, killed in July 1938, a mathematician and son of L. Haden Guest, Labour M.P. for North Southwark, 1923-7, and North Islington, 1937-50. Lewis Clive (1911-38), was a signatory of a letter sent to the Labour Party from the front line in Spain a few days before his death, urging greater effort in aid of Spanish liberty. (See *Report of Thirty-eighth Annual Conference of the Labour Party, 1939*, 114). Dr Alexander Ethan Tudor Hart, M.R.C.S., L.R.C.P. Ronald Malcolm Loraine Dunbar (1912-63), was a son of Sir Loraine Geddes Dunbar, of Whitehill Lodge, Harrogate.

39. The Stukas were Ju or Junkers 87 two-seat precision dive-bombers of 1937-45 that, tested in the Spanish War, contributed to the success for the German *Blitzkrieg* in Poland and France in 1939-40 but suffered disastrous losses in the Battle of Britain.

40. The Garibaldi Battalion of anti-Fascist Italians in the XIIth Internationsl Brigade played a leading part in the Spanish Republican victory over Mussolini's troops at the battle of Guadalajara in March 1937.

41. The Geneva Convention, an international agreement regulating the treatment of the wounded in war, was first made at a conference in 1864 and was later extended to cover the treatment of the sick and of prisoners and the protection of civilians in wartime. The rules were revised in 1906 and 1929 (and more recently, in 1949). The use of particular weapons was prohibited in a series of agreements – e.g., gas and dum-dum bullets.

42. Dolores Ibarruri, La Pasionaria (1895-), orator and perhaps the best known leader of the Spanish Communist Party, wife of an Asturian miner, imprisoned several times for her political activities, a member of the Cortes or parliament before the Civil War and President of the Communist Party for many years after it, she seemed to many to personify Spanish resistance to Fascism. After the Civil War she went into prolonged exile in the Soviet Union.

43. Henderson was lost in April and Lobban in September 1938. Alexander, op.cit., 268, 270.

44. Georgi Dimitrov (1882-1949), Bulgarian Communist leader, tried but acquitted on charges of burning down the German Reichstag or parliament building a year earlier. The Hunger March was to London.

45. *Daily Worker*, Communist paper, January 1930 – April 1966, then continued as *Morning Star*.

46. See above, Note 2. André Marty (1886-1956), a leader of the French Communist Party and member of the Executive Committee of the Third International had led a mutiny in the French Black Sea Fleet in 1919 against supporting White Russian forces. Marty was commandant of the International Brigades base at Albacete. He was expelled from the French Communist Party shortly before his death.

47. Bob Cooney (1910-84), was one of a family of eight. He was brought up in Aberdeen, where his first job was pawnbroker's assistant. In autumn 1937 he went

to Spain and became political commissar of the British Battalion in spring 1938. During the 1939-45 War Cooney was a gunner in the Royal Artillery. As a Communist he fought the 1945 parliamentary election at Glasgow Central constituency and won 2,709 votes. Blacklisted by building trade employers in Aberdeen, he later moved to Birmingham, where he lived for about fifteen years. His obituary is in *Morning Star*, 18 August 1984.

48. See Note 8 above. Anthony Eden (1897-1977), Conservative M.P., 1923-57, Foreign Secretary, 1935-8, 1940-5 and 1951-5, Prime Minister, 1955-7, created Earl of Avon, 1961.

49. McGuire was killed at Jarama in February 1937. Alexander, op.cit., 270.

50. George Middleton (1898-1971), Secretary of Glasgow Trades Council 1942-9, General Secretary, Scottish Trades Union Congress, 1949-63.

51. Fred Copeman (1907-83). The naval mutiny at Invergordon in September 1931 was against the National Government's cuts in naval ratings' pay. Copeman was one of three dozen leaders of the mutiny who were dismissed from the navy without any charges being brought against them. Copeman's autobiography is *Reason in Revolt* (London, 1948).

52. M. Davidovitch, killed at Jarama, February 1937. Alexander, op.cit., 266.

53. Ralph Campeau. Alexander, op.cit., 265.

54. American film, by R.L. Warner, 1935, based on a novel by Alice Tisdale Hobart, and dealing with the career in China of an American oil company representative, with Pat O'Brien as leading actor.

55. The P.O.U.M. (Partido Obrero de Unificacion Marxista, or Workers' Party of Marxist Unity) had been formed in February 1936 following a breakaway five years earlier by its leaders Andres Nin, Joaquin Maurin and others from the Spanish Communist Party. It joined the Popular Front (see above, Note 13). The P.O.U.M., with between 40,000 and 60,000 members, was the smallest of the four left-wing parties. It had its stronghold in Catalonia and was regarded as Trotskyist by the Communists, although Trotsky himself criticised Nin (his former secretary) for taking part in the Government of Catalonia and for adopting a 'timid and semi-Menshevik' attitude. (See Isaac Deutscher, *The Prophet Outcast: Trotsky 1929-40* (London, 1963), 388). In May 1937 the growing tensions between the P.O.U.M., critical of Stalinism and of alliance with middle class Republican parties and believing that the War would not be won unless the revolution triumphed, and the Communist-dominated P.S.U.C. (Catalan Socialist Unity Party) and also between the latter and the Anarchists, resulted in several days of street fighting in Barcelona in which 500 were killed and 1,000 wounded. The events of those days sharply illustrated divisions on the Republican side in the Civil War, led to the fall of the Government headed by Largo Caballero and to the succession of that led by his fellow-Socialist Dr Juan Negrin, the suppression of the P.O.U.M and the murder in prison of their leader Nin, and also to a decline in the influence of the Anarchists. As one historian (Raymond Carr) has put it: 'The May troubles . . . constituted the watershed in the political life of the Republic.' For full discussion of the complexities of the crisis, its background and consequences, see, e.g., R. Carr, *Spain 1808-1975* (London, 1982), 666-7; R. Fraser, *Blood of Spain* (Harmondsworth, 1981), 340-5, 378-82, 561-2; Gerald Brenan, *Spanish Labyrinth* (Cambridge, 1960), 323-9; Thomas, op.cit., 523. 646-65, 701-09; and George Orwell, *Homage to Catalonia* (London, 1938), chapters 9 – 14.

56. The Olympic Games held in Berlin in August 1936 was the largest festival of sport hitherto in the world, with 4,000 athletes and 100,000 spectators. The French team obliged with the Fascist salute as they marched into the stadium but Hitler was 'highly annoyed' by the remarkable successes of the black American athlete Jesse Owens and declared that blacks should be excluded from future games. Albert Speer, *Inside the Third Reich* (London, 1971), 73.

57. American isolationism resulted in the passing of the Neutrality Act of 1935, at the time of the Italian invasion of Abyssinia. The Act had begun as a Bill proposed by the Roosevelt administration that, while forbidding loans to third parties at war and forbidding American ships to carry arms and munitions to them, left the President with power to decide which side in a foreign war should be subjected to an arms embargo. The Senate, however, amended the Bill to make the arms embargo apply to both sides, no matter which was the aggressor or the victim – a gift to aggressors, usually better prepared for war than their victims. The Act did not forbid the sale to belligerents of raw materials such as oil or coal. Even before the Non-Intervention Committee was established by European states (see above, Note 8) the Roosevelt adminstration declared an embargo on the sale of arms to either side in the Spanish War, and the Neutrality Act as a whole was applied to the War from January 1937. Since the Spanish Republic was supported by (among others) Communists and the Soviet Union, anti-Communism appears a leading motive for the decision, including pressure from influential pro-Franco Roman Catholic figures in Roosevelt's own Party, the Democrats. Though Roosevelt himself appears to have wished later in the War to reconsider United States' policy toward the Spanish Republic nothing in fact was done to change that policy which, like the Non-Intervention of the British and French Governments, contributed to the defeat of the Spanish Republic and the victory of Franco and the Fascist powers. Indeed without the policy of the United States Government 'Non-Intervention' might not have been able to prolong itself throughout the course of the War as it did. The Neutrality Act of May 1937 renewed the non-discriminatory arms embargo, although the President was given discretionary power to add to the list of embargoes oil and certain other commodites useful for making war. See D. Malone and B. Rauch, *War and Troubled Peace, 1917-1939* (New York, 1960), 291-5. On the other hand, Franco's forces received during the Civil War nearly three-and-a-half million tons of oil from the Texas Oil Company and Standard Oil, and 12,000 lorries from Ford, General Motors and Studebaker. Thomas, op.cit., 943. Franco's Under-Secretary for Foreign Affairs told an American journalist in 1945 that "without American petrol, American trucks and American credit, we could never have won the war." Arthur H. Landis, *The Abraham Lincoln Brigade* (New York, 1967), 94.

58. Hugh Pollard, a retired army major, his daughter and another young woman, her friend, flew as cover from London on 11 July 1936 with Luis Bolin, correspondent of the monarchist newspaper *ABC*, in a chartered plane piloted by Captain Cecil W.H. Bebb to the Canary Islands. The four had been suggested to Bolin by the anti-Republican British publisher Douglas Jerrold, chairman of Eyre and Spottiswoode. See Hugh Thomas, op.cit., 203-4, and Luis Bolin, *Spain: The Vital Years* (London, 1967), 17ff.

59. Churchill's view of the War is outlined in, e.g., his *The Gathering Storm* (London, 1948), 191-3. Ivan Maisky, then Soviet Ambassador to Britain, records a conversation with Churchill on 5 November 1936 in which he showed himself "an opponent of the Spanish Republic and openly sympathised with Franco." Maisky, *Spanish Notebooks* (London, 1966), 72. Jessica Mitford, widow of Esmond Romilly, Churchill's nephew, expresses a different view of Churchill's attitude to British imperial interests in the Mediterranean, at any rate from late summer 1937, in her *Hons and Rebels* (London, 1960), 135.

60. Jesus Hernandez (1906-196?), a leader of the Communist Party, was Minister of Education in the Republican Government, 1936-8, and Vicente Uribe, another leading Party member, Minister of Agriculture, 1936-9. Dolores Ibarruri, La Pasionaria, (see above, Note 42) was not in fact a member of the Government.

61. Tom Clarke speaks here of course from his own personal experience. Gerald Brenan, op.cit., 189, refers to "The fanatical hatred of the Anarchists for the Church and the extraordinary violence of their attack upon it during the Civil War ... Without going far wrong one may say that all the churches ... burned in Spain were burned by Anarchists and that most of the priests killed were killed by them. Such a persecution of religion has not been known in Europe since the Thirty Years' War ... It can only, I think, be explained as the hatred of heretics for the Church from which they have sprung. For in the eyes of Spanish libertarians the Catholic Church occupies the position of Anti-Christ in the Christian world. It is far more to them than a mere obstacle to revolution. They see in it the fountain of all evil, the corruptor of youth with its vile doctrine of original sin, the blasphemer against Nature and the Law of Nature ..." Brenan also says, p. 152: "The feeling that rises most quickly to the surface in every Spanish revolution is anti-clericalism. For all the evils of the times the priests and monks are made the scapegoat." Rioting in Barcelona in 1909 had been marked by the burning of twenty-two churches and thirty-four convents. When the monarchy was replaced by the Republic in 1931 102 churches and convents in six large towns alone were completely destroyed. (Brenan, op.cit., 34, 236).

62. The Medical Aid Committee and its work is discussed in Alexander, op.cit., chapter 18, and in Thomas, op.cit., 437. See also Labour Party Annual Report for 1936, 32, 1937, 15-16, and 1939, 7-9. The subject will be included in a forthcoming book by Jim Fyrth on Spanish Aid.

63. See, e.g., above, p. 62. After the battle of Guadalajara in March 1937 women were asked to leave the front. Fraser, op.cit., 286.

64. The Anarchist or anarcho-syndicalist movement had developed particularly strongly in Spain from the mid-nineteenth century, forming in 1910 its own revolutionary trade union movement, the C.N.T. (Confederacion Nacional del Trabajo), estimates of whose numbers by 1936 ranged up to 1,500,000 but whose hard core may have totalled around 200,000. The Iberian Anarchist Federation (F.A.I.), a secret revolutionary elite, was formed in 1927 largely to counteract 'reformism' in the C.N.T. which the F.A.I. came to dominate. The F.A.I. came into the open only at the beginning of the Civil War in 1936. The Anarchists, in contradiction to their tradition, entered the Government of Catalonia in September 1936 and of Republican Spain in December that year, but although the membership of both the C.N.T. and F.A.I. increased to the end of the War, the influence of the Anarchists declined after the street fighting of May 1937 in Barcelona (above, Note 55). For fuller discussion of Anarchism see G. Woodcock, *Anarchism* (Harmondsworth, 1963), 335-75, and Brenan, op.cit., 188-97, 327-8.

65. The editorial seems rather to have been that of 7 November 1936, immediately preceding the unleashing of the Fascist attack on Madrid. On 11 December the *Glasgow Herald* was more concerned with the abdication crisis surrounding Edward VIII in Britain.

66. Sir Daniel Macaulay Stevenson (1851-1944), merchant, philanthropist, coal-exporter, member of Glasgow Town Council, 1892-1914, Lord Provost, 1911-14, Chancellor of Glasgow University, 1934-44, founded a lectureship in citizenship and Chairs of Italian and Spanish at Glasgow University. Toward the end of 1937 Hitler bestowed on Sir Daniel the Cross, first class, of the Meritorious Order of the German Eagle in recognition of his foundation some years earlier of exchange scholarships between Scottish and German students (*Glasgow Herald*, 24 Novem-

ber 1937). According also to the *Glasgow Herald* the Scottish Ambulance Unit in Spain was formed, on the initiative of Sir Daniel, soon after the outbreak of the Fascist rebellion in July 1936. The Unit was organised by an Executive Committee whose chairman was Sir Daniel and whose score of members included several titled people, professors, and Liberals, such as the Marchioness of Aberdeen, the Countess of Oxford and Asquith, Sir Archibald Sinclair, M.P., Professors Glaister and Walton, but also included Bailie William Elger, the General Secretary of the Scottish Trades Union Congress. The Unit, composed of nineteen men and one woman (Miss F. Jacobsen), with six ambulances and one supply wagon, first left Glasgow for Spain on 17 September. Within a month the *Herald* reported that seven members of the Unit were returning home, two of them voluntarily for health reasons, five others as 'a disciplinary measure', accused evidently by the Republican authorities of looting bodies on the field of battle – an accusation strongly denied by the five. It also appears that Dr Levine, originally in charge of the Unit, had left it while it was passing through France for Spain and there had been 'friction among the members'. The commandant of the Unit after Dr Levine was Duncan Newbigging, a final year medical student. By the later part of October the Executive Committee was formally denying there was any foundation in reports that the Unit was being recalled from Spain. In November one of the ambulances was destroyed by bombing and another badly damaged, while two members of the Unit were made prisoner for some weeks by Franco's troops near Madrid. By Christmas, when they returend home on leave, only two men and Miss Jacobsen remained to the Unit. See *Glasgow Herald*, 9 and 18 September, 14, 15, 17 and 22 October, 2 and 9 November and 21 December 1936.

67.   Miss Fernanda Jacobsen. Cecil Phillips, *The Spanish Pimpernel* (London, 1960), 85, describes her as "a picturesque and exhilarating character ... a little middle-aged sandy-haired woman who ... presented herself to the world in a man's kilt, tartan hose, bare knees and a Glengarry. She spoke bad Spanish with a broad Scots accent." The *Glasgow Herald* in its reports on the Scottish Ambulance Unit described Miss Jacobsen as its liaison officer, but from July 1937 as its commandant.

68.   Sir George Arthur D. Ogilvie-Forbes (1891-1954), of Aberdeenshire, K.C.M.G., D.L., was not Ambassador but Counsellor at the British Embassy in Madrid, 1935-7, and Chargé d'Affaires in Madrid and Valencia, 1936-7. He became Counsellor at the British Embassy in Berlin, 1937-9.

69.   The disappearance that month of Baron de Borchgrave, First Secretary of the Belgian legation in Madrid gave rise to rumours that he had joined Franco's forces. He was found dead at Fuencarral, on the outskirts of the city, the circumstacnes of his death unknown. *The Times*, 29 and 30 December 1936.

70.   Dr Leonard Crome, M.C., B.Com., L.R.C.P., L.R.C.S., L.R.F.P.S.

71.   Captain Edwin Christopher Lance (1892-1970), D.S.O., a civil engineer, had fought for Kerensky against the Bolsheviks in 1919, worked as a railway engineer in Spain from 1926 for a time and then returned there again in 1931. Lance, the subject of *The Spanish Pimpernel*, op.cit., arranged escapes and rescues of anti-Republicans.

72.   George Green's wife Nan was a hospital administrator in Spain and afterwards was for many years Secretary of the International Brigade Association.

73.   These Spanish divisions were named after their Communist generals, El Campesino (pseud. of Valentin Gonzalez), who died in exile in Mexico in 1972, and Enrique Lister.

74. The *Glasgow Herald* reported on 24 July 1937 that Sir D.M. Stevenson and other members of the Executive Committee had written Miss Jacobsen in Spain requesting the Scottish Ambulance Unit to return home "as they had now been on duty for six months and were obviously in need of a rest." The Unit returned to Glasgow on 30 July "to refit". It was stated that Manuel Azana, President of the Spanish Republic, had recently "expressed his gratitude personally to Miss Jacobsen for the work of the Unit". The Executive Committee decided unanimously that the Unit should return to Spain and it did so, arriving on a British destroyer at Barcelona on 13 September. The Unit, again led by Miss Jacobsen, had eight men, one of whom had been in both previous expeditions and three of whom had first gone out to Spain at the same time as Roderick MacFarquhar. A photograph of the Unit in the *Glasgow Herald* of 28 October 1937 shows five ambulances and a lorry, and the caption states: "The Unit has done valuable work in Spain for both sides." The Committee are said to have thought of "winding up the work" of the Unit at the end of 1937 but were said to have been "bombarded with requests" from "the people of Madrid" as well as from members of the Government asking that the Unit carry on. Miss Jacobsen was quoted as saying "she was at a loss to understand the criticism levelled at the Unit by certain people in Scotland." Distributing food and evacuating invalids and women and children from Madrid appear to have become the main work of the Unit from the summer of 1937. The Unit seems to have finally returned home in July 1938. *Glasgow Herald*, 30 July, 4 August, 15 and 20 September and 28 December 1937, and 16, 23, and 30 July 1938.

75. Dr Norman Bethune (1890-1949) died while working as a doctor with the Chinese Communists. A biography of him by Ted Allan and Sydney Gordon is *The scalpel, not the sword* (London, 1954).

76. Winifred Bates (1898-?) and her husband Ralph (1899-?) were writers who were in Spain when the Civil War began and who put their writing abilities at the service of the Republicans. Winifred Bates helped in the refugee camps in France at the end of the War. Alexander, op.cit., 41, 221, 234, 248.

77. A magnificent royal palace thirty miles north-west of Madrid that was built between 1563 and 1584 by Philip II, King of Spain.

78. Discussion did take place between Moroccan nationalists and the Spanish Republican Government in the autumn of 1936 but came to nothing as the Government did not want to antagonise the French Government or the Spanish middle class by proclaiming support for Moroccan independence from both Spain and France. Thomas, op.cit., 579, and Fraser, op.cit., 330.

79. On 26 April 1937. The Republicans were falsely accused by the Fascists of either blowing up or bombing Guernica themselves. The destruction of the town was immortalised in Picasso's painting later that year.

80. Archie Dewar was killed in March 1938 in the fighting on the Ebro. Alexander, op.cit., 266.

81. Canadians had been fighting with the International Brigades since January 1937. The Mackenzie-Papineau Battalion, named after the two leaders of the Canadian rebellion of 1837-8 against Britain, was the last English-speaking battalion formed in Spain and joined the XVth International Brigade in September 1937.

82. Smith, who had been in the Canadian army, was promoted to major early in 1938 and commanded the Mackenzie-Papineau Battalion from then until he was wounded in September that year. Landis, op.cit., 354, 383, 569.

83. Paul Robeson (1898-1976), concert singer and actor. His wife, née Eslanda Cardozo Goode, died in 1965.

84. Jawaharlal Nehru (1889-1964), a leader of the Indian nationalist movement and President of the Indian National Congress, 1929, 1936-7, 1946, 1951-4, and Prime Minister and Minister for External Affairs, 1947-64.

85. The Munich Agreement of September 1938 between the governments of Britain, France, Nazi Germany and Fascist Italy forced Czechoslovakia (which, like the Soviet Union, had not been invited to attend the Munich conference) to cede the Sudetenland, the German-speaking part of the country, to Hitler. Six months later Hitler sent his troops into Prague, the Czech capital, and established a 'protectorate' over the provinces of Bohemia and Moravia. The British Government then appeared to reverse its policy of appeasement by giving a military guarantee to Poland, Rumania and Greece – with fateful consequences when Hitler invaded Poland in September that year. The Munich Agreement was a major factor in the decision by Stalin to make, in August 1939, the Non-Agression Pact with Nazi Germany. By removing, at the expense of Czechoslovakia, the possibility of war in 1938 between the two Western Powers and Nazi Germany, Munich removed the prospect of the Spanish War becoming part of a general European War that might have saved the Spanish Republic from Fascism.

86. Charlotte Haldane (1894-19??).

87. Leon Blum (1872-1950), Socialist Prime Minister in the Popular Front Government of France, 1936-7 and March-April 1938, and again very briefly Prime Minister in winter 1946-7.

88. S.I.M. – Servicio de Investigacion Militar, counter-espionage and political police service established by the Republican Government after the crisis in Barcelona in May 1937 (see above, Note 55). Fraser, op.cit., 444 and 459; and Thomas, op.cit., 776-8.

89. Scottish Painters' Society, formed 1898, amalgamated in 1963 into the Amalgamated Society of Painters and Decorators, which in turn merged in 1972 into the Union of Construction and Allied Trades and Technicians.

90. *L' Humanité* was founded as a Socialist paper in 1904 but became the leading organ of the Communist Party after its formation in 1920/1.

91. *Garde-à-vous* – stand at attention.

92. Hugh Slater had originally gone to Spain as correspondent for *International Press Correspondence (Inprecorr)*, a Communist weekly. Later, at the battle of Brunete, he succeeded Malcolm Dunbar as commander of the anti-tank unit, and in 1938 became Chief of Operations of the XVth Brigade. Landis, op.cit., 626; Alexander, op.cit., 128, 201.

93. Not much more information has so far been gleaned about Williams. Eddie Brown recalls that he "was with the doctors in the Battalion and was in almost every front that the Battalion was in. Williams was not a doctor but did all the bandaging." It is possible he was Alun Menai Williams from Tonypandy. See Hywel Francis, *Miners against Fascism: Wales and the Spanish Civil War* (London, 1984), 136.

94. Dugald McLean, General Secretary of the Society from 1924 to 1946.

95. Bill Alexander, author of *British Volunteers for Liberty: Spain 1936-39* (London, 1982), and presently Secretary of the International Brigade Association.

96. The Left Republican Party, one of those in the Popular Front, had been formed in 1934 as an amalgamation of three formerly separate liberal republican parties, and was the Party to which belonged both Manuel Azana, the President of the Republic, and Casares Quiroga, Prime Minister at the outbreak of the Civil War. With 79 seats won in the elections of February 1936 it was the second largest Popular Front Party in the Cortes or parliament. The Party had members in the Republican Government throughout the Civil War. See also above, Note 55.

97. Maurice Winnick, who died in 1962 aged 59.

98. See above, Note 2.

99. George Aitken, a Communist Party organiser, was a Scots engineer who had served in the 1914-18 War. Along with four other British Battalion or XVth Brigade British leaders among whom sharp differences of opinion had taken place he was sent back to Britain after the battle of Brunete and did not return to Spain. Alexander, op.cit., 67, 74, 130-1; Judith Cook, *Apprentices of Freedom* (London, 1979), 97-8.

100. John or Jack Black, a Scots miner and member of the Labour Party, was second-in-command of the anti-tank battery. Alexander, op.cit., 125.

101. Nan Green – see above, Note 72.

102. Creations of the literary genius of Miguel de Cervantes (1547-1616), Don Quixote and his squire Sancho Panza are the most widely known characters in Spanish literature.

103. Captain, later Major, Allan Johnson, a Regular officer in the United States army, arrived in March 1937 in Spain and became Operations Officer of the XVth Brigade. He was the highest ranking American army officer to volunteer to serve with the Spanish Republican army. He had evidently applied for and received a year's leave of absence from the American army. He left Spain for some months in the summer of 1937 in order to purchase supplies for the Spanish Government, and took command of the base at Tarazona on his return in September. He was badly wounded in the retreat in the Aragon in March 1938 and remained out of action for the rest of his time in Spain. Landis, op.cit., 109-10, 162, 443.

104. Offsink was captured with some of his men by Franco's forces in the retreat in the Aragon at the end of March 1938. They were executed one by one by machine gun – except the last man in line who, though wounded, made a successful dash for freedom, was later picked up by an ambulance of the Franco forces whose crew, sympathetic to the Republican forces, murdered a wounded Fascist inside the ambulance, gave the American his place and uniform and took him to hospital where, knowing no Spanish, he feigned loss of voice. He was eventually repatriated. Landis, op.cit., 461, and further information from John Dunlop.

105. T.H. Wintringham, former commander of the British Battalion (see above, Note 9), describes this incident in his *English Captain*, op.cit., 143: ". . . when moving to take up position for a second stand, near Gandesa, the whole battalion

marched straight up to a large group of Italian tanks. The battalion had no advance guard. It had been told that the Fascists were twenty miles away; but this and the weariness that follows weeks of heavy fighting, and the fact that many men were new recruits who had only just joined the unit, cannot excuse the disastrous slackness of its march. The foremost company seems to have gone right past the tanks before anything happened – although these machines had Italian lettering on their sides. No preparations had been made by the battalion for action; no hand-grenades were fused. Most of the first company were cut off and captured. More than a year before, at Madrigueras, I had circulated and posted up a silhouette of the Italian light tank, which is easy to distinguish from the types of tank used by the Republican forces. This training, I suppose, had later been neglected." About 150 British were killed and 100 taken prisoner, among them Frank Ryan (see above, Note 14) and Garry McCartney (see above, p. 249).

106. Digger – guardhouse or gaol.

107. Wild, a Manchester labourer, born 1908, had joined the Royal Navy at age 15 but after some years deserted and was discharged. He was active in the National Unemployed Workers' Movement and anti-Mosley agitation before going to Spain. George Fletcher, from Crewe, a sergeant in the British army, was promoted to captain in Spain and was in command in the absence of Wild on sick leave at the time of the disastrous encounter of the British Battalion with Italian tanks mentioned in Note 105 above. Judith Cook, op.cit., 23-4; Alexander, op.cit., 154, 178-9.

108. Jennie Lee (1904-), daughter of a Fife miner, widow of Aneurin Bevan, M.P., was Labour M.P. for North Lanark, 1929-31, and Cannock, 1945-70, and was a Minister in the Labour Governments of 1964-70. She was created a life peeress as Baroness Lee of Asheridge in 1970.

109. General Walter (pseud. of Karol Swierczewski) (1897-1947), a Pole who had fought with the Soviet Red Army, was commander of the 35th Division in Spain. He was Minister of Defence in Poland from 1945 until his assassination by Ukranians in 1947. Alexander, op.cit., 85, 144; Thomas, op.cit., 954.

110. Johnny Hall, from Rutherglen, was killed in March 1938 at Belchite. Alexander, op.cit., 268.

111. José Calvo Sotelo (1893-1936) was Minister of Finance during the dictatorship of General Primo de Rivera, 1923-30, and leader of the Monarchists from 1934. His murder on 13 July 1936 became the signal for the rebellion four days later against the Republican Government. The left-wing Assault Guards officer whose murder on 12 July, evidently by Fascists, provoked that of Calvo Sotelo was Lieutenant José Castillo.

112. Paddy O'Daire, who had fought with the International Brigades since December 1936, was a former member of the Irish Free State army, had emigrated for a time to Canada, then worked as a labourer in Britain, became second-in-command then commander of the British Battalion in the summer of 1937. In the following year he became Director of Operations of the XVth Brigade. In the 1939-45 War he joined the British army as a private and reached the rank of major. Alexander, op.cit., 44, 144, 149; O'Riordan, op.cit., 81.

113. John Peet was son of the editor of the Quaker periodical *The Friend*. After the 1939-45 War he was a journalist in Berlin, publicly denounced the Western press,

and took East German nationality. (Further information from John Dunlop).

114. For father and son see above, Note 38.

115. Gates, a steel workers' union organiser aged 23, had arrived in Spain with some other Americans in February 1937, during the battle of Jarama, and became commissar of the American Lincoln Battalion of the International Brigade in spring 1938, soon after which he had to swim the river Ebro to reach safety during the Republican retreat in the Aragon. He was subsequently made commissar of the Brigade, and addressed the meeting John Dunlop refers to on 24 July 1938. Landis, op.cit., 77, 476, 517, 521.

116. Glyn 'Taffy' Evans was a South Wales miner and had fought with the International Brigade through the battles of Jarama and Brunete in the previous year. Alexander, op.cit. 167.

117. Johnny Power, one of three brothers from Waterford in Ireland who fought with the International Brigades, had gone to Spain in December 1936, was wounded at the battle of Brunete, and was promoted to captain in September 1938. Power was interned at Curragh during the 1939-45 War. O'Riordan, op.cit., 58, 88, 134, 139.

118. William Paynter (1903-85), Hunger Marcher in the 1930s, was elected to the Executive Committee of the South Wales Miners, 1936, became Agent, 1939, President, 1951, and was General Secretary from 1959 to 1969 of the National Union of Mineworkers. He was author of *My Generation* (London, 1972).

119. For Pollitt and Gallacher, see above, Notes 31 and 33 respectively. William Rust (1903-49), Secretary, Young Communist League, and editor of *Young Worker*, 1924; imprisoned, 1925, for twelve months for incitement to mutiny, was editor of the *Daily Worker*, 1930-49.

120. John Londragan mistakes here the Ju or Junkers 88, which entered service with the Luftwaffe only from late 1939, with the Ju 87 or Stuka, a two-seat dive bomber in service with the Luftwaffe from 1937 to 1945 and first tested out in the Spanish Civil War.

121. Bill Cranston is mistaken here: Harold Fry was killed at Fuentes del Ebro in October 1937. Fry had been a sergeant in the British army and later a shoe-repairer. Alexander, op.cit., 93, 267. See also below, Hugh Sloan, p.217.

122. Ramage & Ferguson Ltd were shipbuilders and engineers at Leith.

123. Ben Glaser, from London, killed on the Ebro in September, but evidently by a shellburst, not a bullet. Information from Hugh Sloan (and see below, p.235).

124. Dunbar seems in fact to have gone into the army and John Dunlop recalls him as a sergeant in the Tank Corps.

125. Alexander, op.cit., 271, gives Mason's first name as Robert.

126. Gallabears – *galabia*, a loose-fitting cloak.

127. Arthur Nicol or Nicoll, who returned home for medical treatment after the battle of Brunete, thereafter actively recruited volunteers in Dundee for the International Brigade. He returned to Spain taking his younger brother with him, and

became the commander of the anti-tank unit until it went out of existence during the retreat of the Aragon early in 1938. Alexander, op.cit., 138, 171-2.

128. A. Winter (sic), Glasgow, was killed at Brunete in July 1937. Alexander, op.cit., 276.

129. See also above, p.138, for John Dunlop's and below, p.206, for Hugh Sloan's recollection of this incident. Dickson was brother-in-law of George Watters.

130. John McArthur (1899-1982), a founder member of the Communist Party, full-time student, 1920-1, of the Clydeside revolutionary John Maclean at the Scottish Labour College, a militant leader of the Fife miners between the Wars, and District Secretary of the National Union of Mineworkers in Fife until his retirement in 1964.

131. The United Mineworkers of Scotland, 1929-36, was a left-wing union, based largely in Lanarkshire and Fife and in rivalry with the existing federal organisation of the county unions, the National Union of Scottish Mine Workers.

132. *Everybody's*, London, 1913-59, assumed that title in 1930 after four successive different titles including originally *The Competitors' Journal*.

133. Maurice Thorez (1900-64), General Secretary of the French Communist Party for over thirty years from 1933 and its President for two months before his death.

134. George Orwell (pseud. of Eric Blair) (1903-50), novelist and essayist, fought and was wounded in the Spanish Civil War, his own experiences in which he published as *Homage to Catalonia* (London, 1938).

135. Unity Theatre, London, was a left-wing amateur group, founded in 1936, when it produced Clifford Odets' play, *Waiting for Lefty* written the previous year.

136. Black Agnes, wife of the Earl of Dunbar and March, defended Dunbar Castle against an English army for five months in 1338. See also above, Note 38.

137. Buenaventura Durruti (1896-1936), Spanish Anarchist leader, killed during the defence of Madrid in November 1936.

138. The Francoist offensive against the Basque Provinces in the north of Spain had begun on 31 March, the bombing of Guernica being one consequence (see above, Note 79). The Basque Provinces finally fell to Franco's troops at the end of August and the province of Asturias, to the west of them, in the later part of October 1937.

139. George Brown (1906-37), born in Ireland but moved as a child to Manchester, where he became an active trade unionist and member of Manchester and Salford Trades Council and an organiser of the unemployed. O'Riordan, op.cit., 84.

140. The Means Test, introduced by the so-called 'National' Government in 1931, was bitterly resented by the working class as an inquisition into the earnings as well as savings and pensions of members of the household (including sons and daughters) which were then deducted from any unemployment payments. Any member of the family in employment had to support those at home who were unemployed. Consequently families broke up as employed or unemployed left home to avoid being means-tested.

141. Nicola Sacco (1891-1927) and Bartolomeo Vanzetti (1888-1927) were executed in the United States seven years after being found guilty of murder and robbery. Both had been left-wing agitators. The executions took place despite world-wide protests, conflicting and circumstantial evidence at their trial, and the confession of another man to the crime.

142. Estenson, a seaman from Stockton-on-Tees, was later second-in-command of the anti-tank battery. Alexander, op.cit., 154, 164.

143. George Nathan, brave, competent and highly respected, had served in the British army, first as a sergeant major during the 1914-18 War, later as an officer in the Guards. He arrived in Spain in December 1936 and was successively a company and battalion commander, then became a major and Chief of Staff of the XVth International Brigade before the battle of Brunete, in which he was mortally wounded by aerial bombing. He had unsuccessfully applied earlier in 1937 to join the British Communist Party. During his service in the British army he had been in Ireland, and it has been claimed he was attached to the Black and Tans and was responsible for the murder of two leading Irish nationalists. Thomas, op.cit., 490 and n., 713 and n.; J. Delperrié de Bayac, Les Brigades internationales (Paris, 1968), 99; Alexander, op.cit., 36, 38, 65, 85, 86, 87, 88, 101, 129.

144. Steve Nelson, "one of the best liked officers in the 15th International Brigade", had worked in a slaughterhouse in Philadelphia from the age of 12, and later in shipyards there. He had become a leading member of the American Communist Party and was the most senior member of it to volunteer to fight in Spain. He was immediately made political commissar of the Lincoln Battalion and arrived in Spain in April 1937. After the battle of Brunete he became commissar of the XVth Brigade. He was seriously wounded at Belchite in September and returned to the United States. Landis, op.cit., 164-6, 248, 299.

145. Delperrié de Bayac, op.cit., 99, says Nathan was homosexual and called his men not 'Comrades' but 'Ladies'.

146. Peter the Painter, otherwise Peter Straume of Riga, was believed by the authorities to be an anarchist responsible for the shooting of three police sergeants in London in December 1910. The 'Siege of Sidney Street' by police and troops in the following month conducted by Winston Churchill as Home Secretary resulted in the deaths of two anarchists, but of 'Peter the Painter' there was no sign. See, e.g., G. Dangerfield, The Strange Death of Liberal England (London, 1970), 91-2.

147. No one of either name is listed by Alexander among those killed in Spain, although Jim Brewer from South Wales was a member of the anti-tank unit, survived the War and later became a Labour councillor. Alexander, op.cit., 171, 240, 246, 264, 266.

148. Eric Whalley, a leader of the unemployed in Mansfield, Notts. Alexander, op.cit., 35.

149. Nelson's successor was his fellow American, Dave Doran, an organiser of the steelworkers and a member of the National Executive of the Young Communist League, who was captured and executed during the Republican retreat in the Aragon in spring 1938. Landis, op.cit., 249, 464.

150. Robert Hale Merriman (1908-38), of Scots-American parentage, a graduate of the University of Nevada, lecturer in economics at University of California, had

been studying European agricultural problems in the winter of 1936-7 but gave up his project and went to fight in Spain with the International Brigade. He was adjutant of the Lincoln Battalion but later became Chief of Staff of the XVth Brigade. Merriman, who was 6ft 2½ins tall, was captured and executed with Dave Doran in spring 1938. Landis, op.cit., 33, 351, 464.

151. Boyle, an East Fife miner now aged about 80, still lives at Methil.

152. Paddy Ryan, i.e. Frank Ryan (see above, Note 14).

153. See above, Note 135.

154. Dr Juan Negrin (1889-1956), Socialist, Minister of Finance in the Republican Government, 1936-7, Prime Minister, 1937-9, and of the Spanish Government in exile until 1945.

155. *The Times*, 26 July 1963, reported that a body found about three weeks earlier on a deserted beach at Milford-on-sea, near Bournemouth, had been identified as Malcolm Dunbar. He was cremated at Southampton on 30 July. As for Dunbar's 'disappearance' from the train at Versailles, John Dunlop recalls meeting Malcolm Dunbar in 1939 or 1940 in Glasgow when Dunbar said he had gone from the train straight back to Spain where he remained in Valencia as correspondent of the *Daily Worker* until the end of the Civil War.

156. Sir Hugh Roberton (1874-1952), founder of the Glasgow Orpheus Choir, 1906, and its conductor from then until his retirement in 1951.

157. John Penman (1908-54), active in the Fife Mineworkers' Reform Union in the 1920s, the United Mineworkers of Scotland and the Communist Party, lived in the Soviet Union 1931-6, working in the pits in the Donbass, as well as on the building of the Moscow underground, and at Novosibirsk in Siberia. He joined the International Brigade in Spain in 1937, was captured and imprisoned at Burgos and San Sebastian, returned home to Bowhill, Fife, early in 1939, and worked for some years in Dundonald pit. Penman suffered from Bright's Disease after his return from, but apparently not as a result of, his experience in Spain, and was an invalid for the last four years of his life.

158. Rt Hon. Thomas Kennedy (1876-1954), Scottish organiser from 1903 and General Secretary from 1919 of the Social Democratic Federation, M.P. for Kirkcaldy Burghs, 1921-2, 1923-31, 1935-44, held junior office in the Labour Governments of 1924 and 1929-31.

159. Edouard Daladier (1884-1970), a leading French Radical politician, Prime Minister, 1933, briefly in 1934, and 1938-40, Minister of Defence and War, 1936-40, Minister of Foreign Affairs, 1939-40.

160. Cable Street, in the East End of London, was the scene of a confrontation on Sunday, 4 October 1936, when an estimated 300,000 people blocked streets against a march by Mosley's blackshirts. The Home Secretary had refused to ban the march but after much baton charging by the police and barricade building by the crowds the Chief Commissioner of police decided on the day that the march would have to be abandoned. Noreen Branson and Margot Heinemann, *Britain in the Nineteen Thirties* (St Albans, 1973), 317-20.

161. Riley was killed in the battle of Teruel in January 1938. Alexander, op.cit., 273.

162. The Foreign Enlistment Act, 1870, prohibited the enlistment by a British subject in the army or navy of a foreign state at war with a friendly state. The Act also prohibited anyone from leaving Britain so to enlist. The British Government decided in January 1937 to forbid under the Act recruitment of British subjects for service in Spain (in effect, Republican Spain), but no volunteer was in fact prosecuted. See C.L. Mowat, *Britain between the Wars* (London, 1955), 575; and Alexander, op.cit., 45.

163. Moore was killed at the battle of Teruel in January 1938. Alexander, op.cit., 271.

164. Sam Russell (pseud. of Sam Lesser) had been one of the first British volunteers to fight for the Republic in Spain. He later worked with a Spanish news agency and became *Daily Worker* correspondent in Spain. Alexander, op.cit., 222.

165. For *Daily Worker*, see above, Note 45. The Dependants' Aid Fund gave weekly allowances to dependants in need. The Communist Party played a major role in this work. In June 1937 the Dependants' Aid Committee was set up on a broader base, with sponsors including several Labour, Liberal and Conservative M.P.s, and trade union and Co-operative leaders. By September that year some 1,100 wives and children of British volunteers in Republican Spain were being helped by the Committee, and through street and factory, etc., collctions over £43,000 had been raised by the Fund by November. Alexander, op.cit., 141-2.

166. Ivan Mikhailovich Maisky (1884-1975), Soviet Ambassador to Britain, 1932-43, Assistant People's Commissar for Foreign Affairs, 1943-6.

167. Gibbons was one of three brothers fighting with the International Brigades. Alexander, op.cit., 122.

168. Lieutenant Colonel Edward Cuthbert De Renzy-Martin (1883-1974), C.M.G., D.S.O., M.C., Inspector of Albanian Gendarmerie, 1927-34, Hon. Attaché and Secretary, British Embassy, Madrid, 1938-40. He had himself been wounded and a prisoner-of war in 1914-18.

169. Jack Jones was a miner from the Rhondda and later became a full-time official in the miners' union. Alexander, op.cit., 187, 245.

170. Going down on one knee would be at the consecration or elevation of the host.

171. *Arriba, Espana!* – Up Spain!

172. Paavo Nurmi (1897-1973), athlete known as 'The Flying Finn', won the 10,000 metres race in the 1920 Olympic Games and dominated long distance running for years afterward.

173. Horatio, Viscount Nelson (1758-1805), lost his right eye at the battle of Calvi in 1794 and his right arm was amputated in 1797 after an encounter at Santa Cruz.

174. The Spanish Aid Committee, or Aid Spain Committee, existed in almost every town in Britain, collected food, money for medical aid, and held meetings to explain the cause of Republican Spain. The composition of the local committees varied but often included delegates from union branches, Co-operative Guilds, and Labour parties. See, e.g., Branson and Heinemann, op.cit., 340.

175. Flynn was killed at Cordoba in April 1937. Alexander, op.cit., 267 (where Flynn's initials are given as J.F.).

176. For Phil Gillan, see above, pp.13-19. David MacKenzie, a medical student from Edinburgh, had gone to fight in Spain at the beginning of October 1936. He had been reported killed in action but turned up afer a memorial service had been held for him. Addressing a public meeting at Coatbridge on 6 January 1937, he said that while helping to defend Madrid he had only once seen Spaniards fighting against Republican troops at the front – "all the rest were either Moors or Germans." McKenzie also said that the Soviet Union had supplied the Republicans with "arms the Allied armies had left behind in their hurry to leave the U.S.S.R. in 1921." When he addressed a meeting at City Hall, Glasgow, on 10 January, "the audience got to their feet and in a remarkable display of enthusiasm, hats, caps and scarves were waved in the air." He said that during the siege of Madrid by Franco's forces "many dud shells came over from the German batteries. Several had been opened by men of the International column and in one of them was a note – 'This gun is not going to fire. Welcome from the anti-Fascist workers.'" See *Glasgow Herald*, 7 and 11 January 1937. Johnny Lochore had been a leader of the 1936 Hunger March to London and had recruited in Glasgow a dozen other volunteers for Spain where he had arrived at the end of 1936. Alexander, op.cit., 37, 53, 59.

177. Twenty-nine foodships were sent as gifts to Republican Spain from Britain. Branson and Heinemann, op.cit., 340.

178. Finlay Hart (1901-), a veteran West of Scotland trade union and Communist activist, who joined the Workers' International Industrial Union in Beardmore's Dalmuir Yard on the Clyde and also the Socialist Labour Party during the 1914-18 War, emigrated in the 1920s to Canada for three years and became active in the Plumbers' and Boilermakers' unions, etc., after his return.

179. Joe Norman, an engineer from Manchester, was later taken prisoner in the retreat in the Aragon in spring 1938. Alexander, op.cit., 187.

180. Vladimir Copic (1891-1938), a Croat or Yugoslav Communist and former officer in the Austro-Hungarian army, was commander of the XVth International Brigade from early in 1937 until July 1938. He then returned to the Soviet Union where he was executed by Stalin. Landis, op.cit., 40, 505; Thomas, op.cit., 953.

181. The Labour College Movement, which flourished from 1908 until 1964 when it was merged into the Trades Union Congress educational service, was supported by the bulk of the organised labour movemnet and ran a wide range of independent working class education classes and postal courses. Charles L. Gibbons (1888-1959), born in London, later became a miner in South Wales and an active Socialist. He attended the Central Labour College in London from 1911-13 and was appointed in 1924 and long remained organiser in Edinburgh and District for the National Council for Labour Colleges.

181. Fred Douglas, who left the Communist Party c. 1945, and later ran a bookshop in Edinburgh, died in 1971.

183. Julius Lipetz (1903-72), and his elder brother Sam (1897-1983), were well known Edinburgh doctors of left-wing views who ran a joint medical practice in Edinburgh from the 1920s until their deaths.

184. The Plebs Club was a Saturday evening discussion and social group that met first in George Street then in Candlemakers' Hall in Edinburgh, and which included Labour Party and Co-operative members and a few Communists.

185. S.A.I. – Scottish Agricultural Industries Ltd.

186. John Wheatley (1869-1930), an Independent Labour Party leader, was M.P. for Shettleston, 1922-30, and Minister of Health in the Labour Governemnt of 1924. The general election Steve Fullarton recalls was almost certainly that of 1929, when he was nine years old.

187. Michael O'Riordan, from Cork, interned during the 1939-45 War at the Curragh Camp, later Secretary of the Communist Party of Ireland, author of *Connolly Column*, op.cit., 124; Alexander, op.cit., 246.

188. Maurice Ryan.

189. C.A. Bennett, from Walsall, was killed. Alexander, op.cit., 263.

190. Alexander, op.cit., 268, gives G. Kelly, from Greenock.

191. Lord Halifax (1881-1959), Viceroy of India, 1926-31, Foreign Secretary, 1938-40, Ambassador to U.S.A., 1941-6.

192. Willie Joss died in 1967, aged 88.

193. No. 1 Lichfield Street also housed, on the floor above, the office of the Dependants' Aid Committee. It seems likely that Tom Murray was interviewed by R.W. Robson, an official of the Communist Party. Alexander, op.cit., 44, 141.

194. The man from Kirkcaldy was Smith – see above, p.291.

195. The New Model Army in the English Civil War had its elected radical Agitators, representing the rank-and-file soldiers. See, e.g., C. Hill, *The Century of Revolution, 1603-1714* (Edinburgh, 1961), 113, 114, 130, 189; and A.S.P. Woodhouse (ed.), *Puritanism and Liberty: the Army Debates (1647-49) from the Clarke Manuscripts* (London, 1938), passim.

196. Jack Nalty, from Dublin, was a member of the Communist Party of Ireland, of the Irish Republican Army and the Republican Congress (see above, Note 14). He had taken part in the last stages of the Irish civil war in the early 1920s and had been imprisoned twice in Ireland for his political activities. He was one of the first group of Irish volunteers to arrive in Spain in December 1936. He was badly wounded then at Cordoba and was killed on the last day of the last fighting in which the International Brigade took part in September 1938. O'Riordan, op.cit., 57, 58, 60, 66, 132.

197. *Las Noticias*, was a newspaper of the Catalan group of the U.G.T. (Union General de Trabajadores, or general Union of Workers), the Socialist trade union.

198. Sir David Low (1891-1963), born in Dunedin, New Zealand, worked as a cartoonist for the *Evening Standard*, 1927-50, and later for the *Daily Herald* and *Guardian*. The cartoon in question was published in the *Evening Standard* on 11 May 1938.

199. The Thirteen Points were issued as a declaration on 1 May 1938 listing the war aims of the Republican Government. They included the absolute independence and integrity of Spain; liberation of Spanish territory from foreign occupation

and foreign influence; a people's republic; the organisation when the War ended of a plebiscite on the form of government; respect for the national liberties of the peoples of Spain, compatible with Spanish unity; full social and civic rights for every Spaniard, including freedom of religious worship and conscience; complete agrarian reform; and amnesty for all Spaniards who proved they desired to co-operate in the work of reconstruction (the amnesty to include common soliders of the rebel army). Thomas, op.cit., 820; Landis, op.cit., 487.

200. *Cabo* – corporal, *sargento* – sergeant.

201. Tom Murray seems mistaken here. Marxism was coming to be known to socialists in all the countries associated with the International Working Men's Association, or First International, at roughly the same time. He may be thinking of the controversy between Marxism and Bakuninism, which was particularly lively in Spain, or at least in Catalonia.

202. Jack Larkin Jones, born 1913, Liverpool City councillor, 1936-9, member of the General Council of the Trades Union Congress, 1968-78, General Secretary, Transport & General Workers' Union, 1969-78, was wounded in the fighting on the Ebro in August 1938.

203. Mehemet Shehu (1913-81), Deputy Prime Minister and Minister of Internal Affairs of Albania, 1948-54, Prime Minister, 1954-81.

204. The annual conference of the Labour Party was not held in 1938 because of a decision to change the normal month of its meeting from October (as in 1937) to May, when it met in 1939. The conference in Edinburgh to which Tom Murray refers seems to be that held for Labour councillors and Parliamentary candidates, on the issue of restoring peace and the sending of a foodship to Spain. The conference is reported in, e.g., *Edinburgh Evening News*, 24 September 1938.

205. Tom Murray took ill and died before he could resume and complete the tape-recording of his recollections.

Some further reading

Alexander, Bill, *British Volunteers for Liberty: Spain 1936-1939* (London, 1982)

Brenan, Gerald, *The Spanish Labyrinth* (Cambridge, 1960)

Carr, Raymond, *Spain 1808-1975* (Oxford, 1982)

Delperrié de Bayac, Jacques, *Les Brigades internationales* (Paris, 1968)

Francis, Hywel, *Miners against Fascism: Wales and the Spanish Civil War* (London, 1984)

Fraser, Ronald, *Blood of Spain: The experience of Civil War, 1936-1939* (Harmondsworth, 1981)

Jackson, Gabriel, *The Spanish Republic and the Civil War, 1931-1939* (Princeton, 1965)

Landis, Arthur H., *The Abraham Lincoln Brigade* (New York, 1967)

Orwell, George, *Homage to Catalonia* (London, 1938)

Thomas, Hugh, *The Spanish Civil War* (London, 1977)

INDEX